The Unofficial Guide®

DISNEY
Cruise Line 2023

Photo: Erin Foster; sandcastle by Luciana Misura/AmoCruzeiroDisney.c

Erin Foster and Len Testa with Ritchey Halphen

The *Disney Dream* docked at Castaway Cay
(Photo: Erin Foster)

The *Disney Wonder* leaves Nassau in the twilight after a day in port.
(Photo: Laurel Stewart)

Castaway Cay hosts the *Disney Fantasy.*
(Photo: Erin Foster)

The *Disney Magic* sails out of New York City in the fall. This photo shows it leaving the harbor.
(Photo: Erin Foster)

Bingo is a popular diversion on all the Disney ships. (Photo: Ivonne Ramos)

The *Wish*'s atrium hosts character greetings and has a small performing stage.
(Photo: Erin Foster)

The *Dream* is decked out in holiday finery.
(Photo: Erin Foster)

The decor gets spooky on Halloween cruises.
(Photo: Erin Foster)

...ald's Pool on the *Fantasy*. You can see ...AquaDuck waterslide and Mickey's Pool ...he background. (Photo: Laurel Stewart)

The *Magic*'s Twist 'n' Spout waterslide (Photo: Len Testa)

...e *Fantasy*'s dedicated teen pool at the ...e youth club (Photo: Erin Foster)

The *Fantasy*'s AquaLab splash area (Photo: Ricky Brigante)

...ests on the *Dream* and *Fantasy* can play ...ofy-themed minigolf on Deck 13. ...oto: Laurel Stewart)

The *Wish*'s Toy Story Splash Zone is a water-... area for preschoolers (Photo: Erin Foster)

...e pools on the *Wish* are staggered on several ...els. (Photo: Erin Foster)

Most sailings of the *Wish* feature a pool-deck... pirate party with live rock music. (Photo: Erin Foster)

The ships' Bibbidi Bobbidi Boutiques offer makeovers plus a large selection of princess dresses. (Photo: Erin Foster)

Many Disney characters wear nautical garb on board. (Photo: Ivonne Ramos)

All Disney ships have fitness centers equipped with a wide range of cardio and weight machines. (Photo: Erin Foster)

The Walt Disney Theatre is the site for major events and stage shows. (Photo: Erin Foster)

It's a Small World Nursery has a quiet room just for napping. (Photo: Erin Foster)

The *Dream*'s kids' clubs include a replica *Millennium Falcon* bridge. (Photo: Erin Foster)

The ships' Oceaneer Clubs feature themed play areas. (Photo: Erin Foster)

Vibe is the ships' teen hangout. This is the *Wish*'s version. (Photo: Erin Foster)

...er-the-top treats await you at the ships' ...ecialty sweets shops. (Photo: Ivonne Ramos)

The Hero Zone on the *Wish* is home to the Incredi-Games obstacle course. (Photo: Erin Foster)

...r of the ships have a restaurant called ...nator's Palate, which celebrates the joy of ...ey animation while you eat. (Photo: Erin Foster)

Enchanté is the most elegant adult-dining experience on the *Wish*. (Photo: Erin Foster)

...e Hyperspace Lounge on the *Wish* serves ...nks from across the *Star Wars* universe. ...oto: Erin Foster)

Big-city vistas unfold behind the bar at Skyli... on the *Dream* and *Fantasy*. (Photo: Erin Foster)

...e Bayou is the *Wish*'s New Orleans–themed ...r. (Photo: Erin Foster)

Tiana's Place on the *Wonder* serves New Orlea... style cuisine with a live jazz band on stage. (Photo: Erin Foster)

ur stateroom couch can become a twin bed. ome rooms have Murphy beds built into a wall. hoto: Erin Foster)

Some inside staterooms on the *Dream* and *Fantasy* have a so-called virtual porthole. (Photo: Erin Foster)

eluxe Oceanview Stateroom with Verandah on e *Wish* (Photo: Erin Foster)

rge-portholed Oceanview staterooms can el just as airy as Verandah staterooms—and ten at a much lower cost. (Photo: Erin Foster)

Many family staterooms include hidden bunk beds for children. (Photo: Erin Foster)

our stateroom attendant will leave surprise visitors in your cabin each evening. (Photos: Erin Foster)

Castaway Cay's Pelican Plunge is a floating platform of fun.
(Photo: Erin Foster)

ssau's Atlantis resort is the site of many hamian port adventures. (Photo: Erin Foster)

Ample refreshment is available on Castaway Cay. (Photo: Ivonne Ramos)

ach chairs, umbrellas, and gorgeous sand are included at Castaway Cay. (Photo: Erin Foster)

Private cabanas on Castaway Cay's Serenity Beach are an adult oasis. (Photo: Erin Foster)

Many Northern European sailings depart from the charming city of Copenhagen, Denmark. (Photo: Erin Foster)

The glorious stained glass windows of the Basílica de la Sagrada Família are a highlight port stops in Barcelona, Spain. (Photo: Erin Fos

Canadian Coastline cruises visit picturesque fishing villages. (Photo: Erin Foster)

Mush! Dogsledding in Alaska (Photo: Erin Foster)

On this Adventures by Disney (AbD) Rhine River cruise, you can canoe through the center of lovely French village. (Photo: Erin Foster)

Excursions to Incan ruins are part of some *Fantasy* intineraries. (Photo: Erin Foster)

AbD river-cruise ships are significantly smaller than DCL ocean ships. (Photo: Erin Foster)

AmaWaterways' *AmaViola* river-cruise ship is used by AbD. (Photo: Erin Foster)

THE *unofficial* GUIDE®

TO Disney Cruise Line

2023

ERIN FOSTER with
LEN TESTA and RITCHEY HALPHEN

Every effort has been made to ensure the accuracy of this book, and its contents are believed to be correct at the time of publication. Nevertheless, please be aware that these contents are subject to change after publication, owing to numerous factors that influence the cruise industry. The publisher therefore cannot accept responsibility for errors or omissions; for changes in prices, itineraries, and other information presented in this guide; or for the consequences of relying on this information. We strongly suggest that you write or call ahead for confirmation when making your travel plans.

The authors' assessments of restaurants, shows, port adventures, and the like are subjective—they may not reflect the publisher's opinion or align with a reader's own experience. Readers are invited to write the publisher with ideas, comments, and suggestions for future editions.

Note: COVID-19 infection is a risk in any public space, regardless of your vaccination status. The authors and publisher are not liable for any illness or injury resulting from your cruise—*your health and safety are your responsibility.* Before booking travel, you must decide whether you are willing to accept these potential risks. For the latest CDC guidelines, please see cdc .gov/coronavirus/2019-ncov/prevent-getting-sick/prevention.html; for the latest information about Disney Cruise Line's health and safety measures, see tinyurl.com/DCLKnowBeforeYouGo.

The Unofficial Guides
An imprint of AdventureKEEN
2204 First Ave. S., Ste. 102
Birmingham, AL 35233

Editor: Ritchey Halphen
Cover and color-insert design: Scott McGrew
Text design: Vertigo Design, with updates by Annie Long
Maps and illustrations: Steve Jones
Proofreader: Jenna Barron
Indexer: Frances Lennie/Indexing Research

Cover photo: The brand-new *Disney Wish* docks at Disney's private island, Castaway Cay, during every sailing. Photo: Erin Foster

To contact us from within the United States, please call 888-604-4537 or fax 877-374-9016. You may also contact us at info@theunofficialguides.com; @TheUnofficialGuides on Facebook; @TheUGSeries on Twitter, Instagram, and Pinterest; and TheUnofficialGuideSeries on YouTube.

AdventureKEEN also publishes its books in a variety of electronic formats. Some content that appears in print may not be available in electronic formats.

ISBN 978-1-62809-141-0 (pbk.), ISBN 978-1-62809-142-7 (e-book)

Distributed by Publishers Group West

Manufactured in the United States of America

5 4 3 2 1

CONTENTS

LIST *of* DIAGRAMS *and* MAPS

ABOUT
the AUTHORS

ERIN FOSTER researched and responded to more than 11,000 guest questions as a charter member of the Disney Parks Moms Panel (now the planDisney Panel). Erin has visited Walt Disney World; Disneyland; Disneyland Paris; Hong Kong Disneyland; and the Disney Vacation Club properties at Hilton Head, South Carolina; Vero Beach, Florida; and Aulani in Hawaii. She has also taken Adventures by Disney journeys to four continents, including AbD's European river cruises. And, of course, she has been on many Disney Cruise Line sailings on the *Magic, Wonder, Dream,* and *Fantasy,* and she was among the passengers on the maiden voyage of the *Wish* in 2022. Erin is a regular contributor to the blog at TouringPlans.com. When she isn't traveling, you can find her attending theatrical performances in New York City.

LEN TESTA is the coauthor of the Unofficial Guides series, covering Walt Disney World, Disneyland, Las Vegas, Universal Orlando, and Washington, D.C. While Len has published works in travel, computer science, and endocrinology, it's widely acknowledged that he's just the pretty face for a group of people way more talented than he is (and "pretty face" is a stretch at best). Len sends love to his daughter, Hannah.

RITCHEY HALPHEN is an editor at AdventureKEEN, publisher of the Unofficial Guides. His only cruise so far has been on Norwegian Cruise Line's late, lamented SS *Norway,* originally the French Line's SS *France.* A Disney cruise is on his bucket list—for research purposes, of course.

ACKNOWLEDGMENTS

FIRST AND FOREMOST, thank you to the cast members of Disney Cruise Line—always, but especially during these trying and unprecedented times. You not only make the magic, you *are* the magic.

Thank you to the team at TouringPlans.com, particularly Christina Harrison, Annette Jackson, and Jennifer Heymont, for their research and analysis of Walt Disney World and DCL information. Scott Sanders provides invaluable news and updates on his Disney Cruise Line Blog. The women and men of the planDisney Panel provide generous and thoughtful insight into all aspects of Disney vacation planning. The Mascardo, Harrison, and Guha-King families have helped with reporting on DCL's current kids' club practices.

As always, thank you to my husband, Jeff, and my daughters, Charlie, Josie, and Louisa, for reminding me that the camera eats first.

—*Erin Foster*

IT TAKES A LIFEBOAT FULL OF PEOPLE to produce this book and its companion web content. David Davies created our website for DCL information, wrote our Fare Tracker tool, and lent an expert eye to the proofreading of the text. Thanks to CruiseWatch.com for providing cruise-fare data. Scott, Emily, and Isabelle Sanders provide in-depth coverage of DCL at DisneyCruiseLineBlog.com. We relied on Tammy Whiting of Storybook Destinations and our Touring Plans travel agents (touringplans.com/travel) for updates as DCL's policies changed . . . often. Finally, much love to Matt Hochberg of RoyalCaribbeanBlog.com for his comparison of DCL and Royal Caribbean. No matter which line you're sailing, Matt's website has tons of useful information about the towns, ports, and excursions common to all cruise companies.

—*Len Testa*

INTRODUCTION

CRUISING *in the* TIME *of* COVID

THE GLOBAL TRAVEL INDUSTRY—and the cruise industry in particular—continue to weather the aftereffects of the COVID-19 pandemic. While much of the Disney Cruise Line experience has returned to pre-COVID norms, there are still areas where veteran cruisers will notice modifications to their previous sailing experiences (see pages 2 and 3 for details). These adjustments may last through 2023, or they may fall by the wayside entirely. Most likely, however, COVID-related protocols will simply continue to evolve, being updated and tweaked as conditions warrant.

As you read through this book, you'll notice descriptions of pre- and post-pandemic practices on board. (These references include **COVID Tips,** accompanied by the Unofficial Guides' mascot, the Wuffo, in a mask, sunglasses, and beachwear.) Depending on when you sail, you might expect to see pre- or post-pandemic practices implemented—but more likely, with much about the virus still in flux, you'll experience something along a continuum, with more-restrictive practices in play while infection is more pervasive and more-relaxed practices coming into play as the virus abates and as new treatments become available.

SHOULD YOU CRUISE RIGHT NOW?

AT THE TIME OF THIS WRITING, young, healthy, vaccinated people have a limited chance of catastrophic COVID outcomes stemming from cruise travel, provided they adhere to public safety advice. In a 2022 *New York Times* article on this topic, one cruise passenger observed:

> *When you're on a plane, or in a hotel or at a theme park, you don't know who has COVID around you. . . . On a cruise, it's detected right away and the positive cases are isolated, so you can continue your vacation in a COVID-free bubble. I really don't know a safer way to travel.*

A summer 2022 article in the *Miami Herald* noted:

Cruise industry leaders have acknowledged that having coronavirus cases on ships is the new normal, but say the infection rates are less than in the general population and the industry's public health safety protocols are more stringent than most public settings.

While breakthrough cases have occurred on every major cruise line, the point remains that most DCL cruisers must be fully vaccinated and all passengers must undergo pre-embarkation testing—a level of scrutiny not seen with most other forms of vacation travel.

If you have an underlying medical condition (such as asthma or diabetes) or a compromised immune system (for example, due to an organ transplant or treatment for cancer), cruising will likely continue to be a suboptimal vacation choice in 2023. Remember, however, that we're not doctors: any decisions you make related to travel should be in consultation with your personal healthcare provider.

SHOULD YOU CRUISE *DISNEY* RIGHT NOW?

IF YOU'VE DECIDED TO SAIL, the next logical question is, "Should I sail Disney Cruise Line?" The answer to this, as with most Disney travel questions, is, "It depends." Most guests who had a Disney cruise on their radar pre-pandemic will find that the DCL experience has essentially returned to its former glory. Although not all sailings have been completely free of COVID incidents, Disney continues to do as well as—or better than—other major cruise lines when it comes to keeping guests and crew as safe as possible.

While many aspects of sailing DCL are back to normal, two protocols that persist at press time (albeit with frequent tweaks) are **mandatory vaccination and pre-trip COVID testing.** If you're an adult who's unable or unwilling to get a COVID-19 vaccine, your only alternative for a cruise vacation at the time of this writing is to book with another line where exemptions are allowed (**Carnival, Princess, Virgin Voyages**), or where vaccination requirements have been dropped entirely (**Norwegian, Oceania**) or for specific sailings (**Royal Caribbean**).

COVID TIP

If you test positive for COVID during your DCL sailing, you and any other guests in your stateroom will likely be moved to a COVID isolation cabin on Deck 2 for the remainder of your trip.

Also consider that, aside from what's happening on the ship, you might arrive on board to find, say, that your dream destination has unexpectedly closed its borders to foreign travelers or that a bucket-list excursion has been canceled due to COVID concerns. Modified Mickey plus a possibly abbreviated shore experience may mean you need to think especially hard about how you'd be spending your vacation dollars before you book a DCL experience.

WHAT WERE 2021 AND 2022 LIKE ON DCL?

LIKE NEARLY ALL MAJOR CRUISE LINES, DCL suspended operations from mid-March 2020 to mid-2021. The first cruises after sailing resumed were a handful of short "staycation" voyages of the *Disney Magic* in the UK. Test sailings of the *Disney Dream* were conducted in mid-2021, with the first regular sailing of the *Dream* embarking on August 9, 2021—marking the end of 513 days without a regular US departure of a DCL ship. The *Disney Fantasy* then resumed sailing on September 11, 2021, followed by the *Disney Wonder* on October 1, 2021.

COVID TIP

DCL's **Know Before You Go** webpage (tinyur .com/dclknowbefore yougo) contains the most up-to-date information about Disney's current COVID vaccination and testing requirements.

The ships returned to service with dozens, if not hundreds, of changes to procedures, protocols, and physical spaces. Most of these have been lifted as of the time of this writing, but it's possible that Disney could bring them back, in whole or in part, in response to a future COVID outbreak or other medical emergency. With this possibility in mind, here's a recap of the more-restrictive practices implemented on DCL at various points during 2021 and 2022:

- Sailings without port stops
- Mask requirements for all indoor and outdoor venues on board, except when eating or drinking
- Reservation requirements for kids' clubs and limits on time spent in them
- Closure of the onboard nurseries
- Fewer stage performances and movie screenings to allow for social distancing in the theaters
- Suspension of deck parties and other mass gatherings
- Use of spa and fitness center by timed reservation only
- Suspension of character greetings
- Delayed sail-away times
- Capacity restrictions for pools and/or reservation requirements for pool access
- Cafeteria-style service at the buffets

ABOUT *This* GUIDE

WHY "UNOFFICIAL"?

THE MATERIAL HEREIN originated with the authors and has not been reviewed, edited, or approved by the Walt Disney Company Inc. or Disney Cruise Line. To the contrary, we represent and serve you, the consumer: if a ship serves mediocre food or has subpar entertainment, we say so. Through our independence, we hope that we can make selecting a cruise efficient and economical and help make your cruise experience on-target and fun.

Toward that end, our *unofficial* guide offers the following:

- Assessment of how COVID-related modifications will affect your DCL experience
- Our recommendations for which ship to choose for your first cruise
- When to book your cruise to get the cheapest fares
- What to pack, including travel documents for you and your children

- Color photos from throughout the ships, along with deck and stateroom plans
- Unbiased reviews of onboard restaurants, live entertainment, and nightlife
- Our recommendations for the best family activities: kids' clubs, games, outdoor sports, and more
- Coverage of Disney's private island, Castaway Cay, along with chapters about ports of call and shore excursions
- Tips on how to choose the best stateroom for your needs
- Comparisons of DCL vacations with Royal Caribbean cruise vacations, Walt Disney World vacations, and Adventures by Disney (AbD) river-cruise vacations

DISNEY CRUISE LINE:
An Overview

DISNEY CRUISE LINE SHIPS IN A NUTSHELL					
	Disney Magic	*Disney Wonder*	*Disney Dream*	*Disney Fantasy*	*Disney Wish*
YEAR LAUNCHED	1998	1999	2011	2012	2022
CAPACITY					
PASSENGERS (*maximum*)	2,713	2,713	4,000	4,000	4,000
CREW	950	950	1,458	1,458	1,555
TOTAL CAPACITY	3,663	3,663	5,458	5,458	5,555
PASSENGER DECKS	11	11	14	14	14
STATEROOMS					
INSIDE	256	256	150	150	121
OCEANVIEW	362	362	199	199	185
OUTSIDE VERANDAH	259	259	901	901	948
TOTAL STATEROOMS	877	877	1,250	1,250	1,254
DESIGN/DECOR	Art Deco	Art Nouveau	Art Deco	Art Nouveau	"Enchantment"*

*Gothic, Baroque, and French Rococo

IN 1998 THE WALT DISNEY COMPANY launched its cruise line with the 2,400-passenger **Disney Magic.** An almost identical ship, the **Disney Wonder,** entered service in 1999. Two larger ships, the **Disney Dream** and the **Disney Fantasy,** joined the fleet in 2011 and 2012, respectively. In 2016 DCL announced that they would be building two additional ships. A year later this was amended to include a third new ship. The first of this new generation of ships, the **Disney Wish,** set sail during summer 2022, and coauthor Erin was fortunate enough to be one of her first passengers. Erin's reporting is woven throughout this edition; for specific topics, see the table of contents (page iii) or check the index (page 360).

In starting a cruise line, Disney put together a team of industry veterans, dozens of the world's best-known ship designers, and its own unrivaled creative talent. Together, they created the DCL ships, recognizing that the smallest detail would be critical to the line's success.

The result? They succeeded, starting with the ships' design aesthetic: simultaneously classic and innovative. Exteriors are traditional, reminiscent of the great ocean liners of the past, but with some quintessentially

Disney twists. Inside, the ships feature up-to-the-minute technology and brim with novel ideas for dining, entertainment, and cabin design. Even DCL's exclusive cruise terminal at Port Canaveral, Florida, is part of the overall strategy.

For Bahamian cruises, Disney chose **Castaway Cay** (see Part Ten) as the site of its private island to avoid the hassle of tendering. As for dining, Disney practically reinvented the concept for cruises when it introduced rotational dining (see Part Seven, page 186), where each evening you not only dine in a different restaurant with a different motif, but your waiters and dining companions also move with you.

The foundation of DCL's business is built on **Bahamian** and **Caribbean** cruises out of Port Canaveral, about 90 minutes from Walt Disney World, and Miami. Disney also offers **Alaskan, Bermudan, Canadian, European,** and **Pacific Coast** cruises; **Panama Canal** and **Transatlantic** cruises; and **Hawaiian** cruises (during some seasons). And coming in late 2023 are **Oceanian** cruises in the South Pacific, Australia, and New Zealand (see the next section for more information).

Other DCL departure ports include Barcelona, Spain; Civitavecchia (Rome), Italy; Copenhagen, Denmark; Southampton, England; Galveston, Texas; New Orleans; New York City; San Diego; San Juan, Puerto Rico; and Vancouver, British Columbia, Canada. **Port Everglades,** a new departure port at Fort Lauderdale, Florida, will open in late 2023.

Bahamian cruises originating in Port Canaveral and Miami make at least one port call at Castaway Cay. DCL's Alaskan and European itineraries are well conceived and interesting; by comparison, its Bahamian and Caribbean itineraries are comparable to other cruise lines', but they're still good for first-time cruisers.

THE NEXT GENERATION OF DISNEY SHIPS

DCL'S FIRST NEW SHIP IN MORE THAN A DECADE, the *Disney Wish,* made a splashy debut in 2022. When DCL's third wave of ships (the *Triton* **Class**) was announced, there was initial speculation that the new vessels would be substantially different from their older sisters. As it turns out, the *Wish* adheres to the model of the first four ships, both in outward appearance and interior spaces, albeit with a more modern, high-tech feel and an even greater reliance on Disney imagery in her theming.

During Disney's D23 Expo fan event in September 2022, DCL announced that the sixth member of the fleet will be called the *Disney Treasure.* It will be similar in size to the *Wish,* but with "adventure" decor and theming, drawing inspiration from *Aladdin*'s fictional land of Agrabah as well as real-life places in Africa and Asia.

More-pressing questions remain about how the introduction of two more ships will impact Disney's original fleet. We've already seen some changes: the *Magic,* which once spent summers in Europe, now sails in the Caribbean and Bahamas, and in 2023 it will be making the Panama Canal crossing to sail on the West Coast. The *Dream,* which was based almost exclusively in the Bahamas for a decade, has taken over European routes formerly plied by the *Magic.* And the *Wonder,* which used to winter in the Caribbean, will be on the West Coast for much of 2023; then, following her normal Alaska season, DCL's second oldest ship will spend late 2023 and early 2024 in the South Pacific, Australia, and New Zealand. These are exciting new waters for DCL.

We wonder what else lies in store as the *Treasure* and DCL's as-yet-unnamed seventh ship set sail. The *Magic* and *Wonder* are now more than 20 years old—an age at which many cruise ships tend to be retired, repurposed, or sold to a smaller line. Will these two ships become less popular than their newer siblings? Will they be substantially rethemed at some point?

For the answers to these and other burning questions, keep an eye on **DisneyCruise.com** and the **Disney Parks Blog** (disneyparks.disney .go.com/blog). Also check the **Touring Plans blog** (blog.touringplans .com) for our takes on future announcements from Disney.

New Ships, New and Updated Ports

In May 2019 Disney signed an agreement with the Canaveral Port Authority, which runs DCL's primary home port, to increase the number of sailings departing from there each year. The number of DCL sailings from Port Canaveral was 150 per year in 2019 and is expected to grow to 216 sailings per year by about 2024.

A planned $45 million cruise-terminal improvement project was expedited during the pandemic, allowing construction to proceed unimpeded by guest traffic. The updates included expanding the passenger arrival area, filling gaps in the pier, adding and replacing mooring fixtures, strengthening the pier deck, and installing a new passenger gangway. To facilitate additional improvements, Port Canaveral will receive an estimated $72 million of investments from the Florida State Coronavirus Fiscal Recovery Fund.

Moving forward, one member of DCL's original fleet (the *Fantasy*) and two members of the newer Triton Class will sail out of Disney's home base at Port Canaveral. In recent years, Disney has used Miami as an ancillary Florida departure point, but long-term continuation of this arrangement seems unlikely.

In 2022 Disney entered an agreement with **Port Everglades** (in Fort Lauderdale) to have at least one ship make its home port there, beginning with the 2023–24 cruise season and continuing for at least 15 years. The agreement gives DCL rights to a dedicated terminal and direct highway access, indicating a substantial investment in this new location.

Port Everglades will be DCL's first year-round port outside of Port Canaveral. The *Dream* will be based there starting in late 2023, followed by a second ship in 2025.

The full expansion of the DCL fleet also means that Disney's original private island, Castaway Cay, will soon be insufficient to handle full guest capacity. To help entertain all of these new cruisers, in May 2019 Disney purchased a second major property in the Bahamas: **Lighthouse Point,** a 700-acre parcel of land on the southern tip of the island of Eleuthera, about 132 miles southeast of Castaway Cay. Disney has acquired all necessary permits to begin construction at Lighthouse Point, and the initial building phase began in March 2022.

According to Disney, Lighthouse Point will have a "seaside adventure camp" feel with authentic Bahamian influence, not some "pirate cove" or other imaginary concept slapped onto the existing beauty of the island. Disney has pledged to develop just 20% of the land it has purchased and return about 190 acres to the Bahamian government for use as parkland, maintaining much of the rest in its pristine, undeveloped state.

DCL has also committed to using sustainable building practices and ensuring strict environmental standards. At the D23 Expo in September 2022, Disney announced that the development will be 90% solar-powered. (A 550-page environmental-impact study for Lighthouse Point is available at lighthousepointbahamas.com.)

In addition to protecting the environment, Disney has pledged to make a positive impact on the Bahamian economy with Lighthouse Point. The project will provide 120 construction jobs, approximately 80% of which will be Bahamian. Additionally, DCL has a goal of creating about 150 well-paying operations jobs once the site opens. As a step toward the second goal, DCL now has a partnership with Junior Achievement Bahamas. The program will provide services to nearly 1,000 high school students on Eleuthera and will include education on financial literacy, entrepreneurship, and college preparedness. Additionally, DCL has awarded $150,000 in grants to small businesses on Eleuthera, designed to fund training in topics such as developing marketing plans and understanding financial statements.

According to the project's spokespeople, Disney's goal is to have a ship at the Lighthouse Point port three to five days a week, with the destination having room for just one vessel at a time. Weekly visitors are expected to number approximately 11,400–26,600, depending on the season and which ships are in port.

IS DISNEY CRUISE LINE RIGHT FOR ME?

MANY TRAVELERS, particularly adults traveling without children, may wonder if they'll enjoy a Disney Cruise Line vacation. It's a legitimate concern: Disney charges a premium for its voyages, particularly in the Caribbean, banking on brand loyalty and its reputation for high-quality family experiences.

Disney offers great service, has some of the most attractive ships sailing, and goes out of its way to make sure everyone has a great time. While other cruise lines may be better in some areas, travel and general media outlets give DCL among the most consistently strong marks across all categories. Among its most recent accolades are the following:

- *Travel + Leisure*'s 2022 Best Large-Ship Ocean Cruise Line and 2021 Best Cruise Line for Families
- *U.S. News & World Report*'s 2022 Best Cruise Line for Families and Best Cruise Line in the Caribbean

A ROYAL CARIBBEAN FAN SPEAKS OUT

We asked our good friend **Matt Hochberg** *from RoyalCaribbeanBlog.com to weigh in on key differences between DCL and Royal Caribbean. A lifelong Disney fan who's been running Disney-related podcasts and websites for more than a decade, Matt has an in-depth perspective on both cruise lines.*

EVEN DISNEY CRUISE LINE FANS AGREE that a Disney cruise isn't cheap, and a Royal Caribbean family vacation cruise is arguably a better value when you consider that RCI offers more ships, destinations, and more of the newest innovations in the cruise industry than DCL.

Royal Caribbean's fleet consists of 26 ships (with a new one to be added in 2023), providing more choices throughout the year for where to sail in the Caribbean, Alaska, Northern Europe, and the Mediterranean, not to mention that RCI's ships offer so much more to do on board than DCL does for families of all ages. Indeed, Royal pushes the envelope in terms of onboard activities—surfing, bumper cars, rock walls, waterslides, ice skating, and more—in ways that Disney doesn't.

Families often look to DCL first because they have kids, but RCI's kids' offerings get better and better each year; each new ship has more space dedicated to children and more programming options than before. **Adventure Ocean,** the onboard youth program, lets kids enjoy supervised games, events, and activities throughout the day and evening. In addition, enhanced kids-only facilities and programming are available on RCI's refurbished ships.

But beyond all that, most families have a budget, and Royal Caribbean will cost you significantly less than Disney—likely **30%–50%** less. When you consider that DCL and RCI are more similar than different, it can be hard to justify Disney's prices. Both lines offer a great family cruise option, but Royal Caribbean is a far better value.

- *Condé Nast Traveler*'s 2021 Readers' Choice Awards: #1 Top Large Cruise Line in the World
- *Porthole Cruise and Travel Magazine*'s 2020 Readers' Choice Awards: #1 Best Cruise Line for Families, #1 Best Children's Programs, and #1 Best Cruise Ship Entertainment
- *Newsweek*'s 2020 award for America's Best Company for Customer Service—not just in the cruise industry, but for companies overall
- The **Port of Vancouver**'s 2020 Blue Circle Award for voluntary efforts to conserve energy and reduce emissions
- The highest-ranking line for 2021 in **Friends of the Earth**'s Cruise Ship Report Card (see foe.org/cruise-report-card)

While awards are great, none of them mean anything if DCL isn't the right cruise line for *you.* Obviously, *we're* fans. We (Erin and Len) have nearly 40 Disney cruises between us, and we keep booking more. But we do concede that you, gentle reader, have many other fine options for cruise vacations—and that some of them may fit your needs and tastes better than DCL.

- If you're looking for the *ne plus ultra* in cruise ship technology, choose **Royal Caribbean.** Its megaships are marvels.
- If you're looking for a sedate cruise experience, with relatively few children or younger families, choose **Holland America.**

- If you're a solo traveler looking to economize, choose **Norwegian** or another line that doesn't charge you extra to book a cabin for one.

- If you want an adults-only European experience, choose a **Viking** river cruise.

- If you wanna rock-and-roll all night and party every day, choose **Carnival** or **Virgin Voyages.**

- If you belong to a niche demographic, or you're a fan of a particular sports team, entertainment genre, or movie franchise, choose a **specialty cruise.** Examples include DCL's TCM Classic Movie Cruises (see page 237); Pride Party at Sea (LGBTQ) sailings on Celebrity; *Playbill*'s Broadway-themed charters on luxury cruise lines such as Seabourn and Silversea; Royal Caribbean's cruises for *Star Trek* and San Francisco 49ers fans; and charters for LDS (Mormon) church members on Carnival and other lines. There's even Margaritaville at Sea, an entire cruise line themed to Jimmy Buffett's lifestyle brand.

- If you're looking for that sweet spot between family-friendly and upscale, choose **Celebrity.**

- If you're accustomed to your butler Jeeves carrying your steamer trunk for you, choose **Cunard.**

- If you're looking for Disney service on a smaller, more intimate scale, choose an **Adventures by Disney** river cruise. See Part Thirteen for details.

- If you're unvaccinated, whether by necessity or by choice, choose **Norwegian, Oceania,** or select sailings on **Royal Caribbean.**

- If you love all things Disney but you'd rather avoid cruising until the pandemic is over, opt for a **Walt Disney World vacation** instead (see our discussion starting on page 81).

DCL'S TARGET MARKET

DISNEY CRUISES ARE TAILORED to families who are new to cruising. But like the theme parks, the cruise line is a Disney product for kids of all ages. Each ship has at least one alternative restaurant, swimming pool, and nightclub just for adults.

*un*official **TIP**
Because DCL ships' decor and entertainment are based almost entirely on Disney films and characters, we don't recommend a Disney cruise to anyone who isn't at least mildly fond of Mickey and the gang.

Initially, cruise experts questioned whether DCL could fill its ships when kids are in school, but Disney determined that if 1%–2% of the estimated 40 million annual visitors to its resorts and parks bought a Disney cruise vacation, the ships would sell out. Disney was right, and after more than two decades of success, no one is questioning them.

COMPETITORS AND PRICES

DCL USES ITS REPUTATION for high quality, service, and entertainment to dispel novices' doubts about cruise vacations. Disney's main competitor is **Royal Caribbean International** (**RCI**), which offers Caribbean, Mediterranean, and Alaskan cruises similar to Disney's, with most of the same departure and destination ports. The two cruise lines often have ships departing within days—sometimes hours—of each other, headed mostly to the same places.

Beyond staterooms, you'll find everything from bars and lounges to small art galleries, expansive spas, dedicated shopping areas, and specialty restaurants on both cruise lines. Here's how those offerings, plus pre- and post-cruise services, compare between DCL and RCI's newer ships, such as *Allure of the Seas, Oasis of the Seas,* and *Wonder of the Seas.*

AREA VARIETY OF ITINERARIES

WHO'S BETTER: Royal Caribbean Even after DCL adds two ships to its fleet, RCI will still have more than three times as many vessels in service. This enables Royal to more broadly cover the globe with, for example, sailings to China, Australia, and the Middle East, none of which DCL visits. If you're a frequent cruiser who wants a wide variety of port experiences, you may find that Royal Caribbean better suits your needs.

AREA YOUTH CLUBS

WHO'S BETTER: Disney The kids and teens we've interviewed, including our own, prefer Disney's youth clubs by a wide margin. During our observations, DCL staff ensured that every child new to the club was introduced to the existing members, and the staff actively participated in planning and keeping organized a continuous set of games, crafts, and playtime. If structured activities for kids and teens are an important consideration in planning your cruise, this is all you need to know.

AREA PRE-TRIP PLANNING AND RESERVATIONS

WHO'S BETTER: Disney Disney's website is easier to use than Royal Caribbean's—booking is simple, and information is clear and generally easy to find. Pre-pandemic, both DCL and RCI had exemplary phone-based customer service. During most of 2022, however, both lines—indeed, nearly all cruise lines and many airlines—became bogged down with staffing shortages at their phone centers. Waits of several hours became shockingly common. To avoid such frustrations, now may be the time to use a well-regarded travel agent, even if you've handled things on your own in the past. Agents will endure phone waits so you don't have to.

AREA BOARDING PROCESS

WHO'S BETTER: Royal Caribbean Its boarding is faster and more efficient, even on ships such as the *Allure of the Seas*—one of the largest passenger vessels in service—which holds 50% more passengers than Disney's largest ships.

AREA GETTING AROUND AND GETTING ORIENTED

WHO'S BETTER: Disney The free **DCL Navigator app** (see page 136) lets you see quickly what's going on at any time of day. We do like Royal Caribbean's touchscreen maps, located near the elevators.

AREA THEMING AND DETAIL OF PUBLIC SPACES

WHO'S BETTER: Tie DCL's stem-to-stern theming, based on the decor of classic ocean liners, makes its ships far prettier than RCI's, which, as one of our dinner companions once remarked, feel like "a really nice mall."

On the other hand, RCI's largest ships are big enough to host scaled-down versions of New York City's Central Park and Atlantic City's boardwalk. Likewise, RCI's collection of onboard art, curated from contemporary artists worldwide and displayed in walkways and stairwells, is more interesting to many adults than DCL's collection, which is inspired by Disney's animated films.

AREA DINING

WHO'S BETTER: Depends Both cruise lines provide breakfast, lunch, and dinner in standard restaurants as part of your fare. Service is excellent on both lines, but Disney's food is tastier and its restaurants more creatively themed.

On the other hand, Royal Caribbean's larger ships offer more than 20 optional dining locations (where you pay extra to eat), while DCL's ships have just 2 at the most. If you think you'll tire of eating at the same restaurants again and again, Royal is a better choice.

AREA IN-ROOM DINING

WHO'S BETTER: Disney Royal Caribbean charges guests $7.95 for basic room-service fare (Continental breakfast is free), while most of Disney's offerings are free.

AREA LIVE ENTERTAINMENT

WHO'S BETTER: Disney for kids, Royal Caribbean for adults Both lines put on extravagant stage shows: RCI's lineup includes Broadway staples such as *Cats, Grease, Hairspray,* and *Mamma Mia!;* DCL generally presents live adaptations of its musical animated films. RCI's shows are more varied than DCL's and appeal to adults; kids and Disney-loving kids at heart will love DCL's offerings.

AREA NIGHTCLUBS, BARS, AND LOUNGES

WHO'S BETTER: Disney Surprised? Where Royal Caribbean's bars tend to be large, open to pedestrian traffic, and barely themed, Disney's are more intimate and have appropriately atmospheric music and decor, and many sit in a dedicated adults-only area, far away from crowded public spaces. Plus, service is more personal on DCL.

AREA SHOPPING

WHO'S BETTER: Royal Caribbean Its larger ships carry a wider variety of men's and women's clothing, art, household items, and other goods. Both DCL and RCI sell men's and women's jewelry, resort wear, and sundries.

AREA SPA

WHO'S BETTER: Disney This is another area where DCL wins on theming and detail. While the Senses Spas on the *Dream* and the *Fantasy* are smaller than the spas on RCI's ships, Disney's overlook the ocean and have more heated-stone loungers, more themed showers, and better steam rooms. The *Wish* features an elegant outdoor spa retreat with loungers and space for doing yoga.

AREA POOLS

WHO'S BETTER: Disney for children, Royal Caribbean for adults The kids' play areas, slides, and water rides on the DCL ships are better than those on RCI's. The newer RCI ships have larger adult pools and more of them, spread across an even wider area than on Disney's largest ships. Both lines take safety seriously, with lifeguards on duty whenever the pools are open.

AREA PRIVATE ISLAND

WHO'S BETTER: Depends (for now) DCL and RCI both have award-winning private islands in the Bahamas. Whereas Disney's Castaway Cay (see Part Ten) is known for pristine, serene beaches, RCI's **Perfect Day at CocoCay** can be frenetic. Its Thrill Waterpark has 13 slides and a wave pool—along with an admission fee. The extra charges for things like beach rentals, zip lines, balloon rides, and the spa can also add up if you're not careful. Which experience is best depends on the mood you're after—but keep in mind that Disney is building a second private-island area that will likely make a giant splash (see page 6 for details).

AREA DEBARKATION

WHO'S BETTER: Royal Caribbean Both DCL and RCI can get you off the ship quickly, although RCI does it a bit faster. Disney's baggage-claim area is better organized, however, making it easier for you to find your checked luggage.

AREA GAMBLING

WHO'S BETTER: Depends Many RCI ships have full casinos with slot machines and tables dedicated to poker, blackjack, roulette, craps, and more. Admission is limited to guests ages 18-plus on most sailings. In contrast, the only onboard gambling offered on DCL is a bingo game once or twice a day, at which kids are welcome (see page 262 for details). If you like to gamble—or you don't—the choice is obvious.

AREA HEALTH AND SAFETY

WHO'S BETTER: Depends DCL ships consistently receive outstanding health and safety marks from the US Centers for Disease Control and Prevention (CDC), whose inspections include assessments of illness outbreaks. In the most recent CDC inspections, the *Dream* and *Wonder* both received perfect scores of 100 (on a 0–100 scale), and the *Magic* and *Fantasy* both scored in the high 90s. During the same inspection period, one of Royal Caribbean's 24 ships, the *Rhapsody of the Seas,* received a 100, with all others in the 90s, indicating a major improvement in RCI's cleaning protocols compared with previous inspections. When we first started covering cruises in 2014, a few RCI ships rated just barely above the CDC's failing score of 86.

In addition, be aware that both DCL and RCI fare better than some other cruise lines: in recent years, Princess Cruises, Norwegian Cruise Line, and even the upscale Silversea Cruises have had ships fail inspection.

For inspection updates, go to wwwn.cdc.gov/inspectionquerytool (*wwwn.* is correct). If you're interested in cruise ship safety, check out

ProPublica's report at projects.propublica.org/cruises. Their inspection data is out of date, but they do an excellent job of explaining what good ship safety looks like.

AREA COVID HEALTH AND SAFETY

WHO'S BETTER: Depends Both DCL and RCI tinkered with their vaccination and testing requirements several times while this edition was in production. As of September 2022, DCL requires that guests **ages 12 and older** be fully vaccinated for cruises originating in the US. Unvaccinated children under 12 must take a lab-processed COVID test one to three days before sailing. Unvaccinated guests on all sailings originating in the US are exempt from testing altogether as of November 2022.

For European sailings, Disney required that guests **ages 5 and older** be fully vaccinated at the time of this writing. Unvaxxed kids under 5 were required to take a test before embarkation day and a second test at the cruise terminal before boarding; vaccinated guests were required to take a pre-trip test but were exempt from the second test. These requirements could easily change after press time, though.

In September 2022, Royal Caribbean dropped its vaccination requirement for cruises sailing from American ports (with the exception of cruises visiting Bermuda and Canada) as well as European ports (with the exception of transatlantic sailings to the US). For US sailings, unvaccinated kids under 5 are required to take a COVID test one to three days before sailing. When it comes to vaxxed guests, RCI was actually a little stricter than DCL at press time: these guests were exempt from testing, but on cruises of nine nights or fewer rather than across the board.

Disney currently requires masks for unvaxxed kids in its youth clubs and in the ships' Bibbidi Bobbidi Boutiques; all guests ages 2 and older must wear masks on Castaway Cay (see Part Ten) in specific areas and situations. In contrast, Royal Caribbean generally makes masks optional for all guests in all situations, except as required in port.

If you insist on sailing with a cruise line that requires vaccination for most guests, then go with DCL—for now, anyway.

AREA INTERNET

WHO'S BETTER: Depends Technically, **Royal Caribbean** wins. Its Voom high-speed Wi-Fi—touted as the fastest internet at sea—lets you stream your favorite movies and TV shows, something you can't do using DCL's Wi-Fi. Disney is making strides to catch up, though. At press time, the *Fantasy, Magic,* and *Wish* had begun offering Wi-Fi packages by the day or for the length of your cruise, with three tiers based on your usage needs (see page 137 for details). The packages are pricey for what you get, but the service is faster and more stable than on the other ships. We expect the new system to roll out to the entire DCL fleet over the next year. If you don't want to get sucked into binging *Stranger Things* while you're at sea, then Disney will help you unplug . . . and isn't that the point of a cruise anyway?

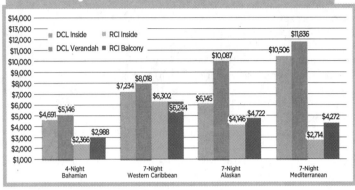

Price Differences Between Disney and Royal Caribbean Cruises

Legend: DCL Inside | RCI Inside | DCL Verandah | RCI Balcony

	4-Night Bahamian	7-Night Western Caribbean	7-Night Alaskan	7-Night Mediterranean
DCL Inside	$4,691	$7,234	$6,145	$10,506
RCI Inside	$5,146	$8,018	$4,146	$11,836
DCL Verandah	$2,366	$6,302	$4,722	$2,714
RCI Balcony	$2,988	$6,244	$10,087	$4,272

Cost Considerations

Money can't buy happiness, but it **can** *buy you a yacht big enough to pull up right alongside it.*

—David Lee Roth

Disney's fares include unlimited fountain soda, plain coffee, tea, and water (bottled soft drinks and water cost extra); Royal Caribbean doesn't charge for tap water, plain coffee, or tea, but it does charge for fountain soda. For 2022, RCI's least expensive beverage package, which is limited to fountain drinks, averaged $14 per person, per day—that works out to almost $400 for a family of four for a seven-night cruise. Adding mocktails, bottled water, fresh-squeezed juice, and premium coffee to the package cost $29–$38 per day in 2022, or upwards of $800 for the same family of four on the same cruise.

Needless to say, we don't recommend RCI's beverage package. For starters, their free coffee is better than DCL's, and although RCI officially prohibits bringing soda on board, they rarely enforce the ban when it comes to small quantities (say, a six-pack).

Beyond all that, though, it's hard for us to wrap our heads around drinking $400 worth of soda in a week. If you and your family limited yourselves to an occasional Coke with meals, you wouldn't spend anywhere close to $400 over the course of your trip.

So why, you may ask, are we nattering on about soda? Because when it comes to the cost of a cruise, that's virtually the only area where DCL has the advantage over RCI.

Make no mistake: Disney cruises are expensive. We discuss at length in this book the importance of figuring out if a DCL cruise is right for you and your family, and depending on what you're looking for in your cruise vacation, you may find—as many others do—that the benefits of sailing with Disney are worth the premium price tag.

We admit, however, that the value proposition isn't always clear-cut. Case in point: Disney charges more than Royal Caribbean for cruises that visit the same areas; DCL's ships, however, are often older and smaller than the ones RCI uses for equivalent sailings.

*un*official **TIP**
If a DCL cruise is out of your price range, or if you strongly prefer a newer ship with lots of bells and whistles, Royal Caribbean is a great alternative.

The chart at the top of the previous page shows the lowest fares available for cruises departing June 15–August 15, 2022, to four popular destinations served by Disney and RCI, for two adults and two kids ages 6 and 8; prices reflect the cheapest inside stateroom and the cheapest stateroom with an ocean-facing balcony, including taxes and fees. All cruises except the Mediterranean ones are round-trip, and all sailings depart from the same port except for the Alaskan cruises (DCL uses Vancouver, RCI uses Seattle). The ports visited are either exactly the same or similar.

Bahamian cruises out of Port Canaveral on the *Disney Wish* cost up to 90% more than comparable cruises on Royal Caribbean's *Independence of the Seas*. In this case, the price difference is partially explained by the ships sailing these routes: a brand-new DCL vessel versus an RCI ship that entered service in 2008.

The "new ship" argument doesn't hold water (so to speak) for seven-night **Caribbean** cruises on the *Disney Fantasy* and Royal Caribbean's *Wonder of the Seas*. In this case, DCL's cruises are roughly 15%–30% more expensive than RCI's, but *Wonder of the Seas* is a brand-new ship—not to mention it's the largest cruise ship in the world at the moment. Conversely, the *Fantasy* is more than a decade older and a good bit smaller than *Wonder of the Seas.*

The price differences for **Alaskan** and **Mediterranean** cruises are likewise a head-scratcher. For every sailing, Royal Caribbean's ships are newer, bigger, and flashier than Disney's, yet in every case, DCL charges considerably more than RCI—almost **$8,000** more, in fact, for a Mediterranean cruise in an inside stateroom.

And get this: for the price of a seven-night Mediterranean cruise in a Verandah stateroom on DCL, you could book not only a comparable Mediterranean cruise but also a seven-night Alaskan cruise *and* a four-night Bahamian cruise on RCI.

When you cruise with DCL, what you're really paying for is the Disney brand—that is, a unique experience designed to appeal to families and fans of Disney's theme parks and movie/TV franchises. Branding aside, though, we suspect another factor is at play: specifically, we think DCL assumes its target market isn't bothering to comparison-shop.

HOW *to* **CONTACT**
the **AUTHORS**

MANY WHO USE THE UNOFFICIAL GUIDES write to us with questions, comments, or their own travel strategies. Readers' comments are frequently incorporated into revised editions and have contributed immeasurably to their improvement. If you'd like to get in touch, you can write or email us at the following addresses:

Erin, Len, and Ritchey
The Unofficial Guide to Disney Cruise Line
2204 First Ave. S., Ste. 102
Birmingham, AL 35233
info@theunofficialguides.com

You can also look us up on social media: **@TheUnofficialGuides** on Facebook; **@TheUGSeries** on Twitter, Instagram, and Pinterest; and **TheUnofficialGuideSeries** on YouTube.

STAY UPDATED WITH THE LATEST NEWS

WHEN IT COMES TO DISNEY CRUISE LINE, the only constant is change, so it's important to stay abreast of the latest developments even after this book goes to press. The **Touring Plans blog** (blog.touringplans .com) posts regular DCL updates; we'll also aggregate this information and post updates and corrections for this edition of the print book at a special webpage: see tinyurl.com/UGDisneyCruise2023.

READER SURVEY

OUR WEBSITE HOSTS A QUESTIONNAIRE you can use to express opinions about your Disney cruise: touringplans.com/disney-cruise-line /survey. The questionnaire lets every member of your party, regardless of age, tell us what they think about attractions, restaurants, and more. If you'd rather print out the survey and mail it to us, send it to **Reader Survey** using the street address above.

PART ONE

DOLLARS *and* SENSE

WHAT'S INCLUDED *in* YOUR DISNEY CRUISE FARE

AS WE TOLD YOU EARLIER, a Disney cruise isn't cheap. Given the cost, you might be wondering how much more you'll have to pay once you're aboard the ship. Here's a quick rundown of what is and isn't included in your cruise fare. We've included some rough estimates of the optional items to help you with budgeting.

FOOD

INCLUDED: LOTS OF FOOD All meals, including snacks, are free at all of the ship's restaurants *except* the adult-dining venues **Enchanté, Palo, Palo Steakhouse,** and **Remy.**

NOT INCLUDED: FANCY RESTAURANTS **Remy** and **Enchanté** cost an additional $125 per person for dinner and $75 for brunch. **Palo** and **Palo Steakhouse** cost $45 per person at brunch and dinner. Palo's dinner is fixed-price, but be aware that many popular dishes are no longer included in the cost of your meal—they're now à la carte only. Keeping that in mind, and figuring in tips and alcohol, you'll likely pay considerably more than the quoted $45.

INCLUDED: MOST ROOM-SERVICE FOOD Your fare includes room service meals, except as noted xref. Room service is a great option if you're in the mood for breakfast on your verandah or you don't feel like dressing up for dinner.

INCLUDED: ALL-YOU-WANT SOFT DRINKS AND ICE CREAM Soda, coffee, water, cocoa, and hot and iced tea are free and unlimited at meals, as are beverages served from the drink dispensers on deck. Soft-serve ice cream is also free, but the specialty ice creams sold at **Vanellope's Sweets & Treats** on the *Dream,* **Sweet on You** on the *Fantasy,* and **Inside Out: Joyful Sweets** on the *Wish* cost extra, as do the specialty smoothies at the pool-deck windows and in the spas.

THE BEST BANGS FOR YOUR BUCK ON A DCL CARIBBEAN CRUISE

1. Porters for your bags The $2–$5 per bag you'll tip your porter both boarding and returning home is money well spent. When you're boarding, not having to handle your own bags is one less hassle in a hectic process. When you debark, it helps you end your cruise on a high note.

2. Oceanview staterooms If the prospect of three to seven nights in a cabin with no natural light is more than you can bear but a Verandah room is beyond your budget, we recommend a room with a porthole. Located on the lower decks, Oceanview staterooms not only offer a closer view of the sea, they don't sell as quickly as Inside rooms (least expensive) and Verandah rooms (often in the highest demand). Oceanview cabins also have the best access to the main dining rooms, Guest Services, and the adult lounge areas.

3. Cabanas on Castaway Cay *Hold up! How can you possibly recommend something that costs at least $400 as a bang for your buck?* Here's the thing: the amenities that come with a cabana equal more than the sum of its parts. If you have enough people to fill a cabana or you can find someone to share with, the free equipment rentals, shelter from the sun, dedicated beach (Family Beach), and personalized service make this something well worth checking out. Our only qualm in including the cabanas here is the fact that they're notoriously difficult to book. See page 315 for details.

4. Brunch at Palo or Palo Steakhouse A quiet, no-rush brunch or dinner for adults with great service and fantastic food for just $45 plus tip? *Yeah, baby!*

5. Room service Most items on the room service menu are free. For the price of a tip, you can get a cheese plate to stave off the afternoon munchies, fresh coffee and pastries in the morning, or warm cookies and milk in your stateroom before bed, among other treats. That's our idea of pampering!

6. Castaway Ray's Stingray Adventure It's a winner with kids and adults. There's no time wasted getting back and forth to your port adventure because it's on Castaway Cay—just show up at your appointed time and have fun interacting with the rays. See page 330 for more info.

7. Coffee The swill at the beverage stations can best be described as a tepid, vaguely coffee-flavored substance that could sap you of your will to live. Pony up for the good stuff at **Cove Café, Vista Café,** or the coffee bar at the buffets. Sure, it's around $3–$6 plus tip, but that's less than you'd pay at Starbucks. Ask for a **Café Fanatic** rewards card and get every sixth coffee drink free. (For us, that's sometime early in day two of any cruise.)

8. Castaway Cay 5K This port adventure is free, and you can take pride in knowing that you've gotten your exercise in for the day. There are plastic medals, regardless of how fast or slow you "run." To keep it real, try to beat your personal best every time you come to the island.

9. Gratuities DCL ships are full of enthusiastic cast members, who work hard to make your trip magical. To ensure great service, please give generous tips not only to your servers and stateroom attendants but also your baristas and bartenders. And don't forget these folks when you're filling out your comment cards at the end of the cruise.

NOT INCLUDED: BOTTLED DRINKS, PACKAGED SNACKS, ALCOHOL, AND FANCY COFFEES Bottled water, soda not served as part of meal service or on the pool deck, and alcoholic beverages cost extra, as do packaged snacks such as popcorn and peanuts. You'll also pay out of pocket for specialty coffees, espresso, cappuccinos, and teas from bars and cafés (such as the **Cove Café**). Adults ages 21 and older may bring a limited amount of beer and wine aboard in their carry-on luggage; a $25 corking fee applies if you bring your own wine to a full-service restaurant on board.

NOT INCLUDED: THEATER SNACKS A kiosk outside the movie theaters and live-production venues sells soft drinks, beer and wine, packaged snacks like M&M's, and fresh popcorn before showtimes. The prices are a smidge less than you'd pay at your local cineplex—but you can always grab a soda and a plate of chicken nuggets and fries from the top deck to nosh on for free.

NOT INCLUDED: SOME BAR SNACKS Many onboard bars offer free nighttime nibbles such as chips and salsa, cut veggies, or mini hot dogs. If you want more-substantial or themed bar food (bangers and mash at **O'Gills,** for example), expect to pay $8–$12 per item.

ENTERTAINMENT AND ACTIVITIES

INCLUDED: LOTS OF ENTERTAINMENT There's no extra charge for the live shows, movies, and character sightings.

NOT INCLUDED: BINGO The only form of gambling offered on DCL, bingo games start at about $15 for a three-pack of paper cards and go up to about $75 for a family pack of two 24-chance electronic handsets, plus bonus paper-card packs.

NOT INCLUDED: SOME ONBOARD SEMINARS The most notable examples of fee-based seminars are the many adult-beverage tastings. Most cost $40–$50 per person, with a few climbing into the $100 range. Other examples include hands-on instruction in things like decorating gingerbread houses.

INCLUDED: GYM FACILITIES Covered in your fare is use of the fitness center, which has weights, cardio machines, and floor equipment along with changing rooms with showers and a sauna.

NOT INCLUDED: PERSONAL TRAINING AND SOME FITNESS CLASSES Body Sculpt Boot Camp packages, for example, consist of two 30-minute sessions for $69 or four 30-minute sessions for $119. Personal training is offered at $89 for a 45-minute session. An 18% gratuity may apply depending on the class.

NOT INCLUDED: SPA AND SALON SERVICES Spa treatments (including massages, facials, steam rooms, and upscale showers) cost from $118 to more than $500 per person, per treatment. Salon services range from $50 to $70 for manicures and pedicures and from about $35 to $75 for hairstyling, depending on hair length.

INCLUDED: POOLS AND MOST SPORTS Pools, waterslides, and many outdoor hot tubs are included, as are activities such as miniature golf, basketball, and shuffleboard (when available).

INCLUDED: CASTAWAY CAY BEACHES AND RESTAURANTS Food, lounge chairs, and beach umbrellas are free, as is the island's 5K road run.

NOT INCLUDED: CASTAWAY CAY RECREATION AND ALCOHOL DCL charges for bike rentals, floats, snorkeling, and use of watercraft. Private cabanas are also available for an upcharge (see page 315). Alcohol pricing on Castaway Cay is comparable to that on the ships.

KID STUFF

INCLUDED: KIDS' CLUBS (AGES 3 AND UP) These include the **Oceaneer Club/Oceaneer Lab** for kids ages 3–12, the **Edge** club for tweens ages 11–14, and the **Vibe** club for teens ages 14–17.

NOT INCLUDED: CHILDCARE FOR KIDS UNDER 3 It's a Small World Nursery charges $9 per hour for the first child and $8 per hour for a second child in the same family.

NOT INCLUDED: MAKEOVERS AT THE BIBBIDI BOBBIDI BOUTIQUE Kids' salon services start at about $70 for the Swashbuckle package available on Pirate Night; basic princess hairstyling, makeup, and nail-polish application starts at about $100; and princess packages top out at **more than $1,000** for multinight experiences with several costumes. (Yes, we love our kids. But perhaps not *this* much.) All makeovers are available to both boys and girls.

NOT INCLUDED: TEA PARTIES AND SUCH Some DCL ships offer special dining experiences for children—the **Royal Court Royal Tea Party** on the *Fantasy,* for example—at a substantial additional charge. See page 285 for details.

SCOTT'S MONEY-SAVING STRATEGIES
by Scott Sanders

IT'S COMPLETELY POSSIBLE to go on a Disney cruise and not spend a dime aside from gratuities. The ships offer essentially everything you need and more while you're on board, but there are plenty of opportunities to enhance your vacation. That said, I suggest budgeting for some onboard spending—it *is* a vacation, after all.

My favorite money-saving strategy is to book shore excursions via third parties. The catch: sticking to the all-aboard time so you don't miss the ship. If that sounds too stressful, just explore on your own where it's safe to do so.

Not picky about where you sleep? Then book an inside stateroom—the money you save here can go toward splurges on other fun stuff. If you're just using your room for sleeping, showering, and changing clothes, why spend more?

To save 10% on your next cruise, buy a "placeholder" for a future cruise (which is really simple with the DCL Navigator app), or book your next cruise while you're on the ship. Onboard booking saves you money on not only the overall price of your cruise but also the amount of your deposit for voyages of seven nights and longer.

MISCELLANEOUS

INCLUDED: SOME TEXT MESSAGING The **DCL Navigator app** (see page 136) lets you communicate over Wi-Fi with other Navigator users on board. Owners of iPhones and iPads can use **iMessage** (see pages 70 and 71) to text other Apple devices both on and off the ship (you can't send photos or videos, though).

NOT INCLUDED: INTERNET Except for accessing the Navigator app and a limited free trial on embarkation day, you must pay to use your ship's Wi-Fi network. See Part Four (page 137) for pricing information and tech tips.

NOT INCLUDED: SHIP-TO-SHORE CALLS Each stateroom has a landline-style phone (remember those?) with voice mail; ship-to-shore calls from these phones cost an astronomical $7–$9.50 a minute. See Part Two (page 69) for our advice on using your cell phone during your cruise.

NOT INCLUDED: PHOTOS Similar to the Memory Maker packages at Walt Disney World, DCL offers packages of photos taken by onboard photographers. Most packages are expensive, and none are included in the price of your cruise. See page 308 for details.

NOT INCLUDED: SHORE EXCURSIONS Known in DCL-speak as **port adventures,** these cost anywhere from about $13 for a 1-hour bike rental on Castaway Cay to about $3,400 for the 4-hour private Elite Whales and Glaciers Photo Safari in Juneau, Alaska. Be aware that shore excursions often carry extra-cost options such as photo packages; also note that meals may not be included. Bring cash to tip your guides.

NOT INCLUDED: LAUNDRY It costs $3 to wash and $3 to dry a load of clothes in the onboard laundry rooms. Soap, fabric softener, and dryer sheets are available for $1 each, per load. Dry-cleaning is also available for an additional fee. Typical pricing is about $6 to dry-clean a man's shirt. Garment pressing is available for about half the price of dry-cleaning.

NOT INCLUDED: TIPS Disney automatically adds gratuities of around $13.50 per person per day to your onboard account. A 18% gratuity is automatically added to bar and beverage tabs. See the section starting on page 140 for our tipping guidelines.

NOT INCLUDED: TRANSPORTATION TO THE PORT Round-trip service between Walt Disney World and Port Canaveral runs $78 per person; transportation costs between any city's cruise terminal and airport will vary. See the section starting on page 119 for details.

CRUISING *With* KIDS

LET US START BY SAYING that your kids will almost certainly have a blast on a DCL cruise. (See pages 153 and 267 for more advice on cruising with teens and tweens.)

As parents, we know that one of the most difficult parts of planning a vacation with kids is ensuring that they stay entertained. For us, this usually means making sure that every travel day has at least a couple of things specifically designed to appeal to our kids and their friends—things that we'd prefer didn't involve shopping or sitting passively in front of a screen.

It can be exhausting to plan this way (and we're *professionals*!). And it's one of the main reasons that a trip to Disney World is so appealing to parents: Disney's theme parks provide nearly constant, wide-ranging entertainment options for both kids and adults. A family that hasn't planned a thing beyond making a park reservation can show up and find something fun to do. Disney cruises work the same way: family activities, including trivia contests, scavenger hunts, and shuffleboard, are scheduled throughout the day, on virtually every day of every sailing.

DCL provides nearly nonstop organized activities for kids ages 3–17. Some activities for younger children get started as early as 7 a.m., while activities for older teens can run until 2 a.m. on some sailings.

COVID TIP

During the height of the pandemic, the kids' clubs were open by timed reservation only. While this restriction had been lifted as of press time, keep in mind that Disney could bring it back in the event of a future virus surge.

Off the ships, Castaway Cay (see Part Ten) has designated recreation area for families, teens, and tweens, plus a splash pad area for little ones. There are also shore excursions created just for families; plus, some port stops include teen-only excursions and sightseeing events.

While the youth clubs on the *Magic* and *Wonder* are substantially smaller than the ones on the *Dream, Fantasy,* and *Wish,* note that DCL frequently runs concurrent, age-appropriate activities within the same club. For example, the Ocean-eer Club accepts children ages 3–12; however, the younger kids may gather for a game with marshmallows in one area of the club while the older kids sing karaoke in another.

Our own children have found Disney's kids' activities much more fun than hanging around with us on the ship. It may be a cliché, but it's true: we saw the kids only during meals, at bedtime, or when we specifically scheduled things to do as a family. Thanks to the internet, our kids are still in contact with the friends they've made on their cruises, even though some are an ocean away.

On the other hand, if your kids aren't interested in the clubs, or if you're determined to make your cruise a time for family togetherness, there are still plenty of activities that you can enjoy as a family. These include structured things like family game shows and trivia contests, and unstructured things like board games and scavenger hunts.

■ CRUISING *Without* KIDS

GIVEN THAT DISNEY IS SYNONYMOUS with *family-friendly,* it's natural for those who travel without children to wonder if DCL is a good choice for them. Happily, just as with the Disney parks, there's something for folks of all ages to enjoy on a Disney cruise. Disney ships have an adults-only pool and coffeehouse. Some entertainment districts are adults-only after 9 p.m., and the spas are limited to ages 18 and up (with the exception of teens in the Chill Spa). Likewise, every ship has restaurants that don't allow kids (see Part Seven). Castaway Cay has an adult beach with its own dining, bar, and cabanas (which must be reserved in advance). We recommend traveling when school is in session if you're looking for a more adult-oriented vacation; the good news is that these times tend to be far less expensive.

 ***unofficial* TIP**
According to Disney cast members we've talked to, the long ship-repositioning cruises (such as the Panama Canal itinerary) and Transatlantic voyages tend to have the fewest children on board.

If your idea of a fun cruise is a party barge, then DCL probably isn't for you—there's no casino, and honestly the nightlife is more mild than wild. If, on the other hand, raucous exploits aren't your thing, then the sedate nature of Disney cruising could be just what you're looking for. Spend some time at the spa, skip the stage shows, dine at the adult restaurants, and enjoy some downtime. We've traveled several times with just adults in our party and had a fantastic time.

WHERE *to* FIND MORE INFORMATION

DISNEY CRUISE LINE'S official website is **DisneyCruise.com** (the longer version is disneycruise.disney.go.com). Here you can see which itineraries are served by each ship; search for cruises by destination, month, and length; and check stateroom prices. After your sailing is booked and paid for, this is also where you'll make reservations for port adventures, restaurants, and children's activities.

Free **trip-planning videos** for DCL, Walt Disney World, Adventures by Disney (including AbD river and expedition cruises; see Part Thirteen), and other Disney destinations are available at disneycruise .disney.go.com/cruise-planning-tools. (*Note:* You'll need to fill out a short survey before you can watch the videos.) The DCL video can also be accessed through the **My Reservations** area of the DCL site (see page 47). Besides being a good planning tool, the video is a good way to prepare kids who've never cruised before.

The **Disney Parks Blog** (disneyparks.disney.go.com/blog) is the official public source for news about the Disney theme parks worldwide, Disney Cruise Line, Adventures by Disney, Disney's Aulani resort in Hawaii, and more. To find DCL stories, click "Destinations" at the top of the page, and then scroll down to "Disney Cruise Line," or look for articles with the orange ship symbol in the upper-left corner.

DCLNews.com posts official news and PR about Disney Cruise Line. Though intended for the media, most of the site is open to the public. The information resources include fact sheets and press releases, as well as photos and videos of the ships.

Scott Sanders's **Disney Cruise Line Blog** (disneycruiselineblog.com) posts almost-daily updates, including everything from rumors about new itineraries to the skinny on new shopping merchandise. The site also has a cool feature that lets you see the current location of every ship in the Disney fleet. In addition, you'll find tips and advice from Scott throughout this book. For up-to-the-minute DCL news, Scott's Twitter feed, **@TheDCLBlog,** is another terrific resource.

The **planDisney Panel** (plandisney.disney.go.com) is staffed by veterans of many DCL voyages. Trained by Disney cast members, the planDisney team can answer virtually any DCL planning question, big or small. The site also hosts short videos on Disney trip planning, including content specific to DCL (see plandisney.disney.go.com /plandisney-video-library).

Some popular unofficial Disney sites with dedicated DCL discussion forums include **DISboards** (disboards.com); **WDWMagic** (wdw magic.com; choose "Forums" and then "Disney Cruise Line"); and, for Brits, **The DIBB** (Disney Information Bulletin Board; thedibb.co.uk).

If you enjoy listening to podcasts, three that focus specifically on Disney cruising are *The DCL Dude* (thedcldudepodcast.libsyn.com), the *DCL Podcast* (dclpodcast.com), and *DCL Duo* (dclduo.com). Our friend Matt Hochberg hosts the *Royal Caribbean Blog Podcast* (royal caribbeanblog.com/podcast), which offers useful tips about cruising in general as well as insights about some of the ports that DCL visits. Want the inside scoop on all things Disney? Check out *The Disney Dish,* hosted by Len Testa, the coauthor of this book, and Jim Hill, an entertainment writer and Disney historian. (Go to podcasts.jimhillmedia .com and click on "Disney Dish Podcast.")

MouseSavers (mousesavers.com) offers discounts and money-saving tips for all aspects of Disney trip planning, shopping, and entertainment. Click on the "Disney Cruise Line" tab for the latest information about DCL promotions and special offers. Speaking of deals and discounts, online travel guru **The Points Guy** (Brian Kelly) has a section on DCL at his website (thepointsguy.com/cruise/disney-cruise-line).

The **US government** offers a wealth of online resources for citizens traveling to other countries. For example, the **Department of State**'s travel website (travel.state.gov) features weather and safety advisories, advice on what to do if you've lost your passport, information on visa requirements, and more.

COVID TIP
You can find the CDC's COVID-era guidelines for cruise ships at tinyurl .com/CDCCovidCruise.

The **CDC Traveler's Health** website (cdc .gov/travel) includes both a general section about cruise-related health concerns (wwwnc .cdc.gov/travel/page/cruise-ship) and a section with COVID-specific resources (tinyurl .com/CruiseTravelCOVID19). *Note:* In a somewhat controversial move, the CDC discontinued its COVID-19 reporting program for cruise ships in July 2022; however, the agency continues to provide general guidance regarding testing, vaccination, quarantining, and preventative measures.

The **World Travel Guide**'s country reports (worldtravelguide.net /country-guides) are an easy-to-read source of information about foreign ports. Though the site is geared primarily to British and European travelers, Americans will also find it helpful.

If you're flying to your cruise's embarkation point, check both your airline's website and the **Transportation Security Administration** website (tsa.gov) to make sure you're up to date on current air-travel rules and procedures. We find the list of prohibited travel items (tinyurl.com /TSAWhatCanIBring) particularly helpful. Be aware, however, that acceptable items for air travel and DCL boarding vary (see page 75).

If you're interested in the legal nuances of cruising, maritime attorney Jim Walker's **Cruise Law News** blog (cruiselawnews.com) discusses issues related to passenger and crew legal rights on most major cruise lines.

The **Sitata Travel Safe** app (iOS and Android) spotlights travel-safety issues by country; it also provides information on medical assistance and warnings about tourist traps.

If you're interested in learning more about the types of jobs available on DCL and other cruise lines, take a look at the **Florida-Caribbean Cruise Association**'s Cruise Industry Onboard Employment Overview booklet (tinyurl.com/FCCAGuide).

Finally, try searching **Facebook** for a group specific to your DCL sailing. Many cruise-specific groups share tips on excursion booking, pricing changes, and other information, as well as organizing private mixology classes or gift exchanges. It's a great way to meet new friends before you sail. The DCL board on **Reddit** (reddit.com/r/dcl) is another excellent source of up-to-the-minute news and advice.

IS IT WORTH IT?

AS YOU PLAN YOUR CRUISE, you may find yourself asking questions along these lines:

*un*official **TIP**
In a nutshell, worth is achieved when benefits exceed costs.

• Is it worth paying a higher price for Disney versus another cruise line? • Is splurging on a cabana worth the (considerable) expense? • My child wants to go to the princess tea. Is it worth it? • Is the food at Palo Steakhouse worth the upcharge? • This photo package seems expensive—should I skip it? • Is that helicopter excursion *really* worth $4,000? • Should I spring for a second stateroom for my family with teens?

You may also have some non-money-related questions:

• Do I want to keep my preschool-age daughter up late to go to the fireworks show on Pirate Night? • Should we get off the ship in Nassau? • Is meeting Cinderella worth the wait in line? • Is a Disney cruise worth the trouble if it means taking my child out of school?

The dirty little secret most travel writers won't tell you is that our answers to these questions is, "We don't know"—and we say that even after having asked ourselves about all of these things and paid for them out of our own pockets.

Here's what we *do* know: We can tell you what the charge on your Amex card will be. We can tell you our (and other guests') personal perceptions of the quality of the food, the service, and the attention to detail. We can tell you what the views are like, how long waits are likely to be, and which experiences were worth it *to us*—but we can't tell you whether they'll be worth it *to you*. (Heck, even the coauthors of this book disagree about the worth of some DCL activities and expenses.)

Because vacation time and money are scarce commodities, you want to be reassured that the benefits you'll gain from your experiences will be greater than your investment in those experiences, in terms of both money and time. You want to be reassured that your investment will be worth it. But we can't tell you if a Disney cruise will be worth it *to you*, because we don't know you.

As an example, consider the Senses Spa Ultimate Indulgence package, which costs a hefty $600 and includes a fancy facial, a deep-tissue massage, time in the Rainforest saunas, and all the herbal tea you can choke down. Len loves it, but there's absolutely no way this $600, 3-hour investment would be worth it to Erin, who doesn't like being touched by strangers and prefers coffee over tea.

So how do you determine whether any specific Disney cruise experience will be worth it *to you?* Here are more questions to consider:

1. **What is your income and/or vacation budget?** If you make $50,000 a year, then spending 10% (or a lot more than 10%) of your total annual income on a cruise vacation would be a significant expense. If you make $500,000 a year, it would take far less of a bite out of your bottom line.

2. **What is the financial opportunity cost of the experience?** Will spending money on a cabana mean you'll have less money to spend on things like port adventures and adult dining? If push comes to shove, which would you rather have?

3. **What is the time opportunity cost of the experience?** Is going on that 8-hour port adventure more important than experiencing the ship's amenities to their fullest?

4. **What are the real financial costs of the experience?** Have you researched the options for promotions and discounts? What are the hidden taxes, gratuities, or other fees that would make the experience more costly? How could you make the experience *less* costly?

5. **Will you have opportunities to experience this event again, or is it a one-time-only experience?** For example, if Christmas is the only time your extended family, including your aging parents, are available to travel, then the extra expense of a holiday cruise might be well worth it.

6. **Are there aspects of your personality that will affect the experience?** If you detest having to dress up for dinner, then Remy wouldn't be worth it to you, no matter how good the food is. (For us, it's *1,000%* worth it.)

7. **Are there aspects of other family members' personalities that will affect the experience?** What would you do if your child didn't want to go to the kids' clubs? Would your vacation be affected (positively or negatively) if you had less opportunity for adult time?

8. **Is a reasonable facsimile of this experience available elsewhere?** If, say, you've experienced that cool zip line course back home, then you can probably skip the zip line excursion in port.

9. **Why do you want to cruise?** Do you value relaxation? Convenience? Novelty? Adventure? Indulgence? Quality or quantity of food? Ease of planning? Family time? Private time? If the cruise doesn't push one or more of these buttons, then it's probably not worth it.

10. **Will you feel frustrated if you have to do without something you're used to?** If, for instance, you dread having to sleep in the same room with your kids, then the extra expense of a second stateroom may well be worth it.

11. **Will these experiences make for great memories down the road?** A princess or pirate makeover for your kids at the Bibbidi Bobbidi Boutique might seem like an unnecessary indulgence. But if you know your Disney princess-obsessed 5-year-old will be overjoyed to get the royal treatment and will talk about it for months afterward, then it could be worth the expense after all.

12. **How disappointed would you be if the cruise didn't go as planned?** Let's face it—things don't always happen as we expect them to: the weather doesn't cooperate, kids get sick, and so on. If you think the experience will be a total bust if it's not absolutely perfect, then a cruise may not be for you.

13. **Would you do this even if it were free?** We have friends who are deathly afraid of heights. Even if someone gifted them with a parasailing excursion at Castaway Cay, they wouldn't take it.

14. **Will you feel guilty or foolish if you spend your time or money on the experience?** There can often be waits of well more than an hour for the AquaDuck waterslides on the *Dream*-class ships. If it were Erin's favorite slide in the universe, she had nothing but time on her hands, and she knew that she'd never get to experience it again, she'd still hate herself for waiting that long for a water ride that lasts just a couple of minutes. Likewise, we have family members who think blowing money on fancy food is ridiculous—they would feel guilty if they spent $200 to eat at Remy, even if it was the best food they'd ever tasted.

By asking yourself these and similar questions, you may be able to determine on your own whether a particular DCL experience will be worth it to you. If you still have questions, try these tips:

Get advice from someone in a situation similar to yours. If you have three kids who are crazy about the Disney princesses and you're trying to decide whether to shell out hundreds of dollars for makeovers at the Bibbidi Bobbidi Boutique, a parent whose kids are obsessed with football and the Marvel superheroes probably wouldn't be much help. Likewise, if you have a taste for luxury, chances are that someone who travels as frugally as possible would tell you *not* to spring for a Concierge-level suite.

Someone with circumstances similar to yours will likely have the most useful perspectives. Finding someone you can relate to is particularly important when lurking on message boards, reading reviews at travel sites, and scanning social media posts.

Ask your advisor(s) for a benchmark. If you're seeking DCL advice from someone you don't know personally, try to get their opinion on something you're both familiar with. If, say, you both like restaurants X and Y, then chances are good that you'll agree with their assessment of restaurant Z.

In one recent social media discussion, a would-be DCL cruiser posed this question: "We're new to cruising, and my husband is losing his mind over the several-thousand-dollar price difference between

Disney and another cruise line for nearly the same route on the same dates. What are you getting on Disney for all that extra money?"

The responses included the following:

We love Disney and wish we could cruise with them all the time, but we think Royal Caribbean has a lot to offer for less money.

*Disney has the best food, the best ships, the best shows, the best crew, the best **everything**. You feel like royalty the second you walk on board.*

*I've cruised on Royal Caribbean as well as Disney, and the easiest way to sum up the difference is this: When we cruised with Royal Caribbean, I felt like I was on a floating mall. When we cruise with Disney, we feel like we're **on vacation**.*

When it comes to comparing DCL with other cruise lines, think Disney World vs. Universal Studios—both are super-entertaining and have lots to offer guests, but they have a totally different feel.

*We started cruising with DCL and have been on three cruises with them so far. We decided to try Royal Caribbean for the first time this year, and we were so disappointed that we've vowed never to cruise with anyone but Disney from now on. **The price is well worth it.***

A pure bottom-line analysis is important when planning any expenditure such as a vacation—you can only afford what your budget allows, after all—but you should also consider what your vacation goals are. Do you want your children to be fully occupied during your trip, or do you want to travel without kids? Do you want a certain type of food on the ship, or do you not care just as long as it's there when you get hungry? Do you want to go on port adventures, or do you just want to relax, sip fruity cocktails, and stare at the ocean? Depending on your answers to these questions and more, the extra cost of cruising with Disney might well be worth it to you . . . or it might not.

Don't take an online reviewer's word for it. We'd like to thank our friend Matt Hochberg of the Royal Caribbean Blog (see page 8) for pointing us to a *New York Times* article called "Why You Can't Really Trust Negative Online Reviews." It starts with a bemusing fact: "The Great Wall of China has more than 9,000 Google reviews, with an average of 4.2 stars. Not bad for one of the most astonishing achievements in human history."

The point here, however strange, is that when it comes to online comments, you can't please everyone. The *Times* also notes, "Reviews are subjective [even ours], and the tiny subset of people who leave reviews aren't average." So if you see extremely biased comments about DCL online, know that they're not necessarily the last word, and weigh them against other, more balanced commentary.

PART TWO

PLANNING YOUR CRUISE

CHOOSING *an* ITINERARY

DISNEY CRUISE LINE OFFERS more than 50 different itineraries that cover 11 geographic regions or major routes, classified as follows: **Alaska, Bahamas, Bermuda, Canadian Coastline, Caribbean, Europe, Hawaii, Mexico, Pacific Coast, Panama Canal,** and **Transatlantic.** (A fifth region, **Oceania,** is being added in 2023; see page 6 for details.)

These cruises don't necessarily fit neatly into their assigned geographic categories as defined by Disney, however. For example, the sailings that DCL classifies as Canadian stop only along the Atlantic Coast; and DCL's Alaska cruises include Vancouver, British Columbia, as a port of call.

Further muddying the waters, so to speak, Disney breaks out a number of these cruise regions into subcategories. For instance, Caribbean cruises

> **unofficial TIP**
> The average DCL cruise lasts five nights, sails somewhere in the Caribbean, and stops at Disney's Castaway Cay island in the Bahamas.

encompass Eastern, Western, and Southern Caribbean itineraries, while European cruises comprise Northern European, British Isles, Mediterranean, Norwegian Fjords, and Western European itineraries—which are sometimes subdivided even further into trips named things like "Mediterranean with Greek Isles" and "Norwegian Fjords with Iceland."

DCL uses **repositioning cruises** whenever it needs to move a ship between the US and Europe, between the Atlantic and the Pacific, or from one base port to another within a geographic area (say, from San Juan, Puerto Rico, to Port Canaveral, Florida). Any cruise that starts at one port and ends at another is a repositioning cruise, the most notable being DCL's **Transatlantic** and **Panama Canal** cruises.

To appeal to as wide an audience as possible, Disney cruises vary in length (and price) within each geographic area. Guests interested in visiting the Bahamas, for instance, can choose from cruises of three, four, or five nights.

To help fit its ships into the ports' schedules, DCL offers multiple versions of many itineraries, each of which visits exactly the same ports but in a different order. Consider the many four-night Bahamian cruises out of Port Canaveral on the *Wish:* all visit Nassau and Castaway Cay and include a day at sea, but at the time of this writing they can be configured in the following six ways:

4-NIGHT BAHAMIAN CRUISE ITINERARIES (*WISH*)				
ITINERARY	**NIGHT 1**	**NIGHT 2**	**NIGHT 3**	**NIGHT 4**
Version 1	Port Canaveral	Nassau	Castaway Cay	At sea
Version 2	Port Canaveral	Nassau	At sea	Castaway Cay
Version 3	Port Canaveral	At sea	Nassau	Castaway Cay
Version 4	Port Canaveral	At sea	Castaway Cay	Nassau
Version 5	Port Canaveral	Castaway Cay	Nassau	At sea
Version 6	Port Canaveral	Castaway Cay	At sea	Nassau

As long as the itinerary you choose offers the ports you want, there's little need to worry about the order in which you experience them. Simply choose your cruise based on the dates and pricing that make the most sense for you and your family.

IDEAL ITINERARIES FOR FIRST-TIME CRUISERS

IF YOU'VE NEVER CRUISED BEFORE, we recommend an itinerary of **four or five nights on the *Dream.*** Why? It's a larger ship, with good restaurants, bars, and a spa; ample space for kids' activities; and plentiful areas on deck for pools and lounging.

The *Fantasy* is equal to the *Dream* in these respects but sails primarily on seven-night itineraries. If you're looking for a slightly longer cruise vacation, then it's another excellent choice.

The ***Wish*** sails itineraries similar to the *Dream*'s, with a preponderance of three- and four-night sailings in the Bahamas. So why aren't we recommending the shiny new star of the Disney fleet for your first cruise? Because "shiny and new" comes with a steep price tag: for many stateroom categories and dates in 2023, the *Wish* is priced from $500 to $1,000 more per trip (for a party of two adults) than the exact same itineraries sailed by the *Dream* (except the *Dream* is sailing from Miami or Port Everglades instead of Port Canaveral).

Having experienced the *Wish* for ourselves, we can tell you it doesn't lack for a wow factor—but for now, we think first-time cruisers will be just as wowed by the *Dream,* and for a lot less money.

GENERAL RECOMMENDATIONS

IF YOU'RE TRYING TO DECIDE among Eastern Caribbean, Western Caribbean, and Bahamian cruises, then you have just a couple of questions to answer:

1. Are you interested in exploring the culture of the ports you're visiting?
2. If so, are you more interested in Caribbean towns or Mayan history?

If you're interested in local color, either DCL's **Eastern Caribbean** or **Western Caribbean** itineraries fill the bill. The Western Caribbean cruises visit the Mexican ports of Costa Maya and Cozumel, notable for their Mayan ruins (visited on DCL port adventures). If those interest you more than Caribbean beach towns, then choose the Western itinerary. Our advice here is based on the industry's tendency to overbook the same Caribbean ports over and over again—which has led to a certain sameness of experience regardless of the cruise line.

Alaskan itineraries, served by the *Wonder,* are virtually identical. Choose whichever sailing suits your budget and schedule.

Mediterranean cruises range from 4 to 12 nights. Most leave from Barcelona or Civitavecchia (Rome), but there are other departure points to choose from. In 2023, in addition to its usual port stops in France, Italy, and Spain, DCL is once again sailing in **Greece,** with port stops in Katakolon, Heraklion (Crete), Piraeus (Athens), Santorini, Kefalonia, Chania, and Mykonos. Again, choose the sailing that best suits your budget and schedule.

unofficial **TIP**
If your preferred itinerary is fully booked, check back often to see if other guests have canceled, or ask your travel agent to check for you.

Northern European itineraries have more variety than those in any other region. These sailings range from 5 to 11 days, with some focusing on Norway and Iceland and others visiting Germany, Sweden, Denmark, Belgium, the Netherlands, and the British Isles. Limited availability of some itineraries makes them particularly popular, with some ports visited on only one or two sailings per year.

Specific Recommendations

Here are some additional questions to ask yourself to help narrow down the right itinerary for you—along with our recommendations.

- **Are you a first-time cruiser?** Choose a **three-, four-, or five-night cruise.**
- **Do you want a long, relaxing vacation?** Choose a sailing with multiple consecutive sea days, such as a **Panama Canal** or **Transatlantic crossing.**
- **Do you want to do lots of sightseeing?** Choose a longer **Mediterranean** or **Northern European cruise.**
- **Do you want to lie on the beach as much as possible?** Choose a **seven-night cruise on the *Fantasy.***
- **Don't like hot weather?** Choose an **Alaskan, Canadian Coastline,** or **Northern European cruise.**
- **Do you want to sail DCL in a new part of the world?** Choose an **Oceanian cruise** (South Pacific, Australia, and New Zealand; see page 6).
- **Do you like museums and the city scene?** Choose a **Mediterranean DCL cruise** or an **Adventures by Disney (AbD) river cruise** (see Part Thirteen).
- **Are you prone to motion sickness?** Choose an **AbD river cruise** or a **three-night cruise on the *Dream* with no sea days.**
- **Do you *really* like Castaway Cay?** Choose a **double-dip sailing** with two stops on DCL's private island.
- **Don't have a passport and don't want to get one?** Choose a **closed-loop cruise** (see page 62).

- **Do you hate to fly?** Choose a cruise from **the embarkation point closest to your home.**

- **Do you have a small budget?** Choose a **two-night cruise on the _Wonder_** (if you live on the West Coast) or a **three-night cruise on the _Dream_** (if you live on the East Coast).

- **Are you looking for the experience of a lifetime?** Choose a **Concierge stateroom** on a **European cruise.** Or opt for **Suite 14000,** the largest Concierge cabin on the **_Wish,_** for a family reunion over the holidays.

NEW ITINERARIES

DISNEY USUALLY ANNOUNCES its ships' schedules in seasonal blocks—spring, summer, and so on— about 12–15 months ahead of the first sailings of that season. For example, early-2023 sailings (beginning in January 2023) were announced on October 12, 2021, and became available for booking to the general public on October 14, 2021. Summer 2023 sailings (beginning in May 2023) were announced on April 27, 2022, and booking opened to the general public on May 2, 2022. Fall 2023 sailings (beginning in September 2023) were announced on July 21, 2022, with booking available to the general public on July 28, 2022.

> _**unofficial** TIP_
>
> DCL's new **Oceanian** cruises (South Pacific, Australia, and New Zealand) were announced September 11, 2022, with general booking availability beginning October 6, 2022.

Based on how Disney publicized the inaugural sailings of the _Wish,_ we think they'll hold a separate announcement for the corresponding sailings of the two as-yet-unnamed new ships. But despite the stand-alone announcement, the release schedule for the _Wish_ followed the typical pattern of 13–15 months in advance: the first itineraries were announced on April 29, 2021, for sailings beginning in July 2022.

Knowing when new itineraries are released is useful if you're trying to get the lowest possible price for a specific cruise. (See "Saving Money," page 34.) It's also helpful if you want to book a specific type of stateroom for a typically popular sailing (such as a Christmas cruise) or if you want a low price or specific stateroom type for a new route. For example, when Disney introduced its Northern European itineraries, several stateroom categories sold out almost immediately; a similarly rapid sellout happened when Disney announced its first sailings out of New Orleans.

ITINERARY CHANGES

THE PANDEMIC NOTWITHSTANDING, itineraries can change for a number of reasons. Fortunately, these changes don't happen often. When they do, it can be frustrating and disappointing—particularly if they happen on a cruise you've been planning for years—but understand that in nearly every case, Disney makes these changes with your safety and well-being in mind.

Occasionally, DCL has altered itineraries as little as hours in advance because of issues in a foreign country (for example, political unrest in Turkey during a 2015 Mediterranean sailing on the *Magic*) or weather conditions (for example, iceberg activity in the Atlantic Ocean during the *Magic*'s 2015 eastbound Transatlantic crossing). We've also been on cruises where the itinerary changed midtrip due to the weather: on one of our trips on the *Fantasy*, the seas were too rough for tender travel into port, so a scheduled stop in Grand Cayman became a sea day instead.

Less common pre-pandemic were cancellations or reschedulings of entire sailings. A few published sail dates for 2015, for example, were canceled and rescheduled due to problems with a planned regular-maintenance dry dock of the *Dream*. Guests whose travel plans had been affected by the cancellations—which were announced nearly a year in advance—were offered assistance with rescheduling and given a $250 onboard

unofficial **TIP**
If you're sailing just after a dry dock, it may be prudent to book a flight for very late in the day or a post-cruise stay at a hotel close to the port.

credit. A similar situation happened in 2022, when the *Wish*'s first sailings were postponed by six weeks: guests whose cruises were impacted by the delay were generously compensated with 50% off any rebooked sailing.

The 2017 hurricane season was particularly troublesome for the cruise industry in general, with Hurricanes Franklin, Irma, and Maria all necessitating ship rerouting and the latter two storms causing substantial damage to popular ports. Some storm-related DCL itinerary changes in 2017 included a canceled stop in Cozumel, some *Dream* and *Fantasy* sailings returning early to Port Canaveral, and other *Dream* and *Fantasy* sailings being scrapped completely; Eastern Caribbean sailings on the *Fantasy* were subject to itinerary changes well into 2018.

Even when wholesale itinerary changes can be avoided, changes may still be necessary in parts of a sailing. For example, during the middle of a March 2018 sailing of the *Fantasy*, several planned port adventures in Cozumel, including a popular excursion to the Maya ruins in Tulum, had to be canceled due to travel-safety warnings issued by the US Embassy in Mexico. In summer 2019, the *Fantasy* swapped a scheduled stop in San Juan for a visit to St. Thomas due to political unrest in Puerto Rico. And after Russia invaded Ukraine in February 2022, port stops in St. Petersburg and several countries adjacent to the conflict were dropped from European sailings for 2022 and 2023.

Somewhat more common are changes to arrival and departure times—we hear several stories a year about ships docking late due to bad weather or other factors. For example, heavy fog caused a December 2018 *Wonder* sailing to arrive at Galveston several hours behind schedule, causing many passengers to miss their early-afternoon flights home. In 2019 Hurricane Dorian forced the cancellation of one sailing of the *Dream*, while a different sailing that started as a three-night trip ended up as a six-night trip to keep the ship out of harm's way. And in August 2022, a sailing of the *Wonder* left Vancouver about 8 hours late due to a labor strike by tugboat workers.

Again, such itinerary disruptions are rare, typically affecting fewer than a handful of sailings each year. They're unlikely to happen on your cruise, but we mention them here because they may affect your decisions about whether to book excursions through Disney or another vendor (see Part Twelve), whether you want to buy travel insurance (see page 58), and whether you want to add some buffer time to your scheduled flight home.

SAVING MONEY

FOR THIS EDITION we analyzed more than 1.3 million cruise fares. One of the big trends we saw in 2022 was the return of last-minute fare discounts, especially on Bahamian and Caribbean cruises. Before the pandemic, both Disney and Royal Caribbean had adopted a policy called "pricing integrity," which all but guaranteed that prices could go up only after cruises went on sale.

unofficial **TIP**
When you're combing through the DCL website for deals, keep an eye out for discount codes **IGT, OGT,** and **VGT.** These indicate heavily discounted Inside, Oceanview, and Verandah staterooms.

Like cats walking across keyboards on Zoom calls, last-minute cruise discounts were something to look forward to during the pandemic. In particular, you could get the best prices on Bahamian cruises by booking anywhere from 30 to 90 days out.

Likewise, prices for Alaskan cruises were about the same at the 60-day mark as they were 15 months in advance. Even the *Fantasy* had low-cost cabins available for seven-night Caribbean cruises from around 60 to 150 days in advance of sailing.

Pandemic-related pricing trends aside, here are the strategies we recommend for saving money on a Disney cruise:

1. **Book early if possible.** For newer ships like the *Wish,* cruise fares start low and begin to rise as the ship fills up. Booking early can save you 10% or more on the price of a stateroom; keep in mind, though, that this strategy may be tricky to pull off depending on the itinerary, ship, and timeframe. Many families begin booking their cruises about 8–15 months out—and we don't think it's a coincidence that this is also when prices start to creep upward, especially on the *Fantasy*'s longer cruises. (We wouldn't be surprised if Disney adjusts its prices according to spikes in website traffic and similar metrics.) See page 36 for further discussion.

2. **If you can't book early, try booking at the last minute.** Late-breaking deals can be found across all stateroom categories, particularly for Bahamian and Caribbean cruises, but it helps if you're not choosy about a specific room or deck. And because airfares often go *up* at the last minute, this strategy works best if you live within a day's drive of your departure port. Look for last-minute deals at **DisneyCruise.com** and **MouseSavers.com,** or use the **Cruise Price Drop** tool at **CruiseWatch.com.** Start checking the fares daily two months out, and consider booking as soon as you see even a small drop or increase in price.

3. **Book your next cruise during your current one.** DCL offers onboard-booking discounts of up to 10% off the lowest prevailing rates. Stop by the

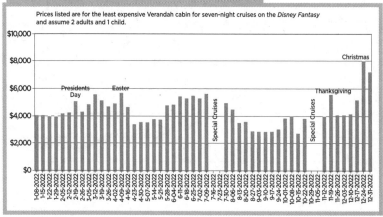

DCL Year-Round Pricing

Prices listed are for the least expensive Verandah cabin for seven-night cruises on the *Disney Fantasy* and assume 2 adults and 1 child.

Future Cruise Sales Desk for details. Note that blackout dates may apply: when we tried to book a cruise coinciding with Easter, we were told that the standard 10% discount was unavailable. We did, however, get a discount on our deposit. See page 48 for more information.

4. Depart from a less popular port on an older ship. Disney offers aggressive discounts on cruises from ports that aren't in heavy demand. At the time of this writing, for instance, off-season four-night cruises out of Miami on the *Dream* were selling for 15%–20% less than similar cruises on the *Wish* out of Port Canaveral, for the same stateroom categories. Granted, the *Dream* is 10 years old, but it's still a really nice ship, and you'd be saving hundreds of dollars versus sailing on the *Wish*. (See the section starting on page 119 in Part Four for more tips on choosing a port.)

5. Take advantage of onboard credit offers. While pricing is generally consistent among DCL, independent travel agents, and sites such as **Orbitz** and **Expedia,** some outfits can sweeten the pot with generous onboard credits. Shop around for the best deals.

6. Use your special status. Discounted fares and "sweeteners" are often available to military personnel, residents of Florida, and the like. These deals are typically noted on DCL's **Special Offers** page (disneycruise.disney.go. com/special-offers). As one notable example, **AAA** and **Costco** members traveling with a large group (at least eight staterooms or 16 adults) may qualify for perks such as special gifts and private parties. For more information, call ☎ 800-511-6333.

7. Sail during an off-peak time. The same cruise on the same ship often costs twice as much on peak dates than during the off-season. The *Fantasy* makes a good point of comparison because it primarily serves two itineraries: seven-night Eastern and Western Caribbean cruises out of Port Canaveral. The chart above shows the cost of the *Fantasy*'s standard seven-night cruises for all of 2022, based on two adults and one child in a Verandah stateroom. (Prices for 2023 show the same seasonal patterns, but at generally higher prices.)

Not surprisingly, it's most expensive to sail during the winter holidays and cheapest to sail when the kids are in school—specifically, during early fall, the beginning of December, and right after New Year's.

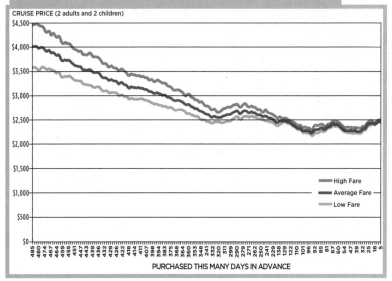

Disney Dream 4-Night Bahamian Cruises: 2022 Price Trends

CRUISE PRICE (2 adults and 2 children)

PURCHASED THIS MANY DAYS IN ADVANCE

High Fare
Average Fare
Low Fare

Other than holidays, the middle of summer is the most expensive time to cruise (even ignoring special, longer itineraries). If you want to cruise with your school-age kids, try to book as closely as possible to the start or end of summer vacation. Your fare won't be as low as when school is in session, but if you want to cruise during the summer, these options are as good as it gets.

What's truly astounding is the difference in prices for seven-night cruises between December 9 and December 23, 2022. That two-week difference will cost you nearly double if you want to spend Christmas aboard the *Fantasy*. To put it another way, you could sail back-to-back in August—14 nights—for $2,000 less than you would for the seven-night Christmas cruise. We know which option *we'd* choose.

PRICE TRENDS BY SHIP AND ITINERARY

YOU KNOW, OF COURSE, THAT "BOOK EARLY" AND "BOOK LATE" are complementary suggestions—if you can't do one, do the other. In the following section, we show how these strategies work for each ship in the Disney fleet on some of DCL's most popular itineraries. The bar graphs in this section represent our analysis of more than 1 million prices gathered from DCL's website for every combination of family size, stateroom category, ship, and itinerary.

To simplify our discussion, we'll use pricing trends for two-adult, two-child families in DCL Verandah staterooms for sailings in 2022, from 15 months to a few days in advance, as follows:

- Four-night **Bahamian** cruises on the *Wish*
- Four-night **Bahamian** cruises on the *Dream*

Disney Wish 4-Night Bahamian Cruises: 2022 Price Trends

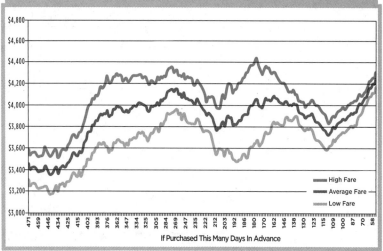

If Purchased This Many Days In Advance

- Seven-night **Western Caribbean** cruises on the *Fantasy*
- Seven-night **Alaskan** cruises on the *Wonder*
- Seven-night **Mediterranean** cruises on the *Magic*

The price of a stateroom is largely tied to the deck it's on; staterooms on a higher deck usually cost more than the same stateroom on a lower deck. The bar graphs illustrate pricing trends for the most- and least-expensive fares for DCL Verandah (balcony) staterooms on all decks in 2022–23. The graphs use a 30-day rolling average for the prices to smooth out tiny variations.

Bahamian Cruises

For cruises on the *Dream* in 2022, booking early wasn't quite as useful as in years past. A typical family would have saved up to $2,000, or almost 45%, by booking a year in advance rather than at the earliest possible opportunity—that is, 15 months out. That trend holds true for cabins on all decks: the highest fares declined at the same rate as the lowest fares.

In 2022 Verandah rooms on the *Dream*'s lower decks started off at a 20% discount over those on higher decks. Those prices tended to converge, however, as departure dates approached—and at 120 days out, there was virtually no difference in prices. In this instance, we would've suggested a stateroom on a higher deck.

Disney's newest ship, the **Wish,** also offers four-night Bahamian cruises. Because the *Wish* is Disney's newest ship, you'll pay considerably more to sail compared with the *Dream,* but you can sail for less by booking early.

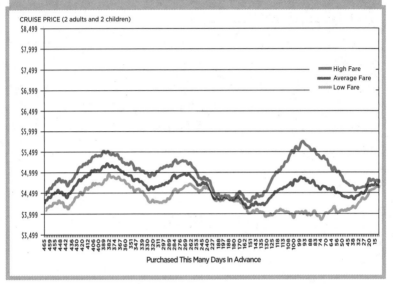

Caribbean Cruises

Price trends for seven-night sailings varied considerably in 2022. Fares were higher closer to departure versus 15 months in advance, but prices tended to bottom out at different times, depending on the deck location. For Verandah rooms on higher decks, the lowest prices were found both at 15 months out and again 5–8 months in advance. Cabins on lower decks achieved their cheapest pricing roughly 2–5 months in advance.

Alaskan and Mediterranean Cruises

As we note on page 15, DCL isn't price-competitive for these itineraries—equivalent cruises on Royal Caribbean cost substantially less and sail with newer ships. Even so, if you had wanted to book a Disney cruise to Alaska in 2022, you could've gotten the cheapest fares by booking either early or late: prices for Verandah cabins were roughly the same 14 or 15 months out as they were within 60 days of sailing.

On the other hand, prices for DCL's 2022 Mediterranean sailings were all over the map—so much so that it wasn't useful to graph them for this edition. This was almost certainly because of the European Union's constantly evolving COVID policies regarding travel. Before his young-adult child left for a Mediterranean cruise in summer 2022, coauthor Len gave them a step-by-step, 14-page itinerary noting every document, test, and procedure they would encounter along the way. Aside from one flight cancellation, everything went well. Back to the

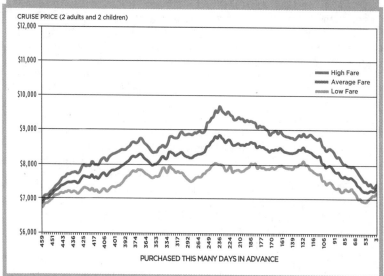

Disney Wonder 7-Night Alaskan Cruises: 2022 Price Trends

CRUISE PRICE (2 adults and 2 children)

High Fare
Average Fare
Low Fare

PURCHASED THIS MANY DAYS IN ADVANCE

matter at hand, though, it's hard for us to predict prices for DCL's Mediterranean cruises in 2023 based on how they shook out in 2022.

Cruise Costs from a Different Perspective

While researching price trends during summer 2022, we found that the least expensive single-stateroom choice for 2023 was a three-night Baja cruise in early January on the *Wonder:* **$2,056,** or about $171 per person, per night, for two adults and two children in an inside stateroom. The most expensive choice? A jaw-dropping **$67,203,** or about $1,527 per person, per night, for an 11-night Mediterranean/Greek Isles cruise on the *Dream;* in this case, the price reflects two adults and two children in a one-bedroom Concierge suite. (The even-pricier two-bedroom suite had already been booked, so we couldn't check rates for that option.)

Right about now you're probably contemplating the myriad things that you could spend $67K on besides a two-week vacation—a down payment on a house, for instance—but be aware that total costs aren't always the most helpful gauge of whether a particular cruise is a good value. Instead, think in terms of **cost per person, per night.**

As noted above, that low-priced Baja cruise for four works out to about $171 per person, per night—certainly not a bad price for a cruise. But in many port cities that DCL visits, you could book a land-based vacation with a decent hotel, several nice meals, and a few extras for that same per-person, per-night price, whereas on the cruise most of your money would be going toward a small cabin. Granted, that may be exactly what you want, but it's still worth weighing the pros and cons.

As it turned out, the least expensive per-person, per-night choice we found for 2023 was a **13-Night Eastbound Transatlantic Cruise** sailing from Miami on the *Dream* (inside stateroom). Of course, prices will vary depending on when you search, but during summer 2022 we found this cruise for a reasonable **$7,422** for two adults and two children, or about $142 per person, per night. As a reminder, that price includes your room, your meals, the onboard entertainment, and use of the kids' clubs, but it doesn't include excursions, alcoholic drinks, or spa treatments.

DO THE MATH (OR, FOREWARNED IS FOREARMED) It's possible to have a perfectly lovely cruise without paying for a thing beyond the cost of your stateroom plus customary tips and the costs of traveling to and from port. More likely, however, you'll incur added costs for extras— port adventures, adult dining, childcare, rum cakes for your coworkers—so factor at least some of these into your budget. (See page 17 for what is and isn't included in the price of your cruise.)

To use a personal example from a few years ago, I (Erin) took a five-night cruise with my husband on the *Dream*. The base price for two adults, including Disney bus service from Port Canaveral to Orlando International Airport and prepayment of baseline tips, was about $4,900.

unofficial **TIP**

Pricing information for most cruise add-ons is available at DisneyCruise.com.

Our onboard spending during this sailing was relatively restrained—or so we'd thought: just under $100 in purchases at the gift shop; one brunch and dinner each at Palo; one port excursion (a parasailing adventure for two at Castaway Cay); a daily pass for one to the Rainforest in Senses Spa; a bingo game; a mixology class; snacks at a movie screening; additional tips for our stateroom host and server in the main dining room; and a couple of rounds of drinks for us and three other couples who were our travel companions. All of those extras added up to around $950 in stateroom charges—or about a 20% bump in the total cost of the cruise.

▌ **SURF** *and* **TURF, DISNEY-STYLE**

COMBINING YOUR CRUISE WITH A WALT DISNEY WORLD VACATION

DISNEY SELLS PACKAGES THAT COMBINE A DISNEY CRUISE with a trip to Walt Disney World for cruises departing from Port Canaveral. Called **Land and Sea** packages, these itineraries include the Bahamas, the Caribbean, and Bermuda in 2022–23.

Land and Sea packages include lodging at a Walt Disney World resort hotel; theme park admission, the Disney Dining Plan, and other components can be added to the Disney World portion of the trip. For more information, see disneycruise.disney.go.com/featured/packages/land-sea.

Because you don't have much flexibility when you book a Land and Sea package through DCL, and because you save money when you book individual components à la carte, we recommend making reservations for each part of a theme park–cruise vacation separately. Regardless of whether you book Land and Sea together or separately, you can arrange bus transportation between Port Canaveral and your Walt Disney World resort for a fee.

The most frequent question we're asked about combining a theme park vacation with a cruise is whether to visit Walt Disney World before or after the cruise. Pre-pandemic, we found that most people who did both preferred to relax on the cruise after the more-hectic park visit. But given COVID-era pre-cruise health requirements, you may find it easier to cruise first. This not only allows you to complete any required pre-sailing testing requirements at home but also reduces your risk of acquiring COVID at a bustling theme park.

Even pre-COVID, some guests still preferred to experience Walt Disney World second, either because they just really love cruising (as Erin does) or they liked the faster pace of WDW after the relaxation of a cruise. Doing WDW second can backfire, though, particularly if you have small children in need of frequent naps. A reader from Houston shares her experience:

We added two days at WDW to the end of our Disney cruise. We were struck by two things: First, the heat is a lot less fun when you're waking up at 6 a.m. to get off the ship, and second, not being able to check in to our hotel room at WDW until late afternoon was really rough on everyone. We were too exhausted after the cruise to enjoy our time at WDW.

BACK-*to*-BACK CRUISING

HAVE YOU EVER ended a cruise and thought, "*Waaah*, I don't want to go home! Can't I just stay on board forever?" That's almost exactly what you do when you book back-to-back cruises—cruises on the same ship in which the second cruise begins the day the first cruise ends. And we think it's *glorious*.

Other than not wanting to leave, why might you consider a back-to-back cruise?

1. **The ship you like doesn't offer longer cruises.** Our first back-to-back cruises were three and four nights on the *Dream*. Back-to-back bookings on the *Wish* are quickly becoming popular with veteran DCL cruisers who want a longer timespan in which to explore the new ship.

2. **You want to see more ports.** Want to see both the Eastern *and* Western Caribbean? Book two consecutive cruises on the *Fantasy*. The Baltics *and* the Mediterranean? The *Magic* has you covered.

3. **You want to save on transportation costs.** Combining two itineraries can be less expensive (assuming you're planning to do both in the first place). For instance, it's much less expensive to fly to Vancouver, British Columbia; do a 7-night Alaskan cruise immediately followed by a 10-night cruise to Hawaii;

and then fly home from Oahu than to book round-trip airfare to Canada *and* round-trip airfare to Honolulu.

4. **You're amassing Castaway Club credits.** We're not saying that one of our researchers booked a back-to-back cruise just because the second cruise was the one that pushed her into Platinum Castaway Club status. But we're not saying she didn't either.

5. **You *really* love Castaway Cay.** A significant subset of Disney cruisers finds DCL's private Bahamian island to be the best part of their trip. If you're a Castaway Cay devotee and the few itineraries with "double dips" (two stops at Castaway Cay on one sailing) don't line up with your vacation schedule, then you can cobble together your own double-dip vacation by scheduling a four-night and three-night sailing on the *Dream* or the *Wish* back-to-back.

So how does it work?

First a caveat: not every consecutive cruise can be booked back-to-back due to federal maritime law. The specifics are a bit confusing, and they apply only to ships registered outside of the United States, including DCL's ships, which are registered in the Bahamas: if your first cruise leaves from a US port, your next cruise ends in another US port, *and* you haven't visited "a distant foreign port" along the way, you're in violation of the Merchant Marine Act of 1920. (We know, it's complicated.)

unofficial **TIP**

The Points Guy has an informative discussion of the legal issues involved in back-to-back cruising. See tinyurl.com/TPGBackToBack.

Oddly, the DCL website lets you book back-to-back cruises that violate the law, but once Disney catches your mistake, you'll be forced to choose one cruise or the other. Countries that this affects include the United States, Italy, and Norway. At the time of this writing, no DCL cruises depart from Norway (though they do visit there), so you'll need to pay close attention if you're booking a back-to-back trip that travels to either US coast, or if you're booking a back-to-back that includes southern Europe.

Here's a back-to-back that works: an Alaskan cruise starting in Vancouver, followed by a Pacific Coast cruise from Vancouver to San Diego—you're good to go because you start in Canada.

Not OK: Honolulu to Vancouver, followed by Vancouver to San Diego—you start in one US city and end in another; plus, Vancouver, despite being in Canada, is too close to the United States to be considered a *distant* foreign port.

Note that when booking back-to-back, you may or may not be able to keep the same stateroom for both cruises—basically, it's the luck of the draw. If you're moving to another cabin for your second sailing, you'll pack your bags and leave them in your current room before debarking. You'll find them waiting in your new room on your return.

Pre-pandemic, back-to-back cruisers whose rooms stayed the same could leave their stuff unpacked and exit the ship with anything they might need in the meantime (such as medications). In the COVID era, however, you may be asked to pack your suitcases and leave them in your room. If you were to test positive for COVID and couldn't reboard, the steward could simply retrieve your luggage instead of having to handle your belongings.

Assuming you've been cleared for your second sailing, you'll check in again (in the Castaway Club Platinum Lounge) and then walk back on board. You may find the ship deserted upon your return. (That once prompted Len to do impromptu carpet angels in the atrium.)

The BOOKING PROCESS

GETTING STARTED

ONCE YOU'VE SETTLED ON A SHIP, an itinerary, and dates, it's time to book your trip. You have three ways to do this:

> **1.** Use the DCL website.   **2.** Call DCL at ☎ 800-951-3532.   **3.** Use a travel agent.

Most guests will be happier if they book online or use a travel agent. The main advantage to booking online yourself is that you can usually do it immediately. If you've booked a cruise before, you have easy access to each traveler's information, you don't have questions about the ship or itinerary, and you want instant gratification, this may be your best option.

The main advantage of using a travel agent is that they can save you time by doing most of the tedious legwork for you; plus, the agent may also offer a discount in the form of onboard credit—money you can use to pay for items like adult beverages, port excursions, or photo services. Many agents have booked dozens, if not hundreds, of cruises, and have a single-page form for you to fill out, where you provide your preferences for everything from what time you prefer to board the ship to when you prefer to eat. Some travel agencies will also rebook your cruise automatically if a lower fare becomes available; a travel agent might also be able to save you money because he or she might have access to group space for a particular cruise. (You're not required to participate in any group activities, but you do get the price advantage of the group booking.) Finally, a seasoned travel agent may be able to help you find rooms with special characteristics, such as an oversize verandah, a particular view, or one of the few sets of Inside Staterooms connected to Oceanview Staterooms.

When it comes to booking by phone, we've heard countless reports of being put on hold for several hours. If you have questions that require a human response, you may want to have a travel agent handle them.

USING THE DCL WEBSITE
TO FIND THE RIGHT CRUISE

IN ADDITION TO ABUNDANT INFORMATION about the ships, onboard amenities, and port adventures, **DisneyCruise.com** makes it easy to understand and compare prices for different sailings, party sizes, stateroom configurations, and more. By playing around with filter criteria, you can narrow down which cruises are right for your budget, schedule, and destination preferences.

Get started by clicking "Plan a Cruise" at the top of the homepage; then choose "Find a Cruise" from the pull-down menu. The options on the next page are as follows:

LEAVING (DATE) Narrowing down your search by date is a good first step if you already know the month when you want to cruise, because it eliminates a lot of unnecessary scrolling through lists that don't fit your needs.

SAILING TO Narrow your search further by checking the box(es) only for places you know you'd like to visit.

DEPARTING FROM If you have a strong preference for a particular departure port (say, one near your home), select it here.

GUESTS The default search is for two adults. To get accurate pricing, adjust the party size and composition (children and adults) to reflect your travel group. This is also where to search for wheelchair-accessible staterooms, if you need one, or to add additional staterooms for your party. Pay particular attention to "Add Another Stateroom" if you're traveling with more than two people—it could be worth your while to split your party between two rooms. The price of two smaller rooms is often equivalent to that of one larger room, with the bonus of an extra bathroom and more square footage. (See page 95 for more on stateroom categories and configurations.)

MORE FILTERS This tab asks you for your preferences regarding the number of nights you want to sail, the ship you want to travel on, and whether you want to limit your search to voyages with themed events such as Marvel Days at Sea (see page 232 for information on themed cruises). Again, check the boxes here according to your preferences. If you have a young daughter who's obsessed with Rapunzel, for example, you might want to sail only on the *Magic,* which has a *Tangled* stage show and a *Tangled*-themed restaurant. Or you might want to explore only Disney's newest ship, the *Wish*.

DEPOSIT TERMS AND CANCELLATION POLICIES

MOST DISNEY CRUISE RESERVATIONS require you to put down a deposit equal to 20% of the cruise's price (not including taxes) for each passenger ages 3 and older in your party on a given reservation. Some DCL promotions, however, such as booking a follow-up cruise while you're on your current cruise (see "Onboard Booking," page 48), require only a 10% deposit.

During the pandemic, as subsequent waves of cruises were canceled and guests became wary of sailing in general, DCL tinkered with its cancellation policy on several occasions, typically allowing guests to extend their final payment deadline and relaxing the typical penalties for late cancellation. For example, on August 5, 2022, DCL temporarily changed its final-payment and cancellation policies for guests booked on sailings through March 31, 2023. The amended terms are as follows:

- For guests booked in non-suite and non-Concierge rooms for sailings through March 31, 2023, Disney temporarily rescheduled the cancellation policy to take effect **59 days before sailing.**

- For guests booked in unrestricted staterooms for specific sailings on the *Magic* and the *Wonder,* Disney temporarily rescheduled the cancellation policy to take effect **29 days before sailing.** For the *Magic,* this applied to sailings between May 8, 2022, and June 27, 2022; for the *Wonder,* this applied to sailings starting or ending in a non-US port between April 21, 2022, and May 30, 2022.

- Reservations for Inside, Outside, and Verandah categories with restrictions (see next page) remain nonrefundable and nontransferable, per normal DCL policy.

Additional DCL pandemic-related policy relaxations included the following:

- Within 14 days of sailing, booked guests with COVID-19-related health concerns (symptoms, exposure, or a positive test) could either receive a full refund or apply their cruise fare toward a future sail date within a specific time period. Guests could not change their reservation back to the original sail date after taking advantage of this policy, and blackout dates applied. Third-party cancellation fees (for airfare and the like) were nonrefundable.

- Guests found to have COVID-19-related health concerns (symptoms, exposure, a fever of 100.4°F or more, or a positive test) at boarding time were issued a full refund, either as a voucher or a reimbursement, for which cancellation fees were waived. Guests who were quarantined or who tested positive after boarding were eligible for a prorated refund or a prorated credit toward a future cruise.

We expect that some version of these accommodations will stay in place for as long as the pandemic persists; that said, you should expect changes to these policies as conditions evolve.

Before booking *any* cruise—on DCL or otherwise—make sure that you understand the prevailing cancellation policies, and recheck them periodically before you sail. To do this, check the **DCL Terms and Conditions** page (tinyurl.com/DCLTermsAndConditions), do a search for "cancellation" and/or "COVID" at the DCL website, and carefully read the **DCL Cruise Contract** (tinyurl.com/DCLCruiseContract). Note that slightly different terms and conditions apply for guests from the US, guests from the UK, and guests from other countries.

For reference, the following cancellation policies apply during normal operations:

DCL CONCIERGE CANCELLATION POLICY

Full payment required 120 days (trips 1–5 nights) or 150 days (trips 6+ nights) before sailing.
Cancel 90 days or more before sailing, charge is **deposit per guest.**
Cancel 89–56 days before sailing, charge is **50% of vacation price per guest.**
Cancel 55–30 days before sailing, charge is **75% of vacation price per guest.**
Cancel 29 days or fewer before sailing, charge is **100% of vacation price per guest.**

Standard cancellation policies are less restrictive:

DCL STANDARD CANCELLATION POLICY: 1–5 NIGHTS

Full payment required 90 days before sailing.
Cancel 89–45 days before sailing, charge is **deposit per guest.**
Cancel 44–30 days before sailing, charge is **50% of vacation price per guest.**
Cancel 29–15 days before sailing, charge is **75% of vacation price per guest.**
Cancel 14 days or fewer before sailing, charge is **100% of vacation price per guest.**

DCL STANDARD CANCELLATION POLICY: 6 NIGHTS OR LONGER
Full payment required 120 days before sailing.
Cancel 119–56 days before sailing, charge is **deposit per guest.**
Cancel 55–30 days before sailing, charge is **50% of vacation price per guest.**
Cancel 29–15 days before sailing, charge is **75% of vacation price per guest.**
Cancel 14 days or fewer before sailing, charge is **100% of vacation price per guest.**

Cruises booked with a **restricted-rate** discount code (see page 104) are always nonrefundable and nontransferable—you eat the cost of the entire cruise if you don't sail.

Airfare and port-hotel bookings arranged through Disney have their own unique cancellation policies. Check with DCL or your travel agent for specifics.

AGE REQUIREMENTS FOR BOOKING

DCL ALLOWS ADULTS ages 18 and up to travel unaccompanied and book their own staterooms. However, **guests ages 17 and younger must be booked into a room with an adult ages 21 or older.**

DCL's age requirement is liberal compared with, say, Carnival's (tinyurl.com/CarnivalMinorPolicy), which allows only adults ages 21 and older to book and travel unaccompanied and requires guests under 21 to travel with an adult who's at least 25. Additionally, Carnival imposes restrictions on the number of people of certain ages who may travel together: for example, an adult over 25 may chaperone no more than eight people under 21. The exceptions to Carnival's rules—young married couples and military personnel—must provide careful documentation of their circumstances. Disney's policy affords under-21 married couples, young servicepeople, and most college students the ability to travel unchaperoned and unencumbered by extra paperwork.

Nevertheless, any group that includes minors needs to consider the implications of the age requirement when planning a Disney cruise. For example, a single parent who wants to travel with four minor children would have to book at least a Verandah stateroom on the *Magic* or *Wonder*. That's often more expensive than booking two individual Inside or Oceanview cabins, but it's the only option in this case because DCL doesn't allow minors to stay by themselves in a different stateroom, even if the rooms are connected by an inside door.

In the case of a couple who want to book more than one room but are traveling with just one minor child, Disney requires that one parent be booked into a room with the child. Further, if the parent who is registered in a different room wants to leave the ship with the child, that parent must first sign a waiver at the Guest Services desk.

A few situations would either be a no-go or require altering to meet the age requirement:

- High school and college spring breakers, some of whom are 18 and some of whom aren't • Young adults ages 18–20 who want to travel with younger siblings but without their parents • Families traveling with an under-21 nanny whom they wish to book in the same room as the child • Guests wanting to travel with minors who aren't in their immediate family—say, a grandchild or a child's friend (whom you might not want sleeping in the same room as you)

In general, DCL requires that guests be age 21 or older to drink alcohol. Guests ages 18–20 may drink on some European cruises with a parent or guardian's written consent, provided that the adult is present when the alcohol is purchased and consumed.

MANAGING YOUR CRUISE ONLINE

ONCE YOU'VE BOOKED YOUR CRUISE, either directly with Disney or through a travel agent, you'll be making ample use of the "Already Booked" tab at the top of the DCL homepage. The following items appear under this tab:

- **My Reservations** includes all the vital information about any sailing you have booked: dates, stateroom numbers, reservation number, members of your travel party, ports or call, and so on.

  The **Cruise Details** subtab provides a diagram of where your stateroom is on a deck plan of your ship, as well as your assigned dinner seating and the ability to request a change in seating time. This is also the place for information about choosing the Vacation Protection Plan (DCL's trip insurance; see page 58) and for information about reserving Disney transportation to or from your port to another destination such as an airport or Walt Disney World hotel.

  The **My Plans** subtab is a running list of the reservations you've made for port excursions, adult dining, spa treatments, and other activities/experiences.

- **Your Guide to Updated Experiences** This page aggregates the latest information about health and safety requirements and protocols. There are separate pages for sailings departing from the United States, Canada, and Europe. Much of this content is duplicated in an identically named subsection of DCL's **Know Before You Go** page (tinyurl.com/DCLKnowBeforeYouGo).

- **Make a Payment** Here, not surprisingly, is where you pay for your cruise. If you've booked through a travel agent, you'll get a message here stating that you need to contact your agent to arrange payment.

- **Book/Manage Cruise Activities** Click here to make reservations for adult dining, port adventures, spa treatments, and so on. Note that you won't be able to book activities until after you've paid in full and your booking window (based on your Castaway Club status; see page 85) opens.

- **Air and Ground Transportation** provides information on booking pre- or post-cruise air travel and hotel/airport shuttle service through DCL.

- **Online Check-In** This becomes available after you've paid in full *and* your booking window opens. At press time, online check-in was available 30 days before sailing, but be aware that the booking window has changed a few times since sailings resumed in 2021. Check the DCL website for the latest information. *Note:* Online check-in used to be optional but is mandatory at the time of this writing.

- **Download the Navigator App** Here's where you'll find download links to the DCL Navigator mobile app for iOS and Android (see page 136 for an in-depth description). The app is invaluable for communicating with your party, staying abreast of what's going on aboard the ship, and keeping informed about the ports you'll be visiting. It offers much of the same functionality as the "Already Booked" section of the website for managing the details of your cruise, including payments, booking activities, and more.

- **Onboard Gifts** Here you can buy flowers, gift baskets, and other goodies and have them delivered to your stateroom (see pages 134 and 302).

- **Photography** provides information about photo opportunities on the ship (see page 308).

- **Getting to the Port** includes GPS addresses and driving directions to all DCL embarkation ports. (See pages 119–124 for individual port instructions.)

- **Travel Documentation** outlines the citizenship documentation, passports, and/or visas required for each DCL embarkation location.

- **Packing Checklist** offers basic suggestions for various DCL destinations. (See page 72 for more packing tips.)

ONBOARD BOOKING

BOOKING YOUR NEXT CRUISE while you're taking your current cruise is a great way to save money, but you need to understand the fine points of the process. **Tammy Whiting,** owner of **Storybook Destinations** (storybookdestinations.com), a Disney-specialist travel agency, shares the following tips.

unofficial **TIP**
For maximum flexibility and cost effectiveness, make your first round of onboard bookings with an eye to everyone who *might* go instead of only the people you *know* will go. You can always fine-tune the details later.

HOW TO BOOK Your ship's **Disney Vacation Planning Desk** handles in-person bookings. Alternatively, you can complete a brief intake form and drop it in the box at the Planning Desk (someone will get back to you), or you can use the DCL Navigator app.

THE BENEFITS When you book a future cruise on board, you get a 10% discount on the fare. In addition, onboard booking lets you put down a smaller deposit on cruises of seven nights or more: 10% instead of the normal 20%.

Just to be clear: these benefits are available *only* if you book on board—there are no equivalent deals for booking at home.

You can book up to two staterooms on board. Once your cruise is over, you can't book additional rooms on top of these two, but you can tinker with other details. You can change your sail date as long as it's within **exactly 24 months** of the date of the original booking.

THE EXCEPTIONS If you're booking a Concierge stateroom *or* you want to book a cruise during a period when blackout dates are in effect, you don't get any price breaks. Also, onboard discounts can't be combined with other discounts, such as military rates; Florida-resident rates; or IGT, OCT, or VGT rates (see page 104). All of these exceptions also apply to placeholder bookings (see below).

unofficial **TIP**
If you're on a long sailing, try to make your onboard-booking arrangements on one of the last days of your cruise. This could give you a week or more of time on the back end to take advantage of the two-year use window.

HOLD THAT THOUGHT If you're not sure when you want to cruise next but you do know that you want to do it within the next two years, you can make what DCL calls a **placeholder booking** for a flat $250. As the name implies, a placeholder will apply your onboard discounts to a future sailing, again within 24 months of this booking. When you're ready to reserve in earnest, simply contact DCL to confirm your travel date and pay the remainder of your deposit. In addition to the exceptions noted above, placeholders can't be used for two-night sailings.

If you make a placeholder booking but you end up not sailing within the two-year window, your $250 will automatically be refunded. If you've already used your placeholder to book but then you decide to rebook for a date beyond the original two-year window, your cruise won't be canceled, but you also won't get any discounts.

REAL BOOKING VS. PLACEHOLDER BOOKING The main advantage to booking a specific sailing on board is that it locks in your fare. Even with discounts applied, you may end up paying more for your cruise if you delay booking with a placeholder, depending on the time of year and overall pricing trends.

A LITTLE HELP FROM YOUR FRIEND You can book on board directly or you can use a travel agent. If you'd like to use a different agent from the one who booked your current cruise, or you booked your current cruise yourself, you can transfer your booking to a new agent within 30 days; the agent will have a form ready for you to fill out. Disney is strict about the 30-days part, so don't delay.

When Your Activities Window Opens

Non-Concierge guests may start booking cruise activities online based on their **Castaway Club** status (see page 85) after they've paid in full. Booking windows open at midnight Eastern time, and many eager guests go online at exactly that moment, endeavoring to snap up their preferred activities before all spots become fully claimed. If there's a particular activity that you consider a must-do, then plan to be on the DCL website at the appointed hour. If you've booked through a travel agent, he or she may offer to do this for you.

If you've booked a Concierge stateroom, you can email your activity requests to the DCL shoreside concierge 130 days before you sail. Activities are automatically added to your account

> *un*official **TIP**
> Reserve bikes, floats, or snorkels for Castaway Cay once you're on the island; DCL has enough of these on hand that they hardly ever run out. If you book them online, you'll have to pay for them whether you end up using them or not.

at the 120-day mark; the concierge may contact you beforehand to clarify your requests. Platinum Castaway Club members can book activities 120 days before they sail.

Whether you're a Concierge guest or a Platinum Castaway Club member, we recommend that you first try for **private cabana reservations** on **Castaway Cay.** We also recommend booking the following as early as possible:

- **Adult-dining reservations,** as well as **spa reservations,** on sea days
- **Nursery reservations** during dinnertimes
- **Bibbidi Bobbidi Boutique** appointments
- **Port adventures** to major tourist sites on DCL European cruises

If you can't get what you want on the first try, keep checking back, both online before your trip and at the Guest Services desk on board—usually there are cancellations.

OTHER PREP WORK

HEALTH CONSIDERATIONS: COVID AND MORE

COVID Vaccination and Testing

DCL'S COVID POLICIES have been in a veritable state of flux since cruising resumed in 2021—and they changed several times before this edition went to press. Disney's vaccination requirement has a moving target in particular: at the outset, it applied to guests ages 12 and older, but it was extended to guests ages 5 and older after the CDC approved vaccination for younger kids in late 2021. In August 2022, however, DCL announced that it was returning to its original 12-and-up policy.

COVID TIP
When it comes to vaccination and testing, assume that Disney may change its rules at any time.

DCL also announced two major changes to its pre-trip COVID-testing policy before press time. As of November 2022, vaccinated guests no longer have to submit proof a negative test before they sail. Unvaxxed kids must still submit proof of testing before they sail, but they are no longer required to take a second test at the terminal before they board the ship.

(*Note:* These updates apply to DCL cruises originating from ports in the US. DCL's European cruises have different vaccination and testing policies at the time of this writing; see page 54.)

So you don't get caught off-guard if the rules change again in the future, we strongly recommend that you and your family get all vaccinations that you qualify for.

Bottom line: it's *your* responsibility to stay informed about the rules that apply during your cruise. Check DCL's **Know Before You Go** page (tinyurl.com/DCLKnowBeforeYouGo) for the most up-to-date information.

VACCINATION REQUIREMENTS DCL currently requires that guests **ages 12 and older** provide proof of full COVID-19 vaccination—no exceptions. Disney also highly recommends vaccination for children under 12.

COVID TIP
The vaccines accepted by DCL at press time are **Pfizer, Moderna, Johnson & Johnson, AstraZeneca, Covishield, Novavax, Sinopharm (BBIBP-CorV), Sinovac-CoronaVac,** and **Covavaxin.**

In accordance with the CDC and the World Health Organization, DCL considers guests **ages 5 and older** to be fully vaccinated 14 days after (1) a second dose of an accepted two-dose vaccine (see Unofficial Tip); (2) a single dose of Johnson & Johnson (ages 18 and older only); (3) a second mix-and-match dose of any accepted vaccine; or (4) two doses of AstraZeneca or Novavax received as part of those vaccines' US clinical trials. (*Note:* Different criteria apply for children under age 5. See tinyurl.com/KnowBeforeYouGo for more information.)

The CDC's recommended interval between doses of a two-dose vaccine is 17 days to four weeks. This means that in most cases, your vaccination process should begin **at least five to six weeks** before your cruise, depending on which vaccine you receive. If you're planning a Disney cruise in Europe, you may also need a booster shot, depending on the country and itinerary (see pags 54 and 55).

GETTING CLEARED TO SAIL Safe Passage by Inspire Diagnostics (dcl .safepassage.com/account/register), an independent company, manages vaccination and testing compliance for DCL in the US. In order to sail, every adult guest (ages 18 and up) must individually create a Safe Passage account and link it to their DCL reservation (or reservations, for guests with back-to-back sailings).

A Safe Passage account can't be created **sooner than 15 days** before sailing; check the specifics of your cruise, as this window has changed a few times. Each adult must have a unique email address in order to register with Safe Passage—if you're making travel arrangements for an adult who doesn't use email (a person with a disability or a senior citizen, for example), you'll need to create an email account for them. Parents and legal guardians of guests younger than age 18 may use their own accounts to submit required documents on behalf of their children.

Guests ages 12 and older, along with vaccinated guests under 12, must submit proof of vaccination to Safe Passage **no later than 24 hours** before they sail. Vaccination documents must include your full name and date of birth, along with the specific vaccines you received and the dates they were administered.

In general, "proof of vaccination" means a CDC vaccination card. If your proof consists of multiple documents (such as state-certified immunization records), you will need to provide those in full.

To submit your proof of vaccination, upload an image file (such as a photo taken with your phone) to the Safe Passage website; the same procedure applies for submitting your children's pre-trip test results (see next section). After uploading the required files, log into you DCL account to check your status; if Safe Passage has approved your documentation, you'll see "Clear to Sail" under the Port Arrival heading.

COVID TIP

Note: The name and birthdate on your proof of vaccination must match the name on your cruise booking *and* the name on your passport or other legal ID. Safe Passage has been known to reject vaccination cards issued with a nickname or without a birthdate.

Once everyone in your party has been cleared, they'll each receive a QR code at the email addresses used to register their accounts—you'll need these codes at the port, so either print them out or save them to a phone or mobile wallet. Also be sure to bring your proof of vaccination and hard copies of your test results to the port. (See page 129 for more information about pre-boarding procedures.)

If you need assistance, contact Inspire Diagnostics at ☎ 877-250-5132 (daily, 8 a.m.–8 p.m. EST) or dclsupport@inspirediagnostics.com. When emailing, indicate that you're a DCL guest in the subject line, and include your full name, reservation number, and phone number in your message.

TESTING REQUIREMENTS AND METHODS Parents of unvaccinated children under age 12 must submit proof of a negative PCR or NAAT test—*not* **a rapid antigen test**—taken **three days-24 hours** before sailing.

COVID TIP

If your child's 12th birthday falls within five weeks of sailing, that's not enough time for them to be fully vaccinated. Kids in this situation are currently subject to the same testing rules as unvaccinated kids under 12.

As with proof of vaccination, proof of COVID testing must include your child's full name (not a nickname) and birthdate, the date the test was taken, the type of test, the name and address of the testing facility, and the test result. (As noted earlier, though, DCL no longer requires that unvaxxed kids take a second test at the cruise terminal before boarding.)

You may arrange your child's test on your own or order an at-home PCR test from Inspire Diagnostics through your Safe Passage account. Inspire's PCR test kit ($98.33) includes instructions on how to obtain and submit your test sample.

The test must be completed **three days** before you sail and immediately mailed back to Inspire in the prepaid UPS envelope provided with your kit. You must mail your kit from an official UPS drop box or take it to a UPS store—*not* a UPS Access Point at a drugstore, gas station, or the like.

You may also arrange an in-person PCR test with Inspire **one to three days** before your cruise at **Sheraton Suites Orlando Airport;** the **Cape Canaveral Radisson Resort;** the **Holiday Inn Port of Miami;** the **Sinclair Centre** in Vancouver, British Columbia; or the **Hyatt Regency Waikiki Beach Resort and Spa** in Honolulu. For hours and other information, go to tinyurl.com/DCLKnowBeforeYouGo, then click "Before Leaving Home." Test results are available within 24–48 hours of receipt; allow enough time for Inspire Diagnostics to receive and process your child's test sample.

POSITIVE TESTS Guests who test positive before their trip—and, more than likely, the other members of their party—will not be allowed to sail. Disney occasionally grants some leeway in making this decision, but such cases are few and far between.

If your child tests positive before your sail date and you need to cancel or reschedule your cruise, call DCL at ☎ 888-325-0168 or 407-566-7475, Monday–Friday, 8 a.m.–10 p.m. EST, and Saturday and Sunday, 9 a.m.–8 p.m. EST.

The possibility of a child testing positive for COVID could be an important consideration in deciding whether to link your family's stateroom reservations with those of another party. For further discussion, see page 116 in Part Three, "Staterooms."

DEBARKATION, AND POST-CRUISE TESTING As of November 2022, unvaccinated children on back-to-back cruises (see page 41) are no longer required to take a COVID test after debarking and before reboarding. However, unvaxxed kids *may* still need to take a rapid test before debarking on sailings of **five nights or longer.** The DCL website used to list this as a requirement, but the wording was removed in late 2022. Given Disney's history of changing its rules on a dime, though, you'll want to check the specifics for your sailing.

In early 2022, Inspire Diagnostics began offering a new service for guests who must provide proof of a negative COVID test before flying home to certain countries or US states. When booking their appointment with Safe Passage, guests are responsible for knowing what type of test they need and when they need to take it. Testing is conducted at the terminal after debarkation; results are available in about 45 minutes–2 hours, depending on the type of test.

CAN I CRUISE IF I'VE HAD COVID RECENTLY? WHAT IF I'M STILL TESTING POSITIVE? If you've recovered but have tested positive within **11–90 days** of your sail date, you may qualify as what DCL calls **90-Day Recovered.** If approved to sail, you'll be exempt from testing.

To find out if you qualify as 90-Day Recovered, you'll need to upload the following documents to Safe Passage and, if approved, bring them with you to the port:

- Proof of a positive COVID-19 test taken between 11 and 90 days of your expected sail date. The test result must include your date of birth. At-home antigen tests must be proctored by a telehealth provider.

- A signed letter from a licensed healthcare provider or public health official stating that you've recovered from COVID-19 in the last 90 days and are clear for travel. The document must be on official letterhead and include the provider's name, address, and phone number.

- Proof of vaccination, if applicable (mandatory for guests ages 12 and older)

REQUIREMENTS FOR DCL CRUISES VISITING CANADA Guests on DCL sailings originating from or visiting Canada must adhere to both Disney's and the Canadian government's vaccination and testing requirements. See tinyurl.com/CanadaTravelRules for full details. Some key points to be aware of:

- All visitors ages 12 and older must provide proof of full vaccination.

- Your proof of vaccination, along with your citizenship and travel documents, must be uploaded to **ArriveCAN,** which works similarly to Inspire Diagnostics' Safe Passage website (see page 51). You must create an ArriveCAN account and upload your documentation **within 72 hours** of entering Canada. For more information, see canada.ca/arrivecan.

- Pre-trip COVID tests are not required, but you may be selected at random to undergo testing at the border.

- Masks must be worn at all times in public spaces such as airports, testing sites, and cruise terminals.

Requirements for DCL European Cruises

At press time, these sailings have different vaccination and testing requirements from DCL cruises originating in the US, as outlined below.

Proof of full vaccination is required for all guests **ages 5 and older;** accepted vaccines are the same as those for US sailings (see page 50).

Parents of unvaccinated children under age 5 must submit proof of a negative PCR or NAAT test—*not* **a rapid antigen test**—taken **three days–24 hours** before sailing. Unvaxxed kids must also take a rapid test (paid for by DCL) at the port before they can board.

In addition, vaccinated guests must submit proof of a negative COVID test taken **two days–24 hours** before they sail. PCR, NAAT, and at-home rapid antigen tests are all accepted, but rapid tests must be supervised by a telehealth provider (see below).

Some European cruises accept guests who are **90-Day Recovered** from COVID (see previous page). Check the specifics for your sailing.

SAIL SCREEN BY PRENETICS This UK-based company (projectscreen.co.uk/portaldcl) handles vaccination and testing compliance for Disney's European cruises. You may register for a Sail Screen account **no sooner than 14 days** before sailing. Submitting documents and getting cleared to sail work basically the same as they do on Safe Passage (see page 51). Sail Screen also offers a proctored at-home antigen test and pre-trip testing at sites near the cruise terminals.

PROCTORED TESTING FOR VACCINATED GUESTS Sail Screen's proctored test costs $32 US/£30 UK. *Note:* The Sail Screen website says this test is available only within the UK, but the DCL website doesn't mention this. In case you can't order through Sail Screen, tests from other providers, such as eMed and Quest Diagnostics, are also accepted.

Regardless of the provider, your test kit will include instructions for scheduling a teleconference with a healthcare provider; you should also receive an email confirming your appointment. You'll need a computer or smart device with a video camera and a stable internet connection; check YouTube for videos walking you through the testing process.

Vaccinated guests who don't upload their test results by **midnight before their sail date** must pay for a rapid test ($74) at the port before they can board, plus a second test ($125) if the first test is positive.

Again, guests who test positive—and, most likely, the other members of their party—will not be allowed to sail. Call DCL as soon as possible if you need to cancel or reschedule your cruise (see page 52).

POST-CRUISE TESTING If your sailing ends in **Barcelona** and you need to be tested before you can fly home, you can book an appointment with **CERBA International.** Go to cerba.com and click "Make An Appointment"; on the next page, click the flag for Spain, then select "Centro Paris" from the drop-down menu.

COUNTRY-SPECIFIC REGULATIONS Many European nations have vaccination, testing, and documentation requirements that differ from DCL's. In addition to your passport, you may need to provide any or all of the following (or more): proof of a booster shot, proof of a negative COVID test taken within a specific timeframe, or documentation such as an **EU Digital COVID-19 Certificate** (tinyurl.com/EUCovid).

DCL's **Know Before You Go** page includes links to current entry requirements for 18 European nations that Disney visits; go to tinyurl .com/DCLKnowBeforeYouGo, and click "Europe Sailings" at the top of the page. Three more excellent resources are the US State Department's **COVID-19 Country-Specific Information** page (tinyurl.com/World CovidInfo), **Visit Europe** (visiteurope.com; click "COVID-19 Info" at the top of the page), and **Re-Open EU** (reopen.europa.eu). These web-sites aggregate COVID-related policies for all 27 countries in the European Union and include links to additional information.

*un*official **TIP**
If your cruise visits a country that requires booster shots for entry, get it at least two weeks before you arrive.

VACCINE CONSIDERATIONS FOR INTERNATIONAL GUESTS During the initial return to sailing, people outside the US sometimes found themselves blocked from cruising with DCL due to restrictive vaccination rules (usually pertaining to kids) in their home countries. Health authorities around the world have been gradually loosening these rules since 2021, but international guests still need to make sure that the vaccines they've received are approved by Disney. The website **VisaGuide.world** has a handy tool for checking whether a particular vaccine is accepted in a given country: see tinyurl.com/VisaGuideVaccineChecker.

Mask Requirements

At press time, DCL didn't require most guests to wear masks on board (masking is still required for cruise staff). Unvaccinated children under age 5 are required to wear face coverings in the kids' clubs and in the Bibbidi Bobbidi Boutique; DCL also recommends that unvaxxed kids wear masks in all other indoor locations.

In the US, face coverings are optional on motorcoach transportation (such as port-transfer shuttles) and in cruise terminals; masks may, however, be required in ports of call and cruise terminals outside of the US, depending on local regulations.

On Castaway Cay, face coverings are mostly optional, but they're still required for guests ages 2 and up—regardless of vaccination status—on trams and other island transportation, in areas where merchandise is sold, in dining pavilions when you're not actively eating or drinking, and in restrooms.

Where masks are still required, DCL's specifications for them are as follows:

All face coverings must fully cover an individual's nose and mouth and allow the guest to remain hands-free; fit snugly but comfortably against the side of the face; be secured with ties or ear loops; and be made of at least two layers of breathable material, either disposable or reusable, that is not elastic in nature such as spandex and elastane. At this time based on guidance from health authorities, neck gaiters, open-chin triangle bandannas, and face coverings containing valves, mesh material, or holes of any kind are not acceptable face coverings. Costume masks are not considered appropriate and are prohibited from being worn.

Health Insurance

US residents traveling internationally should contact their insurance providers to check their health coverage for emergencies outside the country (see page 58 for an in-depth discussion of travel insurance). While Disney offers its own insurance (called the **Vacation Protection Plan**), it limits coverage to $20,000 per person for medical and dental emergencies. If you're going to pay for additional insurance, make sure it's enough to be helpful in an emergency.

Residents of most European Union countries who are planning a Disney cruise in Europe should consider getting the **European Health Insurance Card** (see tinyurl.com/euinsurancecard).

The Health Questionnaire

Before boarding, adults are asked to complete a mandatory questionnaire. Pre-pandemic, this was a paper sheet you were handed at the port; post-pandemic, the form is available online on embarkation day, both on the DCL Navigator app and at a link that will be emailed to you.

The questionnaire we received during a summer 2019 cruise asked just two questions:

- Are you or is any occupant of your stateroom experiencing a fever *and* any one of the following symptoms: sore throat, cough, runny nose, muscle aches, or headache?
- Within the last three days, have you or has any occupant of your stateroom developed symptoms of vomiting or diarrhea?

When there are global health issues, Disney adds questions to the intake form. For example, when Ebola outbreaks surfaced pre-COVID, Disney asked passengers whether they had traveled to western Africa or had contact with Ebola patients.

DCL's first oblique acknowledgment of COVID on the health questionnaire appeared in late January 2020 with the question, "Have you been to Wuhan, China, or been in contact with anyone who has been in Wuhan, China, in the past 14 days?" By February 6, 2020, more-pointed questions were added:

- Have you or any occupant of your stateroom traveled from or through China, including Hong Kong or Macau, in the past 14 days?
- Have you or any occupant of your stateroom had close contact with, or helped care for, anyone suspected or diagnosed as having Novel Coronavirus, or who is currently subject to health monitoring for possible exposure to Novel Coronavirus, in the past 14 days?
- The Bahamas will not allow anyone who has been in China in the past 20 days to disembark at any Bahamian port of call. Have you or any occupant of your stateroom been to China, including Hong Kong or Macau, in the past 20 days?

As sailings resumed during summer 2021, guests were asked if they had experienced symptoms of COVID-19 or had been in contact with anyone suspected of or confirmed as having COVID-19 within the previous 14 days.

The health questionnaire at press time reads as follows:

- Will anyone in your travel party be pregnant 24 weeks or more at any point during your sailing?
- Have you or any person in your party had a positive COVID-19 test within the past 10 days?
- Within the past 14 days, have you or any person in your party had close contact with or helped care for anyone diagnosed with or suspected of having COVID-19?
- Are you or any person in your party currently subject to health monitoring for possible exposure to COVID-19?
- Do you or any person in your party have symptoms commonly associated with COVID-19? This includes a fever (100.4°F/38°C or higher), feeling feverish, chills, cough, shortness of breath or difficulty breathing, fatigue, muscle or body aches, headache, new loss of taste or smell, sore throat, congestion o runny nose, nausea or vomiting, or diarrhea.

Answering "yes" to any of Disney's questions will trigger an interview at the cruise terminal and may prevent you from boarding—so be sure that everyone in your party is in excellent health, not just COVID-free. Disney states the following in the contract that you were required to sign when you booked your trip:

> The Carrier [DCL] reserves the right, without liability whatsoever, to refuse passage . . . to any Guest whose physical or mental condition . . . is considered a risk to the Guest's own well-being or that of any other Guest, crew member, or person.

Before the pandemic, Disney offered no refunds or reimbursements to guests who couldn't board the ship due to last-minute health issues. At press time, however, remediation was offered to guests with travel-week positive COVID tests. This is another area where you can expect that policies will evolve as the pandemic continues, so check the DCL website frequently for updates.

A pre-cruise check-in with your doctor is a prudent step to make sure that you're set for ocean travel. If you need help with a pre-travel medical consultation, **Passport Health** (passporthealthusa.com) is a network of clinics in North America specializing in travel readiness. Even if you're using your own doctor, you may want to consult their easy-to-read lists of travel precautions and required immunizations for nearly every country in the world.

If you get sick in port, the **International Society of Travel Medicine** has an online directory of clinics that specialize in treating travelers: see tinyurl.com/istmclinicdirectory. The **International Association for Medical Assistance to Travelers** (iamat.org) also maintains a list of clinics and English-speaking doctors worldwide. **InternationalSOS** (international-sos.com/personal-travel) is a fee-based service (sign up for it before your trip) that provides medical and security assistance for international travelers. If you work for a large corporation, check with your HR department to see if they have a contract with a similar service.

If you've purchased DCL's **Vacation Protection Plan** (**VPP**) trip insurance (see below), you're entitled to 24-7 global assistance during your trip. Services include medical assistance and emergency service. To access this feature, call ☎ 877-303-5909 within the United States and Canada, or call ☎ 515-342-4594 outside the US and Canada.

*un*official **TIP**

If you receive medical treatment on your cruise, save any records such as prescriptions, lab reports, and X-rays, and share them with your regular doctor once you're back at home.

Before your cruise, create a document with key medical information and share it with others in your travel party. Include contact information for your doctors at home, your medications and their dosages, any allergies (for example, to medication or food), your insurance information, and any past surgeries or major illnesses. If you become incapacitated, having ready access to this information could save your life.

Also consider installing an app like **Life 360** or Apple's **Find My Friends** on the phones of everyone in your party—these can help you locate each other in an emergency.

TRAVEL INSURANCE

IN PREVIOUS EDITIONS OF THIS BOOK, we recommended travel insurance for Disney Cruise Line guests, but only vociferously so for those on long and expensive trips. We're now recommending it for nearly everyone.

COVID TIP

Some countries require travel insurance for visitors, for both COVID- and non-COVID-related reasons. If you're planning to travel internationally before or after your cruise, check the requirements for these countries at tinyurl.com/travelinsurancerules.

There are risks associated with any kind of travel, but cruises are unique because they're all-or-nothing propositions. If your flight to Orlando is delayed and you miss the first day of your week-long Walt Disney World vacation, you'll be disappointed, but you'll still be able to have a great time for six of the seven days. Not so with a cruise: if your flight is delayed and you miss boarding the ship, your entire vacation is over before it starts. Similarly, medical or weather issues that might be minor annoyances on land can completely derail a cruise, where there are fewer forms of remediation.

Most importantly, the cruise lines themselves are becoming increasingly aggressive—and understandably so—about enforcing health and safety precautions, meaning cruisers now face a greater-than-ever chance of being denied boarding for illnesses of *any* sort.

For all of these reasons, we now strongly recommend that you buy trip insurance for your cruise, even if you wouldn't normally buy it for a land-based vacation and even if you're fully vaccinated for COVID-19.

DCL offers its own trip insurance, called the **Vacation Protection Plan** (**VPP**). If you'd like to buy it, you must do so before you pay in full for your vacation (see tinyurl.com/dclvacationprotectionplan for details). Note, however, that many other reputable companies offer travel insurance at a variety of price points and coverage levels.

Providers reviewed in recent "best of" articles in *Forbes* magazine and at TheWirecutter.com (the *New York Times*'s product review website) include **AIG Travel Guard** (aig.com/travel-guard), **Allianz Global Assistance** (allianztravelinsurance.com), **American Express Travel Insurance** (tinyurl.com/AmericanExpressInsurance), **C&F Travel Insured** (travel insured.com), **Seven Corners** (sevencorners.com), **Travelex** (travelex insurance.com), and **Travel Guard** (travelguard.com). **InsureMyTrip** (insuremytrip.com), **SquareMouth** (squaremouth.com), and **Visitors Coverage** (visitorscoverage.com) can help you compare and contrast plans from many providers.

If you travel frequently, consider getting annual trip insurance, which provides coverage for multiple trips and is available from many of the previously listed companies. In addition, check whether you already have some travel coverage through your credit cards, your regular insurance provider, or your employer.

In general, when you're researching travel insurance, consider the following:

KINDS OF COVERAGE Plans are available that cover medical issues, with or without coverage for preexisting conditions; evacuation due to political unrest or weather; flight delays or cancellations (plus the cost of meals and/or hotels stemming from these); luggage replacement; trip cancellation due to unexpected events such as family emergencies; and various combinations of the above.

> *un*official **TIP**
> The **International Association of Medical Assistance to Travelers** has a helpful glossary that defines many of the terms you'll encounter when reading about travel insurance. See iamat.org /travel-insurance.

In the pandemic era, pay particular attention to whether your policy covers cancellation due to COVID or other diagnoses immediately before traveling; emergency care if you become ill while traveling; and accommodation coverage if you get quarantined at your destination, on board, or in port. Also, check whether some COVID-related aspects of the plan have time limits or other exclusions.

> *un*official **TIP**
> **MedJet** (medjetassist.com) provides insurance specifically for medical evacuation when overseas. Short-term and annual memberships are available.

PRICE Trip insurance is expensive—often 4%–8% (or more) of the cost of your vacation (see next page)—so be sure to compare quotes from different agencies to ensure that you're getting the best price for the coverage you need.

TIMING OF PURCHASE Some companies offer discounts if you buy insurance within a week or two of placing your deposit on a trip.

REIMBURSEMENT LIMITS If a policy caps your reimbursement, consider whether the maximum amount would be sufficient to cover the cost of your vacation or your medical care in an emergency.

FINE PRINT Make sure that you understand *all* the details of the policy you're purchasing, including your deadline for submitting a claim.

How Much Will Travel Insurance Cost?

Expect to pay between 4% and 8% of your total prepaid, nonrefundable trip expenses for a travel insurance policy. That range reflects a wide variety of coverage options: you'll find some basic plans that cost even less than 4% of your trip expenses but provide only limited coverage, as well as deluxe plans, costing as much as 12% of your trip, that cover anything and everything you can think of. Reputable insurance companies will offer a brief "try before you buy" period during which you can review the policy you've selected, then return it for any reason within the period allotted for a full refund, minus a small administrative fee.

MOTION SICKNESS AND GASTRIC DISTRESS

THE DISNEY SHIPS ARE LARGE VESSELS with sophisticated stabilizers and other technology that keep motion to a minimum, and the navigation staff does as much as possible to minimize the impact of weather on ship motion. Most of the time, you'll feel no different on the ship than you would if you were strolling across your own front yard; nonetheless, there may be times when you feel the motion of the ocean.

*un*official **TIP**

If you find yourself disoriented on the ship, *look down.* In the stateroom hallways on the *Dream, Fantasy, Magic,* and *Wonder,* the point of the star and the north direction of the compass point toward the bow, or front, of the ship. On the *Wish,* look for a small Mickey Mouse symbol in the carpet pattern—Mickey is upright when you're facing forward on the ship.

Depending on your level of sensitivity, the ship's route, the conditions at sea, and other factors, your perception of this situation might range from mild amusement to abject misery.

If you know that you're prone to motion sickness in other situations (such as during long car rides and on roller coasters), you may want to speak to your healthcare provider before you sail. They may suggest natural or over-the-counter remedies such as ginger supplements, Queasy Pops, or peppermint essential oil; acupressure tools such as SeaBands; Seetroën motion-sickness eyeglasses (less-expensive equivalents are available on Amazon and the like); electrical-stimulation tools such as ReliefBands; over-the-counter medicines such as Bonine or Dramamine (in regular and nondrowsy versions); or, in severe cases, prescription remedies such as scopolamine patches.

We're not doctors, but in our experience it can be more effective to stave off motion sickness before it starts than after. Erin has had success with starting a daily dose of Dramamine two days before sailing and continuing to take it through the voyage. You may have to experiment a bit to find the best solution for you.

Regular and kids' versions of Dramamine are available for sale in the ships' gift shops, as well as in single-dose form at Guest Services and at the onboard Health Center, but you'll likely save a few dollars if you buy it at home.

Another aspect of motion sickness may be the location of your stateroom. The rule of thumb is that midship staterooms experience the least rocking, followed by aft and then forward staterooms. Lower decks are more stable than high decks. If you're prone to motion sickness, a Deck 2 midship cabin may be more comfortable than a Deck 9 forward cabin. The exception to this might be if you find that fresh air helps you, in which case a midship stateroom with a verandah on Deck 6 might be your best bet.

While motion-sickness medications are sold at the onboard shops, you'll have to head to the ship's infirmary to get medicines for gastric distress, such as Imodium or Pepto-Bismol. DCL wants to reassure guests that they're on top of possible outbreaks of norovirus and the like, so if you have unexpected stomach or intestinal issues, do the safe and sane thing and go to the Health Center. But if you know that you typically experience minor GI upsets in any travel situation and you don't need a doctor, bring your own over-the-counter meds.

*un**official* **TIP**
News of a guest's GI distress will result in a report to the onboard medical staff and a likely 24-hour quarantine.

Again, preventing "traveler's tummy" is preferable to combating it once it's started. Here are a few suggestions

- **Make good decisions your first day aboard.** If you traveled from home the same day you boarded the ship, chances are you got up several hours before normal, packed yourself onto a plane or into a car, maybe ate something healthy (but probably didn't), and headed to the cruise terminal. What are you going to do first? Start stuffing your face with the all-inclusive food, of course! It's great to start your cruise off with a bang, but remember that you can always get more food if you're still hungry later.

- **Stay hydrated.** Carry a water bottle and keep it filled throughout the day. Then refill it at night and keep it in your cabin's beverage chiller for morning.

- **Take a walk.** Stretch your legs on the outside decks and enjoy the sea air. It may be just what you need.

- **Take an antacid.** Tums and Zantac are typically stocked on board, or you can bring your own.

- **Lay off the soda.** Yes, fountain drinks are included in your cruise fees, but just because you can have all you want doesn't mean you *should.* Bubbly beverages put air in your stomach, and as anyone who's ever fed a baby knows, that's not a good thing. Water is good. Add some lemon if you like.

- **Pack some loose-fitting clothes.** Be sure to bring along at least one dinner-appropriate outfit that you know will fit no matter what's going on in your gut. Maybe that's a caftan or palazzo pants with a drawstring waist. (Guys, you're on your own—just try to leave a few notches to spare on your belts and you should be OK.)

- **Make good choices in port.** Stick with bottled water and cooked foods. (Drinking from a water fountain in Mexico is probably playing with fire.) Additionally, if you're prone to motion sickness or GI issues, avoid port adventures involving things like rides on small boats or jeep trips down bumpy roads.

- **Wash/sanitize your hands.** The disinfecting wipes handed out every time you come within 20 feet of food are only a start. The very best way to avoid major and minor bugs is to wash your hands and visit the hand-sanitizing stations at every opportunity.

- **Chat with your doctor.** Before your cruise, ask your healthcare provider for advice about prescription and over-the-counter remedies. (For example, some dietary supplements, such as Travelan, are advertised as promoting digestive health and preventing travelers' diarrhea.)

PASSPORTS AND TRAVEL DOCUMENTS

EVERYONE IN YOUR PARTY, including babies and children, must present proof of citizenship before boarding the ship. **A passport is your simplest, safest bet because it covers all your bases.** Depending on the situation, it's either mandatory (see Unofficial Tip, left) or good to have but not absolutely necessary.

If you don't have a passport and (1) you're a US citizen traveling from a US port (such as Port Canaveral, Miami, Galveston, San Diego, New Orleans, or New York); (2) you're traveling only within the Western Hemisphere (the US, Canada, Mexico, or the Caribbean); and (3) you're on a so-called closed-loop cruise—that is, you're embarking and debarking from the same US port on the same ship—you may be able to use alternative documentation.

unofficial **TIP**
You **must** have a passport if you're a US citizen flying from home to a foreign cruise port, or vice versa.

According to US Customs and Border Protection (see tinyurl.com /WesternHemisphereTravel), adult cruisers meeting these conditions may present government-issued photo ID *plus* proof of citizenship: an original or copy of a state-issued birth certificate, a Consular Report of Birth Abroad, or a Certificate of Naturalization. US citizens under age 16 (or under age 19 if traveling with a school group, religious group, or other organized youth group) need present only proof of citizenship. Be aware, however, that you may still need a passport to enter the countries your cruise ship is visiting, so check before you go.

For adult US citizens who don't have a passport, acceptable alternatives on a closed-loop cruise include the following:

- **A US Passport Card.** This limited-use document lets you enter the United States by land or sea from within the Western Hemisphere. At the time of this writing, a new (nonrenewal) card costs $65 for adults ages 16 and over, versus $165 for a first-time US Passport book. Expedited processing and shipping may be available for an extra fee.

- **An Enhanced Driver's License (EDL).** An EDL provides proof of both identity and citizenship in addition to certifying you to drive. Currently available only to US citizens in Michigan, Minnesota, New York, Vermont, and Washington, EDLs contain security features such as a radio frequency identification (RFID) chip.

- **A Trusted Traveler Program Card** (NEXUS, SENTRI, or FAST).

- **A Uniformed Services ID Card** for US military traveling on official orders.

We recommend that all members of your party obtain passports if possible, even for a closed-loop cruise. Let's say you're on a port adventure in Nassau and you learn of an urgent family emergency. If you have a passport, you can hop on a plane and be back home within hours. If you don't, you'll first have to go to the US Embassy, apply for an expedited passport, and wait for it to be processed.

Documentation requirements for Canadian citizens are similar: a Canada passport, Enhanced Driver's Licence, or Trusted Traveler Card. Citizens of other countries may be required to present a passport or visa to enter a port even if US and Canadian citizens aren't.

As of May 3, 2023, all US citizens flying domestically must present either a **Real ID**–compliant driver's license/state ID card or an alternative such as a passport at their airport's Transportation Security Administration (TSA) checkpoint; see tsa.gov/real-id for details.

Converting a noncompliant license to the Real ID version can be a huge hassle—we've heard of waits at the DMV that are even more soul-crushing than those for a routine license renewal—so get this straightened out well in advance of your cruise if it includes domestic air travel. **AAA** offers upgrading assistance for its members in Massachusetts, New York, and Rhode Island (see tinyurl.com/AAARealID).

One particularly confusing issue regarding ID requirements applies to US citizens on DCL Alaskan cruises from Vancouver. The Western Hemisphere Travel Initiative specifies that you can drive from the United States to Vancouver with only an Enhanced Driver's License or a US Passport Card, but you may be required to present a full passport *book* to board the ship in Vancouver, depending on whether you're on a closed-loop cruise, a repositioning cruise, or a back-to-back sailing. Be sure to confirm your exact documentation needs well before your trip—when in doubt, a passport book will always work.

Check the specifics of your sailing when choosing excursions. Again, if you're an American citizen and you're flying to your cruise's embarkation point from a non-US port, you'll need a passport to get there. Also, note that some DCL port adventures on Alaskan cruises require a valid passport because you cross into Canada during the trip. Plus, some foreign ports require not only passports but also special visas for guests who plan to explore on their own versus with an approved excursion group or tour guide.

Whichever forms of ID you bring, be sure to secure them when traveling—either in your stateroom/hotel-room safe when you're not in port or on your person when you're out and about. Some guidebooks recommend leaving your passport on board at all times, but we've seen too many instances of people being left behind because of a taxi breakdown or other unforeseen mishap. If you have your passport and a credit card, you can fly to the next port to meet the ship if needed. That beats searching for an embassy, possibly having to wait for it to open after a weekend or holiday, and then paying for and waiting on an expedited replacement.

*un*official **TIP**
In most cases, you must book a cruise departing from the United States **at least three days in advance.** Department of Homeland Security rules require cruise lines to submit their passenger lists 72 hours before sailing.

Also be sure to take precautions in the unlikely event that your ID is lost or stolen. Make photocopies of your passport or other documents; keep one set of copies in your luggage and another set at home with a trusted friend or relative. We also email digital copies of our ID and travel documents to ourselves or upload them to the cloud.

unofficial **TIP**

If you'll be working during your vacation abroad, check the **FBI**'s safety tips for conducting business overseas. See tinyurl.com/FBIBizTravel.

GETTING A PASSPORT US citizens may obtain passports themselves by following the steps at tinyurl.com/HowToApplyForAPassport. In the COVID era, there have been substantial waits for processing passport applications. In normal times, passports typically took about 6–8 weeks to process— at press time, waits in excess of 16 weeks were common. If you want to get a passport, plan to do so far in advance of your trip. If you already have a passport, be sure to check the expiration date to make sure you have time to renew it if needed. You may be able to get a passport more quickly by applying in person at an official passport office. See tinyurl. com/USPassportAgencies for locations. Note, however, that there may still be delays even with expedited passports.

While Disney offers no additional passport advice beyond working directly with the US Department of State, many other major cruise lines (including Royal Caribbean, Holland America, and Norwegian Cruise Line) refer guests needing passport assistance to **Visa Central** (877-535-0688, visacentral.com). This reputable fee-based service can help with passport processing and offers one-day turnaround on passport renewals. If you find the application process too complicated to tackle on your own, Visa Central may be worth the cost.

PASSPORT EXPIRATION Many countries require your passport to be valid for up to 6 months after your cruise. To avoid complications, check the passport policies in the countries you plan to visit ahead of time, and make sure that you have ample time remaining on your passport before it expires.

EXPEDITING YOUR TSA CHECK If you fly at least a couple of times per year, you may want to consider registering for **TSA PreCheck** (tsa.gov /precheck). This service shortens your waits in line to less than 5 minutes in most cases; it also lets you skip headaches such as removing your shoes and unpacking liquids from your carry-on luggage. Membership costs $85 for five years—in our opinion, it's money well spent.

If you don't mind tinkering with credit card or mileage points, you may be able to obtain TSA PreCheck and/or Global Entry (see next page) membership at no cost. While offers vary, there are currently nearly 50 credit card, airline, or hotel affinity programs that offer credits or reimbursements for TSA PreCheck fees. Other programs let you pay for PreCheck access with points or miles instead of cash. See tsa.gov /precheck/credit-cards-offer for more information.

If you fly often, consider **Clear** (clearme.com), a higher-fee service that provides even faster screening, letting you skip to the front of the TSA

PreCheck line. Rates are currently $189 per year, $50 for each additional adult family member, and free for children under age 18 who are flying with an adult member; the student rate is $50 per year, with no age restrictions (see tinyurl.com/ClearStudentRate). Clear also has a **Health Pass** component that you can use at entertainment and tourist venues that require proof of COVID-19 vaccination for entry, such as New York City's Madison Square Garden and San Francisco's Oracle Park.

Frequent travelers may want to download the **MyTSA** app (tsa.gov /app), which provides estimates of security-line waits at US airports, as well as information about packing rules and ID requirements. We're also keeping an eye on a new free app called **Whyline** (whyline.com), which lets you reserve a security-line time slot and jump to the front of the line. At press time, participating airports included Orlando International, Los Angeles International, Dallas–Fort Worth, JFK, and Newark, among others.

You also have some options for speeding up customs processing after you return to the US. **Global Entry** (tinyurl.com/USAGlobalEntry) is a fee-based adjunct to TSA PreCheck; approved travelers can use automated kiosks to proceed through US Customs stations at some airports. The free **CBP Mobile Passport Control App** (tinyurl.com/US CustomsApp) makes processing more efficient by letting you fill out some of the necessary paperwork ahead of time.

EUROPEAN TRAVEL UPDATE As of May 2023, US citizens visiting Europe, as well as passport-holding citizens of several other nations, will need a **European Travel Information and Authorization System** (**ETIAS**) visa waiver to enter countries in the European Union (EU). For DCL passengers, this includes almost everyone sailing on the *Dream* during the summer.

An ETIAS waiver is *not* a tourist visa; rather, it's a prescreening registration for travelers visiting the EU from countries that don't require a visa. It's very similar to the US Electronic System for Travel Authorization, which most EU nationals must obtain in order to travel to the United States.

*un**official* **TIP**

Join the US State Department's **Smart Traveler Enrollment Program** (step.state.gov/step) to receive updates on safety conditions abroad and facilitate contact with US embassies in case of emergencies.

Valid for three years, an ETIAS waiver costs €7 (less than $10 US) for adults and is free for children under age 18. For more information, see schengenvisainfo.com/etias; to apply online, go to etiasvisa.com /etias-form-application.

TRAVELING WITH MINORS If you're an adult age 21 or older traveling with someone else's minor child, Disney Cruise Line requires written permission from the child's parent or legal guardian in addition to proof of the child's citizenship. DCL's **Minor Authorization Form** is available as a PDF at tinyurl.com/DCLTravelWithMinor. Present a signed printout at check-in at the cruise terminal.

If you're cruising outside the United States with your own minor child but without the child's other parent—whether you're a single parent or your spouse/partner couldn't make the trip—US Customs and Border Protection strongly recommends that you also bring along a signed, notarized permission letter in addition to proof of the child's citizenship. (See tinyurl.com/CBPChildTravel for details.) Adults traveling with someone else's minor child are advised to do the same in addition to filling out the Minor Authorization Form.

The permission letter isn't legally required, and many cruisers, including Erin, report that they've never been asked for it. That said, customs reserves the right to investigate situations that it deems suspicious, so better safe than sorry.

The letter should include (1) the child's full name and birth date; (2) your and the other parent's full name, address, and phone number; (3) a description of the entire trip (dates, countries, and cruise information); (4) the purpose of the trip; (5) the other parent's original signature, in ink; and (6) the date of the signing.

Don't put off getting the letter notarized until the last minute. Banks and post offices often have notaries on staff, but some will come to you (Google "mobile notaries" in your area). The notary will have to witness the other parent signing the form, so it's best to have the other parent present the form to the notary. DCL doesn't require that the Minor Authorization Form be notarized, but if you're already getting a permission letter notarized, it can't hurt to get this form notarized, too, while you're at it.

Pre-Cruise Mailings and Cruise Contract

Several years ago, DCL mailed large spiral-bound booklets to all travelers a few weeks ahead of their trips. The booklets included information about reserved activities such as adult dining and port adventures, a printed copy of your cruise contract, suggested items to pack, and assorted marketing fluff.

As an environmental measure, Disney was already winnowing down the number of these paper mailings pre-COVID. You may still receive a few items in the mail, such as luggage tags, but in an effort to reduce physical items of contact, most of your communication with Disney Cruise Line will now be electronic. This makes it all the more important to explore the DCL website at length.

Of particular importance should be your **Cruise Contract** (see tinyurl.com/DCLCruiseContract), which details the legal aspects of your relationship with DCL. Agreeing to cruise means you agree to abide by the contract. Note that there are slightly different versions for residents of the US, the UK, and other countries, so make sure you're looking at the contract that applies to you.

PAYMENT METHODS

YOU CAN PAY FOR YOUR initial cruise package in US dollars, British pounds, or euros. The DCL website will display cruise and transportation prices in one of these three currencies depending on your geographic location where you access the site. To change to a different one of these currencies, use the selector at the top of the home page, next to the "Sign In" button. On the DCL website, all other purchases such as spa services, port adventures, and adult dining are priced in US dollars. These charges will be billed to your **folio,** or room account.

Payment methods accepted on DCL ships are cash (as detailed following), Visa, MasterCard, American Express (both charge cards and traveler's checks in US dollars), Discover, Diners Club, and JCB. They also accept Disney gift cards, Disney Rewards Dollars (available to Disney Chase Visa holders), and Disney Dollars (which were officially discontinued in 2016 but are still redeemable). When you complete online check-in for your cruise (see page 69), you'll choose your preferred way to pay for incidentals on the ship: cash or a credit card.

If you prefer cash, note that you can't use it to pay directly for beverages, spa or salon services, photos, laundry, or retail purchases. What you'll need to do first is stop by the Guest Services desk to set up a **cash account**—you'll use this to fund onboard charges made with your Key to the World (KTTW) Card (see page 133), which functions somewhat like a credit card on the ship.

You'll be asked to sign an agreement that lets you charge up to a specific amount on your KTTW Card before you can make additional charges. For a three-night sailing, you'll likely hit a $300 limit before being asked to deposit more cash into your account. You can also top up your account using Disney gift cards. But even if you'll be using a credit card to fund your folio and pay for stuff in port, you may still want to keep some cash on hand for gratuity envelopes or on-the-spot tipping (say, for luggage assistance or room service). You can cash checks and obtain change from the Guest Services desk; you can also use other credit cards on board.

unofficial **TIP**

If you're traveling in the same stateroom with friends, you can arrange to have your respective onboard charges go to your individual credit cards or other payment methods. Arrange this during online check-in or at Guest Services at the beginning of your trip.

unofficial **TIP**

To prevent any sudden stops on your accounts, let your bank and credit card companies know that you're traveling abroad before you leave home

US dollars are widely accepted in most of the Caribbean and the Bahamas, and most prices are quoted in dollars. Credit cards from US-based banks are also accepted at many shops and stores, but don't count on smaller stores, bodegas, markets, and taxis taking them.

If you're traveling to Europe, Mexico, or Canada, you generally have three options:

- **Ask your local bank to convert your US dollars before you leave home.** Many banks will do this at a reasonable exchange rate; some charge a small exchange fee. Give your bank about a week to obtain the currency you need, because many branches don't keep euros, pesos, or Canadian dollars on hand. Your bank will likely convert any unspent currency back to dollars when you return.

- **Use a local ATM that's part of your bank's network.** If you're traveling in Europe and you're not sure how much cash to bring along, you can usually get a fair exchange rate by withdrawing money at a local cash machine. **Visa's** website has a handy worldwide ATM locator (visa.com/atmlocator), and in our experience there are usually many more ATMs available than the ones listed online. Keep in mind that your local bank will probably add a withdrawal fee and a foreign-transaction fee, so it's better to make a few large withdrawals than lots of small ones. If you plan to use ATMs abroad, make sure to review *The Overseas Traveler's Guide to ATM Skimmers and Fraud,* published by the US Department of State. Download a PDF of this document at tinyurl.com/guidetoatmskimmers.

• **Exchange traveler's checks for local currency when you disembark.** Traveler's checks are safer than carrying cash because they can be replaced if lost or stolen. The downside: converting them to local currency takes more time than using an ATM or obtaining local currency before you leave home.

If you want to convert traveler's checks to cash, do it a reputable local bank—*not* a currency-exchange stand—and do the math yourself on-site to verify that you're getting the correct exchange rate. We've heard from readers who were promised one rate but got another, lower one when the conversion was done.

Passengers on DCL ocean cruises and Adventures by Disney (AbD) river cruises in Europe should take extra care to understand the currency used in all of the countries they will be visiting, both during their cruise and during any pre- or post-voyage travel. Of particular note, not all countries in Europe use the euro as legal tender.

AbD's Rhine River cruises begin in Switzerland, which uses the franc, and its Danube River cruises either start or end in Hungary, which uses the forint. DCL European ports that don't use the euro include stops in Denmark, Iceland, Norway, the United Kingdom, and several other countries. An important distinction in the British Isles: the UK (including Northern Ireland) uses pounds, but the Republic of Ireland uses euros.

The US dollar is unofficially accepted by many markets, bodegas, and taxi drivers throughout Mexico, but you'll rarely get a good deal that way. You'll probably be offered a simple exchange rate of 10 or 15 pesos per dollar, whereas at press time the actual exchange rate was about 20 pesos per dollar, a significant difference from what you're likely to be offered.

If you're a frequent international traveler, check with your credit card companies to see if they charge a currency-exchange fee for purchases made with your cards in other countries. Some cards don't charge any exchange fees, so it could pay to shop around.

Having a credit card lost or stolen is an annoyance at any time, but it can be particularly upsetting when you're traveling and relying on your card for food and lodging, or for paying off your bingo and bar bill on board. We've had to cancel cards while on vacation more than once due to suspected identity theft. Replacing a compromised card on the road (or in the middle of the ocean) is much more complicated and stressful than simply having a new card delivered to your home or office. For this reason, we strongly suggest that you or members of your party travel with at least two kinds of credit and/or debit cards, with enough access to funds to pay for several days of your trip. Keep one card with you and the other tucked in your stateroom or hotel safe.

Be aware that the Disney ships have no ATMs, but you can exchange small amounts of money (bills only, not coins) at the Guest Services desk, at prevailing exchange rates. DCL takes no commission on these transactions.

Disney Visa Card Discounts

DCL cruisers who use a Disney Visa Card to fund onboard purchases are entitled to various discounts on the ship; register your card during online check-in (see below) or at the cruise terminal. Your Key to the World Card will then indicate that you're eligible for discounts such as 10% off select photo packages (see page 308), 10% off most merchandise purchases over $50, 10% off some Castaway Cay rentals, and 20% off some spa treatments. Offers are subject to change, and they can't be combined with other discounts. See disneyrewards.com/vacation-perks/disney-cruise-line-savings for more information.

ONLINE CHECK-IN

IN THE PRE-COVID ERA, online check-in at the DCL website was optional, but at the time of this writing it's mandatory. In addition to performing pre-cruise tasks such as inputting flight and credit card information, guests must upload photos of numerous travel documents, including passports and other identity verification items, to reduce the amount of time guests spend in the cruise terminal.

unofficial **TIP**
You'll need to bring all of your travel documents with you to the port in addition to uploading them to the DCL website.

Guests must also upload photographs of themselves for ID purposes when entering and exiting the ship, and to match adults with their associated minors. Previously, these photos were taken at the port.

Note: The document-review system can be finicky, so make sure the photos of your documents are in focus and free from glare; also make sure the documents themselves aren't wrinkled or folded. An Unofficial Guide team member had their birth certificate rejected due to a slightly folded corner on the original document. After they smoothed out the corner and took a new photo, the birth certificate was accepted.

Be sure to print out copies of any port-arrival documents that you receive; these contain QR codes that will need to be scanned first thing when you arrive. In addition, make sure your phone is running the most up-to-date versions of its operating system and the **DCL Navigator app** (see page 136). At press time, online check-in could be completed **3–30 days** before sailing.

PHONE SERVICE

WHEN IT COMES TO STAYING CONNECTED to the outside world during your cruise, you should first figure out exactly *how* connected you want to be. Do you want to be accessible only in an emergency? Do you want to check email once or twice a day? Do you want to post on social media? Do you want to listen to music or watch videos? Are you willing to put in the effort to search for Wi-Fi in port, or do you want to be fully connected at all times?

Note: Connectivity on the ship and in port are two entirely different animals. Depending on your needs, you may have to set up two separate phone/data plans—one for use while you're at sea and another while you're on land.

ON BOARD Every DCL stateroom has a landline-style phone with voice mail that you can use to call other rooms and contact onboard services such as Room Service or Guest Relations. Your can also use your stateroom phone to make ship-to-shore calls; we recommend this only as a last resort, though, because rates are outrageous (see below). DCL's Wave Phones, cell phone–like devices that could be used to call and text other guests onboard and at Castaway Cay, were retired in 2019. Their functionality has been replaced by the text function of the **DCL Navigator app** (see page 136) and (for iPhone/iPad users) by **iMessage** (see below).

> *un*official **TIP**
>
> The number for incoming calls to your stateroom is ☎ **888-322-8732** in the US or ☎ **732-335-3281** outside the US; callers must provide a credit card number, along with the name of your ship and your stateroom number.

Cell service is available through DCL's **Cellular@Sea** satellite wireless network. The rates for pay-as-you-go talk, text, and data roaming on board vary depending on your carrier, but they're expensive compared with a standard phone plan. Turn off roaming when you don't need it or, better yet, turn off your phone completely when you're not using it.

> *un*official **TIP**
>
> If you have a older smartphone that you don't use anymore, give it to your school-age kids to use during your cruise. Having access to texting via the Navigator app will greatly increase your ability to communicate with them.

Most cellular carriers offer special cruise-ship packages. While these are more expensive than a regular wireless plan, they've become more affordable over the past few years, and they're definitely cheaper than using Cellular@Sea. As a typical example, **AT&T** offers two versions of its cruise package: (1) 30 days of unlimited shipboard and ship-to-shore talk and text, with 200MB of data included, for a $100 one-time charge (data overage is charged at $2 per megabyte), and (2) 30 days of unlimited shipboard and ship-to-shore texting (no data included), with 50 minutes of talk time included, for a $50 one-time charge (talk over the first 50 minutes is charged at $2 per minute).

If you have pressing work issues or family members you might need to reach to while you're at sea—particularly if you have a non-Apple cell phone—buying at least the cheaper of these two packages would probably make sense for your peace of mind. And it would definitely be less expensive than using your stateroom phone to call from ship to shore: that costs a sky-high $7–$9.50 per minute, charged to your room. (On the upside, calls are limited to 10 minutes.)

A FREE PERK FOR IPHONE USERS In 2019 DCL added free **iMessage** capability to its ships. It works both on the ship and from ship to shore. Assuming that all parties have iPhones, you can text your teens while they're in your stateroom and you're at Palo, or you can text your housesitter while you're floating in the Caribbean. DCL's iMessage is text only—you can't send photos or video—but it's nevertheless a huge boon for iPhone users whose primary contacts are other iPhone users. To use it, just put your iPhone in airplane mode and connect to DCL's onboard Wi-Fi at no extra charge. *Note:* We've had good luck using iMessage in the Caribbean and other areas close to land, but some guests report that it's less reliable farther out at sea.

IN PORT Most wireless carriers in the United States offer international talk, text, and data at rates far more reasonable than paying roaming charges. Note that if you purchase a cruise package from your wireless carrier (see previous page), it won't cover the use of your mobile phone while you're in port—it's an entirely different set of charges.

International plans vary slightly from carrier to carrier, but **AT&T**'s **International Day Pass** is typical: it includes unlimited talk and text in most countries for $10 per day (plus $5 per day for each additional family member on your plan, used on the same day); data availability is based on your regular AT&T plan. **Verizon**'s international plans are similar to AT&T's, while **T-Mobile** includes limited "buckets" of international text and/or data in some standard plans.

Our general advice is to thoroughly research your carrier's options, paying particular attention to differences in rates and coverage on board the ship versus off of it. Again, international phone plans used in port are nearly always a better value than special shipboard plans, and they're definitely a better value than just letting your cell phone roam indiscriminately.

If you've chosen either a land package or a sea package but not both, pay attention to what type of service your phone is actually using. When the ship's cellular network is on, the display on your device will show **Cellular@Sea, 901-18,** or **NOR-18,** which indicates that you're roaming on Cellular@Sea. When you start roaming on a land carrier, your device will display that carrier's network information.

The easiest ways to keep your wireless bill from spiraling out of control both on and off the ship are as follows:

1. **Keep your phone turned off when you're not using it.** If you don't have the patience or tech savvy to tinker with settings, this is the simplest way to ensure that your phone doesn't connect to a cellular network without your consent—and possibly leave you with a whopper of a phone bill later on.

2. **Put your phone in airplane mode.** This shuts off voice, text, and data but still lets you take pictures, listen to music, and connect to Wi-Fi (see next page).

3. **Turn off data when you don't need it.** Look for an icon or button called "Settings" on your phone, and from there look for "Cellular," "Wireless and Networks," or the like. Under that, look for "Data Usage," "Cellular Data," "Data Roaming," "Mobile Data," or something similar—*make sure that's unchecked or turned off*. Airplane mode (see above) disables talk and text as well as data.

4. **Use Wi-Fi calling.** The three major US wireless carriers offer free Wi-Fi calling to the United States from international locations, depending on your plan. You need a phone that supports Wi-Fi calling; check with your carrier for details. The catches, of course, are finding a hotspot with a strong signal and deciding

whether you want to pay for Wi-Fi versus scrounging around for free access (try Googling "free Wi-Fi in cruise ports"). If you do find a free hotspot, say, at a restaurant or shop, keep in mind that you may be expected to buy something in return. (DCL's onboard Wi-Fi generally isn't reliable enough for making calls.)

DCL ships have a dedicated internet desk to answer questions about **Connect@Sea** Wi-Fi packages (see page 137). The staff has printouts available detailing specific phone settings that will reduce your data consumption. If you're planning to be online during your vacation, it's well worth stopping by the internet desk for information.

Depending on your cruise destination, you may not need to make any changes to your cell service when calling in port. Some US carriers include land-based calling to and from Mexico and Canada in their standard plans; again, confirm the specifics with your carrier.

unofficial **TIP**
Disney's onboard Wi-Fi is free to use with the **DCL Navigator** app (see page 136).

Finally, in Alaska, Hawaii, Puerto Rico, and the US Virgin Islands, you won't need to make changes to your cell service just for a cruise, but signal quality may fluctuate compared with your service at home. For example, our AT&T service in Skagway, Alaska, was OK, but our travel companion's Verizon service in the same area was spotty at best.

PACKING

HAVING TRAVELED WITH lots of people over many years, we realize that asking "What do I need to pack?" is like asking "What is art?" Everyone will have their own answer based on their experience and preferences.

unofficial **TIP**
If you're not absolutely sure that you're going to use something on your cruise, **leave it at home.**

Some people assume they're going to do laundry on the ship and pack three days' worth of clothes for a seven-night cruise; others would rather pay for an extra suitcase to carry more clean clothes. *Bottom line:* It's up to you.

Knowing what to pack is equally important, and the range of opinions regarding packing essentials varies wildly. The DCL website has a helpful page (tinyurl.com/dclpacking-list) with suggestions on appropriate clothing for the ship's restaurants and ports of call, along with a short, reasonable list of incidentals to pack (as well as stuff you can't bring aboard).

When you're looking at the packing tips on the DCL website, be sure to consult the list for your destination—not surprisingly, you'll need to pack a bit differently for Alaska than you would for the Caribbean. In addition to general packing lists, you may want to consider the particular port adventures you've selected. For example, if you're touring in Rome, you may want to dress more stylishly than you would if you're just hanging out at the beach, or if you're planning to visit churches and cathedrals, you'll want to take a moment to research their dress codes.

Beyond that, just type "Disney Cruise Line packing list" into your favorite search engine, and you'll see myriad lists with a wide range of items. Some of these read more like an Amazon jungle–trek prep list (yes, mosquito netting appears on more than one of them). It's useful to read through a couple of lists to see if they mention anything you can't live without.

Our most important packing advice is this: don't drive yourself crazy trying to pack for every scenario. You're going to be lugging those bags a lot farther than you might think.

You can buy many personal-care products and OTC medicines on board (see page 304 for more info). You may not find your preferred brands at the best prices, but if, say, you run out of ibuprofen or you forgot to pack anti-itch cream, you'll appreciate the convenience. Notably, however, remedies for gastric distress *aren't* sold on the ships—see page 60 for more about that.

Besides appropriate clothing, our packing list includes the following essentials:

- **Face masks** In the COVID era, you never know when protocols will change. Even if you'll be sailing during a period when face coverings are not required, we recommend being prepared just in case.

- **Prescription medications** Pack these in carry-on luggage, in their original containers. (Also see pages 75 and 162–163.)

- **Tablet computer** Load enough books, music, movies, TV shows, and games for the cruise, plus the trip to and from the port. At the time of this writing, DCL's Wi-Fi speed and pricing make video streaming all but impossible. If your child must have access to particular content, download it to your device *before* you set sail.

- **Games and diversions** Pre-COVID, many DCL lounges kept board games on hand. To limit high-touch surfaces, these have now been removed. If you, like us, enjoy a family game night, then plan to bring your own deck of cards, Apples to Apples, Scrabble board, or the like. Other relaxing diversions for kids and adults might include paperback novels, magazines, coloring books, yarn crafts like knitting, puzzle books, or sticker books.

- **White-noise mobile app** This is useful for drowning out noise from hallways, next-door cabins, and ship machinery.

- **Sun hats and sunglasses** Sunscreen is reasonably priced on the ships in case you don't want to pack it.

- **Water shoes or flip-flops** You'll need these for the pool and beach.

- **Some large zip-top plastic bags** Store damp, sandy swimsuits, shoes, and such in these so they won't get the rest of your packed luggage dirty on the trip home.

- **Chewing gum** As is the case at the Disney parks and the Orlando airport, gum is not sold on DCL ships (though mints and other candies are). If you need to chew gum to relieve ear pressure during air travel, whether for your flight home or a port excursion that involves a seaplane or helicopter, bring your own.

If you're traveling with young children or someone with special needs, you may also want to pack the following items:

- **Sippy cups and/or drinking straws** Disney Cruise Line has largely moved away from serving beverages with lids and straws, and during our most recent sailings, we couldn't find sippy cups for sale on board. If you're cruising with toddlers or anyone who needs assistance with drinking liquids, then bring your own supplies.

- **Regular and swim diapers** The onboard shops carry these in maybe a couple of sizes at the most.

- **Earplugs** The ship's horn can be *loud*. Also, some of the music amplification during the deck parties may be too intense for sensitive ears. If anyone in your party has auditory sensitivities, bring ear protection.

- **Favorite snacks** Yes, the Mickey-shaped cheese crackers sold on the ships *look* a bit like Pepperidge Farm Goldfish, but they don't *taste* exactly the same—and that could trigger a tantrum in a persnickety toddler. (*Note:* Any food you bring on the ship must be factory-sealed in its original packaging.) To cut down on lots of open bags and boxes, stock up on single-serving snacks. A great place to get them online is **Minimus.biz**, a one-stop shop for individually packaged food items along with travel-size toiletries, easy-to-pack games and toys, and small travel accessories.

- **A night-light** There are no night-lights in the bathrooms on the *Magic* and *Wonder,* nor do most DCL staterooms have night-lights elsewhere to soothe children who may not be accustomed to sleeping in total darkness. Battery-operated tea lights or fluorescent glow sticks cost less than a dollar, will keep outlets free for phone charging, will prevent stubbed toes on the way to the bathroom, and will help anxious kids sleep better in an unfamiliar place.

Solutions for Lots of Stuff

Some guests may find that they have more luggage than they can reasonably transport to the ship on their own; this often happens to guests with small children sailing on longer voyages with bulky items such as diapers and wipes.

If you need to bring bulky items onto the ship but you don't want to incur excess-baggage fees by flying with them, you have a few alternatives, particularly if you're going to Walt Disney World before your cruise (see page 149).

- **Drive a rental car to the port instead of flying,** or use a car service that allows stops. On the way to the port, stop at a grocery store to stock up.

- **Ask if your pre-cruise hotel accepts packages.** If it does, have your items shipped there. (All Walt Disney World hotels accept packages.)

- **Amazon Prime** members can have groceries, baby-care products, and the like same-day-delivered to their Orlando-area hotels. Also, **Garden Grocer** (gardengrocer.com) and **Turner Drugs** (turnerdrug.com) offer delivery service in the Orlando area.

Alcoholic Beverages

Some guests choose to economize on booze by bringing their own. Guests age 21 or older may bring a maximum of two bottles (no larger than 750 milliliters) of unopened wine or Champagne or a six-pack of beer (bottles or cans no larger than 12 ounces each) on board at the beginning of the trip *and* at each port of call. These beverages must be packed in carry-on bags. Any alcohol packed in your checked luggage will be removed and stored—the next time you'll see it will be when you're getting ready to head home.

unofficial **TIP**
You can bring sealed nonalcoholic beverages onto the ship in any reasonable quantity that you can carry on yourself. Bottled water, canned soda, iced tea, and the like are all fine.

If you bring hard liquor, powdered alcohol, or beer or wine on board in excess of the allowed quantity, it will be likewise stored until the end of your cruise. If you plan to buy the local hooch while in port, ask to have it packaged for travel (for example, in bubble wrap).

Be aware that if you bring alcohol on board, you can't drink it in a bar or other public area. The one exception is wine or Champagne that you want to drink with a meal, but the dining rooms charge a corking fee of $25 per bottle.

Note: Many readers have asked us if it's OK to bring aboard single-serving "hard" beverages like hard cider, Truly, White Claw, and Mike's Hard Lemonade. Technically, they're not allowed, but cast members may not bother to confiscate them.

Banned Items

While you're packing, it also makes sense to review the fairly extensive list of items that are prohibited aboard DCL ships. Not surprisingly, you can't bring weapons, fireworks, or illegal drugs, but did you also know that you can't bring pool noodles, musical instruments, in-line skates, fishing gear, or kites? Other prohibited items include candles; clothes irons; balloons; toy guns (including Disney-themed guns such as *Star Wars* blasters); remote-control drones; Christmas lights; skateboards; fresh fruit or flowers; inflatable mattresses; TV-streaming devices (such as Apple TV, Roku, Amazon Fire TV Stick, and Google Chromecast); and medical marijuana.

*un**official* **TIP**
For a complete list of items banned on DCL ships, see tinyurl.com/dclbanneditems.

Even if you've cruised with DCL before, make sure to review the banned-items list, which is updated fairly regularly. We've seen posts on social media that advise packing seemingly mundane items that are against the rules—a common example is over-the-door shoe racks.

Likewise, exercise common sense and leave at home anything that would be difficult or impossible to replace: expensive or sentimental jewelry, for instance, or your young child's one and only "lovey"—we had a daughter's beloved plush bunny, Pinky, go missing on a cruise, much to the distress of the entire family. If items such as these must make the trip, label them with your contact information (sew a soft tag on a stuffed toy) and stow them in your stateroom safe when not in use. This applies to favorite toys as well as jewelry: Pinky vanished when a housekeeper inadvertently carried her away with the sheets after stripping the bed.

*un**official* **TIP**
If you lose something on board, stop by Guest Services and have them check their lost-and-found box. If you realize you've left something on the ship after your cruise is over, file a report with **Chargerback,** Disney's third party lost-and-found service (chargerback.com/dcl).

Traveling with Prescription Medications

A hot topic on many online cruise boards is whether prescription medicines must be transported in their original containers or can be transferred to handy daily-dose containers. Some guests with complex medical conditions say they'd need an additional suitcase to pack all of their bottles and claim they've never been questioned about their meds. Honestly, we've never been questioned either over the course of many cruises—but we also realize that it takes just one challenge to derail your otherwise-relaxing vacation.

DCL recommends keeping medicines in their original bottles, as do the FDA and US Customs. If, like most cruisers, you'll be visiting countries other than your own, be aware that they have their own regulations as well and that foreign airlines may also have restrictions. If you choose not to transport your medications in their original containers, bring copies of your prescriptions and/or a note from your doctor listing the meds you take. In short, err on the side of caution.

ELECTRICAL OUTLETS

OUTLETS ON DCL SHIPS conform to the North American 110V/60Hz standard. If you live in the United States or Canada, any electrical device you have that operates normally at home should work fine on board.

All staterooms have hair dryers, so if you're tight on space and not overly attached to your own dryer, you may not need to pack one. Look for the dryer in a drawer in your stateroom desk—if it's missing, ask your stateroom host to bring you one. In addition to these dryers, which are newer models with plenty of power, the *Magic* and *Wonder* have older dryers (attached to some bathroom walls) that may not do much if you've got a lot of hair to dry, so don't overlook that newer-model dryer in the desk drawer.

unofficial **TIP**
We recommend bringing one converter per person, two if you're traveling alone.

If you're visiting from outside the US, you may need an adapter or a converter for your electric gadgets. What's the difference? An adapter ensures that the plug on your device will fit into the electrical receptacle in the wall, but it doesn't change the electrical voltage. A converter does both (and costs more). Your local version of Amazon likely has an excellent selection.

There is a significant scarcity of electrical outlets in most DCL staterooms. If two people in your party over age 8 will be sharing a room, you'll almost certainly need to bring along some means of adding outlet access—the problem is, power strips and extension cords are on DCL's list of prohibited items. A good workaround is a plug-in USB hub. Many inexpensive models allow four or five USB devices (phones, tablets, and the like) to charge on one outlet. If you're bringing a laptop, you can use that as a charging hub too.

Another possible workaround is an international electrical converter, even if your cruise takes place in the United States. Most staterooms have a 220-volt outlet near the desk, which is intended for the hair dryer provided on board. If you have a converter, you can use this outlet for your 120-volt US devices.

WEATHER

AS MUCH AS WE'RE SURE THEY'D LOVE TO, Disney can't control the weather. You're probably envisioning spending your Caribbean cruise sipping piña coladas on the pool deck, but the reality is that you may encounter inclement weather during your sailing. Don't worry if it rains; there are plenty of indoor activities for children and adults. Disney also does a terrific job of providing extra indoor programming if conditions warrant. Check the **DCL Navigator app** (see page 136) for up-to-the-minute changes in the schedule.

In extreme-weather situations, DCL will alter plans more substantially than just running a few more games of bingo. On rare occasions, sailings have left their embarkation port a day or two late, returned to port a day or two early, cut or substituted a midtrip port stop, ended a voyage at a port other than the one planned, or even canceled a sailing, all in the interest of guest safety.

While Walt Disney World has an official hurricane policy (disney world.disney.go.com/faq/hurricane-policy), there's no comparable one for Disney Cruise Line. DCL does, however, have an admirable record of assisting guests with refunds and remediation for missed sailing days and fees at skipped ports. For example, in the case of Hurricane Irma in 2017, DCL offered refunds on the missed days for the sailings that returned early and were offered a 25% discount on a future sailing in 2017 or 2018. Those on the canceled sailings were given a full refund and the same 25% discount on future sailings.

If your itinerary changes, it may be easier to get refunds for excursions booked through Disney rather than for those booked on your own (see the discussion on page 327). Also, keep in mind that if you're flying to your DCL sailing, weather can also impact your airline, and guests with pre- or post-cruise hotel stays may also see those plans affected by weather issues.

If you encounter a storm, rest assured that the chance of any real danger at sea due to a hurricane is virtually zero. Weather tracking is such that cruise lines typically know about impending severe weather at least three days before it hits, giving the captain and crew plenty of time to change course. Captains also have great latitude to reroute ships to avoid areas of concern. Large ships such as those in the Disney fleet even have the ability to outpace the danger zone of a storm: most hurricanes travel at a speed of about 10 knots, and the ships are able to sail at more than 20 knots.

If you want to delve into the minutiae of maritime weather tracking, **PassageWeather** (passageweather.com) is a terrific source of information about phenomena that affect ships: surface winds, wave height and direction, sea-surface temperatures, and more. The **National Weather Service** also offers detailed current information at its **Ocean Prediction Center** (ocean.weather.gov).

Whenever possible, build in a day or two on both sides of your sailing to account for unexpected weather situations. This is another reason that we highly recommend buying trip insurance (see page 58). Depending on the policy, it may cover flight-change fees and/or unexpected hotel stays. Be sure to read the fine print on any trip-insurance contract to understand exactly what it covers before you purchase.

On the other end of the spectrum, some guests, equating cruising with the tropics, are wary of booking a sailing to colder-weather regions such as Canada, Alaska, and Northern Europe. We've sailed itineraries to these areas and rank them among our favorites. During a Norwegian Fjords cruise on the *Magic,* we often heard the maxim, "There's no bad weather, only bad clothing"—as long as you're dressed appropriately, touring in a cooler climate can be a fabulous experience, with more variety in the sights than you're likely to find on a beach-intensive voyage in the Caribbean. Plus, the ships feel particularly cozy on cold-weather routes. For example, on the glacier-viewing days of Alaskan sailings, the DCL staff places piles of fleece blankets on deck and rolls around a cart stocked with hot cocoa, Irish coffee, and hot toddies. Cuddling up with your honey, sipping a warm beverage, and watching seals and whales swim by makes for a truly memorable day. We're with Elsa on this one: "The cold never bothered us anyway."

Weather in Port

Knowing approximately what the weather will be like at your cruise destinations can help you fine-tune many aspects of planning, your trip, including packing, your choices of port adventures, and the type of stateroom you select.

unofficial **TIP**
No matter where you're headed, we suggest that every member of your group bring at least one light sweater or jacket that can be worn on board—the dining rooms can get downright chilly.

Starting about 10 days before your cruise and then again 2 or 3 days before, take a look at the current short-term weather forecasts for the ports you're scheduled to visit. Sites such as **Weather Spark** (weatherspark.com) and **Holiday Weather** (holiday-weather.com) list the weather averages for cities around the globe; look not only at daytime and nighttime temperatures but also at typical rainfall and the number of days with clouds or sun.

PREPARE YOURSELF AND YOUR HOME FOR TRAVEL

IN ADDITION TO CRUISE-SPECIFIC PREPARATIONS, you should also be aware of general guidelines for international travel. If you want to be comprehensive, **Pinterest** is filled with hundreds of travel-prep hint lists, but a few of our favorite tips are as follows:

- Consult with your doctor about whether you're up to date on vaccinations.
- Confirm all travel and transportation arrangements; double-check that the names match on all documents.
- Consider adding the numbers of foreign embassies or consulates to your phone contacts. (If you lose your passport, you'll need this information.)
- Make sure that your credit/debit cards will work in a chip-style reader (the standard outside the US) rather than a swipe-style reader.

- Download maps of your destination cities to your phone before your cruise.
- Arrange to stop mail and newspaper delivery.
- Line up pet sitters or housesitters.
- Unplug electric appliances such as coffee makers and toasters. If you're a worrywart who needs extra reassurance that everything is safe and sound, take photographs of large appliances such as ovens and stoves just before you leave home.
- Hire someone to maintain your yard or remove snow so that your absence isn't immediately apparent to strangers.
- Clean your refrigerator of perishable items, and arrange grocery delivery for the day of your return.
- Turn off (or turn down) the heat/AC while you're gone.
- Load your mobile devices with plenty of content for your flight, drive, or poolside lounging.
- Make sure you have ample quantities of any prescribed medications you'll need during your trip.
- Give a trusted friend or family member your itinerary information and a way to contact you in an emergency. You may also want to give them the ship-to-shore phone number (see page 70) in case they can't reach you easily by phone, text, or email.

MAKE SURE YOUR CHILD IS READY TO CRUISE

IT'S NO SECRET that many Disney Cruise Line guests are families with young children. Most of these guests have a fabulous time, but the small subset of DCL cruisers who have a neutral or even negative experience while cruising are typically those whose expectations are disconnected from the reality of traveling on a cruise ship.

When you're considering a Disney cruise with kids, know first that travel with small children is almost always more challenging than travel with older kids or grown-ups. Adults who are used to traveling solo or with other adults may be surprised at the difficulties they experience when traveling with young children.

Rest assured, however, that whatever issues you encounter aren't specific to Disney or cruising but rather par for the course when it comes to travel in general. Whenever you travel with young kids, you're carrying their stuff, making sure they eat what they're supposed to, hovering over them at the pool, and making sure they get something approximating sleep. This always-on feeling can be hard to reconcile with the "cruise as ultimate relaxation" ethos that many expect.

To figure out if you and your child are ready for a cruise vacation, ask yourself these questions:

- **Can my child comply with health and safety rules?** Since cruising resumed, DCL's COVID protocols have included mandatory masking for either all guests or a specifc group (such as kids under age 5). When these requirements are in place, DCL means business about enforcing them—if your child breaks the rules, both of you could get confined to your cabin. Additionally, some countries or specific attractions within countries have their own masking or social-distancing mandates. If your child has trouble keeping a mask properly situated over their nose and mouth for extended periods, then you should strongly consider postponing your trip.

- **Is my child a good sleeper?** Or are there specific situations in which he or she *doesn't* sleep well? For example, would your child be frightened by the motion of the ship? Would she feel anxious about sleeping in an unfamiliar room or bed? Would sleeping in the same room as your child affect his or her ability to sleep—or yours?

- **How does my child react to changes in his or her schedule?** Many younger children have trouble coping with changes in their nap or eating schedule, particularly if that schedule is disrupted for several days in a row. Most activities on the ship take place at set times—times that may not align with your child's schedule. Can your child deal with the disruption, or are tears and tantrums inevitable? Are you willing to forgo eating in the main dining rooms if your child's schedule requires it?

- **Do I have any claustrophobia issues? Does my child?** On any cruise ship, spaces are more compact than those in most land-based locations. Staterooms are smaller than many typical hotel rooms; stateroom bathrooms may be smaller still than what you're used to.

- **Does my child have issues with characters?** By elementary school, most kids will have outgrown any reticence about meeting Santa or the Easter Bunny. But a quite a few toddlers and preschoolers find such encounters terrifying.

    Characters are difficult to avoid completely on the Disney ships. Many character greetings take place in public areas such as the atriums or theater exits; plus, characters sometimes make surprise appearances in the kids' clubs. Given the closed-in nature of a cruise ship, you'll likely run into characters at some point during your trip. If your young child has a serious character phobia, you may want to hold off on booking until they're older.

- **Is my child easily overwhelmed in new situations?** On a ship, there are new foods, new people, new activities, and loud ship horns—the list goes on and on. (I've heard several stories about children becoming upset on seeing the yellow lifeboats.) It may be difficult to predict what exactly will unsettle a 3-year-old, but chances are that you already know if your child becomes easily upset or overstimulated. Additionally, you may want to consider that on sea days, there may be few options for separating your child from other people other than staying in your stateroom.

- **Will childcare eat into my vacation budget?** DCL's kids' clubs are included in your cruise price for potty-trained children ages 3 and up. The nurseries (for infants–age 3) charge a fee—currently $9 per hour for the first child and $8 per hour for each additional child in the same family. It may be relatively easy to leave your 10-month-old in the nursery while you enjoy the sunshine, but be aware that those fees can sneak up on you over the course of a long sailing.

- **Will I be able to find childcare when I need it?** Children ages 3–17 have unlimited use of the kids' clubs whenever you and they want, with no reservations necessary (although in the COVID era, that could be subject to change). The nurseries, however, accept only a limited number of children per hour, and reservations are required. Depending on how crowded your cruise is and what level of Castaway Club status you've attained, you may not be able to arrange babysitting for your young child when you want it.

- **Is my child in a particularly active phase?** Given the constraints of the ship, space is limited for many large-motor activities. Additionally, there are many expectations for restrained behavior while on board (sitting still in a restaurant, for example). The kids' clubs offer some physical activities, but they may not be exactly the type of activity your child is used to. Further, opportunities for ball play, climbing, and running are fairly limited for young children, and what there is on board takes place almost entirely in the kids' clubs. If you have a child with separation issues who also needs lots of physical activity, or a child with separation issues with an aversion to water play, then you may want to think hard about whether this is the right time to book a cruise.

- **Does my child require lots of gear for personal maintenance or stimulation?** Yet again, it bears mentioning that staterooms are small. Boxes of diapers, strollers, play mats, and the like may seem quite large in a confined space. Consider whether it might be more practical to cruise when these items are no longer necessary.

- **Traveling with my child means I wouldn't get to experience everything the ship has to offer. Would I be wasting my money by booking a cruise in the first place?** *Absolutely not*—some of our most memorable cruise experiences haven't involved a specific activity or event. Given factors such as a young child's sleep schedule, however, you may find that most adult activities—and even many family activities—are inaccessible to you. If you're in for the night because your child is asleep at 8 p.m., then you're going to miss the stage shows, family game shows, and many similar experiences that take place later in the evening. There are some partial workarounds: for example, the main stage shows are available on closed-circuit TV in your stateroom.

- **Who else are we traveling with? What are their needs?** Travel with a small child may go better, or worse, depending on your traveling party. Many folks with young children cruise with extended family. This can be a boon for Mom and Dad (or Mom and Mom or Dad and Dad) if Grandma offers to babysit while the parents enjoy Palo or the margarita-mixing class. It can be a struggle for the parents if Grandma expects the entire clan to sit still for a 3-hour dinner every evening, or if Grandma needs physical assistance or has medical needs of her own.

- **What ports will the ship be visiting? Are there appropriate excursions or other activities in port?** If you're planning to leave the ship while it's in port, review your shore-excursion options carefully. At some stops, there may be limited offerings for children under age 5 or even under age 8. At other ports, excursions may technically be available to younger children but aren't very practical. (For example, a 5-hour bike tour probably isn't appropriate for a 4-year-old.) With younger kids, you may want to consider arranging your own excursions or just going for a leisurely walk near the dock area. The counterpoint to this is that some families find cruising to be one of the easiest ways for a young child to experience a distant land.

By the time a child is 6 or 7 years old, he or she has usually developed strong enough coping skills to deal with separating from family, meeting new people, waiting his or her turn, and sitting still for extended periods of time. Additionally, a school-

*un*official **TIP**
See our thoughts about food issues with young kids on pages 194–196.

age child likely has a broader palate, little need for special equipment, and enough language skills to effectively communicate in productive ways. Each of these capabilities will serve to make cruising, or any travel, more relaxing for the entire family.

DISNEY WORLD *vs.* DISNEY CRUISE LINE: *How to Decide*

WHILE MANY DCL GUESTS CHOOSE TO COMBINE a cruise with a visit to Walt Disney World (see page 40), we also get many questions from readers trying to decide if they should choose a Disney cruise *or*

Disney World, rather than both. Here are some factors to consider as you make your decision:

- **Travel to the vacation.** Disney World is in Florida, but you can hop on a Disney cruise in many locations. If you live near a DCL departure port, the savings in time and money compared with traveling to Florida for your vacation could be substantial. You'll also save on time off from work if you board DCL near your home. Coauthor Erin, who lives near New York City, cruised DCL out of Manhattan and was home, unpacked, and back at work by 9:30 a.m. on debarkation day.

- **Weather.** Some vacationers are leery of sailing during hurricane season, making Walt Disney World potentially more attractive during that time. If you're limited to summer travel (because you're a teacher, for example) but you're heat-averse, one of DCL's many cool-weather itineraries may make sense.

- **Motion sickness.** While most folks find they have minimal motion-sickness issues on a Disney cruise, any cruising may be too much for severe sufferers. Disney World (with a focus on the tamer rides) or an Adventures by Disney river cruise (see Part Thirteen) will make more sense for you.

- **Mobility issues.** The average Disney World visitor walks 7–12 miles per day. You could rent a wheelchair or an ECV, but that's still a *lot* of miles to cover each day. On the other hand, the ships are large but contained. If you have difficulty walking long distances or transferring in and out of mobility devices, then DCL could be a convenient solution.

- **Access to healthcare.** DCL ships have basic medical facilities (see page 140), but if you have complicated medical needs, you may find that ready access to hospitals on land makes Disney World a safer option. In the COVID era, guests with compromised immune systems or other medical issues should take particular care to consult with their medical providers about the pros and cons of *any* vacation, WDW, DCL, or otherwise.

- **Access to childcare.** Here's where DCL has the clear advantage: group childcare is unavailable at WDW, and hiring a babysitter can get really pricey really fast. On a Disney cruise, however, high-quality group childcare is included in the price of your trip and is available throughout the day and evening for kids ages 3–17. (Infant and toddler care are available for a small extra fee.) This may be particularly appealing for a single parent who needs some occasional downtime to recharge during vacation, or for the parent(s) of an only child who might benefit from interacting with other children, rather than just adults, during an extended vacation.

- **Variety of accommodations.** There are many stateroom categories, but nearly all are variations on a box. If you want to stay with extended family in one unit or have access to residential-style amenities like full kitchens, private communal living spaces, or large outdoor play spaces, then you're out of luck with a cruise. With a Disney World vacation, however, you have your choice of hundreds of thousands of hotel rooms, villas, and rental homes—accommodations to meet every need.

- **Pace of the vacation.** It's a near-cliché to come home from Disney World and say that you need a vacation from your vacation, especially with kids in tow. Disney World trips involve lots and lots (and lots and lots) of running around to take advantage of the countless attractions and entertainment. This is much less true on a Disney cruise, where there are fewer must-do activities and sleeping in and lounging around are much more common.

- **Variety of dining.** The food on DCL is plentiful, all-inclusive, and available anytime you want it, but your choices are limited. If you like exploring a wide variety of cuisines, or if you have an extremely picky eater in your group, Disney World may be a better choice. Guests on special diets may find the lack of in-room kitchen facilities restrictive on a cruise ship.

- **Need for planning.** When it comes to a Walt Disney World trip, planning is a complicated task. With DCL, there's much less need to map out your time in advance. You can decide on most shipboard activities at the spur of the moment. And it's perfectly fine to wing it and just wander around in most ports. If you prefer a wholly spontaneous vacation, DCL may be the way to go.

- **Shorter lines.** We're professionals at avoiding lines at Disney World, but even we encounter lengthy waits there from time to time. The only times you might wait in line on a Disney ship are for a few photo ops or the occasional turn on the waterslides.

- **Family togetherness.** Because DCL is a smaller-scale proposition than Disney World, family members are less likely to be pulled in different directions due to competing interests. On the other hand, if you want an excuse to separate from your traveling companions, then Disney World is the place to be.

- **Children's age considerations.** Families will find plenty to enjoy together on the DCL ships, but most kids will want to spend at least some time in the onboard kids' clubs. Mostly this is great, but the clubs are strict on age requirements, particularly in the older groups. This could be a challenge if the kids in your party can't go to the same club. If, for example, you have a 10- and 12-year-old, or a 17- and 18-year-old, who want to hang out together on vacation, Disney World will provide more opportunity for this.

- **Pregnancy and babies.** If you're more than 24 weeks pregnant or you have a baby under 6 months old, DCL is off-limits, but you might have a great time at Disney World. Also consider sleeping (or not sleeping) arrangements in a small stateroom with a toddler on an erratic sleep schedule, or feeding arrangements with a baby not eating much solid food. The pros and cons of potty training on a cruise ship are another topic worth considering closely.

- **Connectivity.** Internet access on the ships (see page 137) can be pricey depending on the level of access you want, and service could be spotty depending on the location of your ship. If you must have 100% reliable service 24-7, then a Disney cruise might not be the best choice for you.

- **Disney overload.** If you want your kids to have a Disney experience but you want to limit your own exposure to the Mouse, then DCL is the better choice. If you skip the musical shows and character greetings, your Disney exposure is fairly minimal. Adventures by Disney river cruises (see Part Thirteen) have the least Disney influence.

- **Price.** There are bare-bones and over-the-top luxury versions of both Disney World and DCL vacations. When you're researching costs, try to compare apples to apples (budget DCL versus budget Disney World, not budget DCL versus luxury Disney World, or vice versa). Also consider the prices for all ancillary items you'll consider during your trip (things like Park Hopper tickets at Disney World or port-adventure fees on DCL) and whether those are needs or wants.

If you end up choosing Walt Disney World over a Disney cruise, take a look at our sibling publications *The Unofficial Guide to Walt Disney World* and *The Unofficial Guide to Walt Disney World with Kids,* along with **TouringPlans.com.** These resources can give you the complete scoop on planning a Walt Disney World visit with minimal hassle and maximum fun.

COMPARING PRICES

WE HAD A HUNCH THAT A DCL VACATION is more expensive than a WDW vacation, but we weren't sure by how much. To find out, we did some comparison shopping. (We did our reseach in summer 2022; naturally, pricing will vary depending on when you check.)

Example 1: We priced the September 2, 2023, seven-night Eastern Caribbean sailing of the *Fantasy* for two adults and two children, ages 14 and 9. The lowest rate we found was **$5,320** for an Inside Stateroom. Since that could make for a somewhat cramped experience for four people, we also priced an Oceanview Stateroom (**$5,600**) and a Verandah Stateroom (**$6,048**).

For Walt Disney World, we priced accommodations for four at the Moderate-tier Port Orleans Riverside Resort for seven nights, starting September 2, 2023; we chose a room with a pool view to roughly mirror the space of DCL's Verandah room. To approximate the cruise's onboard activities, we also included seven-day theme park tickets, plus the seven-day Park Hopper add-on, for everyone in the family. At this point, the total WDW price is **$4,695,** or about $1,350 less than the Verandah Stateroom. Finally, we allotted $75 per person, per day—or $2,100 for the entire WDW trip—to approximate the cost of the food included in the price of a DCL cruise. The grand total comes out to **$6,795,** giving DCL the win on price.

Of course, you could save or spend money on either side of the equation. For the DCL cruise, you could go with the inside cabin to save a little money, or you could add port adventures to spend a lot; for the Disney World vacation, you could choose a less expensive hotel or skip the Park Hopper option, or you could add special events like VIP tours or after-hours parties. At WDW, some guests may also add the Genie+ option ($15 per person, per day) to cut down on waits in line; they may also add the Individual Lightning Lane option to skip lines for in-demand rides (typically about $12 per person, per ride).

Adding these features every day of the trip will boost the WDW cost by about $750, making DCL the more solid choice, but again, adding shore excursions, adult dining, and several rounds of bingo could quickly change the balance. **Overall winner on price: DCL, but in practice probably a draw.**

Example 2: We priced the July 3, 2023, four-night Bahamian cruise on the *Wish* for two adults. This is a holiday splurge, so we priced a Concierge one-bedroom suite: **$13,643.** For WDW, we chose an outer-building one-bedroom suite with Club Level access at Disney's Grand Floridian Resort & Spa. A four-night stay for two adults, plus five-day park tickets, a five-day Park Hopper, five days of Genie+ and Individual Lightning Lane passes, and a $150-per-person, per-day dining allowance, costs **$11,125. Overall winner on price: WDW.**

Example 3: We priced the May 4, 2023, three-night Bahamian sailing on the *Dream* for one adult. In this case, we wanted a budget getaway, so we went with an Inside Stateroom (**$1,572**). At Walt Disney World, comparable digs would be a non-Preferred room at the Value-tier Pop Century Resort. A three-night stay for one, plus four-day park tickets, a four-day Park Hopper, and a $75-per-day food allowance, is **$1,671.** **Overall winner on price: DCL by a nose.**

Example 4: We priced the August 8, 2023, four-night Bahamian sailing on the *Wish* for one adult. If our solo traveler in Example 3 chooses an Inside Stateroom, her rate will be **$3,661.** At Walt Disney World, a standard room at Pop Century, plus five-day park tickets, a five-day Park Hopper, and a $75-per-day food allowance, is **$1,851.** Overall winner on price: **Overall winner on price: WDW by a wide margin.**

In Examples 3 and 4, note that DCL's stateroom rate for one guest is only slightly less expensive than the one for two guests. (The rates are technically the same, but the room for two includes some additional taxes and port fees.) That means our solo traveler is effectively paying for all the food and entertainment that her nonexistent companion isn't eating or enjoying. With Walt Disney World, on the other hand, she has to pay only for her own food and entertainment.

In Examples 3 and 4, the price difference is obvious between cruising on the older *Dream and* the brand-new *Wish.* If you want to relax in the Bahamas, the *Dream* is the affordable way to go.

These differences become more pronounced when you look at DCL's itineraries outside of the Bahamas and the Caribbean. Compared with the prices of European cruises, even a higher-end Walt Disney World vacation looks downright thrifty. But as with all things Disney, it makes sense to sit down with a spreadsheet and a calculator to examine the cost comparisons as they apply to your family's unique circumstances and vacation priorities.

CASTAWAY CLUB

DCL USES THIS PROGRAM to reward repeat cruisers. It works somewhat like a frequent-flyer program—the more you cruise, the better your status and the more perks you get.

Castaway Club status is determined solely by the number of DCL voyages you've completed, *not* by how much money you've spent. A guest who's sailed on five 3-day cruises in the smallest Inside cabin belongs to a higher level than a guest who has spent more money on a single 12-day voyage in the largest cabin.

If you've never taken a Disney cruise before, you're a **First-Time Guest.** Guests who have completed 1–4 Disney cruises have **Silver** status, guests who have completed 5–9 Disney cruises have **Gold** status, and guests who have completed 10 or more Disney cruises have **Platinum** status. Most guests will be able to count all of their cruising toward their status level, with a few rare exceptions, such as a Disney cast member cruising on business. (Tough life, eh?)

A number of perks are available to Castaway Club members at the Silver level or higher, including "Welcome Back" stateroom gifts and priority check-in at the port terminal. (*Note:* Priority check-in is paused at the time of this writing, but we expect it to return.) As your membership level increases, so do your benefits. Gold and Platinum guests receive 10% off many onboard merchandise purchases. On sailings of eight nights or longer, Gold and Platinum guests may be invited to a special reception with crew members. Platinum cruisers, along with their guests ages 18 and older staying in the same stateroom, get a free prix fixe dinner at Palo or an equivalent à la carte meal at a discount. While none of these perks are enough incentive to book another trip, they're a nice way to acknowledge loyal customers.

For many guests, one of the chief benefits of Castaway Club membership is that the higher your status level, the earlier you can reserve many aspects of your cruise, including port adventures, onboard dining at the adults-only restaurants, and spa visits. **First-Time Guests** may make reservations **75 days** before sailing, **Silver Castaway Club members** may make reservations **90 days** ahead, **Gold members** may make reservations **105 days** ahead, and **Platinum members** may make reservations **120 days** ahead. Similarly, when new itineraries are released, **Platinum members** may book trips **3 days** before they become available to the general public, **Gold guests** may book **2 days** before, and **Silver** guests may book **1 day** before. (*Note:* DCL modified this policy for the inaugural sailings of the *Wish;* see next page.)

The ability for Castaway Club members to get a jump on booking a just-released cruise itinerary gives loyal customers a greater chance of obtaining their preferred staterooms on new sailings. While cruises seldom become fully booked in the initial days of availability, it is possible that a First-Time Guest could be locked out of a unique stateroom type on a particularly popular voyage.

Castaway Club status may or may not make much of a difference depending on the situation. Take Castaway Cay, for instance: on one hand, nearly everyone will be able to rent a bike here. On the other hand, Platinum Castaway Club members (along with Concierge cruisers) get first dibs on the island's coveted private cabanas. With just 27 cabanas split between the family and adult beach areas, competition for them is fierce. The early-booking benefit for Castaway Club members is also helpful when you're trying to score brunch reservations for Palo or Palo Steakhouse on sea days and babysitting at It's a Small World Nursery during showtimes.

Sometimes not everyone in a single stateroom has the same Castaway Club status. In that case, the benefits for each guest are determined by the Castaway Club member with the highest status in that room. For example, if I (Erin) have been on a few more cruises than my husband and my status is higher than his, I can make reservations for both of us at my level. (Lucky me!) But if we're also traveling with first-timers staying in another stateroom, they *can't* take advantage of my higher status level, even though they're in our party.

Because Castaway Club status is effectively applied by stateroom, not by party, you'll need to keep this in mind when you're booking a cruise for a group. Not everyone will have equal access to reservations for port adventures and the like if members of your party have different status levels—and that could lead to some potentially tense moments.

Let's say, for example, that Chad and Shane are Gold cruisers but their daughters, Karen and Susan, are Silver cruisers. If Chad and Shane are booked in one stateroom and Karen and Susan in another, the dads can make their port-adventure reservations at the 105-day mark, but they can't reserve the port adventures for the kids until the 90-day mark—and in the intervening 15 days, those port adventures could become fully booked, potentially resulting in family friction. But if the dads book staterooms with their respective kids, both staterooms will be able to book their port adventures at 105 days, thus ensuring family harmony.

> **unofficial TIP**
> When it comes to staterooms, Castaway Club status matters only when it comes to booking—once you're on the ship, the cast members don't care who sleeps in which room. Your stateroom attendant will be happy to configure your beds however you like, and Guest Services will issue you keys to both rooms.

Castaway Club and DCL's New Ships

When DCL announced booking availability for the new *Disney Wish,* they knew the ship's first block of sailings would be in high demand. So rather than letting all Platinum Castaway Club members reserve their cruises three days before the general public, per usual Disney policy (see page 85), they took the unusual step of creating special tiers within the Platinum level just for these inaugural sailings. Platinum members with 25 sailings or more could book 10 days before the general public, those with 20-plus sailings could book 9 days before, those with 15-plus sailings could book 8 days before, and those with 10-plus sailings could book 7 days before. Then two more categories opened up: Gold Castaway Club members (5–9 sailings) could book 3 days before the general public (versus 2 days before for regular sailings), and—in a DCL first—Disney Vacation Club (DVC) members and Adventures by Disney (AbD) Insiders could book 2 days before.

Notably excluded from these perks were Silver Castaway Club members, who got nothing beyond the customary one-day jump on booking. Not surprisingly, many Silver members weren't happy with Disney's decision, but it made perfect sense from a purely financial perspective: many Silver members have spent "only" a few thousand dollars with DCL, on quick three-night sailings, while most DVC members and AbD Insiders have spent many multiples of this on their respective Disney vacations.

Two more ships will join the Disney fleet in the near future, and we anticipate that a similar rollout will happen for bookings of their inaugural seasons. To give you a bit of insight into the popularity of a DCL maiden voyage, the very first sailing of the *Wish* was completely sold out to Platinum Castaway Club members—not even Gold cruisers got a swing at them. So if you're a Gold member and you're bound and determined to be on the first sailings of the future ships, you might want to get a few three-night cruises under your belt to bump you up to Platinum level.

PART THREE

STATEROOMS

DISNEY CRUISE LINE'S SHIPS boast some of the largest cabins in the industry, which helps explain (a bit) why its fares are correspondingly high. An inside cabin, generally the least expensive room on any ship, is 169–184 square feet on Disney's ships, compared with 114–165 square feet on Royal Caribbean and 160–185 on Carnival. Disney's Oceanview and Verandah (balcony) cabins are larger than Royal Caribbean's and Carnival's too.

unofficial **TIP**
On the *Dream* and *Fantasy,* (some Inside cabins have **virtual portholes,** or video screens that combine real-time views from outside the ship with animated snippets of Disney characters. Many kids prefer these to actual Verandah views, and Inside cabins are usually much less expensive.

In addition to greater space, DCL's bathroom layout is an improvement over that in staterooms on other cruise lines. All but the smallest inside cabins are configured in a split-bath design, in which the shower and toilet are in separate compartments, each with its own door and sink. The advantage of this design is that two people can get ready at the same time. (Category 11 staterooms have the shower and toilet in the same compartment.)

Clever incorporation of storage space is another plus. Most DCL staterooms have two closets, each one big enough to store one large suitcase or two small ones; under-bed storage for carry-on or soft-sided luggage; and several drawers that are built in to the cabin's desk area. Additional nooks and crannies for storage are scattered throughout each stateroom.

unofficial **TIP**
Wish staterooms have fewer dresser drawers and more storage shelves than staterooms on the other ships. Packing cubes can help you contain and separate family members' belongings on the shelves.

But while Disney staterooms are generally larger than those on other cruise lines, they're still smaller than the typical hotel room. For example, a room at a Walt Disney World Value hotel, such as Pop Century Resort, is about 260 square feet—about 40% larger than a DCL inside cabin. Even a well-appointed Family Oceanview Stateroom with Verandah tops out at 304 square feet, a little smaller than a room at a Disney Moderate hotel, such as Caribbean Beach Resort.

HOW STATEROOM CATEGORY AFFECTS YOUR CRUISE PRICE

ALONG WITH YOUR DEPARTURE DATE and how far in advance you book, the type of stateroom you choose is one of the major factors in determining your cruise's cost.

The chart below shows how much a fare increases, based on the cabin category, for a typical seven-night cruise on the *Disney Fantasy* for two adults and two children in 2022–23.

A stateroom in Category 4A, the most expensive non-Concierge category on the *Fantasy*, costs about $2,000 (30%) more than an Inside Stateroom—and that price spread has doubled since the last edition of this book. On the upside, you get an additional 130 square feet of space and an outside view.

Note the steady upward movement of the lines until you reach Concierge level; this shows that Disney is very consistent in its pricing across stateroom categories. This consistency persists even though

Price-Per-Cabin Categories on a 7-Night Disney Cruise

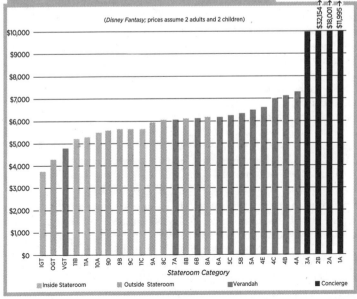

(Disney Fantasy; prices assume 2 adults and 2 children)

Stateroom Category

■ Inside Stateroom ■ Outside Stateroom ■ Verandah ■ Concierge the number of staterooms in each category varies—the majority are Verandah staterooms, but in this case, a larger supply doesn't equal a lower price. Even so, DCL seems to have just enough of each kind of stateroom to meet guest demand.

SHOULD YOU UPGRADE?

FOR MANY DCL CRUISERS trying to decide on a stateroom, the choice comes down to a small Inside Stateroom and a larger Oceanview or Verandah Stateroom. Depending on the ship, itinerary, and time of year, the difference in price can be a little—or a lot.

For this edition, we spot-checked the costs of Disney cruises in different stateroom categories for a family of four: two adults and children ages 9 and 14. The fares in our examples are for summer 2023; prices, of course, will vary depending on when you check.

For our first example, we priced a **3-Night Bahamian Cruise from Port Canaveral** on the *Wish*. For several sail dates in summer 2023, an Inside Stateroom cost $2,980, an Oceanview Stateroom was $3,058, and a Verandah Stateroom was $3,208. Choosing the Oceanview room over the Inside room seems like a no-brainer to us: for $78 more, you get a bigger room, a split bath, and a view of the ocean. The $228 bump from Inside to Verandah gives you even more space plus a balcony—for all but the most frugal of vacationers, we think the Verandah room is the easy choice.

On some longer sailings, however, the cost of jumping from Inside to Verandah is significant. For the July 24, 2023, **9-Night Alaskan Cruise from Vancouver** (*Wonder*), our family of four would pay a whopping $10,319 for an Inside Stateroom. To upgrade to an Oceanview cabin, they'd need to spend at least $12,344, or $2,025 more than the Inside rate; to get a Verandah stateroom, they'd need to spend at least $18,009, or almost **$8,000** more. (For that same sailing, the cheapest Concierge Stateroom still available was $32,278, or about three times the price of the Inside Stateroom.)

Not only are there price differences among stateroom types, there are often differences within the *same* type. For some 2023 three-night Baja sailings on the *Wonder,* for instance, the cheapest Verandah rooms for our family of four cost $2,512, while the most expensive non-Concierge Verandah rooms are $2,859—a $347 difference. For the June 12, 2023, **8-Night Mediterranean Cruise with Greek Isles** (*Dream*), the least expensive Verandah room is $13,861, while the highest-priced non-Concierge Verandah room is $14,692, or $831 more.

WILL A CHEAPER STATEROOM DETRACT FROM YOUR EXPERIENCE? To repeat a familiar phrase, *it depends.* If you're just happy to be on a Disney cruise and you consider your room merely a place to lay your head, then you'll have a great time no matter what. If, on the other hand, you consider an outside view to be non-negotiable, then an Oceanview Stateroom would be worth the bump in price over an Inside Stateroom—you'd just need to figure out how much you'd be willing to pay.

OUR STATEROOM RECOMMENDATIONS

AT 169–184 SQUARE FEET, an **Inside Stateroom** has enough room for two adults, or two adults and one small child. Granted, it's not exactly spacious, but a family of this size shouldn't have much competition for the bathroom. If you're a family of three or four and you have two tweens or teens, you'll appreciate the extra space of a **Deluxe Oceanview Stateroom with Verandah** (218, 243, 246, or 268 square feet, depending on the ship and the location thereon) or a **Deluxe Family Oceanview Stateroom with Verandah** (284, 299, or 304 square feet).

Alternatively, you could book two cabins: two inside connecting rooms or an Inside and Oceanview cabin across the hall from each other. The advantage to two rooms, besides the extra space and extra bathroom, is that the kids can sleep late if they want. Additionally, putting the kids in a different room allows parents to access the verandah (on the kids' side of the room on all ships) and the TV (on the kids' side of the room on all ships except the *Wish*) without disturbing anyone. (See pages 86 and 87 for tips on booking multiple staterooms with differing Castaway Club status and page 46 for age requirements for booking children and teens into different staterooms than their parents.)

CABIN APPOINTMENTS

EVERY DCL STATEROOM is outfitted with the following:

• **Bedside lamps**	• **Ice bucket** and glasses
• **Closet**	• **In-room phone** with voice mail
• **Coffee table** The top opens for storage (*Dream* and *Fantasy* only).	• **In-room thermostat**
• **Custom artwork** Usually depicts Disney characters and themes relevant to the cruise line, ships, islands, or travel.	• **Life jackets**
	• **Minifridge**
• **Desk with chair and dedicated lighting** You'll have enough room to getting actual work done.	• **Privacy curtain** This separates the sleeping area from the sofa.
• **Electronic safe** It's just big enough for storing passports, wallets, and other small valuables.	• **Private bath** with sink, toilet, and shower
	• **Room-service breakfast menus**
	• **Satellite TV** with remote
• **Hair dryer**	• **Sleeper sofa**
• **Hooks** (for towels) and **hangers** (for clothes)	• **Toiletries** H2O+ soap, shampoo, conditioner, body wash, and body lotion are stocked in standard guest rooms.

Cabins with exterior windows have blackout curtains that do an amazing job of blocking the sun. If you need light to wake up in the morning, don't shut the curtains unless you want to sleep until the crack of noon.

Bathrooms are stocked with large pump bottles of shampoo, conditioner, body wash, and lotion; your stateroom host will refill these as needed. DCL introduced the big bottles in 2019 in an effort to reduce waste and plastics use, but not everybody likes them: some guests say they don't squeeze out enough product per pump, others don't like the space they take up in the bathroom, and still others miss being able to take home mini soaps and shampoos as souvenirs. We appreciate DCL's move toward being more environmentally friendly.

unofficial **TIP**

On the *Dream, Fantasy,* and *Wish,* your stateroom lights will work only if you insert a plastic card into a slot on the wall by the door. You're supposed to use your Key to the World Card, but any similar card will do—this is the perfect use for that old Blockbuster card taking up space in your wallet.

KEEPING YOUR COOL DCL staterooms are furnished with minifridges, but some cruisers report that they don't get very cold. Our first suggestion would be to adjust the fridge's temperature control; we've also read that propping the door open slightly with a towel clip or a specially made plastic device can help it cool better by increasing air circulation inside (search for "refrigerator airing card" on Google and YouTube). Disney says the minifridges work well enough that you can use them to store temperature-sensitive medications such as insulin; if you're not sure the fridge in your room is up to the job, check with Guest Services.

Special Features on the *Wish*

Functional updates and fresh design touches distinguish the *Wish*'s staterooms from those of its four older sisters, but there's still no mistaking that you're on a Disney ship. Here's a quick rundown of what's new:

- Instead of a dorm-size minifridge hidden in a cabinet, there's a small refrigerator hidden in a desk drawer.
- Stateroom TVs are full-size flat-screens versus the computer-monitor-size TVs on the other ships.
- The stateroom phone, rather than sitting on your nightstand, is mounted on the wall near the storage shelves.
- Bathrooms have a night light switch and undercounter lighting. The night light is bright enough that you won't need to bring your own.
- The artwork in each stateroom is uniformly themed to a Disney animated film, such as *Frozen, Cinderella, Sleeping Beauty,* or *Moana.*
- Dedicated USB and USB-C outlets are located on each side of the primary bed.
- As on the *Dream* and *Fantasy,* the bed linens are by Frette, but the *Wish*'s have tiny Mickey Mouse images woven into the fabric.
- Buttons on the shower nozzle control the water pressure and temperature. Push and turn the left button to adjust the pressure, or push and turn the right button to adjust the temperature.
- Bathrobes are provided in all staterooms. On the other ships, they're provided only for Concierge-level guests (or you have to buy them in the gift shops).

While most of these changes are welcome, a couple are not. First of all, the plastic dividers in the desk-drawer fridge eat up storage space. If you want to chill that plate of leftover Key lime pie that you ordered from room service, you'll have to take out some of the dividers to get it to fit.

Second of all, the new TV setup strikes us as poorly thought out, to put it mildly. Yes, the stateroom TVs on the other ships are old and dinky, but they're also mounted on a swivel arm attached to the dresser. If you want to watch TV on the couch after your spouse has gone to bed, or your kids are using the foldout bed and want to watch TV while they fall asleep, you can simply point the set toward the sofa. On the *Wish,* however, the TVs are mounted on the wall opposite the foot of the main bed—or, in inside rooms, the wall *beside* the bed. If you have more than two people booked in your stateroom, we don't need to explain how awkward this could get.

Of course, you didn't book a Disney cruise so you could stay holed up watching *The Computer Wore Tennis Shoes* on a loop, but we hope that DCL will find a solution here—and we *really* hope they're not planning to roll out this setup on the other ships.

WHAT YOU *WON'T* FIND Cabins don't have minibars, coffee makers, microwaves, teakettles, steam irons, or ironing boards. Irons are provided in the onboard laundry rooms; you can also have your clothes sent out for pressing (see page 139).

DCL has removed alarm clocks from most staterooms. If you prefer to use a dedicated alarm clock instead of your phone, you may be able to borrow one from Guest Services, but bring your own to be safe. Alternatively, you can request a wake-up call.

BED CONFIGURATIONS Note that the primary beds in DCL staterooms are standard queen-size beds, not the split twins that you might find on some other cruise lines. In addition, all rooms have a foldout sofa bed; some have extra beds that pull out of the ceiling or the wall.

If you have more than two adults in the room, it's likely that two of them will be sharing a sleep surface. This usually isn't a problem for a romantic couple or same-gender siblings, but there are other situations in which people who are comfortable traveling together, even sharing a cabin, might not want to sleep in the same bed: say, a father traveling with a teen or adult daughter, stepsiblings, in-laws, opposite-gender adult siblings, and so on. As you make your decisions about what type of stateroom you need, consider the number and type of sleep surfaces, as well as the stated sleeping capacity of the room.

The beds on **Adventures by Disney** river cruises (see Part Thirteen) are split twins, which means they can be separated with a gap between them. When Erin traveled with her husband, the bed was made up as a queen; when she traveled with her young-adult child, the bed was configured as two twins.

DOOR DECOR AND FISH EXTENDERS The door to your stateroom is made of metal and is thus magnetic. (The exceptions are some of the Concierge-level stateroom doors—these are metal topped with a wood veneer, which makes them decidedly less magnetic.) Many repeat cruisers are fond of decorating their doors with magnets related to family celebrations, the cruise destination, a holiday, or something Disney-related in general. The longer your cruise, the more likely you are to see doors festooned with magnets, sometimes quite elaborately. When cruising in the Caribbean, Erin's daughters like to break out a pirate version of **Magnetic Poetry**'s build-a-sentence kits.

Of course, you're under no obligation to decorate your door, but if you choose to do so, be aware that you can't tack or stick anything to your door—no tape or adhesive wall hangers. Any damage to your door will result in a charge to your folio (room account).

Mounted in a nook beside every DCL stateroom door is a small metal sculpture; on the *Magic, Wonder, Dream,* and *Fantasy,* these sculptures are shaped like either a fish or a seahorse. They're cute, but they're not just for decoration: set away from the wall by a few millimeters, they function as tiny shelves. You'll find your Key to the World Card (see page 133) in your fish on embarkation day; you'll also receive notes and reminders here over the course of your cruise—for example, a note from the spa reminding you about a massage appointment.

A uniquely DCL gadget, a **fish extender** is a vertical strip of fabric with pockets (think a portable shoe rack) that you can hang from your fish to extend its functionality. (According to the discussion forum DISboards.com, a user known as EpcotKilterFan created this ingenious storage solution while preparing for a DCL Panama Canal cruise in 2005.) You can make your own extender or buy one from a site such as Etsy. Some repeat cruisers use their fish extenders to participate in Secret Santa–style gift exchanges arranged online before their trip.

In additional to serving as a tiny shelf, your hallway sea creature can help you remember which side of the ship you're on (except as noted below). If your stateroom has a fish by the door, then you're on the port, or left, side of the ship (and *fish, port,* and *left* all have four letters). If your stateroom has a seahorse by the door, then you're on the starboard, or right side of the ship (and *seahorse* and *starboard* both start with *s*).

Some corresponding sculpture shelves on the *Wish* are shaped like nautilus shells, but others are shaped like items that are decidedly *not* sealife: Cinderella's royal carriage, an owl, a sun, or a crown. Despite this confounding development, guests on DCL's newest ship still seem to be referring to the shelves as fish extenders. (Perhaps "*Wish* extender" will catch on instead?)

UNDERSTANDING STATEROOM CLASSIFICATIONS

DCL USES AN ALPHANUMERIC SYSTEM to indicate different types of staterooms. You might have heard your travel agent say something like, "I could put you in a 6B for this price, or I could book you in a 4C for that price." So what do the codes mean?

There are 23 different stateroom classifications on the *Wonder* and *Magic,* 25 on the *Dream* and *Fantasy,* and 28 on the *Wish.* These can be confusing to veteran cruisers and novices alike.

To demystify the system, here are the key points you need to know:

- In general, **the least expensive staterooms** are designated with the highest category number: **11.**

- The cost and quality of a stateroom generally increase as its category number decreases. For example, a **Category 4** stateroom is typically more expensive than a **Category 5** stateroom.

- When a letter modifies a numeric classification—**Category 4A,** for instance— the letter indicates **the stateroom's location on the ship.** In general, the A staterooms are on higher decks than the Bs, which are on higher decks than the Cs, and so on. An A stateroom isn't necessarily better than a B or C stateroom, however.

- **Midship staterooms,** in the center of the ship on any deck, tend to be more expensive and desirable—and thus tend to have lower category numbers— than other staterooms. This is because (1) the rooms are generally larger and (2) this location is both more convenient to other parts of the ship and less conducive to motion sickness (see page 60) than other locations.

- *Family* in the name of a stateroom category indicates that the room is larger than others without this descriptor. For example, a **Category 4C Deluxe Family Oceanview Stateroom with Verandah** is bigger than a Category **5C Deluxe Oceanview Stateroom with Verandah.**

- *Oceanview* means, not surprisingly, that you have a view of the sea from your stateroom. This could be via a single large porthole, multiple small portholes, or a large sliding-glass door.

- *Inside* means that your room doesn't have a view. Some Inside Staterooms on the *Dream* and *Fantasy* have **virtual portholes** (see page 88).

- **Concierge staterooms** start with the numbers **1, 2,** or **3.** This is a change from the previous system, which used the letters *R, S, T,* or *V.* We think the new system makes more sense, as it's more consistent with the naming conventions for other staterooms.

- Even within the same stateroom classification, you may find as many as **four or five different verandah configurations** (see page 108 for details).

Stateroom Categories

Note: *Due to the shape of the ships, there are minor variations on floor plans even within stateroom categories. In addition to the floor-plan art included in this section, video tours of these rooms are available on YouTube (search for the specific room name).*

- **CATEGORIES 11A–11C** (all ships): Standard Inside Stateroom

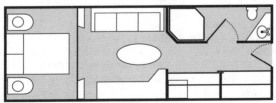

MAXIMUM OCCUPANCY 3 or 4 people
SIZE (square feet) *Magic/Wonder,* 184; *Dream/Fantasy/Wish,* 169

continued on next page

DESCRIPTION These cabins have one queen-size bed, a sleeper sofa, and combined bath with tub and shower. Some rooms have a pull-down upper berth. These cabins are on Decks 2, 5, 6, and 7 of the *Magic* and *Wonder;* Decks 2, 5, 6, 7, 8, 9, and 10 of the *Dream* and *Fantasy;* and Decks 2, 6, 7, 8, 9, 10, and 11 of the *Wish.*

- **CATEGORY 10A** (all ships except the *Wish*), **CATEGORIES 10B AND 10C** (*Magic* and *Wonder*): Deluxe Inside Stateroom

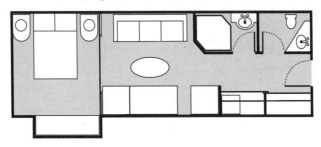

MAXIMUM OCCUPANCY 4 people
SIZE (square feet) *Magic/Wonder,* 214; *Dream/Fantasy,* 204
DESCRIPTION These cabins have one queen-size bed, one sleeper sofa, and split bath. Some rooms have a pull-down upper berth. Category 10C rooms on the *Magic* and *Wonder* are only on Deck 1 Midship and Deck 2 Aft. Category 10B rooms, also found on the *Magic* and *Wonder,* are located only on Deck 2 Midship. Category 10A rooms are on Decks 5 and 7 of the *Magic* and *Wonder* and Decks 5–9 of the *Dream* and *Fantasy.*

- **CATEGORIES 9A–9D** (all ships): Deluxe Oceanview Stateroom

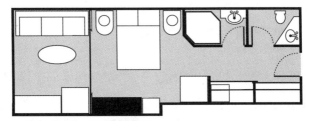

MAXIMUM OCCUPANCY 3 or 4 people
SIZE (square feet) *Magic/Wonder,* 214; *Dream/Fantasy,* 204; *Wish,* 218
DESCRIPTION These rooms are the same size and have the same features as a Category 10 Deluxe Inside, plus a window view of the ocean. These cabins have one queen-size bed. Cabins on all ships have a sleeper sofa and split bath; some rooms have a pull-down upper berth. Categories 9B–9D are found only on Decks 1 and 2 of the *Magic* and *Wonder* and only on Deck 2 Midship of the *Dream* and *Fantasy.* Category 9A cabins are found on the Forward section of Decks 5–7 on the *Magic* and *Wonder* and on Decks 5–8 of the *Dream* and *Fantasy.* The 9A cabins on Decks 6–8 of the

Dream and *Fantasy* are interesting because they're at the extreme Forward and Aft ends of the ships, affording them unique views at a relatively low cost. On the *Wish,* these cabins are on Decks 2, 6, 7, and 8. The far-forward Category 9 rooms on *Wish* Decks 6–8 have unique slanted walls and slanted portholes that follow the curvature of the ship.

- **CATEGORY 8A** (*Dream* and *Fantasy*), **CATEGORIES 8B AND 8C** (*Dream, Fantasy,* and *Wish*): **Deluxe Family Oceanview Stateroom**

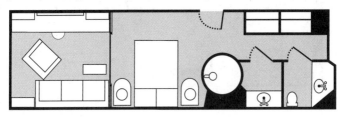

MAXIMUM OCCUPANCY 3, 4, or 5 people
SIZE (square feet) *Dream/Fantasy,* 241; *Wish,* 237
DESCRIPTION These cabins have one queen-size bed. Most also have a one-person pull-down bed in the wall; a few also have one-person pull-down beds in the ceiling. All cabins have a one-person sleeper sofa. Some 8As have a single bathroom, others a split-bath configuration. Many bathrooms have round tubs/showers on the *Dream* and *Fantasy;* the tubs/showers are rectangular on the *Wish.* Category 8 staterooms are on Decks 5–9 on the *Dream* and *Fantasy* and on Decks 6–9 on the *Wish.*

- **CATEGORY 7A** (all ships): **Deluxe Oceanview Stateroom with Navigator's Verandah**

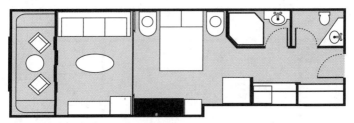

MAXIMUM OCCUPANCY 3 or 4 people
SIZE (square feet) *Magic/Wonder,* 268 (including verandah); *Dream/Fantasy,* 246 (including verandah); *Wish,* 243 (including verandah)
DESCRIPTION Found on Decks 5–7 of the *Magic, Wonder, Dream,* and *Fantasy* and on Decks 6–9 of the *Wish,* these cabins have one queen-size bed, a one-person sleeper sofa, and a split bath; some also have an upper-berth pull-down bed. They may include a **Navigator's Verandah,** a small, semienclosed, teak-floored deck attached to the stateroom and featuring either a large exterior window or open railing. The window doesn't open, so the extra space and teak deck distinguish these rooms from the Category 9

staterooms. On the *Dream* and *Fantasy,* these cabins have Undersize or Obstructed-View Verandahs. (See page 108 for more information about DCL verandah categories.)

- **CATEGORIES 6A** (all ships) **AND 6B** (*Dream, Fantasy,* and *Wish* only): Deluxe Oceanview Stateroom with Verandah

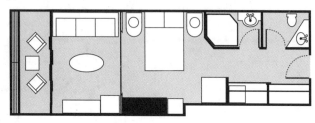

MAXIMUM OCCUPANCY 3 or 4 people

SIZE (square feet) *Magic/Wonder,* 268 (including verandah); *Dream/Fantasy,* 246 (including verandah); *Wish,* 243 (including verandah)

DESCRIPTION These cabins have a queen-size bed; a one-person sleeper sofa; and a one-person pull-down bed, typically above the sofa. All have split baths, most with rectangular tubs/showers on the *Wish* and with round tubs/showers on the other ships. Category 6A cabins are found Aft on Decks 5–7 of the *Magic* and *Wonder;* Aft on Decks 8–10 of the *Dream* and *Fantasy;* and Aft on Decks 8 and 9 of the *Wish.* Category 6B staterooms are found on Decks 8–10 of the *Dream* and *Fantasy* and on Decks 6 and 7 of the *Wish.* These staterooms differ from Category 5 staterooms because they have what DCL calls White-Wall Verandahs, or private verandahs with a short white wall instead of a plexiglass railing.

- **CATEGORIES 5A–5C** (all ships): Deluxe Oceanview Stateroom with Verandah

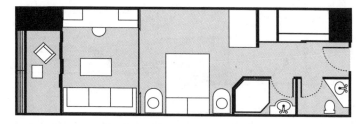

MAXIMUM OCCUPANCY 3 or 4 people

SIZE (square feet) *Magic/Wonder,* 268 (including verandah); *Dream/Fantasy,* 246 (including verandah); *Wish,* 243 (including verandah)

DESCRIPTION There seems to be little difference between these and the Category 6 cabins on the *Magic* and *Wonder*—all have the same square footage and amenities, as well as similar locations. Some Category 5 staterooms on the *Dream, Fantasy,* and *Wish* have Extended Verandahs, which are larger than DCL's Standard Verandahs; a few Category 5s have White-Wall Verandahs.

- **CATEGORIES 4A, 4B, AND 4E** (all ships), **4C** (*Dream, Fantasy,* and *Wish* only): Deluxe Family Oceanview Stateroom with Verandah

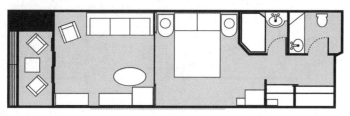

MAXIMUM OCCUPANCY 4 or 5 people

SIZE (square feet) *Magic/Wonder,* 304 (including verandah); *Dream/Fantasy,* 299 (including verandah). *WIsh,* 284 (including verandah)

DESCRIPTION These cabins have a queen-size bed and sleeper sofa (fits one person); most have a pull-down wall bed (sleeps one), and some also have a pull-down upper-berth bed. All have a split bath. One issue with the pull-down wall bed in some of these cabins is that you'd have to move the desk chair to use the bed. Category 4 cabins are found on Deck 8 of the *Magic* and *Wonder;* on Decks 5–12 of the *Dream* and *Fantasy;* and on Decks 6–11 of the *Wish.* On the *Wish,* pay particular attention to your deck plan if you're selecting a Category 4C stateroom (Decks 6 and 7): some of these rooms on the "bumpout" (outward-curving) portion of the ship have significantly larger verandahs than their neighbors.

- **CATEGORY 3A** (all ships): Concierge Family Oceanview Stateroom with Verandah

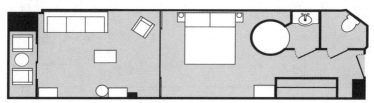

MAXIMUM OCCUPANCY 5 people

SIZE (square feet) *Dream/Fantasy/Magic/Wonder,* 306; *Wish,* 296

DESCRIPTION These cabins have a king (*Wish*) or queen-size bed (*Magic, Wonder, Dream,* and *Fantasy*); a sleeper sofa for two; and an upper-berth pull-down bed that sleeps one. This is the lowest price point that gets access to Concierge-level amenities. Category 3A staterooms are located on Deck 8 of the *Magic* and *Wonder;* on Decks 11 and 12 of the *Dream* and *Fantasy;* and on Decks 12 and 13 of the *Wish.*

- ### CATEGORY 3B (*Wish* only):
  Concierge Family Oceanview Stateroom

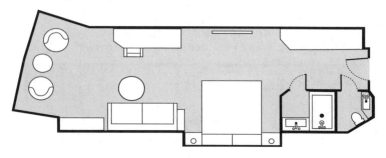

MAXIMUM OCCUPANCY 4 or 5 people

SIZE (square feet) 357

DESCRIPTION With most of the same characteristics of the 3A staterooms, the small group of 3B rooms is located on Deck 11 Forward. While these rooms do not have verandahs, they are significantly larger than the 3As and feature floor-to-ceiling windows with stunning ocean views.

- ### CATEGORIES 2A AND 2B (all ships):
  Concierge 1-Bedroom Suite with Verandah

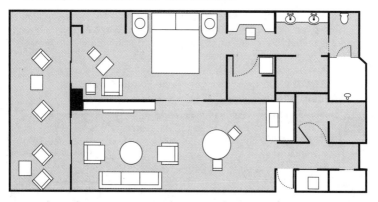

MAXIMUM OCCUPANCY 5 people

SIZE (square feet) *Magic/Wonder,* 614 (including verandah); *Dream/Fantasy,* 622 (including verandah); *Wish,* 608 (including verandah)

DESCRIPTION These cabins feature a separate bedroom with queen-size bed and a bathroom with a whirlpool tub and separate shower. (On the *Wish,* there are two full bathrooms.) The living room sleeps three: two on the convertible sofa and one in the pull-down bed. Category 2 staterooms are found all along Deck 8 of the *Magic* and *Wonder* and the Forward sections of Decks 11 and 12 on the *Dream* and *Fantasy;* on the *Wish,* they're on Decks 12 and 13 Forward.

- **CATEGORY 1C** (*Wish* only): Concierge 1-Story Royal Suite with Verandah

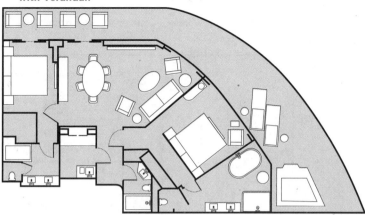

MAXIMUM OCCUPANCY 6 people
SIZE (square feet) 1,507
DESCRIPTION Concierge Royal Suites have two bedrooms with king-size beds and walk-in closets, three full bathrooms, and one half-bath, plus a balcony, a private hot tub, a living room, a dining room with a six-seat table, and a pantry. Category 1C staterooms are located on Deck 10.

- **CATEGORY 1B** (*Wish* only): Concierge 2-Story Royal Suite with Verandah

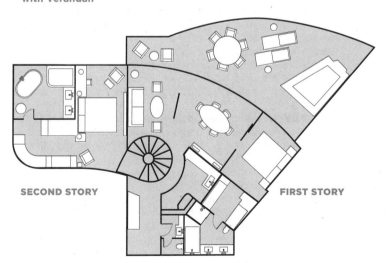

SECOND STORY

FIRST STORY

MAXIMUM OCCUPANCY 6 people
SIZE (square feet) 1,759

continued on next page

DESCRIPTION These suites, located on Decks 13 and 14, have internal spiral staircases connecting the two floors.

- **CATEGORY 1B** (*Magic* and *Wonder*): **Concierge 2-Bedroom Suite with Verandah**

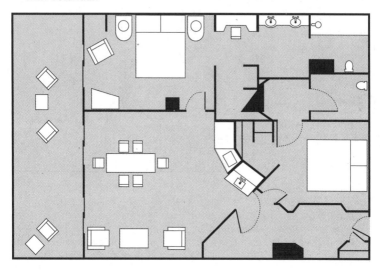

MAXIMUM OCCUPANCY 7 people
SIZE (square feet) 954 (including verandah)
DESCRIPTION The master bedroom has a queen-size bed, a walk-in closet, a vanity, two sinks, and a walk-in shower. The other bedroom has twin beds, a bath with tub and sink, and a walk-in closet. Two others can sleep on the convertible sofa in the living room, and a pull-down bed sleeps one more. In addition, the 2-Bedroom Suite features a large living room with seating for 10 people, a huge private verandah suitable for entertaining a few guests, and another half-bath. Category 1B cabins are on Deck 8 Forward.

- **CATEGORY 1A** (all ships except the *Wish*): **Concierge Royal Suite**
MAXIMUM OCCUPANCY 7 people (*Magic/Wonder*); 5 people (*Dream/Fantasy*)
SIZE (square feet) *Magic/Wonder,* 1,029 (including verandah); *Dream/Fantasy,* 1,781 (including verandah)
DESCRIPTION On the *Magic* and *Wonder,* the master bedroom has a queen-size bed, a walk-in closet, a vanity, two sinks, and a walk-in shower. The other bedroom has twin beds, a bath with tub and sink, and a walk-in closet. Two others can sleep on the convertible sofa in the living room, and a pull-down bed sleeps one more. On the *Magic* and *Wonder,* the Royal Suite includes a separate dining room, living room, and media room, plus a private verandah that you should rent out to other families for birthdays (it'll fit an elephant!) and another half-bath. Royal Suites on the *Dream* and *Fantasy* have one long room separated into dining and living areas. The master bedroom features a queen-size bed and bath with two sinks, a

CONCIERGE ROYAL SUITE

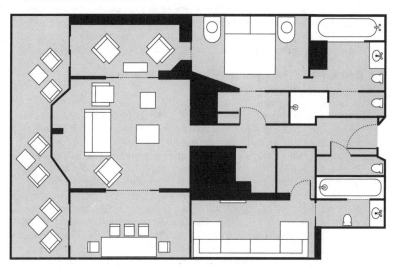

CONCIERGE ROYAL SUITE WITH VERANDAH

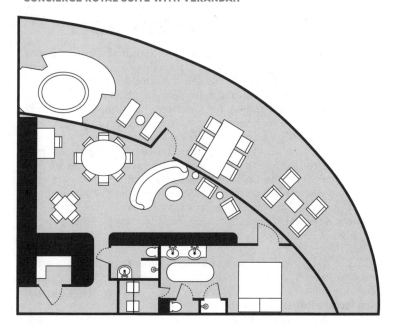

shower, and a tub. An in-wall pull-down double bed and a single pull-down bed in the living room complete the sleeping arrangements. The most impressive feature of these suites on the *Dream* and *Fantasy* may be the verandah, which curves around the suite to follow the contour of the deck. Besides being large enough to land aircraft on, it includes a whirlpool tub.

• **CATEGORY 1A** (*Wish* only): Concierge *Wish* Tower Suite
MAXIMUM OCCUPANCY 8 people
SIZE (square feet) 1,965
DESCRIPTION With subtle *Moana* theming, the *Wish* Tower Suite features two master bedrooms, four full bathrooms, and one half-bath; an eight-seat dining table; a pantry with dishwasher, refrigerator, and coffee maker; a library (which converts to a bedroom if needed); and a kids' room with built-in bunk beds. The lower-level living room affords views across the ship's upper decks through a two-story window wall. The master bedrooms, both on the upper level, have walk-in closets, king-size beds, and floor-to-ceiling windows overlooking the living area below. The main bathrooms each have rain-head showers, double-sink vanities, and spa tubs. All fixtures and finishes are top of the line. The tower is located inside the ship's forward funnel stack on Decks 14 and 15 (this is the only area designated as Deck 15 on the entire ship). (*Note:* No floor-plan art was available for this suite at press time.)

BOOKING A CRUISE *Without* SELECTING A STATEROOM

UNLIKE BOOKING A HOTEL, where you typically don't find out your exact room until you arrive, most guests booking a Disney cruise choose a specific stateroom when they make their reservation. When a preferred stateroom category is nearly full, however, DCL offers what's known as a **GTY reservation.** *GTY* stands for "guarantee," meaning you're guaranteed to be in a particular category of room or a higher category, but you won't know exactly which cabin you're in until immediately before you depart. GTY reservations are often offered close to the ship's sail date.

Other acronyms you might see are **VGT** (Verandah Guarantee), **OGT** (Oceanview Guarantee), and **IGT** (Inside Guarantee), which are typically used when DCL is offering a last-minute discount on a cruise that's not selling well. There are a number of restrictions on these fares—the cruise must be paid in full at booking time, for example—but there are often good deals to be had if you're willing to leave your stateroom selection up in the air.

Note: GTY, VGT, OGT, and IGT rates don't typically appear on the DCL website until about three months before the sailing date, so if you're booking far in advance, you won't see these prices listed. If you have more flexibility, however, booking a GTY room can save you lots of money. In early June 2022, for example, we spot-checked prices for a **5-Night Western Caribbean Cruise** on the *Dream* in August 2022, about eight weeks in advance of the sailing. The lowest available price for a Verandah stateroom for a family of four in a specific location was $7,285. The VGT rate for the same sailing and the same party of four was $4,784—a savings of $2,501. That's more than enough reason for us to gamble on our cabin placement.

CONCIERGE LEVEL: *What You Need to Know, and If It's Worth It*

A DISNEY CRUISE IS ALREADY A FAIRLY LUXE VACATION, but what do you do when you want to plus it up even more? Booking a stateroom on the Concierge level is one option. The amenities offered to Concierge level guests are substantial, as is the price. Not surprisingly, this is one of the areas of cruising where we are most often asked, "Is it worth it?" See page 25 for our thoughts on this topic, but—*spoiler alert*—it depends.

The Concierge levels on the *Dream* and *Fantasy* are nearly identical. The cabins are on Decks 11 and 12, with an exclusive Concierge lounge on Deck 12. The lounge opens to a private outdoor-sunning area (it's right by Satellite Falls).

On the *Magic* and *Wonder,* Concierge staterooms are on Deck 8, while the concierge lounges and staff are on Deck 10. On the *Wish,* the Concierge staterooms are on Decks 10–15. The lounge is on Deck 12, and the Concierge pool and private sundeck are on Deck 13.

The Concierge cabins are described on pages 99–104. Prepare to be wowed upon walking into these rooms, particularly those in Categories 1 and 2. We already think Disney has great staterooms, but the finishing touches in Concierge are beyond our expectations. In fact, if you're considering booking here, we think you'd do well to choose it for an itinerary and ship you've already taken so you're not torn between exploring the ship and port and just hanging out on the Concierge level.

The benefits of booking this level are quantifiable—more space, lounge access, early booking opportunities for specialty dining and port excursions (notably the private cabanas on Castaway Cay)—but they're also intangible when it comes to the added level of service. Also quantifiable is the cost: for an apples-to-apples comparison, plan to pay around 50% more for a Category 3 (Concierge) versus a Category 4 (non-Concierge) stateroom.

Concierge level has perks that range from "really useful" to "just OK." The pampering begins before boarding. The Concierge team will contact you before your booking window for port excursions and dining to ask for your requests. While making adult-dining reservations usually isn't a problem no matter where you're booked, getting a cabana on Castaway Cay is nearly impossible if you're not in Concierge.

On boarding day, Concierge guests check in with Platinum-level guests in a separate area (Port Canaveral only) or line (other ports).

(Pre-pandemic, Platinum and Concierge guests could both board at will, with no waiting for your boarding group to be announced.) Concierge guests are escorted to the lounge by the staff. This helps you get around the usual wait for an elevator on embarkation day.

Erin met a family on the *Wonder* who only travel Concierge—not for the perks or prestige but because the higher level of service and early boarding make the ship less stressful for their son who has autism. If you have a family member with special needs and you can afford the expense, Concierge level could make your cruise easier (see page 158 for more on cruising with people who have autism).

A good rate for a Concierge Family Oceanview Stateroom with Verandah on DCL in 2022–23 is less than $750 per person, per night; for comparison, a good rate for a non-Concierge Deluxe Family Oceanview Stateroom with Verandah is around $350 per night. (From another perspective, if you spent the same amount on a Royal Caribbean Concierge Club room as on a DCL Concierge room, you'd get a multiroom suite rather than a one-room cabin.)

In short, the lowest level of DCL Concierge access costs several hundred dollars more person, per night, than a similar non-Concierge stateroom on Disney and about the same as a Concierge Club suite on Royal. But if you're taking this leap, you're not cruising because it's economical—you're doing so because you enjoy the theming, service, and entertainment.

SO . . . IS CONCIERGE WORTH IT? Being logical types, we like to approach the question methodically. If you accept that (1) a Disney cruise is worth the surcharge you pay over other lines, (2) a Verandah room is worth what you pay over an Inside room, (3) the expense will neither kill your overall bottom line nor negatively impact other aspects of your vacation, and (4) you enjoy personal attention, then the next linear progression is that, yes, the extra space of a Concierge room (we're talking one bedroom) could be worth the price Disney charges. Basically, staying on Concierge level means not just upgraded accommodations but also avoiding all the little annoyances of a cruise vacation—lines, noise, masses of fellow cruisers— by waving them away with a magic wand made of money.

Personally, we wouldn't sail Concierge *every* time, but we do find the one-bedroom Concierge-level suites worth it if we're celebrating something special or we want to take a particularly relaxing or luxurious vacation. To help with your decision, take a look at "Is It Worth It?" (page 25). If you decide to pass, you'll have a great time anyway.

STATEROOM SELECTION *for* LARGER PARTIES

GUESTS TRAVELING WITH NUCLEAR FAMILIES with four or fewer people are often fine staying in one stateroom. DCL offers many options for ship location and stateroom size at a variety of price points—just choose where you want to be and how much you want to spend, and you're good to go. Guests traveling with parties of five or more, and guests traveling with extended family, blended families, or unrelated friends may have more-complicated decisions to make when choosing their staterooms.

A quick glance at DCL's deck plans and stateroom classifications shows that on, for example, the *Magic*, the lowest stateroom category that will sleep a party of five is a **Category 4 Deluxe Family Oceanview Stateroom with Verandah** on an upper deck. Let's look, then, at pricing for a hypothetical family of five—two adults and three kids ages 16, 13, and 9—for the **8-Night Southern Caribbean Cruise** on the *Magic* on May 5, 2023. At the time of our search, the lowest price to put this family in one stateroom was **$10,449** for a **Category 4E** stateroom. If, however, we tried to book that same family of five into two **Category 11C Standard Inside Staterooms,** with one adult and the two older kids in one stateroom and one adult and the 9-year-old in the other, the total price is **$8,436** ($4,742 for the stateroom with three people and $3,694 for the stateroom with two), for a savings of $2,013.

Of course, you have some tradeoffs to consider—the most obvious in this case being that the family gives up access to a verandah. On the other hand, they gain more than 100 square feet of living space and an additional shower and toilet. For many families, the advantages of saving about $2,000 and gaining a bathroom would well outweigh the loss of a room with a view.

Making things even more complicated, the pricing is different if you book the same hypothetical family of five above into the same two Inside Staterooms, but in a slightly different combination. If you book one adult, one teen, and the 9-year-old in the first room, their cost is $4,705, and the cost for the second adult and the second teen is $3,694, for a total of **$8,399.** This slight difference in booking strategy saves $37. (The second person in a stateroom is always charged an adult rate, regardless of age. If the 9-year-old is booked into a stateroom with just one other person, he's priced at the adult rate, but if he's the third person in a stateroom, he's charged the children's rate.)

Granted, a $37 savings is a drop in the bucket for a cruise vacation that costs many thousands of dollars, but if you're traveling with a very large party (a family reunion, for example), such small tweaks can add up in your favor. Again, though, be aware that the Castaway Club status of the travelers also has ramifications for room assignments; if members of your party have different statuses, it may be worth a few dollars to choose a different booking configuration. (See pages 86 and 87 for more information.) Also note that once you're on board, it's easy to tinker with who actually sleeps where, regardless of how the booking was made.

A couple other things to think about when booking staterooms for larger parties:

- **Do we need connecting staterooms?** Guests traveling with small children may prefer them, while guests traveling with well-behaved teens or other adults may find that adjacent rooms or nonadjacent rooms in close proximity are enough.

- **Does it matter if all members of the party have the same type of stateroom?** Is parity needed to keep peace among family members? Are we willing to have an Oceanview Stateroom and an Inside Stateroom, or a Verandah Stateroom and an Oceanview or Inside Stateroom? Is it sufficient if only one room has a verandah that everyone can use?

GET *to* KNOW YOUR VERANDAH

A VERANDAH (note the tasteful *H* at the end) is analogous to a balcony at a hotel. Some cruise lines have verandahs (or *verandas*, depending on the line) that face toward the center of the ship, often toward a pool or open deck stage, but the verandahs on DCL ships face outward toward the ocean.

DCL uses a variety of language to describe the verandahs on its ships. For example:

- **Standard (Family) Verandah** Has a transparent acrylic wall between you and the ocean. You can see the ocean from anywhere, sitting or standing.

- **White-Wall Verandah** An open-air lounge area with a solid white wall from the deck to the railing. You can see the ocean if you're standing up, but you're not likely to if you're sitting down. Most of these staterooms are located in the aft portion of the ship.

- **Navigator's Verandah** An open-air lounge area that has a solid wall from the deck to the railing as well as some enclosure above the railing. Picture a balcony with a large porthole opening to a view of the ocean. You can see the ocean if you're standing up, but you're not likely to if you're sitting down. Most Navigator's Verandahs have one chair and one fixed bench built into the wall rather than two regular chairs.

- **Obstructed-View Verandah** A significant portion of the view is blocked by ship walls or something like the lifeboats.

- **Undersize Verandah** A verandah with smaller square footage than is typical on DCL ships.

- **Extended Verandah** This verandah has greater-than-typical square footage. Instead of room for just two regular chairs, there may be room for lounge chairs or for four chairs.

Also be aware that some staterooms have combinations of these verandah types. For example, many of the far-Aft rooms on Decks 7, 8, 9, and 10 of the *Dream* and *Fantasy* have Extended Verandahs with white walls.

The type of verandah you select can have cost implications. For example, we spot-checked the July 3, 2023, **5-Night Western Caribbean Cruise** on the *Magic* for a party of two adults in a Deluxe Oceanview Stateroom with Verandah. Within eight consecutive staterooms on Deck 7 Aft, there are three different verandah configurations available, each incrementally more expensive than the other:

- **Obstructed-View Verandah:** $4,642   • **White-Wall Verandah:** $4,772
- **Standard Verandah:** $5,652

The same party on the April 29, 2023, **5-Night Bahamian Cruise from Miami** on the *Dream* can choose from among five variants of the Deluxe Oceanview Stateroom with Verandah on Deck 6 Aft:

- **Undersize Verandah:** $2,737
- **Obstructed-View Verandah:** $2,814
- **Standard Verandah:** $2,947
- **Extended Verandah:** $3,146
- **Family Verandah:** $3,299

Note that in this situation, you can get a stateroom with seating for four (Extended Verandah) for just $199 more than a stateroom with seating for two (Standard Verandah)—it's a modest tweak that could make a big difference for some families, although you might be sacrificing other factors such as the stateroom's location on the ship. ("Family Verandah," by the way, is sort of misleading: it's the most expensive option not because of the verandah type—which is Standard—but the room type.)

If you have dreams of sitting with a glass of wine and staring at the sea, be sure you're getting a verandah configuration that will actually allow you to do this. It may well be worth it to spend a few dollars, or even a few hundred dollars, more for better sight lines. Or, if you don't particularly care, you can save yourself a few bucks by choosing a different verandah configuration.

Also note that if your party is staying in two adjacent Verandah staterooms, you may be able to remove the divider separating the outdoor space between them, effectively creating one extra-large verandah. Not all Verandah rooms offer this option, so check with your stateroom host to see if the divider is removable.

Although your verandah is your private outdoor space, please keep in mind the following rules and courtesies:

- **No smoking.** Cigarette/cigar smoke inevitably drifts to neighboring verandahs, so please smoke only in designated areas of the ship (see page 162). The same rule applies to vaping and e-cigarettes.

- **No drying wet clothing or towels.** These items are almost guaranteed to blow away.

- *No nudity!* Verandahs are private, but not *that* private. To the contrary, your naked glory may be visible from other ships, port locations, or nearby verandahs.

- **No loud music or conversation.** You will be heard in nearby staterooms.

If you're sailing to a cold-weather destination, you may find that a verandah is less of an imperative than if you're traveling to tropical locales. It may be nice to stand out on your balcony to view the trees, wildlife, or glaciers for a few minutes, but it may not be comfortable to read or dine outdoors for an extended period of time.

Some guests with small children may have safety concerns. Verandah doors have a lock that's above adult shoulder-height. It is theoretically possible that an enterprising elementary-schooler could climb on a chair or coffee table to reach the lock, but it would take some real ingenuity and strength to open the door. If you're still concerned that you may have a late-night escape artist on your hands, then you may want to save verandah lodging for when Junior is a bit older.

MAKING CHANGES *to* YOUR STATEROOM RESERVATION

GETTING THE BEST RATE FOR YOUR CRUISE often means booking more than a year in advance (see "Saving Money," page 34). But a lot can change in a year, including little things (school and work schedules) and big things (pregnancy, marriage, or divorce). Sometimes these changes mean that you have to cancel the cruise (see pages 44–46 for more on how to do that), but at other times you'll still want to go on the cruise but you may want or need to travel with different people.

Don't worry: Disney Cruise Line lets you change the actual names on a reservation until close to sail time, assuming that one of the originally booked guests remains on the reservation. When Erin's husband, Jeff, had to bow out of an Atlantic Canada (Canadian Coastline) cruise with her due to an unforeseen business meeting that was scheduled during the sail dates, she was easily able to swap in a friend to sail with her.

You may also make changes to the number of guests in your stateroom until your paid-in-full date. The rule of thumb here is that if you're unsure about exactly which friends or family members you'll be traveling with, you should make the reservation for the larger of the possible party sizes. Here's why:

In some cases, your stateroom can physically accommodate more people but DCL won't let you add them to the room; this typically happens when there is a higher-than-average number of guests in your part of the ship. This has to do with lifeboat capacity and other safety issues beyond individual cabin capacity—it's nothing personal.

Another factor in booking your maximum party size and then paring down is that it locks in your booking rate. Even if DCL will allow you to add someone to your room well after the original booking, they might be charged at a higher cost. As long as you make party deletions before your paid-in-full date, you'll be able to reduce the number of guests in your room.

A bit of good news about changing stateroom categories after you've booked a sailing: you lock in prices for your original sailing party once you book. For example, if you book a 4C and later decide to move to a 10A, you pay the price that the 10A was at the time you booked, not the current, likely higher price. If you're sure about your party size and your sail date but not which stateroom type you want, this is a nice feature.

STUFF *to* THINK ABOUT WHEN CHOOSING *a* STATEROOM

THE BEST STATEROOM TYPE is the one that meets your individual needs. Here are some things to think about as you make your decision. A Disney-specialist travel agent can give you advice here as well.

What is your budget? If the sky's the limit, then a Verandah room will likely appeal to you, if only for the extra square footage. If you're prioritizing your pennies, though, an Inside Stateroom would leave you more funds available for excursions or fine dining.

What is the price difference between category types? On some sailings it can be many thousands of dollars, but on other cruises it's minimal (see page 90).

How long is your voyage? You might be able to cope with an Inside Stateroom for a few days, but you might find it oppressive over a week or more. (One of DCL's new Oceanian sailings from Hawaii to Australia in 2023–24 will have *10 straight days* at sea—in this case, we'd recommend booking at least an Oceanview room for your sanity's sake.)

Where are you sailing? The scenery on your cruise—Caribbean ports, glaciers in Alaska, fjords in Norway—might influence your choice of an Inside room versus one with a view. Ditto the weather: the scenery in Alaska, for example, is magnificent, but if you're an Alabama native who's used to warmer climes, you may not enjoy sitting on a verandah when it's 35°F outside. Additionally, consider what it costs to go on port adventures at your destination. Many beach destinations have fun things to do close by that are inexpensive or even free, but on an Alaskan cruise the most appealing excursions—such as helicoptering to a dogsled run—cost hundreds of dollars per person. If you're sticking to a budget but you still want to participate in some off-ship activities, you may want to economize on the room.

How many people are in your party? (See page 106 for further discussion.) If you're traveling with a large group, you'll likely be splitting up into several staterooms. A family may be able to economize by having one group get a Verandah room while the other gets an Inside or Oceanview Stateroom, giving you the best of both worlds. If you're all in one room, then the per-person square footage may be your most important deciding factor.

Do you have claustrophobia? If you don't like compact spaces, you may want to avoid Inside Staterooms, particularly those without a virtual porthole.

Are you an introvert? See page 132 for our thoughts.

Are you prone to seasickness? See page 60 for more information.

Do you love the ocean? If so, you may prefer an Oceanview or Verandah Stateroom over an Inside Stateroom.

How old are the members of you party? If you have little ones, you'll likely be spending a good bit of time in your room while they nap or you get them ready for an early bedtime. In this case, you may find that a verandah gives you a more appealing place to chat with your partner, order room service, or read a book than an Inside or Oceanview room.

Is this your first cruise? If you're a regular cruiser, then you might not need a view or verandah on every trip. If you're a first-timer, depending on your budget and your affinity for cruising, you may be looking for a once-in-a-decade experience on this cruise or an upgraded experience on a trip a year or two from now.

Do you want to do everything the ship has to offer, or do you want to just chill in your room? If your room isn't going to be central to your cruise experience because you know that you'll always be out and about meeting characters, watching shows, playing bingo, and singing karaoke, then an Inside Stateroom will likely meet your needs. But if you want to spend your vacation reading novels and doing lots of nothing, then a room with a verandah might be just the thing you need.

continued on page 114

THE STATEROOM SCOOP

TAMMY WHITING is the owner of **Storybook Destinations,** an Authorized Disney Vacation Planner travel agency. Tammy offers some great insight into specific stateroom categories on the DCL ships.

• *Categories 1 and 2 (see pages 100–104)*

***Magic/Dream* class:** On the *Magic* class, I recommend **8032, 8034, 8532,** or **8534.** In these rooms, the twin pull-down bed is in the living room instead of the master bedroom, giving the latter its own closed-off space. On the *Dream* class, there are six suites with Extended Verandahs: **12006, 12012, 12506, 12512, 11006,** and **11002.** For the absolute best view of Castaway Cay, book **12512.** I prefer the Concierge staterooms on **Deck 12,** which have easier access to the Concierge lounge and sundeck, over the Concierge rooms on Deck 11

***Triton* class (*Wish*):** These rooms are simply spectacular. The *Wish* **Tower Suite,** in the funnel, sleeps up to eight guests and is the best room on any Disney ship. The two-story **Royal Suites** are likewise some of the most luxurious accommodations I've ever been in, either on land *or* sea. The Category 2 staterooms on **Deck 13** are convenient to the sundeck, but a staircase inside the Concierge lounge makes both the lounge on Deck 12 and the sundeck on Deck 13 easy to get to. The Category 2A staterooms with extended verandahs have incredible outdoor space. For these, I recommend Starboard-side staterooms, and **12500** would be my first pick among 2As, with **12000** being a close second because of that giant verandah; **12504** is a particularly nice Category 2B.

• *Category 3 (see pages 99 and 100)*

***Magic/Dream* class:** Category 3 staterooms are essentially Category 4 staterooms with Concierge furnishings and service. On the *Magic* class, I prefer a room on the Starboard side if visiting Castaway Cay. On the *Dream* class, I likewise prefer a Starboard room; I also recommend one of the staterooms on the "bumpouts," or outward curves on each side of the ship: **12008, 12010, 12508, 12510,** and **11004.** If you need to split a group between two staterooms, book **12512** with **12510** to open the verandah partition between the two staterooms for amazing Castaway Cay views.

***Triton* class (*Wish*):** 3B is a brand-new category for DCL—it's the first Concierge stateroom without a verandah. What these rooms lack in verandahs, though, they make up for in views, with breathtaking floor-to-ceiling windows. In particular, Category 3B has three corner staterooms that I call **Secret Suites;** each has a separate bedroom with a door. My first pick of the Secret Suites would be **11006,** which is simply stunning. If you don't absolutely need a verandah, I highly recommend the 3Bs over the 3As—these rooms are so nice, in fact, I have a feeling they'll be recategorized at some point.

• *Category 4 (see page 99)*

***Magic/Dream* class:** Category 4 (Family) staterooms are the biggest non-Concierge rooms on these ships. (The word *Family* in the name means the stateroom is slightly longer and may sleep up to five.) The A, B, C, and D versions of these staterooms (the letter indicates location on the ship) have similar features. Many 4Es sleep just four people instead of five and, on the *Dream* class, lack the round tubs of the other 4s. The *Dream*-class 4Es do have spacious verandahs, while the *Magic*-class 4Es have White-Wall Verandahs.

***Triton* class (*Wish*):** Like the *Dream*-class ships, the *Wish* has bumpouts, or outward-curving areas on each side; unlike the *Dream* class, however, the *Wish* has non-Concierge staterooms in its bumpouts. Category 4's bumpout rooms have large extended verandahs, particularly the rooms in the center of each bump. Similar to Category 3 on the *Dream* class (see above), corner-Aft rooms **6196** and **6696** are **Secret Suites**—these are my top picks in Category 4. Unlike the Secret Suites on the

- **Category 4 (continued)**

Dream and *Fantasy,* however, these have verandahs. Other good Aft options are **10168, 10170, 10668, 9182, 9184,** and **6700;** all afford great views from spacious verandahs.

- **Category 5 (see pages 98 and 99)**

Magic/Dream class: Category 5 is a standard-size stateroom with an unobstructed verandah. I'm very enthusiastic about the 5Es on *Dream*-class ships: they're on the **far-Aft** (back) side of the ship and have huge verandahs, which offer some of my favorite views on board.

Triton class (*Wish*): The hidden gems in Category 5 are the staterooms at the edges of the bumpouts; these have bigger verandahs than other Category 5 rooms on the ship. On **Deck 10,** for example, my picks are **10544, 10546, 10044,** and **10046.** The rooms toward the front of each bumpout have slightly better views facing Forward, while the rooms facing toward the back of each bumpout have slightly better views facing Aft, which means better views of Castaway Cay in particular. Facing all the way Aft are **6198** or **6698.** With their large verandahs and excellent views, these rooms are my top two picks in Category 5.

- **Category 6 (see page 98)**

Magic/Dream class: Category 6 staterooms are like Category 5 staterooms, but they all have Undersize, Obstructed-View, or White-Wall Verandahs. Some of these differences are minor, so if you want to save a little over a Category 5, Category 6 may be for you. Category 6 staterooms on **Deck 6** have slightly larger verandahs than others on the *Magic*-class ships.

Triton class (*Wish*): Category 6A rooms **8192** and **8690** are on the far-Aft side of the ship. They have huge verandahs with stellar views, but be aware that the rooms themselves are quite small. Neither has a couch—only a foldout chair—so keep this in mind when booking your stateroom.

- **Category 7 (see pages 97 and 98)**

Magic/Dream class: There's a big difference between the *Dream*- and *Magic*-class Category 7s. Most Navigator's Verandahs on the *Magic* class are enclosed, with a large circular or oval windowlike opening cut out for viewing purposes. On the *Dream* class, Category 7 verandahs simply have views that are slightly more obstructed than those from Category 6 verandahs. On the *Magic* class, there are four Category 7 staterooms whose verandahs are not fully enclosed: **6134, 6634, 7120,** and **7620.**

Triton class (*Wish*): Category 7A rooms on **Deck 6** have verandahs with slightly smaller obstructions than those on higher decks.

- **Category 8 (see page 97)**

Dream class: Category 8 (Family) staterooms have very large portholes with seating. (Once again, *Family* means these are bigger staterooms that sleep up to five and have round tubs.) Category 8As—which are more like suites than staterooms—have two large portholes and lots of space; many have a divider of some kind between the bed and seating area. Not all Category 8As have tubs, however.

Triton class (*Wish*): There are no Category 8A staterooms on the *Wish*—and that's sad news for those who love 8As on the *Dream* and *Fantasy,* which are known for their massive size and double portholes. I'd be cautious of booking a Category 8 stateroom that's Aft on **Deck 6**—these rooms are directly above the Arendelle restaurant, where the show can get slightly loud.

continued on next page

THE STATEROOM SCOOP *(continued)*

- *Category 9 (see pages 96 and 97)*

Magic/Dream **class:** Category 9s are Oceanview staterooms minus verandahs. On the *Magic* class, I would avoid **Deck 1** if I were staying in a Category 9—this is a short deck with no access to the Aft elevators. The Oceanview staterooms on **Deck 1** also have two small portholes instead of one large porthole, which greatly limits your view. The 9C staterooms that are all the way Forward, like **2504** and **2510**, also have a bit more space due to the curvature of the ship. On the *Dream* class, the 9Bs on **Deck 2** are conveniently located outside Enchanted Garden. The *Dream* class also has some large corner staterooms that are 9Ds: **7006, 7504, 8006,** and **8504.**

Triton **class (*Wish*):** Because of the angle of the ship, 9D staterooms have slanted portholes and terrific views. The largest of these rooms—and thus the ones I recommend first in this category—are **7006, 7504, 8006,** and **8504.**

- *Category 10 (see page 96)*

Magic/Dream **class only:** These Inside Staterooms are basically the same size and have the same setup as Category 9s, but they have no outside views. On the *Dream* class, however, they have so-called virtual portholes, which gives a view (via camera) of what's happening outside, with some occasional Disney magic thrown in. The *Magic* class, however, has its own exciting unofficial category: **"secret porthole" staterooms.** These are Inside Staterooms that actually have a window, albeit with an obstructed view. If you want some natural light for the price of an Inside Stateroom, these are the rooms for you—book **5020, 5022, 5024, 5520, 5522,** or **5524** on the *Magic*-class ships. *Warning:* These staterooms are more popular than a Dole Whip on a sweltering day at Walt Disney World, so book early!

- *Category 11 (see pages 95 and 96)*

Magic/Dream **class:** There are no split baths—standard in all other categories—in Category 11 staterooms. While I highly recommend split baths for families, some people prefer having one large bathroom instead of two smaller ones. Additionally, on the *Magic*-class ships, some 11Bs have a **"sideways" layout.** These staterooms are quite popular because they feel a bit roomier than the typical Inside layout.

Triton **class (*Wish*):** Some *Wish* staterooms on the Starboard side of **Deck 2** have an interesting shape. There are also some, like **7689,** where the entrance is in its own little alcove. If you're looking for quiet, those rooms are good bets.

continued from page 111

How many sea days does your sailing include? Some Disney cruises have none, while others include more than a week of nonport time. If you're participating in land-based activities every day, then the view from your stateroom may not be that important.

Will you be getting off the ship at every port? This is a corollary of the point above. While most DCL Bahamian cruises stop in Nassau, many guests prefer not to get off the ship there (see pages 333 and 334). Still, it can be fun to sit on your verandah and watch the hustle and bustle in port.

Are you a good sleeper? I (Erin) am a poor sleeper at home. In particular, I don't like waking up with the sun. When I'm in an Inside Stateroom, I typically sleep like a log due to the total and complete darkness of a space with no windows.

Are your kids good sleepers? Most verandah staterooms are configured so the verandah is on what would naturally be the kids' side of the room. (The verandah is next to the twin bed rather than the larger, comfier queen bed.)

You may have visions of enjoying a glass of bubbly on the verandah while your kids are snoozing, but if they're light sleepers, you may not be able to do this without disturbing them. In that case, why pay for a verandah if you won't be able to truly enjoy it?

Does your ship offer virtual portholes? Many (but not all) Inside Staterooms on the *Dream* and *Fantasy* have these porthole-shaped video screens, which broadcast what you'd be seeing if your room actually did have a porthole. The illusion is extremely effective—so much so that you may not even notice that it's an illusion after a while. As a bonus for Disney fans, there are often surprises such as Nemo swimming by or Tinker Bell soaring above the sea. Many kids actually enjoy a virtual porthole more than a real one.

Do you want to be on the Port or Starboard side of the ship? This will affect your view when the ship is docked in port.

Do you need special accommodations? The need for a specific type of stateroom that can accommodate a medical issue or disability may trump all of the above. Accessible staterooms are available at a number of price points; if, however, you need to use a device like a walker inside your stateroom, this will be challenging in most of the smaller staterooms.

If you're planning to sail on the *Wish,* do you strongly prefer that your room be themed to a specific Disney character or movie? Room theming on the *Wish* varies by deck. As a general guideline, rooms on **Decks 2, 6, and 7** have either *Cinderella* or *Frozen* theming. Rooms on **Decks 8 and 9** have either *Sleeping Beauty* or *Princess and the Frog* theming. Rooms on **Decks 10 and 11** have either *Moana* or *Little Mermaid* theming. **Deck 12**'s rooms have *Tangled* theming, as do most of **Deck 13**'s; however, Deck 13's **Royal Suites** have *Sleeping Beauty* decor. Finally, the **Tower Suite** on **Deck 14** is *Moana*-themed. (*Note:* Disney doesn't publish a map or a list of specific staterooms with specific themes, but you can call DCL or have your travel agent check for you.)

In addition to the macro decisions about your stateroom selection, here are some specifics to consider:

- Don't book connecting staterooms unless you absolutely need to, although this might be a challenge on the *Wish,* which has many more connecting rooms than the other ships. The connecting doors are less soundproof than an actual wall.

- Depending on how important TV time is to your group—and assuming you'd rather not have everyone piled up on the bed to watch TV—the *Wish* may not be a good choice at press time for groups of more than two sharing a single room (see page 93).

- Rooms next to or across the hall from laundry rooms may be noisy, both because of the washers and dryers and conversation among guests.

- Rooms directly above the theaters will be noisy during the evenings. We've stayed in a room directly above the Walt Disney Theatre on the *Magic* and heard music from the shows loud and clear.

- Some guests find that rooms directly below the pools (**Midship Deck 10** on the *Dream* and *Fantasy,* **Midship Deck 8** on the *Magic* and *Wonder*) are noisy during the day, with guests dragging deck chairs overhead.

- Mechanical noise from elevators is typically minimal, but there will be more foot traffic the closer you are to an elevator.

- Guests with mobility issues may find it helpful to be close to an elevator; those hallways are long and narrow.

- Staterooms at the far-Aft end of the ship will have the most panoramic ocean views. If staring at the sea is priority, these rooms are the ones to get. However, some guests find the far-Aft staterooms on **Deck 10** of the *Dream* and *Fantasy* (**10158–10658**) too noisy—their verandahs are directly below the outdoor seating for the Cabanas buffet.

- The Starboard side of your ship will face the island if you're docked at Castaway Cay. If you have a room with a view, consider whether you'd prefer to gaze at the island or the water.

- Stateroom location may affect your comfort if you have trouble with motion sickness (see page 60).

- Some staterooms come preconfigured with enhanced communication for deaf and hearing-impaired guests.

- In addition to the stated room capacity, also consider the number of separate sleep surfaces. Will the members of your party be comfortable sleeping together on the number of beds in the room? (See pages 106 and 107.)

If particular stateroom features are important to you, you may find it helpful to work with a DCL-savvy travel agent, who is likely to be well versed in the distinct characteristics of specific cabins.

LINKING STATEROOM RESERVATIONS: WHEN COVID CRASHES THE PARTY

PRE-PANDEMIC, THE CONCEPT of a travel party was somewhat fluid. Certainly it included the people in your stateroom. It likely included members of your family booked into other staterooms, if you were sailing with them. Your party might also have included friends, or even acquaintances, with whom you wanted to have dinner or go on an excursion on your sailing. The more people linked to your reservation, the merrier.

In the post-COVID era, however, creating a travel party requires a bit more thought, specifically **if your group includes kids.** Just before press time, DCL dropped its requirement for COVID testing at the port for sailings departing from ports in the US; however, unvaccinated children ages 11 and younger must still get tested before their sail date.

If an unvaxxed child tests positive for COVID, chances are good that everyone in your party will be unable to sail, regardless of whether you've had any in-person close contact with the positive child in the previous weeks or months. (DCL *may* cut you some slack here, but you shouldn't count on it.) This means you'll need to give serious thought to whether you want to tie your long-awaited cruise to the potential medical misfortunes of others—particularly those befalling *someone else's* kids.

Consider the following situations, all of which assume there are unvaxxed kids under 12 in the mix. (*Note:* If you're planning a DCL European cruise, these sailings have different testing requirements at press time. If they're

COVID TIP

If your cruise party includes kids, we strongly recommend that they get all vaccines they qualify for. Vaccination isn't a magic bullet, of course, but it's the best way to prevent a positive test result from taking a wrecking ball to your vacation plans—or someone else's.

still in place when you sail, these requirements could impact adults as well as kids in your travel party. See page 54 for more information.)

- **You, your spouse, and your three kids—ages 6, 13, and 15—live together and are staying in one stateroom.** If the 6-year-old tests positive for COVID, then you'll all be denied boarding. Though it's an unfortunate situation, it's the most cut-and-dried of the ones posed here—the positive child has been in close contact with everyone else in the group, and as a nuclear family, you'd likely want to sail only if the entire party is able to.

- **You and your spouse live together and are booked into the same stateroom. You're traveling with your sister, her wife, and their 11-year-old son, who live together and are booked into another stateroom.** Before arriving at the port, you hadn't seen your sister or her family for a year. Pre-pandemic, you absolutely would have wanted to link your reservations, because it had been a while since you've seen them, and sitting together at dinner would've given everybody a chance to catch up. Post-pandemic, however, if your reservations were linked and your nephew were to test positive for COVID, there's a strong possibility that none of you would be able to board. Do you still want your reservations to be linked in this case? That's a call you'd have to make. We don't know you or your family; thus, we don't know what the implications would be if you took one course of action versus the other.

- **You and your spouse live together and are booked into the same stateroom, and you're thinking of linking your reservations with those of three other couples you met on a previous cruise. One of the couples is traveling with their 8-year-old daughter.** You thought it would be fun to get to know these couples better, though you've had no in-person contact and only minimal online contact with them since your previous trip. Pre-pandemic, you might have linked your reservations so you could eat as a group and maybe experience a few shore excursions together. But if the 8-year-old tests positive before you're due to sail, then there's a good chance that all or at least some of you would be unable to make the trip. Do you still want your reservations linked in this situation? Probably not. If you have little flexibility or vacation time in the coming year to reschedule your cruise (say, because you're a schoolteacher), *definitely* not.

If, out of an abundance of caution, you've decided not to link your stateroom reservations in the second and third examples, there's no reason your party can't have a great time together anyway (assuming everyone gets cleared to sail). Even if you don't do port adventures or eat dinner as a group, you can still eat at the buffet, hang out at the pool, or catch some shows; the grown-ups can also meet for cocktails or book dinner at one of the adult-dining venues.

PART FOUR

ARRIVING, GETTING YOUR SEA LEGS, *and* DEPARTING

TRANSPORTATION *to* YOUR CRUISE

CHOOSING A DEPARTURE PORT BASED ON TIME AND MONEY

THE LOCATION OF YOUR DEPARTURE PORT can affect the transportation cost of your cruise. Driving yourself to the port, of course, is your least expensive option if you live within a reasonable distance. If you'll be flying to the port, though, you need to think about not only money but also time and logistics.

> *unofficial* **TIP**
> If you're flying in from North America for a DCL European cruise, consider arriving two days before you sail. This will not only serve as a buffer against flight cancellations but will also give you a bit of extra time to recover from jet lag.

In past editions, we've recommended flying in at least a day before you sail. Postpandemic, we want to add glow-in-the-dark paint, multicolored glitter, and flashing neon lights to this advice.

At press time, air travel in the United States was, as the kids say nowadays, a hot mess, with flight cancellations and schedule changes at an all-time high. During one particularly fraught weekend during spring 2022, more than 400 guests booked on a sailing of the *Magic* didn't get to cruise due to a raft of canceled flights. **Don't let this happen to you.**

GETTING TO AND FROM THE PORT

MOST NORTH AMERICAN DCL GUESTS have three options for getting to their departure destination: booking transportation through Disney, booking through a third-party service, or driving themselves. The following section covers all three options in detail.

Using Disney Transportation from the Airport or a Disney-Approved Hotel

If you're flying to **Orlando International Airport** (**MCO**), you can use DCL's shuttle service to get to Port Canaveral. Per-person fares are $78 round-trip, $39 one-way, and free for kids under age 3. DCL recommends that your flight into Orlando arrive by **1:45 p.m.** on embarkation day and that your flight out on debarkation day depart after **11:30 a.m.** As we advise above, however, arriving at least a day in advance is ideal.

DCL also provides shuttle service from airports in other cities, as well as to and from select hotels near each port (see next section for information pertaining to Walt Disney World). Depending on the destination, prices range from about $18 to about $55. See tinyurl.com /DisneyCruiseTransfers for details.

The shuttle is convenient, particularly if you're in an unfamiliar country, but understand that the convenience comes at a cost. Before a fall 2016 Canadian Coastline sailing on the *Magic*, for example, guests staying at the Disney-approved New York Marriott Marquis in Times Square were offered transfers to the terminal for $35 *per person,* or $140 for a family of four. The Manhattan Cruise Terminal is only about a mile from the Marriott—easily walkable if you don't have a lot of luggage. (At the time, DCL charged the same $35 to drive Walt Disney World hotel guests to Port Canaveral.) To be fair, Disney later reduced the price from $35 to $20 per person, but it's still 80 bucks for a shuttle when you could walk to the terminal for free.

To arrange a shuttle, call ☎ 800-951-3532 or go to tinyurl.com /DCLMyReservations. Unless you're told otherwise (the DCL website is vague about this), assume that a uniformed greeter will be stationed near the airport baggage-claim area holding either a DCL sign or a sign with your party's name on it.

For additional options for getting from MCO to WDW, Port Canaveral, and other destinations, see the website for the **Greater Orlando Aviation Authority** (orlandoairports.net/parking-transportation).

Using Disney Transportation from Walt Disney World to Port Canaveral

DCL also provides shuttle service from on-property hotels at Walt Disney World. Per-person prices are the same as for the airport shuttle ($78 round-trip, $39 one-way, free for kids under 3).

LUGGAGE TRANSFER If you're taking a DCL cruise after staying at a WDW hotel *and* you've booked your transportation to the port through Disney, cruise representatives can transfer your luggage directly from your hotel room to your ship's stateroom.

Contact DCL at least three days before you leave home to take advantage of this service. They'll ask you how many bags you have and tell you when and where to meet for pickup. They'll also give you instructions on what to do with your bags—typically, you'll simply leave them in your hotel room, with your DCL luggage tags attached, and Disney will transfer them directly to your stateroom.

Surprisingly, this service may not be as efficient as you'd expect, as this reader reports:

> *The staff at Pop Century Resort wants nothing to do with helping you get ready for your cruise. When I stopped at the Concierge desk to ask about luggage transfer, they gave me a card with the DCL phone number on it and told me to call them myself. When I called, I got an automated message telling me what time we would be picked up, but it didn't say where to meet or what to do with our bags. We finally got printed instructions about the port transfer at 9:30 p.m.*

Note: Pre-pandemic, port-transfer buses left Walt Disney World and MCO throughout the morning on embarkation days. Guests sailing immediately post-pandemic received the following notification:

> *For Guests with transfers included with their cruise vacation, motorcoach transportation from the Orlando International Airport to the port in Port Canaveral, Florida, will begin at approximately 11:30 a.m. on the day of embarkation. Walt Disney World Resort Guest motorcoach transportation will begin at approximately 12:00 noon on the day of embarkation.*

If you have a preferred airport (for budget reasons, convenience to where you live, or the like) that isn't served by Disney, you'll have to arrange your own ground transportation to the port. For sailings out of Galveston, Texas, for example, you can arrange transfers from Houston's George Bush Intercontinental Airport but not from its other major airport, William P. Hobby; for cruises sailing from New York City, DCL provides transportation to the terminal from JFK and LaGuardia but not from Newark International (in New Jersey).

MINNIE VANS Disney, in cooperation with Lyft, launched this shuttle service in 2017 as a perk for Walt Disney World hotel guests. Minnie Vans—painted red with white polka dots—shuttle guests between Disney World and MCO; in late 2018, service from WDW or the airport to Port Canaveral was added for guests combining a WDW resort vacation with a DCL cruise.

Note: Minnie Van service restarted at WDW in June 2022 but hasn't yet resumed for DCL guests at the time of this writing. We mention it here assuming that it will return eventually—and when it does, expect it to be expensive. (A one-way trip to Port Canaveral cost a flat $250 in 2019.)

Third-Party Shuttle Services

The easiest, cheapest way to get from the airport to your hotel or to the terminal is likely **Uber** or **Lyft**. Prices are typically for up to four people in a single car rather than the per-person rate that Disney charges. If, however, you have more than four people in your cruise group or you have three people with a lot of luggage, you may want to use a third-party shuttle service instead.

GALVESTON Galveston Express (☎ 409-762-4397, galvestonexpress .com) offers both shared and private transfers, with the former being less expensive. From Hobby Airport in Houston to the Port of Galveston, transfers are about $65 per person, round-trip. **Galveston Limousine** (☎ 409-744-5466, galvestonlimo.com/airport-shuttle) has coach bus service from both Hobby and George Bush Airports several times per day. Round-trip fares are $60–$120 per person, with discounts available for booking online.

PORT CANAVERAL If you have a large party, a third-party service like **Mears Transportation** (☎ 407-423-5566, mearstransportation.com) offers cost savings as well as the ability to schedule your departure at your convenience. Round-trip prices between Orlando and Port Canaveral are about $320 for up to four people in a town car, $380 for up to five people in an SUV, or $410 for up to eight people in a luxury van. The Mears mobile app (iOS and Android) lets you track your driver's location and may also offer discount codes or coupons.

Another well-regarded car service in the area, **Happy Limo** (☎ 407-856-1280, happylimo.com) can provide service from the airport or Walt Disney World to the port in a range of vehicle types.

SAN DIEGO Blacklane (blacklane.com/en/cities-san-diego) offers one-way and round-trip transfers, with up to an hour of complimentary wait time and flight tracking. For shared options, check **Shuttlefare** (shuttle fare.com).

OTHER US PORTS SuperShuttle serves Miami, New Orleans, and New York City. Download its mobile app at supershuttle.com/app. **Mears Transportation** (see Port Canaveral, above) now serves most of the US and much of Canada; see tinyurl.com/MearsTransportation for more information.

Driving Yourself

The following section provides driving directions to DCL ports in California, Florida, New York, Louisiana, Texas, and Canada, along with information on parking rates at the various cruise terminals. See tinyurl .com/DeparturePorts for additional port addresses and customizable driving directions that incorporate Google Maps.

TO PORT CANAVERAL It takes about an hour to drive from Orlando to Port Canaveral under normal conditions. Traffic and road construction on the **Beachline Expressway** (**FL 528**), a toll road, can turn that 60-minute trip into a 3-hour ordeal. And because Port Canaveral and Orlando are linked by just three main roads with only limited connections between them, there are a couple of points along the Beachline Expressway where you have no way of taking an alternative route if traffic is delayed. Our advice is to allow at least 2½ hours for this trip.

If you're using GPS, enter this address as your destination: **Port Canaveral Terminal A, 9155 Charles M. Rowland Drive, Port Canaveral, FL 32920.** If your GPS doesn't recognize Port Canaveral as a city, substitute **Cape Canaveral** for Port Canaveral.

If you're driving from Walt Disney World, the most direct route uses eastbound FL 536 to the Central Florida GreeneWay (FL 417) and then to the Beachline Expressway. The GreeneWay and Beachline are toll roads, so have **$10 in cash** on hand for the round-trip.

*un**official* **TIP**

Text the location and a photo of your parking spot to other members of your group before you leave the lot. This will help you remember where you parked when you return from your cruise.

You'll be on the Beachline almost the entire way to Port Canaveral. Once you arrive, you'll find that the port's terminals function almost exactly like an airport's. The same kinds of signs for airline terminals are posted for cruise-line terminals at Port Canaveral. DCL ships usually depart from **Terminal A,** so you'll be looking for road signs to that effect. If you want to see what the drive looks like, YouTube has videos showing the exits, terminal, and parking options from a car passenger's perspective.

Once you arrive at Terminal A, you'll park and walk to the security checkpoint. Parking at Port Canaveral costs $17 per day, including the days of your arrival and departure. See portcanaveral.com/cruise /directions-parking for details.

TO MIAMI Driving here can be a challenge because of the traffic, one-way streets, and constant construction. Use this GPS address: **Port of Miami, 1015 North America Way, Miami, FL 33132.** Turn off your GPS once you've reached the port's bridge, then stay in the left lane and follow the signs to the parking garage closest to your terminal.

Like Port Canaveral, Miami has both parking garages and open-air lots. Parking is $22 per day; for more information, see miamidade .gov/portmiami/parking-information.asp.

If the lots closest to your ship are full, drop off some of your family and luggage near the cruise terminal, then swing around and find a spot in one of the other garages—the nearest open garages can be half a mile from the terminal, and there's no reason to have everyone haul their luggage that far.

Miami's ports are supposed to have shuttles running between the parking garages and terminals, but we've never seen them operating. (We *have* seen giant iguanas running around, though, so keep your eyes peeled.)

Once you're inside the terminal, you'll be directed to a check-in line. Miami's terminals are older and smaller than Port Canaveral's, but DCL's section is well maintained and efficient. After you check in, you'll go up a set of escalators and then through a long corridor to board the ship.

TO GALVESTON The port is about 71 miles from Houston's George Bush Intercontinental Airport—roughly a 90-minute drive with traffic. If you're just dropping off passengers, the GPS address to use for **Terminal 1** is **2502 Harborside Drive, Galveston, TX 77550; Terminal 2** is at **2702**

Harborside Drive, Galveston, TX 77550. If you're parking, the GPS address is **Port of Galveston Parking, 33rd Street and Harborside Drive, Galveston, TX 77550.** Parking fees range from $65 for four days to $170 for two weeks, with a $5 discount if you prepay online at portgalvestonparking. com. The closest lot to the terminal is **Galveston VIP Cruise Parking** (111 Rosenberg St.; ☎ 409-765-7300, galvestonvipcruiseparking.com). Prices start at $60 for a four-day cruise, and parking may be prebooked online.

TO NEW ORLEANS DCL uses the **Erato Street Cruise Terminal: 1100 Port of New Orleans Place, New Orleans, LA 70130.** From I-10 East or West, take Exit 234A onto US 90 Business West; then, just before US 90 Business crosses the Mississippi River, take Exit 11C for Tchoupitoulas Street. At the end of the exit ramp, turn right at the second stoplight onto Tchoupitoulas Street; then turn left at the next stoplight onto Henderson Street, and drive 2 blocks. Just after you cross the railroad tracks, turn left onto Port of New Orleans Place—*do not* try to access the cruise terminal from the entrance at Julia Street or Poydras Street.

The entrance to the parking garage is on top of the terminal and accessible via a circular ramp that you'll see as you approach the building. On the first floor of the garage (third floor of the terminal building), you'll receive directions to the off-loading area; luggage assistants will take your checked bags and deliver them to the ship. After you park ($90 for four days, $110 for five days, and $140 for seven days), take the elevator to the first-floor check-in and waiting area. You must show your boarding documents to enter the garage.

TO NEW YORK CITY The **Manhattan Cruise Terminal** is located at **711 12th Ave., New York, NY 10019,** about a mile from Times Square. Standard yellow-taxi rates (exclusive of tolls and tips) from area airports are as follows: John F. Kennedy International Airport, $52 flat rate; LaGuardia Airport, $25–$35; Newark International Airport, $80–$100 (negotiate the price with the driver in advance). From the Port Authority Bus Terminal, the fare is $8–$10.

If you're driving, note that cars enter the terminal at the intersection of **West 55th Street** and **12th Avenue/NY 9A** (known locally as the **West Side Highway** and the **Henry Hudson Parkway**). For detailed directions, including a customizable Google map, see nycruise.com/manhattan-terminal/directions.

*un*official **TIP**
For more information about yellow-taxi rates in New York City, see tinyurl.com/NYCTaxiFares.

Parking is located above each of the piers. To reach the official lot, drive up the viaduct ramp at 55th Street to the receiving area adjacent to the berths. Passengers driving themselves must park before bringing in bags to the second level for check-in.

Parking spaces are limited and available on a first-come, first-served basis. The daily rate for up to 10 hours (drop-offs and visitors) is $35; parking for 1–10 nights costs $40 per night, and extended parking (11–14 nights) is a flat $400.

Because hundreds of other parking lots are located within walking or taxi-drop-off distance to the port, it's quite possible to find nearby parking for substantially less than the port's rates. We're fans of the **Best**

Parking app; we have friends who rave about **SpotHero** and **ParkWhiz.** It's worth playing around with the various apps to see if one is better than another for a particular location or a particular day. Using Best Parking, we spot-checked the dates for DCL's 2022 New York sailings and found several lots with rates about 20% cheaper than the cruise terminal's.

The closest **subway lines** to the terminal are the **A, B, C, D,** and **1** at Columbus Circle. From Columbus Circle, walk south on Eighth Avenue, turn right onto 52nd Street, and continue to 12th Avenue and the terminal. The closest **MTA buses** are the **M57–57th Street Cross Town** and the **M31–57th Street/York Avenue.**

TO SAN DIEGO There is no parking directly at the terminal, but several lots are located nearby; some are within walking distance, while others offer shuttle service. See tinyurl.com/SanDiegoCruiseParking for more information.

TO VANCOUVER The port is about a 30-minute drive from the airport: **Cruise Terminal, 999 Canada Place, Vancouver, BC, Canada V6C 3C1.** Traffic in the several blocks surrounding Canada Place can be quite congested on cruise-departure mornings, so budget an extra 20 minutes or so if you're planning to arrive at the port during the late morning of your sail date.

The cruise terminal has 775 parking spaces, which cost $32 CDN (about $25 US) per day. Reservations are recommended and can be made online at canadaplace.westpark.com/reserve-a-space.html.

If you're a group of able-bodied adults with a reasonable amount of luggage, the easiest and cheapest way to get from the airport to the terminal is Vancouver's clean and efficient **subway–light rail service.** A one-way trip costs about $9 CDN (about $7 US) and takes about half an hour, with no transfers needed. Visit translink.ca for more information. (Input **YVR** as your start point and **Canada Place** as your end point.)

Adding Air Travel to Your Package? *Don't!*

*un*official **TIP**
Book your own flight, or use a travel agent who will consider your personal preferences and the logistics of your trip in addition to pricing.

We don't recommend letting Disney book your airfare—it will rarely save you money, not to mention you'll lose control over the details of your flight. We've been cautioned by both Disney-specialist travel agents and a Disney cast member that the booking agents generally don't pay attention to things like layovers, departure times, airports, the type of plane, or other particulars that can turn a good trip into a logistical headache. You may also find that refunds are more difficult to obtain if you arrange your flight through Disney.

If you're looking for bargains on airfare, your first stop should be a website such as **Expedia, Google Flights, Kayak, Orbitz, Priceline,** or **Travelocity;** many of these sites will also find you discounts on hotels and rental cars. Sites like **Airfare Watchdog** (airfarewatchdog.com) and **Scott's Cheap Flights** (scottscheapflights.com) can send you alerts about airfare discounts.

■ *The* **DAY** *Before* **YOUR CRUISE**

STAYING AT A LOCAL HOTEL THE NIGHT BEFORE

YOUR CRUISE WILL START ON TIME whether you're on the ship or not. Again, we strongly recommend arriving at your departure destination one day or more before you sail and spending the night at a local hotel. Yes, it adds another day to your trip's length and lodging adds to your trip's cost—but we think the peace of mind you get from knowing you'll make your cruise is worth it.

You can book your pre- or post-cruise hotel stay through Disney as part of your vacation package, no matter which port you're sailing from. This has its advantages and disadvantages:

THE PROS Disney has vetted the property, so you're unlikely to end up in a dump. Plus, transportation to/from the port will be seamless if you've also purchased ground transfers (see page 119).

THE CONS Your choices of properties and price points are generally limited to chains like Hilton, Hyatt, and Marriott. If you want to stay at a hip boutique hotel, you'll probably have to book it on your own.

For the type A trip planner, booking a hotel through Disney can feel (to use a travel metaphor) like flying blind. Before one DCL Alaskan cruise, for instance, we had Disney book our pre-trip accommodations at the Fairmont Vancouver Airport Hotel. Because we booked through DCL, we received no direct information about our room reservation—not even a confirmation number. Then, about six weeks before our trip, we called the Fairmont to find out what type of room we were booked in, only to be told that they didn't know. As it turns out, Disney doesn't send your hotel your room preferences—or even your name—until about two weeks before you check in.

If you're driving to the port, most hotels near cruise terminals offer inexpensive parking and shuttle transportation. There are exceptions, of course, but parking rates are often substantially less than what you'd pay at the terminal. In Port Canaveral, for example, parking at many hotels costs less than $10 per day, compared with $17 per day to park at the terminal.

If You're Cruising out of Port Canaveral

There are advantages to spending the night in either Port Canaveral or Orlando. Staying in Port Canaveral means you're just minutes from the terminal. You can enjoy a relaxed breakfast on the morning of your cruise, take a swim in the hotel pool, and pick up any last-minute items you might need. The main downside of staying here is that there's not as much stuff to do in Port Canaveral as there is in Orlando. Plus, the attractions may or may not be convenient to your hotel, or they may require booking in advance.

Our favorite hotel in Port Canaveral is the **Residence Inn Cape Canaveral Cocoa Beach** (8959 Astronaut Blvd.; ☎ 855-406-1162,

YOUR DCL ARRIVAL TIMELINE

THE FOLLOWING ASSUMES you'll be arriving at your embarkation point a day before you sail and that you're sailing out of the United States.

2+ Weeks Before Your Trip

- **Double-check DCL's latest vaccination and testing requirements** (see tinyurl.com /DCLKnowBeforeYouGo), and **recheck them religiously** as your sail date approaches. DCL modified its requirements several times while this edition was in production, so make sure you don't get caught off-guard by any last-minute changes that may occur before your sailing.
- **Make sure that you and everyone in your party ages 12 and older are fully vaccinated** (see page 50 for specifics). Also make sure that every adult in your party has a Safe Passage account (see page 51) and that everyone's proof of vaccination gets uploaded to the Safe Passage website. Finally, make sure that all unvaccinated children in your party get tested for COVID before embarkation day. Testing at the port is no longer required, but unvaxxed kids on back-to-back cruises will need to be tested between sailings. **Vaxxed guests are exempt from pre-trip testing as of November 2022.**

    Note: Unvaxxed children under age 12 may be prohibited from leaving the ship, depending on the local regulations in port. See pages 54 and 55 for more information.

3 Days Before Your Trip

- **If you have kids under age 12 in your party,** get them tested for COVID-19 now. **Only PCR or NAAT tests are accepted.** Upload their proof of testing to Safe Passage as soon as the results are available, and print out backup copies of these results to bring to the port.

2 Days Before Your Trip

- **Check in for your flight.**
- **Be sure that you want to commit to any port adventures you've previously reserved.** This is your last chance to cancel without a penalty.
- **Make sure that everyone's passports, vaccination cards,** test results, port-arrival forms, and other necessary ID/documents are packed in your carry-on bags. Also make sure that everyone's Safe Passage QR codes (see page 51) are either printed out and packed or saved to a mobile device.
- **Stock up on face coverings.** At press time, you don't have to wear a mask to get on the ship or in most instances once you're on board, but you will still need face coverings in a few specific circumstances. See page 55 for more information; also see page 73 for our packing checklists.
- **Confirm your transportation to the port.**

1 Day Before Your Trip

- **Put the DCL luggage tags** (that is, the ones you received in the mail) on your bags.
- **Make sure to have some small bills handy** for tipping the porters at the terminal.

Embarkation Day

- **Download the DCL Navigator app** (see page 137) if you haven't done so already. **Don't put this off until you're already on the ship.**
- **Take the health questionnaire** (see page 56), either on the Navigator app or at the link that was emailed to you.

At the Cruise Terminal

- **Show up at your designated arrival time,** with port-arrival forms, passports and ID, Safe Passage QR codes, and all other important documents at the ready. *Remember:* Showing up early means you'll just have to wait to be admitted.
- **Give your large pieces of luggage**—including anything unlikely to fit through the X-ray scanner—to the porters.
- **Make your way inside the terminal** for the ID and security screenings. Have your documentation ready *before* you reach the first checkpoint. Be prepared to present your documents at any point—or at several points—before you board.
- **While waiting to board,** request any stateroom upgrades that you might be interested in. If you're able to connect to your ship's Wi-Fi in the terminal, fire up the Navigator app and start making tentative plans for after the ship leaves port.

tinyurl.com/ResidenceInnCanaveral). Its studio, one-bedroom, and two-bedroom suites sleep up to six people. There's a free breakfast buffet, along with plenty of off-site dining options nearby; other amenities include a fitness center and free Wi-Fi.

The advantage to staying in Orlando, of course, is the plethora of entertainment and dining options at your fingertips. Some hotels, including the **Hyatt Regency Orlando International Airport** (9300 Jeff Fuqua Blvd.; ☎ 407-825-1234, tinyurl.com/HyattOrlandoAirport), also offer transportation to Port Canaveral for cruise guests. The downside to staying in Orlando is that you'll need to allow a couple of hours in the morning for the trip to the cruise terminal. See page 121 for details.

If You're Cruising out of Galveston

Located on a narrow strip of land in the Gulf of Mexico about 50 miles southeast of Houston, Galveston offers beautiful beaches, historic charm, excellent dining and shopping, and family fun at the Galveston Island Pleasure Pier. The century-old **Grand Galvez Hotel & Spa** (2024 Seawall Blvd.; ☎ 409-765-7721, grandgalvez.com) has tastefully appointed rooms, a spa and heated pool, and free shuttle service to the port, which is less than 2 miles away. Open off and on since 1839, **The Tremont House** is located in the Strand Historic District, just a few blocks from the port (2300 Ship's Mechanic Row; ☎ 409-763-0300, thetremonthouse.com). Like the Grand Galvez, the Tremont House is historic and luxurious; while it doesn't have a pool or spa, its location near downtown is better for people who want to explore the area on foot. Both hotels offer AAA, AARP, and other discounts.

If you'd rather spend the night near the Pleasure Pier, the **Clarion Pointe Galveston** (2300 Seawall Blvd.; ☎ 409-356-9853, tinyurl.com/ClarionPointeGalveston) is a 5-minute walk away.

If You're Cruising out of Miami

The advantage to staying in Miami is that it's a big city with plentiful tourist attractions and world-class shopping. The main downsides are traffic and parking: most hotels near the Port of Miami charge about as much for parking (around $20 per day) as the port itself ($22 per day).

The **Holiday Inn Port of Miami–Downtown** (340 Biscayne Blvd.; ☎ 305-371-4400, tinyurl.com/HIPortOfMiami), is located within a mile of the port. Restaurants, shopping, and other activities are just a short walk or drive away; there's also an on-site fitness center and high-speed Wi-Fi. On-site parking is limited, however.

The **Courtyard by Marriott Miami Downtown** (200 SE Second Ave.; ☎ 305-374-3000, tinyurl.com/CourtyardMiamiDowntown) is also conveniently located and offers amenities similar to the Holiday Inn's.

If You're Cruising out of New Orleans

Known for its amazing food, freewheeling atmosphere, and rich history, the Big Easy is a great place to start your cruise. On the budget end of the lodging spectrum, **Hampton Inn & Suites New Orleans Convention Center** (1201 Convention Center Blvd.; ☎ 504-566-9990, tinyurl.com/HamptonInnNolaCC) is within walking distance of the port; a free cruise shuttle is available. The **New Orleans Marriott Warehouse Arts District** (859 Convention Center Blvd.; ☎ 504-613-2888, tinyurl.com/MarriottNolaCC) is slightly more upscale; like the Hampton Inn, it's within walking distance of the port and has a free shuttle.

More-interesting places to stay are located in and around the French Quarter. **Hotel Mazarin** (730 Bienville St.; ☎ 504-851-7300, hotel mazarin.com) offers luxurious boutique accommodations. The **Ace Hotel New Orleans** (600 Carondelet St.; ☎ 504-900-1180, acehotel.com/new-orleans) has a youthful vibe and a fun bar scene.

If You're Cruising out of New York City

A couple of reliable and moderately priced choices near the terminal are the **Row NYC** (700 Eighth Ave.; ☎ 888-352-3650, rownyc.com) and the **Hampton Inn Manhattan–Times Square North** (851 Eighth Ave.; ☎ 212-581-4100, tinyurl.com/hamptoninn-nyc-manhattan). If you have Bonvoy hotel points, the **AC Hotel New York Times Square** (tinyurl.com/ACHotelNYC) typically offers a reasonable exchange rate; the rooms are small, but the service is excellent.

The rooms at the **Sheraton New York Times Square Hotel** (811 Seventh Ave.; ☎ 212-581-1000, sheratonnewyork.com) are somewhat larger by New York standards; plus, the Sheraton is one of the closest major hotels to the port.

If You're Cruising out of San Diego

Disney fans, you're in luck—you can stay at **Disneyland** before your trip! Getting from Anaheim to the San Diego cruise terminal typically takes less than 3 hours (with traffic). The **Disneyland Hotel** (1150 Magic Way; ☎ 714-778-6600, disneylandhotel.com) is our favorite hotel on Disney property, while **Disney's Paradise Pier Hotel** (1717 S. Disneyland Drive; ☎ 714-999-0990; tinyurl.com/ParadisePierHotel) is usually the least expensive choice. The luxurious **Grand Californian Hotel & Spa** (1600 S. Disneyland Drive; ☎ 714-635-2300, tinyurl.com/Grand Californian) is within easy walking distance of the Disney California Adventure theme park.

In addition to Disney's hotels, many good off-site hotels are situated close to the parks. For instance, the **Howard Johnson Anaheim** (1380 S. Harbor Blvd.; ☎ 714-776-6120, hojoanaheim.com) is directly across the street from the park entrance.

In San Diego, try the iconic **Hotel del Coronado** (1500 Orange Ave.; ☎ 800-468-3533, hoteldel.com). Its red-gabled roof and white walls provided architectural inspiration for the Grand Floridian Resort at Walt Disney World; the exteriors were also featured in the 1959 comedy classic *Some Like It Hot*.

If You're Cruising out of Vancouver

The **Pan Pacific Vancouver** (999 Canada Place, Ste. 300; ☎ 604-662-8111, panpacificvancouver.com) is posh and pricey, but it's also incredibly convenient to the port. Also pricey (and fabulous!) is the **Shangri-La Vancouver** (1128 W. Georgia St.; ☎ 604-689-1120, shangri-la.com /en/vancouver/shangrila), which has spectacular

*un*official **TIP**
If you're planning to fly home from Vancouver, you must check in **exactly 1–3 hours** before your departure—you can't check in earlier or later.

views of the ocean and mountains, huge marble baths, and a friendly staff. A more economical option is the **Metropolitan Hotel Vancouver** (645 Howe St.; ☎ 604-687-1122; metropolitan.com/vanc), near the Granville Station Expo Line stop.

GET *in the* BOAT, FOLKS!

CHOOSING A PORT-ARRIVAL TIME

PRE-PANDEMIC, DCL GUESTS were able to check in online for their cruise at least 75 days in advance, based on their Castaway Club level, and while online check-in was recommended, it wasn't required. At press time, however, all guests are required to check in online **no more than 30 days and no fewer than 3 days** befor sailing, using the **My Reservations** section of the DCL website (see page 47). In addition to providing Disney with information about your preferred onboard payment method and travel plans, you'll also select the time you'll arrive at the port, upload all necessary documents, and get your boarding assignment. When you arrive at your assigned time, you should be able to board the ship not long after your party completes the required port-security screening.

At the time of this writing, port-arrival times are tightly regulated—much more so than they were pre-pandemic. To promote social distancing in the cruise terminal, all DCL passengers, including Concierge guests and Platinum Castaway Club guests (who

COVID TIP
In the COVID era, port-arrival times are strictly enforced. **You will not be admitted to the port area if you arrive early**.

were previously allowed to arrive whenever they wanted to), are required to select and abide by a specific port-arrival time.

SCOTT'S ARRIVAL ADVICE *by Scott Sanders*

IF YOU'RE NOT DRIVING YOURSELF TO THE PORT, arrange your pre- and post-cruise transportation yourself in advance. Arriving a day ahead adds to the cost of your trip, but it also creates a safety buffer in the event of a delayed flight or the like.

When it's time to go, assign someone in your party to be in charge of the check-in process, and have each person's government-issued ID in hand to present with the port-arrival QR code. The check-in process is much quicker if you have all your documents ready.

While you wait to board the ship inside the terminal, see if you can connect to your ship's Wi-Fi network (**DCL-GUEST**). If you can, launch the **DCL Navigator app** (see page 136) to browse the embarkation-day activities or see if there are openings for popular onboard activities or port adventures that may not have been available prior to arrival.

Need to change a dinner seating or you don't like your assigned rotation? Check the Navigator app and arrive at the designated location before the listed time to increase your chances of having your change request granted. This is also the time to make adult-dining reservations if you didn't do so previously online, or if you want to make additional reservations.

Take some time to review the deck plans for your ship. This will help familiarize you with its layout and make it easier to get around.

CHECKING IN AT THE TERMINAL

HAVE YOUR TRAVEL AND HEALTH DOCUMENTS, along with your government-issued ID, ready as soon as you arrive. Many terminals, including Port Canaveral, have an initial security checkpoint outside the perimeter to ensure that only ticketed passengers enter.

At Port Canaveral, you'll present your port-arrival forms for scanning, then head to a luggage drop-off zone where you'll unload any luggage you can't carry aboard yourself—just to be safe, drop off any luggage that you're not sure will fit through the X-ray scanner during the security screening. **Note: COVID testing at the terminal has been discontinued for all US sailings as of November 2022.**

After you and your party are cleared to proceed, you'll be directed to the passport/ID checkpoint just inside the terminal's entrance; then you'll pass through a metal detector while your luggage undergoes X-ray scanning. At the terminal, security screening is somewhat like that at the airport, but here they're looking for slightly different things. Not surprisingly, weapons of any sort are forbidden, but you can bring liquids like shampoo or cosmetics in any quantity you like within reason (a half-dozen Costco-size jugs of Head & Shoulders would probably raise eyebrows). You may also bring nonalcoholic beverages (say, a case of water) as long as they're factory-sealed. You can't, however, bring homemade food or fresh produce onto the ship:

they could be contaminated, possibly making you *and* others sick. See page 75 for more information about prohibited items.

After you've passed the security screenings, your party will be issued paper slips about the size of an index card. Each slip has a QR code on it. The code includes your stateroom number, your boarding-group number, and information about your assembly-drill station. When your boarding group is called, head to the gangway, present the cast member with your QR slips, and proceed onto the ship.

unofficial **TIP**

You'll need to provide and scan QR codes at various points both before and during your sailing. If your phone can't read QR codes directly, download an app that can.

BABY, YOU'VE ARRIVED!

JUST BEFORE YOU STEP ABOARD, photographers will offer to take a photo of your party. If this is important to you, a quick mirror check in the restroom and dressing in something you'd like recorded for posterity is a good idea. Otherwise, just politely decline and keep moving.

When you reach the atrium, a cast member will ask for your party's last name and then announce your arrival over the PA system—think a butler announcing VIPs at a fancy party. (When embarking on the *Wish,* kids are given a plastic "Wishing Star" wand as a souvenir.)

Some cruisers get a kick out of the pomp and ceremony of being announced, while others find it cringey and intrusive. It could also be awkward when there are people with different last names in the same party (blended families, for instance).

If you don't feel comfortable giving out your last name, you can provide just your first names, or you can even make something up— it's all in good fun. "Thurston and Lovey Howell" are the preferred aliases of Len and his partner, Laurel; we've also heard of parties calling themselves "The Addams Family," "The Von Trapp Family," and "The Three Amigas." (We don't think "The Seymour Butts Family" would fly, however.)

After your arrival has been proclaimed, you'll be reminded to complete the muster drill (or **assembly drill,** as DCL calls it; see 135) before sail-away time. When you reach your designated lifeboat station, you'll scan a QR code on a sign to verify that you know where your station is. Cast members are on hand to help if you're not sure what to do.

As COVID-19 protocols evolve, you can expect embarkation procedures to be a moving target, with frequent changes and more-than-occasional confusion.

YOUR FIRST AFTERNOON ABOARD

WHILE YOU STILL HAVE ACCESS to your phone's regular data plan, download the latest version of the **DCL Navigator app** (see page 136). If you weren't planning to buy Wi-Fi access (see page 137), you'll have to pony up in order to download it on board. *Note:* For practical purposes, not having the app installed isn't an option.

Disney Cruise Line for Introverts

AS A QUICK GLANCE at the Navigator app shows, a Disney cruise includes lots of activities for people with a social bent: karaoke, dance parties, and so on. All that hustle and bustle could be overwhelming, though, for an introvert or someone with sensory-processing issues. If that's you, here a few suggestions for making your cruise more enjoyable.

- **Choose the right cabin.** A stateroom with a verandah (see page 108) lets you take in the ocean views without your having to venture onto the public decks.

- **Request your own dinner table.** DCL sometimes seats small parties with other guests in the main dining rooms. If eating with strangers isn't your cup of tea, call DCL at ☎ 800-951-3532 to request your own table. Alternatively, you can order room service or eat at one of the restaurants on the pool deck.

- **Time your meals to avoid crowds.** Breakfast and lunch at Marceline Market (*Wish*) and Cabanas (all other ships) can be bustling. Breakfast and lunch in the main dining rooms tend to be less frenetic.

- **Book time in Senses Spa's Rainforest (see pages 300 and 301).** This quiet, relaxing oasis is open to a limited number of guests.

- **Use the adults-only areas as much as possible.** The adult pool areas on board and Castaway Cay's Serenity Bay are much less raucous than the comparable family areas on both ship and shore.

- **Book your own port excursions, explore ports on your own, or just stay on the ship.** Because Disney's port adventures are group events, a private or self-guided tour may be more your speed. Likewise, staying on board when others are in port can feel like having the entire ship to yourself.

- **Don't overshare.** DCL tends to make a fuss about special occasions. If that's not your thing and you'll be celebrating your birthday on board, don't let the cruise staff know. If you're traveling with a group, make sure they respect your wishes.

- **Choose a less-popular sailing date on a less-crowded ship.** Sailings during the school year tend to be more empty than those during the summer and holidays. Take a look at stateroom availability—the more cabins available, the less crowded the ship—or ask a travel agent to help you find a sailing that's sparsely populated.

- **Communicate your needs to your stateroom attendant.** If you need quiet time in your cabin during certain hours, let your attendant know.

- **Make ample use of online communication.** The Navigator app lets you text Guest Services and other staff, minimizing your need to speak to someone in person.

- **Bring a quiet project.** Focusing on your knitting, working on a killer crossword, or reading the entire set of Bridgerton novels can keep you centered during downtime.

Immediately after boarding is a good time to make any last-minute reservations or finesse any aspects of your trip that you couldn't get exactly right online. Your first step should be to use the Navigator app to communicate with **Guest Services** or other ship staff.

Check with Guest Services if you want to tinker with your dining rotation or seating time. On one pre-pandemic cruise, for example, Erin and her husband traveled with three other couples, all of whom had different Castaway Club statuses. That meant they couldn't all reserve Palo for the same seating—they did end up with

unofficial **TIP**

If you need to speak with someone in Guest Services in person, DCL prefers that you use the Navigator app to schedule an appointment first. We've had good luck, though, with just walking up to the desk and asking for assistance.

Palo reservations, but at different seatings. A quick stop at Guest Services right after boarding fixed the issue, though, and the entire group was able to eat together at Palo after all. (See page 116 for our thoughts about linking your dinner plans with those of your friends post-pandemic.)

Many guests make a beeline for **Senses Spa** soon after boarding to check availability for treatments that weren't available earlier online, or to make reservations for the **Rainforest** (see pages 300 and 301).

Once guests have been cleared to go to their staterooms, you can head to your cabin, pick up your party's Key to the World Cards (see below), and drop off any bags you carried on. You may also see your stateroom attendant already sprucing up your cabin for the evening; this is a great time to introduce yourself and let them know if you have any special requests related to your room, such as your child's typical nap hours or your preferred room temperature.

There's a good chance you'll be hungry at this point. If you're in the mood for a buffet, head to **Marceline Market** (*Wish*) or **Cabanas** (all other ships); you can also grab a nosh at the adults-only coffee bar or one of the pool deck's quick-service eateries (on all ships except the *Wish*). Alternatively, check the Navigator app to see if one of the dining rooms is open.

If you're sailing from a warm-weather location, the **pool deck** will be full of guests swimming and lounging. And when we say "full," we mean packed—if you want to relax, don't go there. But feel free to pick up a drink at the beverage station or grab a burger or slice of pizza to tide you over until dinner.

The chaos comes to a head with the **Sail-Away Celebration:** think Champagne and confetti, Captain Stubing and Julie, Charo and Carol Channing. It's a fun way to start your cruise, but it's certainly not a must. (And if these references don't ring a bell, we encourage you to check out reruns of *The Love Boat* on MeTV. The theme song alone may or may not be the reason we're cruise junkies today.)

*un**official* **TIP**

On embarkation day, you'll likely see waiters walking around the pool deck with big trays, passing out fruity cocktails. Though refreshing, these drinks aren't free.

Your Key to the World Card Explained

Similar to Walt Disney World before 2014, Disney Cruise Line still uses the plastic, credit card–size **Key to the World (KTTW) Card** for onboard transactions, unlocking the door to your stateroom, and identification. There is, however, no equivalent of WDW's RFID-powered MagicBands on the ship: children in some of the kids' clubs will be issued wristbands for identification, but they don't have the same functionality as a MagicBand, and you must return them at the end of your voyage.

Pre-pandemic, guests received their KTTW Cards at the terminal. At the time of this writing, DCL guests board the ship with a paper slip containing a QR code (see previous page) and receive their

KTTW Cards in a sealed envelope on a shelf next to their stateroom door (see page 94).

Aside from serving as your stateroom key and an onboard charge card, your KTTW Card contains helpful information about your cruise. The first line just beneath the Disney Cruise Line logo lists the dates of your cruise. The second line lists the name of your ship, and next to that is either **A** for "adult" or **M** for "minor," indicating whether you're old enough to drink. The rest of that line may be blank or, if you've purchased land transfers from Disney, it will list a letter indicating what type of transfer you've paid for: **P** means "port," **R** means "resort" (if you've booked a combination cruise–WDW vacation), and **A** means "airport." Sometimes combinations of letters are used: for example, **PA** indicates a port-to-airport transfer.

The next two lines display your name and **Castaway Club** status (see page 85). A large single letter in the lower-left corner indicates your assigned lifeboat station, which you'll find during the embarkation-day assembly drill (see next page).

Shipboard Gifts Demystified

Many DCL cruisers arrive to find gifts in their staterooms (typically left on the bed) by DCL cast members. If you're a **Castaway Club** member, welcome-aboard stateroom gifts will be awaiting you upon your arrival. Gifts change every couple of years or so, but most recently we've seen seen things like luggage tags, sling-style backpacks, and soft-sided coolers emblazoned with the Castaway Club logo and/or the recipient's membership status. After they board, Platinum Castaway Club members may choose an additional gift such as a box of chocolates or a fruit plate.

On some **special sailings,** such as Marvel cruises and sailings that coincide with Christmas and New Year's Day, you'll receive additional holiday-themed stateroom gifts midcruise—say, a commemorative lithograph or a themed box of candy.

Concierge-level cruisers (see page 105) get exclusive items as well. **Disney Vacation Club** (**DVC**) members can expect to find a gift magnet on their door. DVC members booked on special members-only sailings also receive swag such as travel mugs or Disney-themed board games.

If you booked your cruise through a **travel agent,** you may find that he or she has sent you a token of appreciation such as a bottle of wine or a cheese plate.

If you don't have a particular special status with DCL but you'd like to give someone in your party a nice surprise—or if you'd like to treat yourself—order your own goodies in advance through the **Onboard Gifts** section of the DCL website (see page 302).

DUDE, WHERE'S MY LUGGAGE?

IF YOU'RE CRUISING WITH ANYTHING more than hand luggage—and you probably are—you'll be asked to leave your suitcases for screening when you arrive at the terminal. The next time you see your bags will be in front of your stateroom door, late on embarkation day. Suitcases are delivered to the hallway outside your stateroom throughout the afternoon and into the evening, and it's quite likely that some of your party will receive their bags earlier than others.

On almost every cruise, we've experience an hour or so of controlled panic as everyone's bags trickle in. Just in case, we keep at least one change of clothes, along with must-have items like medications, in a small bag that we carry onto the ship ourselves.

THE ASSEMBLY DRILL

THE US COAST GUARD REQUIRES that all cruise ship passengers complete a safety exercise—known as an **assembly drill** or a **muster drill**—where they learn how to put on a life jacket and where to gather on the ship to board the emergency lifeboats.

COVID TIP
The current assembly drill is far less chaotic and stressful than the pre-pandemic version, particularly for guests with sensory-processing issues.

Pre-pandemic, the DCL assembly drill was conducted entirely in person, with every guest participating at the same time. Post-pandemic, muster is a two-part process: Just after you board, a cast member will direct you to your assembly station, where other cast members are on hand to give you a quick briefing on procedures. You also scan a QR code on a sign at your station; this confirms that you know where the station is located. Later, you listen to information broadcast on your ship's PA system, wherever you happen to be on board

Your KTTW Card (see pages 133 and 134) lists your assigned lifeboat station; you'll also find it listed in the DCL Navigator app.

BARE NECESSITIES

YOUR CELL PHONE ON BOARD

PRE-PANDEMIC, IT WAS PERFECTLY POSSIBLE to take a DCL cruise without packing a cell phone. You could use a camera if you wanted to take photos, rely on paper sources of information, and call or text your family on the ship with a portable device called a Wave Phone.

Post-pandemic, however, managing the key aspects of your cruise while you're on board is virtually impossible without a smartphone or tablet. You'll need the **DCL Navigator app** (see next section) and other functions of your phone to text other members of your party contact onboard services, read restaurant menus, schedule activities, and more.

Many DCL guests lament losing the ability to unplug on a cruise, and we can sympathize. A veteran cruiser posted this comment in a discussion on DISboards:

I'm attached to my phone or computer 90% of the time I'm awake on any given day. I refuse to be a slave to my phone when cruising.

THE DCL NAVIGATOR APP

THE NAVIGATOR APP lists the daily schedule of events and activities on your ship, along with information about onboard entertainment, specials in the shops, and so on. Available free at the Apple App Store and the Google Play Store, the app works through the ships' onboard Wi-Fi, so you can keep your device in airplane mode while using it; you won't be charged for Wi-Fi if you're using it only with the app. To avoid unnecessary data charges, however, be sure to download the app to all of your family's mobile devices *before* you depart.

The app consists of five main categories: **Dining Information** (including the menus for your ship's dining rooms); **Deck Plans** (maps showing each floor of the ship); the hours of the various ship services (shops, gym, and so on); **Activity Schedules; Debarkation Information** (what you need to do at the end of your vacation); and **Onboard Chat.**

Onboard Chat, our favorite feature, allows you to text other passengers at no charge over Wi-Fi. It's as easy and intuitive to use any other messaging app. Choose from DCL-specific emojis featuring Disney, Marvel, and *Star Wars* characters to spice up your messages. You can also now use the Navigator chat feature to interact with Guest Services and other staff departments on the ship.

The Navigator app also shows you **complete menus** for every restaurant on the ship, usually several days in advance. Of course, you could always wait until you sit down at your table to see what's cooking, but in scenarios such as the ones on the following page, it helps to know what's being served ahead of time:

1. If you or others in your crew are picky eaters and the dinner menu on a particular night is a hard pass, you can adjust your dining plans accordingly.

2. If, on the other hand, your dining room will be serving something you really like on a night when you have adult-dining reservations at Palo or Remy, you can try rebooking those for another night.

3. If you see something delish on the menu of a *different* dining room, you can have them bring it to *your* dining room. (Yes, you can order anything served at any of the three main dining rooms—not just the one you're assigned to!)

Other nice features of the app include the ability to set alarms to remind you when favorite activities are starting, plus real-time updates to the ship's schedule.

PRE-CRUISE FEATURES In addition to keeping you in the loop during your cruise, the app functions much as the DCL website does for pre-trip planning. You can link existing reservations, change your stateroom, make payments on your cruise, and complete online check-in (see page 69). You can also modify your dinner seatings, make special dining requests, add Disney's trip insurance (under certain conditions; see page 58), add ground transportation (see page 119), and access details about your air transportation. (*Note:* Some of these features may not be available if you've booked your cruise through a travel agent.)

BON VOYAGE, *PERSONAL NAVIGATOR* From 2018 until shortly before cruising was paused in early 2020, a paper guide called the ***Personal***

Navigator was available at the Guest Services desk by request. (It was delivered to each stateroom before 2018.)

It seems unlikely that DCL will bring back hard-copy *Navigator*s post-pandemic; that said, some guests miss them:

> *Trying to look up activities on a small screen is time-consuming and often frustrating. I think a good compromise would be to have a simple, single-page paper grid of all activities available at Guest Services the night before for those who want it.*

> *I would be totally fine with the app if they would provide a PDF in the same format as the paper* Navigator, *so I could see a bird's-eye view of the events rather than having to scroll to find what I want.*

CONNECT@SEA WI-FI

FOR MANY OF US, being offline for the duration of a cruise simply isn't an option. You can sign up for a special cruise-ship wireless plan with your mobile carrier (see page 70), or you can purchase Disney's onboard Wi-Fi, called **Connect@Sea.**

> *un***official** **TIP**
> See tinyurl.com/DCL NavigatorApp for our step-by-step instructions on using the app.

At press time, Connect@Sea was transitioning to a tiered, flat-rate pricing structure. The new system debuted during late spring 2022 on the *Magic,* continued with the *Fantasy* and *Wish,* and is still rolling out to the other ships.

Packages are available by the day or for the length of your cruise; the prices below are **per device.** Here are the details:

STAY CONNECTED ($10 PER DAY) This package lets you post text and pictures on social media, but you can't browse the web or check email.

BASIC SURF ($20 PER DAY) Adds full web and email access to the Stay Connected package.

PREMIUM SURF ($30 PER DAY) This plan gives you faster speeds than Stay Connected and Basic Surf. Premium Surf lets you do everything you can do using your phone's data plan or your home internet, **except** stream movies and TV shows. (Music and short videos, like Instagram stories and YouTube clips, stream just fine.)

You get small price breaks for multiple devices. For example, a seven-day Stay Connected package is $70 for one device, $126 for two devices, $182 for three, and $238 for four.

Depending on when you sail, your ship may still be selling the old Connect@Sea packages, which give you "buckets" of data in different amounts: **Pay as You Go** (25¢ per megabyte); **Small** (100MB, $19); **Medium** (300MB, $39); and **Large** (1GB, $89). Unlike the new packages, the old ones let you use a single account with multiple devices.

With the old system, the more remote your ship's location, the less reliable your connection was likely to be. For example, during one Northern European voyage that included a long sea day from Iceland to Scotland, we found that service was nonexistent.

In contrast, we've found the new service to be stable and reliable. It's not perfect—for instance, the Premium Surf Plan choked when we tried to upload video to the web—but we think there will be fewer glitches and outages than on the old system.

Here are our tips for using Connect@Sea:

1. Update your apps (including the Navigator app) and download movies, music, and other content **before** you board the ship. To do otherwise is a waste of time and money.

2. If you have a job-critical need for email, put an auto-responder on your account so that people will know your replies may be delayed. (You may or may not choose to state that the reason is that you're being slathered with exotic beauty substances at the spa.)

3. Disney now offers free **iMessage** (text only, not photos or video) to DCL guests. If you have an iPhone or iPad, you can connect with friends and family both on the ship and at home without incurring data charges. See page 70 for more information.

4. If you're having technical issues, check with the onboard Connect@Sea desk.

5. If your ship isn't offering the new Wi-Fi packages yet, note that your data is capped at the amount in your package, and you'll have to pay for more once it runs out. To conserve data, turn off the following settings on your phone or tablet: location services, background app refreshes, automatic app updates, email sync and cloud backup, and automatic video play.

ONBOARD SERVICES

EACH SHIP HAS A 24-HOUR **Guest Services** desk just off the lobby to answer questions, make reservations, and provide other help. You can contact Guest Services from your stateroom by pressing the Guest Services button on your phone; you may also contact them through the Onboard Chat function of the Navigator app.

The crew member you'll likely get to know best is your **stateroom attendant,** who will tidy your cabin after you depart in the morning and turn down your beds each night. You'll almost certainly see them more than any other crew member.

Given the nature of a cruise, you'll find that your stateroom attendant is in and out of your room much more often than a typical hotel housekeeper would be. This makes it particularly important to make ample use of your STATEROOM OCCUPIED sign if you plan to sleep late or nap for a couple of hours, or you don't want to be disturbed for a while otherwise.

AIRLINE CHECK-IN FOR SAILINGS ENDING AT PORT CANAVERAL OR MIAMI

EVEN BEFORE YOU BOARD THE SHIP, you can request airline check-in for your flight home by making arrangements at your terminal's check-in desk. To do this, provide the airline name and flight number(s), departure time and date, names of passengers as printed on their ticket(s), and the confirmation number(s) for each flight segment, or complete the Onboard Airline Check-In Form in your pre-cruise documentation.

While you're on board, you can ask Guest Services to check you in if you're flying home the day that your cruise returns to port; just stop by the Guest Services desk before 10 p.m. on your second night to make this request. This service is available to guests using DCL port transfer service and flying to a domestic location (including the US Virgin Islands and Puerto Rico) on **Alaska Airlines, American Airlines, Delta Air Lines, JetBlue,** or **United Airlines**. For cruises ending at Port Canaveral, the service is available for flights out of Orlando International Airport. For cruises ending in Miami, the service is available for flights out of Miami International Airport.

No matter when you register, your first flight's departure must be **after 11:30 a.m. on the day your cruise ends,** to ensure the ship has enough time to make it back. There's a limit of two bags per person, and each bag must weigh less than 50 pounds. (According to Disney, a few randomly selected passengers may be required to undergo additional screening at the airport; unfortunately, they're ineligible for early check-in.)

LAUNDRY SERVICES

SELF-SERVICE LAUNDRY FACILITIES are available on Decks 2, 6, and 7 of the *Magic* and *Wonder;* on Decks 2, 5, 6, 7, 8, 9, and 10 of the *Dream* and *Fantasy;* and on Deck 8 of the *Wish*. The laundry rooms are furnished with washers, dryers, irons, and detergent for purchase. It costs $3 to wash a load of clothes and another $3 to dry them; detergent costs another $1 per load.

In general, you'll find the laundry rooms less crowded on non–sea days, after 11 p.m., and before 7 a.m.; you will also likely find them easier to access on three- and four-night cruises originating in the US than on longer sailings.

Competition for washers and dryers often reaches *Hunger Games* levels of intensity during the dinner hour on most sailings, and on long European voyages, guests who traveled before their cruises or plan to do so afterward tend to make heavy use of the laundry facilities to keep their packing manageable.

In addition to do-it-yourself laundry, each ship offers **full-service laundry and dry-cleaning,** with pickup from and delivery to your stateroom. Just drop your clothes in the laundry/dry-cleaning bag hanging in your closet, and complete the attached paper form with any special cleaning instructions. Laundry service usually takes 24 hours, but we've had simple requests, such as laundering and pressing a couple of shirts, turned around the same day. There may be an additional charge for rush service.

Prices are subject to change, but for full-service laundry you can expect to pay about $4 for a men's dress shirt and about $2.50 for a T-shirt. Dry-cleaning is available for about $9 for a men's suit and $10 for an evening dress. Pressing is available for half the cost of laundry and dry-cleaning.

PORT ADVENTURES

IN ADDITION TO GUEST SERVICES, a separate **Port Adventures desk** on Deck 3 (*Magic, Wonder,* and *Wish*) or Deck 5 (*Dream* and *Fantasy*) handles booking for shore excursions. The staff is usually knowledgeable about the most popular excursions at each port. In addition to providing information about cost and time, they can typically answer questions regarding the appropriateness of a particular activity for the members of your family; they also can help you reschedule an activity if needed. (See Part Twelve for details.)

HEALTH SERVICES

THE ONBOARD MEDICAL STAFF is experienced in emergency and critical care, and they've developed protocols for COVID-19 screening and treatment. Appointments to evaluate COVID symptoms are free, and the onboard medical facilities are equipped with ventilators, oxygen, and laboratory and pharmacy services should COVID cases arise. The most common shipboard medical complaints are motion sickness and sunburn, although the staff has also seen its share of broken bones over the years.

*uno**fficial* **TIP**

If you have life-threatening allergies, **EpiPens** are available on a case-by-case basis at the Health Center on board and at First Aid on Castaway Cay. If you urgently need an EpiPen, tell the nearest cast member right away, or dial ☎ **7-3000** from any ship phone.

Your ship's **Health Center** (Deck 1 Forward; open 9:30–11 a.m. and 4:30–7 p.m.) can provide doses of basic over-the-counter and some prescription medicines; anything serious, such as surgery, will probably require an airlift to the nearest hospital. Be aware that use of the Health Center isn't free, and the rates are comparable to those of US hospitals (in other words, expensive), so check your insurance coverage before you leave home (see pages 56 and 58 for more on that). However, just like the First Aid Centers in the Disney parks, Health Services will often provide you with a dose or two of Tylenol or motion-sickness tablets at no charge.

Guest Services also stocks OTC medicines and first aid supplies—if all you need is an aspirin or a Band-Aid, that's a good first place to start. Also be aware that when the Health Center and the ship's stores are closed, Guest Services may be the only place to obtain diapers, tampons, or the like; limited supplies are typically available for free.

TIPPING

YOU'LL ENCOUNTER CREW MEMBERS throughout your cruise, many of whom you'll see several times per day and who will have a direct impact on the quality of your trip. Unless you request otherwise at Guest Services, a daily gratuity will be added to your stateroom bill every day for the four crew members most directly responsible for your well-being on the ship: your **stateroom host,** your **dining room server** (in charge of your food), your **assistant server** (in charge of your drinks), and the **head server** (or dining room manager). *Note:* Concierge-level staterooms also have an **assistant stateroom host.** (See pages 143 and 144 for our tipping recommendations for Concierge guests.)

The chart below shows the basic per-day tip amounts for these DCL crew members, for each member of your party. Thus, if you have four people in your family and you're taking a seven-night cruise, budget **$406 ($101.50 times four**) for the personnel listed. (See the sidebar on the next page for details on specific tipping procedures.)

STAFF MEMBER	Suggested Gratuity Per Day	Suggested Gratuity, 3 Nights	Suggested Gratuity, 4 Nights	Suggested Gratuity, 7 Nights
Stateroom Host	$4.75	$14.25	$19.00	$33.25
Dining Room Server	$4.75	$14.25	$19.00	$33.25
Assistant Dining Room Server	$3.75	$11.25	$15.00	$26.25
Head Dining Room Server	$1.25	$3.75	$5.00	$8.75
Total (Per Guest)	**$14.50**	**$43.50**	**$58.00**	**$101.50**

These suggested amounts are automatically added to your folio (stateroom account) based on the number of people in your cabin and your cruise length. Once on board, you can adjust these amounts or pay in cash by contacting Guest Services (open 24 hours a day).

Lines at Guest Services will be long on the last night of your cruise, so plan to make any adjustments sooner rather than later if you wish to avoid a wait. If it makes budgeting easier, you're welcome to prepay many of your gratuities weeks or months before boarding the ship. Call DCL or your travel agent to arrange this.

Here are our suggestions for tipping other DCL crew:

PORTERS People who handle your luggage at the port before or after your cruise should get **$1–$3 per bag.**

BARTENDERS AND DRINK SERVERS An **18%** gratuity is automatically added to all onboard purchases of alcohol, such as in the bars and dining rooms and by the pool deck. If you've received excellent service, by all means tip more.

CAFÉS Specialty-coffee purchases in the onboard cafés (**Cove Café** and **Vista Café**) have an **18%** gratuity automatically added. Again, you may add an additional tip using the Navigator app.

ROOM SERVICE Most room-service food is free, but it's customary to tip the crew member who brings your food: **$1–$2 per item,** or a minimum of **$5,** is the norm.

SPAS Tipping your esthetician, stylist, or manicurist about **20%** is customary. You can add the gratuity to your bill at the time of purchase.

CABANA HOSTS If you were lucky enough to snag a cabana at Castaway Cay, it's attended by a host who will check on you all day, bring you extra towels and snacks, and possibly give you a private golf-cart ride to or from the ship. Tips aren't mandatory but are customary. Tip in cash at a level that feels right to you.

HOW TO TIP ON A DISNEY CRUISE

ON THE LAST DAY OF YOUR CRUISE, you'll find a tip summary sheet in your stateroom, along with four small envelopes labeled "Server," "Assistant Server," "Head Server," and "Stateroom Host," but no instructions are provided on what to do with these items. Guests often find this confusing—here's an explanation.

The summary sheet shows the gratuity amounts billed to your onboard account—or amounts that you've prepaid—for each of these four crew members, plus four perforated strips showing individual gratuity amounts, one for each of these crew members.

If you're satisfied with the gratuity amounts, there's nothing more you need to do—your crew members will automatically receive your tip along with their regular pay; you can throw out the envelopes and keep the summary for your files. The following advice covers what to do in specific tipping situations.

- **If you plan to give your crew members the standard gratuities** but think it feels weird to leave on the last day without handing them anything, place the perforated strip from the summary sheet in the designated envelope, and hand it to the crew member on the last night of your voyage.

- **If you want to give one or more of your crew members an additional gratuity,** you can **(1)** place cash in the envelope and hand it to them on the last night of your voyage; **(2)** place both the perforated strip and the cash in the envelope and hand it to them on the last night of your voyage; **(3)** go to Guest Services and have them add the additional gratuities to your account; or **(4)** go to Guest Services, have them add additional gratuities to your account, and ask for a new summary form. Then remove the perforated strip of the new form, place it in the crew members' envelopes, and hand it to them on the last night of your voyage.

- **You can add a gift card to the envelope instead of cash.** Some guests feel uncomfortable carrying cash and don't want to deal with lines at Guest Services, but they do want to give something of financial value. We'll say up front that cash is the best thing to give a crew member—it's easy to use in ports and send to family back home. But if cash is not your thing, Visa or American Express gift cards or store cards from Walmart or Target are often appreciated.

- **Do any of the above and add a personal note of gratitude to the envelope.**

PORT EXCURSIONS Shore trips are typically run by outside companies, not Disney. Nearly all excursion guides appreciate a cash tip, given at your discretion.

KIDS' CLUB STAFF Gratuities aren't required for nursery or club staff, although you may want to reward a counselor who goes above and beyond for your child. Cash and gift cards are accepted though not expected. Personal notes from your child are a super-thoughtful touch.

Is Tipping Necessary?

A few DCL guests have asked us whether they have to tip at all; these guests are usually from countries outside of the US and Canada, where tipping isn't a norm (usually because restaurant waitstaff in these countries are paid standard wages).

While it's not absolutely mandatory, tipping your crew absolutely *is* the right thing to do: gratuities are an expected part of cruise travel and an important component of crew members' income.

Other guests have asked us whether they should tip the servers in the main dining rooms if they didn't eat in them on their cruise. (Some cruisers on three-nighters on the *Dream*, for example, often prefer to skip the dining rooms and dine once at Cabanas, once at

Palo, and once at Remy.) We recommend tipping at least the base-line amount whether you eat in the main dining rooms at night or not—these same servers not only work in the same dining rooms during the day, but they also work at Cabanas and the food stations on Castaway Cay.

Tipping Extra

When it comes to tipping more than baseline amounts, no, it's not man-datory—but many people do give additional tips to the crew who attend to them most closely.

On one 11-night cruise, our stateroom attendant was fastidious about not disturbing our kids' nap time and left them elaborate towel-animal tableaux each evening. Our serving team brought us our favorite beverages each night before we placed our dinner orders, played logic puzzles with the kids during dessert, and made sure there were six maraschino cherries in our daughter's Shirley Temple because they knew she loved them and it made her feel like a princess. Those crew members all got substan-tial cash tips in their envelopes as we bid them goodbye. (On three-night cruises, where we've had fewer and shorter interactions with the staff, we've tipped the stan-dard amounts.)

*un*official **TIP**
If you really care about your stateroom and dining room teams, the best thing you can do to reward them besides tipping them is to give them rave reviews on your post-cruise comment card.

The next question you'll undoubtedly ask is, "How much extra should I tip?" To that we say, *it's up to you.* For some guests, an extra $10 is a stretch but a meaningful gesture. We've also heard of guests handing several hundred dollars cash to beloved crew members. For most, it's somewhere in between.

Some guests bring candy, magazines, or other personal items as crew gifts. This is a nice thought but probably not the best practice: crew quarters are shared spaces, and your crew's tastes may not be the same as yours. Again, cash is best, gift cards second best. If you really want to give something else, make sure it's in addition to (not instead of) the tip.

Tipping for Adult Dining

At **Palo, Palo Steakhouse, Remy,** and **Enchanté,** a gratuity is automati-cally added for alcohol only; an additional gratuity for dining service is left to your discretion. Because the service at these restaurants is typi-cally impeccable, we tend to tip as if we had eaten at an on-shore res-taurant of their caliber.

Tipping Guidelines for Concierge-Level Guests

The suggested minimum gratuity in this case is **$15.50 per person, per night,** broken down as follows: **$4.75** for your dining room server, **$3.75** for your assistant server, **$1.25** for the head server, **$4.75** for your stateroom host, and **$1** for your assistant stateroom host.

To get a feel for what the norms are when it comes to tipping extra, we decided to consult an expert: **Karen Shelton** a luxury-travel specialist and the owner of **My Path Unwinding Travel** (mypathunwinding .com). Of particular relevance to this topic, Karen also has a PhD in psychology and a background in statistical analysis.

Karen surveyed nearly 200 DCL Concierge-level cruisers about how much they tipped during their sailings. Below are her findings for three different scenarios; all assume accommodations in a Concierge Family Stateroom with Verandah.

The amounts reflect the *modes*, or values most frequently recorded for each scenario; means (averages) and medians (midrange values) were higher or lower depending on the scenario.

- For two adults on a four-night cruise, the most common tip amount is **$200,** or **$25 per person, per night.**

- For the same two adults on a seven-night cruise, the most common tip amount is **$300,** or **$21 per person, per night.** (The key takeaway in this case is that Concierge guests seem to tip more overall the longer their trips.)

- For two adults and two kids on a four-night cruise, the most common tip amount is **$400,** or **$25 per person, per night,** which accounts for the kids as well as the adults.

▌ CHECKOUT *and* DEPARTURE

YOUR LAST NIGHT ON THE SHIP

A DAY OR TWO BEFORE YOUR DEPARTURE, in addition to the tipping-related information discussed in the previous section, you'll receive debarkation information, including luggage tags, instructions on what to do with your bags, information on where to get breakfast on your last morning, and what time you need to be off the ship.

unofficial **TIP**
Look for your final charges on your stateroom TV and the Navigator app. If you want a copy of your final bill for your records, stop by Guest Services for a printout, or download a PDF from the app **before** you leave the ship. Accessing your final bill is much more difficult once you debark.

What to Do with Your Luggage on Your Last Night

Before your departure, you'll be given a set of small, colorful, oval luggage tags decorated with Disney characters: green Tinker Bell, orange Goofy, blue Donald Duck, and so on. If you want Disney porters to carry your luggage for you from the ship into the port terminal upon docking, fill out the information requested on the tag (name, address, stateroom number), attach the tag to your bag, and follow the instructions on your departure-information sheet. (Don't forget which characters were on your tags—you'll need this information later.)

YOUR DCL DEPARTURE TIMELINE

2 Days Before Departure

- **Check your current room charges on the Navigator app** to make sure that you understand them, and make payments as needed. Guest Services gets very busy on the last day, so doing this two days ahead can save you lots of time. **Note:** You will not receive a hard copy of your final bill (see Unofficial Tip below).
- **Make adjustments to your gratuity payments** if desired (see page 140).

1 Day Before Departure

- **Check in for your flight** if you're heading straight home upon debarkation.
- **Give tip envelopes** to your dining room servers and stateroom host (see page 142).
- **Complete your cruise survey** (see pages 147 and 148).
- **Check Lost and Found** for any missing belongings.
- **Leave large luggage outside your stateroom** in the evening unless you're using Express Walk-Off (see next page). **Do not pack** your KTTW Card, ID, electronics, or medications.
- **Return your child's kids' club wristband** to the club before 11 p.m. to avoid incurring a stateroom charge.

Departure Day

- **If you're eating breakfast on board,** go to your assigned dining room or **Cove Café.**
- **Check your final bill** and make sure that your account is in order.
- **Make sure that all photos you've purchased** are either stored on a thumb drive or downloaded to your phone or tablet.
- **Make sure you're not carrying any prohibited items** off the ship (fresh fruit is a commonly overlooked no-no).
- **Have your KTTW Card in hand** as you leave the ship.
- **Complete the US Customs Declaration Form** (see page 147) if you've made any purchases that require it.

If you're sailing into Port Canaveral, you'll typically be asked to leave your luggage outside your stateroom door between 8:30 and 10:30 p.m. Other ports may have slightly different instructions.

You may be asking, "Why do I need Disney to take my bags off the ship?" If you're on a three-night cruise with only a small rolling suitcase, you probably don't need any assistance. But if you have large suitcases or small children, or anyone in your party has special needs, you probably do.

On your departure morning, the same group of 4,000 people who boarded the ship over the course of about 5 hours will be trying to get off the ship over the course of 2 hours. Hallways are narrow and there are zillions of stairs, with the only alternative being the same small, slow elevators that everyone else is using. In short, it's a logistical nightmare if everyone tries to take their bags off the ship themselves. If you have large luggage, avail yourself of this free Disney service.

Packing

As you pack your bags, pay attention to the following:

- Lay out clothes to wear to breakfast and off the ship the last morning.
- If you're flying home, you must pack any alcohol you purchased on the ship in your checked bags.

- **Don't** pack passports, birth certificates, KTTW Cards, or any other travel documents in your checked bags. You'll need them before you can pick up your luggage, so keep them in a bag you plan to carry off the ship.

- Remove any old airline or cruise tags from your luggage before you attach any new ones.

- Keep inside your stateroom any luggage you'll carry off the ship yourself.

- If you have luggage that you want DCL to carry off the ship for you, take a picture of these bags in case you have trouble finding them the next morning.

DEPARTURE DAY

Getting Your Luggage Back in the Morning

If you put oval-tagged luggage outside your stateroom the night before disembarkation, the next time you'll see it is inside the cruise terminal, back on land. Walk off the ship into the terminal, and you'll immediately see many rows of suitcases on the floor and nearby tables sorted by the character and color on the oval tags—all of the green Tinker Bells will be grouped together, along with all of the tan Plutos and so on.

unofficial **TIP**
Guests with flights out of Orlando International Airport before 1 p.m. are required to leave the ship by **8 a.m.**

Theoretically your luggage should be grouped together by stateroom, but if it's not, do a quick scan to check a few bags up and down your section. You should find your bag in the same general area, if not the exact same area, as the other bags with your tag(s). If you still can't find your luggage, speak to one of the many helpful crew members stationed in the terminal. *Note:* Having pictures of your carry-off luggage saved on your phone could come in handy here.

Once you have all of your luggage back in your possession, follow the signs and instructions to the customs area, where your identification will be checked and you will then be allowed back into your debarkation country.

Express Walk-Off

For guests who wish to be among the very first off the ship—those who need to get straight to the airport or who have other time-dependent plans that day—DCL offers Express Walk-Off. As soon as the ship clears customs, you may leave the ship.

You must carry all of your own luggage to take advantage of this service; you may not set it out the night before. Please be considerate and let your stateroom host know that you'll be doing this well ahead of time. (*Note:* Express Walk-Off may not be available on some sailings, so check the specifics for your cruise.)

unofficial **TIP**
Concierge guests may order room-service breakfast on the morning of their departure on some sailings.

Breakfast on the Morning of Your Departure

You'll have the chance to eat one more sit-down meal on debarkation morning. Breakfast will be provided at the restaurants, with assigned, staggered seating times. Typically guests will be assigned to eat breakfast at the same restaurant where they ate on the last night of their sailing. Additionally, **Cove Café** will be open for coffee and **Cabanas** or **Marceline Market** will serve a limited breakfast menu, both from about 6:30 to 8:30 a.m.

Clearing Customs

If your sailing ends in the US—Port Canaveral, Port Everglades, Galveston, Miami, New Orleans, New York City, San Diego, or San Juan—you'll pass through **US Customs and Border Protection** (**CBP**) as you leave the terminal. An agent will check your passport or other identification and will likely ask you a few questions about your trip or your final travel destination.

In years past, everyone disembarking the ship was asked to complete a short but somewhat intimidating paper document asking about purchases made during the sailing (in port and on board), as well as questions like these: "Are you bringing fruit into the country?," "Have you been in close proximity to livestock?," and "Are you carrying more than $10,000 in currency?"

The customs form is no longer distributed to all passengers by default, nor are all passengers asked to fill it out as a matter of course. The forms are available in the terminal if you need to pay duty on your vacation purchases.

If you're not sure whether you'll need to fill out a form, CBP has extensive information about customs duty at its website: see tinyurl .com/USCustomsDuty. If you haven't purchased large quantities of alcohol or cigarettes, you're not bringing home agricultural products or prescription medicines purchased outside the US (Mexico, for instance), you haven't made total purchases of more than $1,600, and you don't have more than $10,000 in cash on you, then you're probably good to go. Nevertheless, read through the rules at least once to make sure you're fully compliant with the law.

See "Doing Your Duty" in Part Nine (page 306) for more information about customs fees.

Comment Cards

On the last night of your cruise, you'll be given a comprehensive survey asking for your evaluation of the ship's cleanliness, the entertainment offerings, the condition of your stateroom, the children's programming, and a number of other aspects of your cruise. You'll also be asked your perceptions of your dining-service team.

Note that the dining staff's performance reviews and pay are often strongly affected by guest input on these comment cards. Because of this, some servers may give guests a high-pressure sell for Excellent ratings, basically begging for high marks. If you really do love your servers, then by all means rate them as Excellent, but don't feel strong-armed into doing so if the service wasn't *truly* outstanding.

The survey also asks you to name any cast members "who made your cruise experience particularly magical." In addition to the obvious dining, stateroom, and entertainment cast members, we like to keep a lookout for cast in minimally guest-facing roles—maintenance crew, for example—and we note when we see them doing a great job.

Flying Out Late on Departure Day from Orlando International Airport (MCO)

DCL asks that guests flying out of MCO from Port Canaveral not schedule flights home before 11:30 a.m. If you can fly out in the early afternoon, you're golden: grab some lunch at the airport and you're good to go. But there may be times where you can't or don't want to fly home until later in the day.

So how do you occupy your time if you disembark at 8 a.m. but you're not getting on your plane until 8 p.m. or later? Here are a few suggestions.

- **Rent a hotel room for the day.** The **Hyatt Regency Orlando International Airport** (inside MCO) has day-use rooms available from 10 a.m. to 6 p.m.; to check availability, call ☎ 407-825-1234.

  You could also rent the cheapest on-property room at **Walt Disney World.** Take the DCL shuttle or a rental car to the hotel. (The room might not be ready until 3 p.m., but if you have a reservation, you can use the pool and other hotel facilities in the meantime.) Then take a third-party shuttle, taxi, or ride-hailing service to MCO just before your flight. (*Note:* WDW discontinued its Magical Express hotel shuttle at the beginning of 2022.)

- **Purchase a day pass for an executive lounge at the airport,** and get some work done in peace and quiet.

- **Visit other Orlando-area attractions.** You have plenty of recreation choices that don't absolutely require booking in advance (but make sure to check availability before you go). Visit **Universal Orlando, SeaWorld, Madame Tussauds,** or the **Kennedy Space Center** (in Cape Canaveral); go horseback riding at Disney's **Fort Wilderness Resort;** or experience **iFly** indoor skydiving (iflyworld.com). If needed, rent a car at the cruise terminal and drop off your luggage at the airport first.

- **Go shopping!** We like **Lake Buena Vista Factory Stores Outlet Mall** (15657 S. Apopka–Vineland Road). The mall also has an outpost of **Orlando Baggage Storage** (☎ 407-539-4742, orlandobaggagestorage.com), which will hold your luggage for the day for a nominal fee.

Flying Out Late on Departure Day from Other Ports

As with Port Canaveral and Orlando, most ports have plenty of interesting things to see and do if you're not flying home until late in the day. If you want somewhere to park your luggage while you're off enjoying the attractions, try **Vertoe Luggage Storage** (vertoe.com), a service with outposts in dozens of cities worldwide, including Barcelona, Galveston, Miami, New Orleans, New York City, San Diego, San Juan, Vancouver, and others.

If you need a place to rest before a long flight home, **Dayuse** (dayuse.com) offers partial-day hotel rentals in cities around the globe.

TRANSFERS TO WALT DISNEY WORLD HOTELS

IN RECENT YEARS, DCL has been tinkering with departure procedures for guests who've purchased transfers from the ship to a Walt Disney World resort hotel. In years past, buses started running from Port Canaveral to Disney World as soon as the ship cleared customs, usually around 7 or 7:30 a.m., but more recently buses haven't begun running to WDW until 9 a.m. If you're an early riser, this can feel like a lot of unnecessary waiting around, so you may want to consider arranging your own transportation to the hotel.

Following one DCL cruise, we took Disney transportation from Port Canaveral to Disney's Wilderness Lodge. Our bus didn't leave the terminal until about 9:30 a.m., and it made several stops at other hotels before ours, so we didn't get to Wilderness Lodge until after 11:30, and we didn't get to the Magic Kingdom until well after noon. Had we scheduled our own transportation, we could have been picked up at 7:30 a.m. and been driven directly to our hotel, putting us at the Magic Kingdom much closer to 10 a.m.

You may also want to arrange your own transportation to the airport if time is tight on the last day of your trip. If, for instance, you really want to squeeze in a couple of extra hours in the parks but you don't want to cut things too close for your flight home, a town car, cab, or Lyft/Uber is probably a better choice than the Disney shuttle.

PART FIVE

TIPS *for* VARIED CIRCUMSTANCES

DCL *for* SOLO TRAVELERS

BECAUSE DCL is targeted to families, roughly 90% of its guests are couples or parents and children. That's about 10 points higher than the cruise industry's average, and it means that there are around 200 solo travelers per cruise on the *Magic* and *Wonder,* and around 400 on the *Dream, Fantasy,* and *Wish.*

unofficial **TIP**
If you're not comfortable walking back to your stateroom at night, ask a cast member to accompany you.

Like the Disney theme parks, Disney Cruise Line is great for solo travelers. The bars, lounges, and nightclubs are clean, friendly, and interesting; the restaurants are welcoming; and the spas are excellent places for grabbing some solo time in public. One aspect that you do have to be vigilant about when traveling alone is shore excursions in foreign countries—more on that a bit later.

If you're interested in meeting other singles, Disney sometimes runs a **Singles Mingle** session on one of the first few days of each cruise. These informal get-togethers last about an hour and are typically held at the Cove Café in the adults-only part of the ship. We've also seen lunchtime gatherings with the name **Cruisin' Solo.**

Single and not-so-single guests ages 18–20 are welcome to attend an **1820 Society** gathering during one night of their cruise. It's a meetup attended by guests and crew, generally during the evening after the second dinner seating, also usually at the Cove Café.

DINING In the immediate post-pandemic return to sailing, single travelers were seated by themselves in the main dining rooms as a means of promoting social distancing. At the time of this writing, however, Disney has resumed its regular policy of seating solo guests with larger parties, unless they specifically request otherwise. (For more on DCL dining, see Part Seven.)

Not everybody enjoys dining with strangers (see "Disney Cruise Line for Introverts," page 132), but we've had great experiences with our tablemates when we've cruised solo. We've met people from many different places, never run out of things to talk about, and have even kept in touch with a few folks when we got back home.

Solo travelers are also welcome at the adult-dining venues, and we've had many fine dinners and brunches there. If you're having difficulty making a reservation for one using the DCL website before your trip, try stopping by the restaurant on the afternoon you board. We've found the staff to be exceptionally accommodating for these requests, especially if you're willing to arrive either early or late.

CRUISE FARES Whereas some cruise lines have staterooms designed especially for solo travelers, cabins on Disney's ships are designed to hold at least two people. Disney also adds a 100% surcharge (or **single supplement,** in cruise-industry lingo) to most solo-traveler fares, making the cost equivalent to two people taking the same trip. You may be able to find last-minute cruise deals that don't require you to pay the full supplement, though; check the DCL website or have a travel agent research for you.

A few of the ships used for **Adventures by Disney** river cruises (see Part Thirteen) have staterooms specifically designed for one occupant. If you're a solo traveler, an AbD cruise could be a more economical alternative to a DCL cruise.

PORT ADVENTURES As with dining, there's a good chance that you'll be paired with other guests for shore excursions. We've experienced everything from cooking demonstrations to snorkeling to city tours as solo travelers, and the Port Adventures staff did a great job of making us feel welcome.

As Len discovered, however, you could be the odd person out if you're doing an excursion with a third-party company and there's not enough room for you on the shuttle vehicle:

unofficial **TIP** If your port adventure involves boating, snorkeling, or any other water-based activity, you'll almost certainly be assigned another traveler or couple as a buddy for safety purposes.

I was once the only solo traveler in a group of nine for an excursion in Mexico that involved a 30-minute bus ride. When we got to the departure point, we saw that not all of us were going to fit on the eight-person bus, so the tour company hurriedly arranged an unmarked, nondescript "taxi" for me.

As I got in this random car on a random street in a random Mexican town, my last words to the others were, "Take a good look—this is what I was wearing the last time you saw me." Of course, I made it to the excursion just fine, and we all had a good laugh once we were reunited. But I wouldn't recommend that others do this, especially women traveling alone.

In the unlikely event that you're asked to travel alone to an excursion, politely request to be accompanied by a staff member or escorted back to the ship.

■ DCL *for* LARGER GUESTS

AS WITH ITS THEME PARK GUESTS, Disney acknowledges that its cruise guests come in all shapes and sizes and makes many accommodations to ensure that they're treated well.

Your stateroom's personal flotation devices (PFDs, or life jackets) are designed to fit most body sizes. With PFDs, chest size, not weight, is the measurement that determines proper fit. Disney's PFDs include a nylon strap that wraps around your body to keep the PFD snug against your chest.

Try on your PFD when you first get to your stateroom to ensure that the strap fits around your body. If it doesn't, ask your stateroom attendant to find you a PFD in a larger size.

The **AquaDuck** waterslides on the *Dream* and *Fantasy* and the **AquaMouse** slide on the *Wish* all seem to be able to accommodate guests of virtually every body size and shape; we've heard success stories from individuals weighing more than 300 pounds and couples weighing more than 400. The **AquaDunk** slide on the *Magic* has a weight limit of 300 pounds.

If an activity or port adventure has a weight limit, it will be printed in the details describing the activity; look for phrases such as "Guests must weigh" or "Weight must be" in the activity's listing. Some shore excursions, including kayaking and some scuba and snorkeling trips, have weight limits of 240 or 300 pounds per person. Segway tours generally accommodate persons of up to 250 pounds.

Many Alaskan excursions involving helicopters or seaplanes have a weight limit of 250 pounds inclusive of all gear (clothing, cameras, and such), but it may be possible to modify this requirement by offering to pay an excess-weight fee for additional fuel. Other activities have weight limits of up to 350 pounds per person. Again, check the activity's details for more information, or check with the Port Adventures desk on board.

Ask for bench seating or chairs without arms at restaurants and lounges. If you don't see any, a cast member may be able to locate them for you.

Wear comfortable shoes. You'll be surprised at the amount of walking you do on board, not to mention the walking you'll do from the cruise terminal to the ship.

■ DCL *if* YOU'RE EXPECTING

DISNEY CRUISE LINE PROHIBITS GUESTS who are **24 weeks pregnant** prior to sailing or who would reach the end of their second trimester during their trip. If you'll be 23 weeks pregnant on embarkation day, a 12-night Transatlantic cruise would be a no-go.

Following are some specific concerns to be aware of on board and in port; be sure to discuss these with your doctor before your cruise.

ON THE SHIP The **waterslides,** both on the ships and on Castaway Cay, are off-limits to pregnant guests.

Certain treatments at the onboard **Senses Spas** are also restricted, but the wording on the DCL website is vague and confusing:

We are unable to provide massage services to pregnant Guests in their first trimester. After the first trimester, Guests may partake of massage treatments, although aromatherapy is not recommended.

When it comes to massages, we assume you're on the honor system if you're in your first trimester but not visibly pregnant. Otherwise, we're not sure how this policy is supposed to be enforced.

As for aromatherapy, reputable sources such as Healthline and WebMD agree that it's safe after the first trimester, provided that you stick with familiar essential oils such as lavender and peppermint. (For a list of oils to avoid, see tinyurl.com/EssentialOilsPregnancy.) Again, though, get your doctor's advice before you sail.

OFF THE SHIP **Shore excursions** such as scuba diving, off-road driving, and parasailing prohibit pregnant guests from participating; in addition, some tour operators have restrictions on snorkeling and dolphin encounters. But even if all you have planned is a day of sightseeing or lying on the beach, be aware that the trip to your destination could involve a lengthy trip in a rattletrap vehicle on a bumpy road.

The pandemic notwithstanding, a lingering health concern for pregnant guests is **Zika,** a mosquito-borne virus that causes catastrophic harm to developing fetuses. The last major Zika outbreak was in 2016, but researchers warn that future outbreaks aren't out of the question. Check the **CDC website** (tinyurl.com/CDCZika) for the latest information.

DCL *for* YOUNGER CHILDREN

DISNEY CRUISE LINE REQUIRES that infants be at **least 6 months of age** to cruise on most sailings from the United States and **at least 1 year of age** on some longer voyages. Here are some key topics to think about if you're traveling with kids ages 5 and younger.

SLEEPING DCL furnishes pack-and-play cribs free of charge to families who need them, along with supplies such as bed rails, bottle warmers, and diaper pails. Call DCL at ☎ 800-951-3532 before your sailing, or check with Guest Services on board.

Families with young children should start thinking about sleeping arrangements ahead of their trip. In particular, a crib could make an already-small stateroom feel even smaller, so consider carefully whether you absolutely need one. If you have a

*un*official **TIP**
For more on cruising with children, see "Cruising with Kids" in Part One (page 21), "Make Sure Your Child Is Ready to Cruise" in Part Two (page 79), and "Special Considerations" in Part Nine (page 267).

toddler who's still sleeping in a crib at home, consider helping them make the switch to sleeping in a bed before your cruise.

unofficial **TIP**

If your preferred seating is fully booked before your cruise, keep checking for openings. You may even be able to switch your seating after you're already on board.

In general, the younger the child, the closer you'll want to stick to their typical eating/sleeping schedule. In most cases, that means choosing the early dinner seating, but depending on where you sail, you may be competing with lots of other families for a table. (A possible exception is some European sailings, where the late seating may be more popular.) And if you'll be cruising far from home, be aware that adjusting to a different time zone could play havoc with your child's sleep schedule.

EATING AND DRINKING The Disney ships serve a wide variety of foods, but naturally they're not going to have *everything* your child likes to eat. Depending on how picky your little one is, that could lead to a tantrum or two. ("*Orange* mac and cheese? I wanted white!") If you have a truly limited eater, you'll need to strategize in advance.

If your child is still learning to drink from a cup, be sure to bring your own lids and straws. As part of its ongoing eco-friendly efforts, DCL has banished plastic straws and cup lids from the ships.

SEPARATION ANXIETY A kindergartner in a clingy phase may not deal well with going to the kids' club, even if you're just a deck or two away. In this case, it can help to adjust your expectations: if you assume that most of your cruise will consist of family time rather than "Mom and Dad at the spa" time, then you'll be pleasantly surprised if your preschooler ends up loving the kids' club.

BREASTFEEDING You're welcome to nurse anywhere on board: the theaters, dining rooms, pool decks, and so on. When it comes to breastfeeding in port, however, you may want to research the cultural norms in the countries you'll be visiting.

DCL *for* OLDER TEENS

SOME FAMILIES WITH 17- AND 18-YEAR-OLDS may encounter frustration during their trip due to Disney's strict enforcement of age restrictions on teen and adult activities. A few years ago, we traveled with a teen just days away from her 18th birthday, and even though she was a high school graduate, she wasn't allowed to dine at Palo— yes, we tried bribery, and no, it didn't work—or go to some of the adults-only cooking demonstrations.

We've also seen 17- and 18-year-old cousins unable to do virtually anything together because the older teen wasn't allowed into Vibe (the teen club) and the younger one wasn't allowed into any of the grown-up activities. We've even met teens who turned 18 during their cruise and were allowed into Vibe for the first part of the trip but then denied entry after their birthday.

Bottom line: If you're the parent of an older teen, consider whether a slightly different travel date would improve your family's shipboard experience.

DCL *for* SENIORS

MOST SENIORS WILL FIND A DISNEY CRUISE less tiring than a Walt Disney World vacation. First, most seniors find there's considerably less walking required on the ship versus the parks. Second, the ships' adults-only areas provide a break from children (and their families) when needed. And even the most energetic onboard attraction—the ship's waterslide—isn't as intense as a ride on Space Mountain.

Because of their flexible schedules, retirees can often take advantage of off-peak cruise fares, especially during fall or spring, when the weather is nicest and crowds are lower because school is in session. If you're cruising to the Caribbean, the Bahamas, or Mexico, be sure to bring a jacket and sweater along with your warm-weather clothing. While temperature averages hover around 70°F in most of those locations, a cold front can drop temps into the upper 40s with little notice, and it's not uncommon to have morning temperatures in the lower 50s.

DCL *for* LARGE GROUPS

A CRUISE CAN BE A GREAT TRAVEL CHOICE for family/class reunions, bachelorette parties, and other groups with diverse interests or dissimilar financial situations. Nobody has to cook or clean, so everybody gets to relax.

COVID TIP
At the time of this writing, there are risks associated with linking the reservations of non-nuclear families into a larger travel party. See page 116 for further discussion.

One potentially awkward issue, however, is the aforementioned dissimilar financial situations. Whereas you can make educated guesses about this on land—you're at Walt Disney World, for instance, and one set of college classmates and their spouses is staying at the posh Grand Floridian and the other is staying at the budget All-Star Sports—on a DCL ship it's not readily apparent from the hallway whether your stateroom has a tiny porthole or an expansive verandah.

The mostly all-inclusive nature of the cruise means there's no "Hey, she ordered the steak but I ordered the salad—why do I have to chip in for an expensive meal I didn't eat?" That said, extra-cost experiences and activities such as port adventures, wine packages, or dining at the adults-only venues could prove to be sticking points later if you don't bring them up now.

In general, when you're planning a cruise for a large group, try to get answers well in advance to such questions as the following:

- Will everyone be able to afford dinner at one of the adult-dining venues, which cost extra?
- Are the adults always responsible for buying their own alcoholic drinks, or do we want to let different groups take turns buying rounds?
- What kinds of excursions do we like/can we afford? Do we have to do all of the port adventures together?
- How much alone time will each person or subgroup (such as teenagers and seniors) need?
- How much supervision will the kids need on board? How much time can the kids can spend in the clubs, and what bedtimes are appropriate?

Many online tools and apps are now available that can help you work out the kinks of large-group travel. Four that we like are **Doodle** (doodle.com), which lets you set up online polls about things like travel dates and preferred excursions; **TripIt** (tripit.com), which can keep everyone's airline and pre- or post-trip hotel information organized; and **Splittr** (splittr.io) and **Splitwise** (splitwise.com), which can track and prorate expenses for things like a round of cocktails by the pool or renting a car in Nassau.

GUESTS *with* DISABILITIES

DCL STRIVES to make its ships accessible to everyone. Virtually the entire ship, from staterooms to restaurants to nightclubs and pools, is friendly to users of wheelchairs and electric convenience vehicles (ECVs). (*Note:* See our observations about accessibility on the *Disney Wish* on page 158.)

Your first step in getting the help you need is to fill out DCL's **Request Special Services** form, available online at tinyurl.com/DCL RequestSpecialServices (a printable PDF is available at tinyurl.com /DCLSpecialServices). This form must be submitted online **at least 60 days before sailing.** You may also contact **DCL Special Services** with specific questions: ☎ 407-566-3602 (voice) or 407-566-7455 (TTY); specialservices@disneycruise.com; or Disney Cruise Line Special Services, PO Box 10210, Lake Buena Vista, FL 32830-0210.

Overall, guests with mobility issues can expect that their needs will be met with courtesy and good design. One guest writes:

I love the accessibility of Disney. I have more freedom and independence at WDW and on board DCL than I do in my own hometown. Being disabled fades into the background, and I can feel just like everyone else.

Stateroom Furnishings

In addition to the standard stateroom amenities, DCL offers a number of features for guests with special needs, as noted on the next page:

• Closed-captioned TV (most stations)	• Portable toilet	• Shower stool
	• Raised toilet seat	• Transfer benches
• Bed boards and rails	• Rubber bed pads	• Sharps container
• A Stateroom Communication Kit, including an alarm clock, door-knock and phone alerts, phone amplifier, bed-shaker notification, strobe-light smoke detector, and text typewriter (TTY)		

WHEELCHAIR AND ECV USERS DCL suggests that guests using a wheelchair or ECV request a wheelchair-accessible stateroom or suite. Found on every Disney ship, accessible staterooms include the following:

• Doorways at least 32 inches wide	• Fold-down shower seating and hand-held showerheads	• Open bed frame for easier entry and exit
• Bathroom and shower handrails	• Lowered towel and closet bars	• Ramped bathroom thresholds
• Emergency call buttons and additional phones in the bath and stateroom		

One advantage to having an accessible stateroom is that its wider door lets you store your wheelchair or ECV inside your cabin when it's not in use. This also makes it easier to recharge the equipment when needed. If you find yourself in a standard stateroom whose door isn't wide enough to accommodate your vehicle, you may be asked to park the vehicle in a designated area elsewhere on the ship, even at night. In practice, we've seen many ECVs parked in a corner of each deck's elevator-landing areas. Chances are that your vehicle will be stored within a short walk of your cabin.

Outside of your stateroom, special areas are designated at most ship activities for guests in wheelchairs. At the Walt Disney Theatre, for example, Disney cast members direct guests in wheelchairs to a reserved seating area. Shops, restaurants, bars, and nightclubs are all accessible, and accessible restrooms are available throughout the ship's public areas. A limited number of sand wheelchairs are available on Castaway Cay, too, on a first-come, first-served basis.

Note that DCL's pools require a transfer from wheelchair to use. For this reason, Disney recommends that guests in wheelchairs travel with someone who can help transfer them to and from the wheelchair.

Another area to be aware of is tendering from ship to shore. Some ports, such as the one at Grand Cayman, aren't deep enough to accommodate large cruise ships such as Disney's. When DCL ships anchor at Grand Cayman, smaller boats, or tenders, pull up next to the ship, and guests board them for travel to and from Grand Cayman.

unofficial **TIP**
Service animals are welcome on all Disney ships, and each ship has a designated animal-relief area on an outside deck.

Some tenders use steps instead of ramps to get guests on board. In those cases, wheelchair passengers must use the steps. Also keep in mind that the Disney ship and tender craft both float freely in the ocean. It's not uncommon for the stairs to move 2 or 3 feet up and down during the course of a transfer. If the seas are too rough, wheelchair guests may be denied transfer.

CRUISING WITH AUTISM

ALISON SINGER, president of the **Autism Science Foundation** (autismscience foundation.org), shares her experiences cruising DCL with her daughter Jodie. DCL provides additional information for guests with autism in a PDF document; see tinyurl.com/DCLAutism.

OUR FIRST FAMILY CRUISE WITH JODIE, who has severe autism, was on the *Disney Magic* when she was 12. I was *very* nervous—as an autism family, we needed a lot more than faith, trust, and pixie dust!

My biggest concern when we first booked the cruise was mealtimes, but the dining staff was incredibly accommodating when I requested Jodie's special foods. One of DCL's strengths is that the waitstaff travels with your family to dinner in the various restaurants each night, so I only had to discuss her needs with one person.

As soon as we would arrive at dinner, French fries, iceberg lettuce, and a small bowl of Russian dressing would magically appear on Jodie's plate. I was also able to order her main course the night before, so she never had to wait, and her plate was always refilled with what at times felt like an overabundance of French fries—but hey, it's vacation!

Most importantly, this accommodation enabled our family to sit together for an entire meal and enjoy our delicious dinners all the way through to the Mickey Bars. Also, we found that letting Jodie wear headphones at the table helped her handle the noise of the busy dining rooms.

Unlike some other cruise lines, though, Disney doesn't provide one-on-one aides for youth activities and doesn't permit adult family members to serve as aides. A similarly aged sibling or cousin could provide support at the kids' clubs, but in most situations a child with autism would need to be high-functioning enough to navigate the youth programs independently. In such cases, families report generally great experiences—few demands are placed on the kids in general, and the activities are all fun and engaging.

Overall, my family's experience was extremely positive, and we look forward to our next Disney cruise!

ON THE *WISH* We spoke with some wheelchair users on early sailings who had six key criticisms regarding the ship's design:

1. **There are no midship elevators.** This means it may take wheelchair users longer to reach various parts of the ship.

2. **The elevators are narrower and deeper than those on the other ships.** This can make them hard to get into and out of in a wheelchair, particularly if you're sharing an elevator with other guests.

3. **Not all elevators go to the top decks.**

4. **The adults-only pool is accessible only via stairs.** The pool has a lift for wheelchair users, but it must be booked in advance through DCL Special Services (see page 156).

5. **The outdoor promenade deck is on multiple levels** that are accessible only via steep stairs.

6. **The main pool area has stadium-style tiers.** These require navigating more stairs than the pool decks on the other ships.

In light of these accessibility issues, wheelchair users should consider carefully whether to book a cruise on DCL's newest ship. If they do, they should be prepared to vigorously advocate for their needs both before and during their trip.

VISUALLY IMPAIRED AND HARD-OF-HEARING GUESTS For guests with visual impairments, DCL provides accessibility aids such as Braille signage and audio descriptions for movies. For guests with hearing loss, in addition to closed-caption TVs, assistive listening devices and printed scripts are available for shows at the ships' main theaters and show stages; contact Guest Services to pick those up. American Sign Language (ASL) interpreters are also available for live performances on some cruise dates. One reader remarked:

> We had two ASL interpreters on board who followed one group around the entire cruise. They signed every show, including the lounge acts. They were spectacular performers—sometimes even better than the featured performers!

ASL interpreters typically work a schedule aligned with the second (later) live performance at the **Walt Disney Theatre,** following the first main-dining-room seating. To request an interpreter for a cruise originating in the United States, contact **DCL Special Services** (see page 156) at least 60 days before you sail. For guests interested in ASL services on international sailings, requests must be made at least 120 days in advance. The following 2023 international sailings will be accompanied by ASL interpreters:

May 20–27, 2023 7-Night Mediterranean Cruise from Barcelona

June 20–27, 2023 9-Night Mediterranean with Greek Isles Cruise from Civitavecchia (Rome)

July 22–August 1, 2023 10-Night France, Iceland, and Norway Cruise from Southampton to Copenhagen

August 1–8, 2023 7-Night Northern Europe Cruise from Copenhagen

September 10–17, 2023 7-Night British Isles Cruise from Southampton

CHILDREN WITH DISABILITIES Disney's youth programs are open to special-needs children ages 3–17. All children must be toilet-trained and able to play well with other kids who are about their same age and size.

The number of special-needs children who can participate is limited and is based on the number of available counselors, the number of other children in the programs, the number of children with special needs already enrolled, and the specific needs of the children to be enrolled. Check with the Youth Activities team for more information when you get on board.

Youth club counselors are unable to provide one-on-one care or specialized medical assistance. Children who can self-address their own medical needs may store their supplies at the Youth Activities desk.

PORT ADVENTURES Many DCL port adventures have mobility requirements. For more information, check at the onboard Port Adventures desk, see disneycruise.disney.go.com/port-adventures, or see Part Twelve, pages 324 and 325.

Guests with mobility issues should be aware of Disney's new partnership with **Accessible Travel Solutions** (accessibletravelsolutions.com). Through this partnership, DCL now offers port adventures specifically designed for ease of access for wheelchair users. To check availability, submit your request to **DCL Special Services** (see page 156) when your cruise reservation is paid in full and you have access to your Castaway Club booking window. A minimum number of participants is required; if the minimum is not met, guests may book the port adventure as a private experience at an additional cost.

Other amenities, such as disabled parking at the Port Canaveral cruise terminal, are also available. See DCL's **Guests with Disabilities FAQ** (tinyurl.com/DCLGuestsWithDisabilities) for more information.

EQUIPMENT RENTALS Guests who need medical equipment on board may find it convenient to rent from **Special Needs at Sea** (specialneedsatsea.com). They deliver to the Disney ships at most embarkation ports, including Barcelona, Copenhagen, Galveston, Miami, New Orleans, New York City, Port Canaveral, San Diego, San Juan, and Vancouver. The available equipment includes wheelchairs, ECVs, walkers, oxygen and respiratory aids, and audiovisual aids.

Another option for mobility rentals is **Scootaround** (☎ 888-971-0665, scootaround.com), which can deliver equipment to hotels or cruise ships at a number of US and international destinations, including Barcelona, New York, Miami, Port Canaveral, and Vancouver.

GUESTS WHO HAVE CANCER An advisory at the onboard **Senses Spas** states, "Guests diagnosed with cancer must obtain medical clearance from an oncologist (in the form of a doctor's note) to partake of massage treatments." We've never heard of anyone being turned away at the spa because of a cancer diagnosis, but if you have concerns, ask your home medical provider for advice. If you're planning to get a massage treatment, bring the doctor's note to be safe.

OTHER CONSIDERATIONS Guests who use electronic devices (insulin pumps or pacemakers, for example) to wirelessly transmit information to medical providers should know that connectivity on board can be intermittently spotty and potentially expensive. If you must constantly monitor these devices, you'll need to make well-informed decisions when planning your cruise.

Additionally, guests with a specific medical condition or care regimen should carry documentation about the nature of care and the contact information of their medical providers. The location of this information should be known to the guest's travel companions.

As noted earlier, DCL no longer stocks plastic straws and cup lids for drinks. Straws, however, can be crucial to quality of life for guests with mobility, eating, and sensory-processing issues, so bring your own if you or someone in your group needs them.

COMPLAINT RESOLUTION To submit complaints, including those regarding disability accommodations, use the following contacts:

Before your cruise DCL Special Services, ☎ 407-566-3602, fax 407-566-3760, TTY 407-566-7455; specialservices@disneycruise.com; PO Box 10210, Lake Buena Vista, FL 32830-0210.

At the cruise terminal Ask for the supervisor at the check-in desk.

On the ship Call or visit Guest Services.

After your cruise Email guest.communications@disneycruise.com, or write to Disney Cruise Line Guest Communications, PO 10238, Lake Buena Vista, FL 32830.

ADDITIONAL RESOURCES AccessibleGo (accessiblego.com/home) is a clearinghouse for information on travel with all types of disabilities; **Wheelchair Travel** (wheelchairtravel.org) is geared specifically to travelers with mobility issues. Both sites provide information that can help disabled travelers plan the noncruise parts of their trip, such as flights to and from DCL port cities and pre- and post-cruise hotel stays.

DIETARY RESTRICTIONS

DCL'S TABLE-SERVICE RESTAURANTS include gluten-free, vegetarian, no-sugar-added, dairy-free, and Lighter Note (lower-calorie) offerings on all menus. (See page 199 and 200 for our vegan and vegetarian dining tips.) With advance notice, DCL can also accommodate low-sodium, kosher, and halal diets, as well as diets that omit food allergens such as eggs, nuts, shellfish, all at no additional cost. Counter-service restaurants and room service may have fewer options for those with dietary restrictions. (See "Special Diets," page 199, for further discussion.)

unofficial **TIP**
DCL makes every reasonable effort to accommodate its guests' dietary needs, but they don't maintain separate kitchen facilities for the preparation of special meals. Most cruisers with food allergies give DCL high marks, but you eat at your own risk.

Notify DCL of your needs at least 60 days in advance using the **Request Special Services** form (see page 156).

On most sailings, a special informational session for guests with food allergies is held on embarkation day, typically at 1 p.m. Call ☎ 800-951-3532 to inquire about whether this is happening during your cruise.

Your best resource for food issues during your sailing may be your dining-service team. Even if you've completed the Special Services form well in advance, you should always make your needs known to dining staff, including your main dining room's head server. Some guests have found they are most comfortable if they stick with the same serving team during breakfast and lunch as well as dinner, and even on Castaway Cay. Feel free to ask your team about their daytime restaurant assignments.

unofficial **TIP**
A wealth of additional information on vacationing at Walt Disney World and Disney Cruise Line is available at **Allergy Free Mouse.** For DCL specifics, see tinyurl.com/allergyfreedcl.

Note that most port adventures are run by independent contractors, not Disney. Your food requests and accommodations will *not* be automatically transferred to excursion contractors, and some providers may not be equipped to work with certain dietary issues. What's more, in many ports you won't be able to bring certain types of food off the ship due to legal and agricultural restrictions. Check with Guest Services for advice on how best to handle your dietary needs in port.

SMOKING *on* BOARD

SMOKING, INCLUDING cigarettes, cigars, pipes, and electronic cigarettes, is prohibited in your stateroom, on your verandah (if your stateroom has one), and in any indoor space on the ship.

unofficial **TIP**
Guests caught smoking in their staterooms or on their verandahs will be charged a $250 cleaning fee.

On the *Magic* and *Wonder,* outdoor smoking areas are located on the Starboard side of Deck 4 between 6 p.m. and 6 a.m., and on the Port side of Deck 9 Forward, excluding the AquaLab area on the *Magic* and the Mickey's Pool area on the *Wonder.*

Smoking areas on the *Dream* and *Fantasy* are on the Port side of Deck 4 Aft, also from 6 p.m. to 6 a.m.; the Port side of Deck 12 Aft, accessed by walking through the Meridian Lounge; and near Currents Bar on Deck 13 Forward, Port side.

On the *Wish,* the smoking areas are on Decks 13 and 14 Forward and on Deck 4 near Lifeboat 14.

TRAVELING *with* MEDICATION

TRANSPORT PRESCRIPTION MEDICINE in its original containers, in your carry-on bag instead of checked luggage. The problem you want to avoid isn't with Disney but with the customs staffs of the

unofficial **TIP**
Marijuana in all forms, including medically prescribed marijuana, is prohibited on DCL ships.

countries you're visiting and US Customs when you return: while it's not likely, you could be asked to provide either the original containers (with your name on them) or a copy of a valid prescription, to ensure that you're not importing illegal or non-FDA-approved drugs. See

tinyurl.com/CBPTravelingWithMeds and tinyurl.com/PersonalDrug Importation for current federal guidelines.

If you'll be taking your medicines with you into port, also make sure to check the policies of the countries you'll be visiting. For example, some over-the-counter medicines commonly used in the US, including Actifed, Sudafed, and Vicks inhalers, aren't allowed into Mexico, nor are medications that contain codeine. See tinyurl.com/Bringing MedicinesToMexico for links to additional information.

In addition, be aware that your ship's onboard Health Center may not to be able to refill prescriptions (especially those for controlled substances) that run out during your cruise, so get them refilled before you leave home.

During our travels, we've had transportation or weather issues delay our arrival home by as many as four days. If you take medication that's critical to your health and well-being, we strongly encourage you to bring several days of extra doses with you whenever you travel, particularly when you travel to countries where medical protocols may be different from what you're used to back home.

Additional questions about traveling with medication are answeredin this informative **US Food and Drug Administration** video: tinyurl .com/FDATravelingWithMedsVideo.

FRIENDS *of* BILL W.

BEER, WINE, AND SPIRITS flow freely on cruise ships, even the relatively tame ones run by Disney. Daily **Alcoholics Anonymous** meetings are held on all cruises; check the specifics for your sailing on the DCL Navigator app. Note that some meetings are held in bars and lounges, but no bottles are out in the open during meetings.

That said, you will almost certainly be confronted with alcohol from time to time on a DCL cruise. If you're in recovery and you need a more fully alcohol-free environment, we encourage you to consider booking a trip with a company such as **Travel Sober** (travelsober.com), **We Love Lucid** (welovelucid.com), or **Sober Vacations International** (sobervacations.com). Some of these trips take place on cruise ships (Travel Sober, for example, uses Norwegian Cruise Line); others offer experiences similar to Adventures by Disney trips.

LGBTQ+ TRAVELERS

DCL IS VERY WELCOMING TO LGBTQ+ GUESTS. Many of our gay and lesbian friends, both with and without children, rave about their Disney cruises. One friend notes:

After about the second day, you can start picking out who's "family." We met more gay people traveling on our Disney cruise than on any of our other non-gay-focused cruises.

We've also met numerous same-sex couples and many LGBTQ+ staff on our **Adventures by Disney** river cruises (see Part Thirteen).

As the reader anecdote above demonstrates, many LGBTQ+ cruisers have good luck finding their tribes while out and about, but if you're traveling solo, it may be worth joining the Facebook group for your cruise or posting to a Disney discussion board to make connections before your trip.

*un*official **TIP**
Unlike other cruise lines, DCL doesn't offer onboard activities geared specifically to LGBTQ guests.

The experiences of LGBTQ+ travelers in port will depend largely on the itinerary. Most places won't present a problem, but there are a few where it may pay to be cautious: socially conservative parts of the Caribbean, for example. The **US State Department**'s resource page for LGBTQ+ travelers includes a wealth of information: see tinyurl .com/USDOS-LGBTTravelAdvice. Other good information sources are **Equaldex** (equaldex.com) and **Destination Pride** (destinationpride .org). You can also Google "LGBTQ+ travel advice" as a starting point for additional research.

RELUCTANT CRUISERS

IF YOU'RE READING THIS BOOK, there's a good chance that you're excitedly planning your first cruise. You may also find yourself dealing with a reluctant cruiser—someone who just can't get on board (ha-ha) with the idea of spending an extended amount of time on a cruise ship.

We love cruising now, but we were once reluctant cruisers ourselves: Erin was afraid of getting seasick, while Len was afraid of being disconnected from work. Despite a few initial missteps, our fears ultimately ended up being unfounded. We hope our experiences can help reassure the reticent cruiser(s) in your family.

A Tale of Two Cruise Converts

ERIN'S STORY *I was woefully underprepared for my first Disney cruise, which was hastily tacked on to a Walt Disney World vacation without much forethought. I'm prone to motion sickness, and my then-3-year-old daughter was in her separation-anxiety phase—but I didn't bother to do any research on these issues beforehand.*

Not surprisingly, I did get seasick, and I wasn't sure what to do when my daughter resisted going to the kids' club. After that first experience, I didn't think cruising was for me.

Fast-forward about eight years: my husband decided that the easiest and most efficient way to introduce our daughters to Europe would be on a cruise. With the carrot of a side trip to Disneyland Paris dangling before me, I reluctantly agreed to a Mediterranean sailing on the Magic.

This time, though, I did my homework: I came armed with an arsenal of anti–motion sickness tools suggested by my doctor, and my daughters had matured enough to enjoy the kids' clubs. Plus, I had researched alternative things to do with them just in case.

We introduced our children to Barcelona, the French Riviera, Rome, Naples, Florence, and Majorca, and I had to unpack only once. **I was hooked!** *I still prefer cruises with calmer waters (typically in Europe and Alaska), but I've gotten my sea legs and am happy to explore the Caribbean anytime. Cruising is a terrific way to see the world . . . as long as you're prepared.*

LEN'S STORY *I'm a workaholic who thinks high-speed internet access is an inalienable right. (True story: I once tried to charter a helicopter at midnight to extract me from a family camping trip to the Outer Banks of North Carolina because there was no air-conditioning or internet.) So I wasn't especially looking forward to my first cruise, on the* Fantasy—*I was envisioning a week spent cut off from civilization while Jimmy Buffett played in the background.*

As it turned out, there were more than enough activities to keep me busy all day, and just enough internet access to stave off any "Get me out of here!" instincts. I even learned to relax in the Fantasy's *Rainforest sauna (relax meaning "catch up on the* New York Times's *mobile edition").*

I don't recommend a seven-night cruise for your first trip on the high seas, but I also think a three-night cruise is too short: you're either packing or unpacking every day. A four-night cruise is the bare minimum for a great experience, as it includes a day at sea so you can explore the ship. A five-night cruise (with two sea days) is probably the best choice.

PART SIX

THE SHIPS *at a* GLANCE

OVERVIEW *and* OUR RECOMMENDATIONS

LAUNCHED IN 1998, the **Disney Magic** holds roughly 2,700 passengers and 950 crew members. The **Disney Wonder** has the same capacity and was launched in 1999. The **Disney Dream** and **Disney Fantasy,** which took their maiden voyages in 2011 and 2012, respectively, hold up to 4,000 passengers and 1,450 crew members. The **Disney Wish** had her inaugural season beginning in 2022. Her guest capacity is identical to that of the *Dream* and *Fantasy,* with a slightly higher crew count of 1,555.

All five ships share sleek lines, twin smokestacks, and nautical styling that calls to mind classic ocean liners, but with instantly recognizable Disney signatures. The colors—dark blue, white, red, and yellow—and the famous face-and-ears silhouette on the stacks are clearly those of Mickey Mouse. Look closely at the *Magic*'s stern ornamentation, for example, and you'll see a 15-foot Goofy hanging by his overalls. (It's Donald on the *Wonder*'s stern, Mickey on the *Dream*'s, Dumbo on the *Fantasy*'s, and Rapunzel on the *Wish*'s.)

A reader offers this tip for getting up to speed on the ships' design:

> *I highly recommend the **Art of the Ship** tour [see page 294] for adults. We learned all about the interior decorating and decor planning on the ship.*

The ships' interiors combine nautical themes with Art Nouveau, Art Deco, and (in the case of the *Wish*) Gothic, French Baroque, and Rococo inspiration. Art Nouveau, popular at the turn of the 20th century, incorporates natural shapes, such as from plants and animals, into its geometric designs; Art Deco has the geometry without the nature—think those sleek, streamlined interiors from 1930s movies. Disney describes the *Wish*'s hybrid design aesthetic as "Enchantment."

Disney images are everywhere, from Mickey's profile in the wrought-iron balustrades to the bronze statue of Helmsman Mickey featured prominently in the *Magic*'s atrium, Ariel on the *Wonder,* Admiral Donald on the *Dream,* Mademoiselle Minnie decked out in full 1920s flapper style on the *Fantasy,* and regal Cinderella on the *Wish*. Disney art is on every wall and in every stairwell and corridor. A grand staircase on each ship sweeps from the atrium lobby to shops peddling DCL-themed clothing, collectibles, jewelry, and more.

Ships have one or two lower decks with cabins; three decks with public areas such as theaters, lounges, and shops; and then three or five upper decks of cabins. Two or three sports and sundecks offer separate pools and facilities for families and adults without children. Signs point toward lounges and facilities, and all elevators are clearly marked as Forward, Aft, or Midship.

Our main complaint concerning the ships' design is that outdoor public areas focus inward toward the pools instead of seaward, as if Disney wants you to forget that you're on a cruise liner. On the *Magic, Wonder,* and *Wish,* there's no public place where you can curl up in the shade and watch the ocean—at least not without a plexiglass wall between you and it. But on Deck 4 of the *Dream* and the *Fantasy,* an open promenade, complete with comfy deck chairs, circles the ship. It's shady and fairly well protected from wind, and it offers you the opportunity to sit back and enjoy the sea without having to look through plexiglass barriers.

DCL CHEAT SHEET

CAN'T REMEMBER, SAY, which ship has the AquaDunk and which has the AquaDuck without looking it up? Neither can we from time to time. The handy charts on the following pages summarize what's the same and what's different across the ships.

All Disney Cruise Line ships have amenities in common, including the following:

FEATURES FOUND ON EVERY DCL SHIP	
• Adult pool and deck areas	• Bars, lounges, and cafés
• Buffet restaurant	• Family pools and water-play areas
• Fitness center	• Full-service spa and salon, with sauna
• Guest Services desk	• Health Center
• Infant, child, tween, and teen clubs	• Venues for live shows and movies
• Basketball court, shuffleboard, and other sports areas	• Outdoor LED screen for movies, concerts, and videos
• One or two upscale restaurants exclusively for adults (ages 18+)	• Opportunities to buy digital photos taken by onboard photographers
• 24-7 soft-serve ice cream "on tap"	• Retail shopping
• Onboard pay Wi-Fi (free to use with the DCL Navigator app)	• A **Bibbidi Bobbidi Boutique** for princess and pirate makeovers

Whereas some amenities are shared by all ships, the new *Disney Wish* has some not found on any other DCL vessel:

FEATURES UNIQUE TO THE *WISH*	
• **AquaMouse** water coaster	• Concierge staterooms above the bridge
• **Palo Steakhouse** and **Enchanté**, two adult-dining restaurants	• A second movie theater (the other ships have one apiece)
• *Star Wars* **Hyperspace Lounge**, a bar themed to the movie series	• **The Hideaway**, a dedicated lounge area for guests ages 18-20
• The **Hero Zone** play area for kids of all ages	• The **Disney Uncharted Adventure** interactive mobile game
• The **Outdoor Oasis**, a retreat attached to Senses Spa, with plush loungers and space for yoga.	• The **Frigidarium**, an ice lounge inside Senses' Rainforest

The sibling *Dream* and *Fantasy* share the following features not found on any of the other ships:

FEATURES UNIQUE TO THE *DREAM* AND *FANTASY*	
• **AquaDuck** water coaster	• Champagne bar (**Pink** on the *Dream*, **Ooh La La** on the *Fantasy*)
• **Meridian**, a martini bar	• Minigolf course
• **Remy**, an upscale French restaurant (adults only)	• **Satellite Falls**, an adults-only area with a splash pool and sundeck
• **Skyline**, a smart craft-cocktail bar with changing virtual cityscapes	• Electronic sports simulators

Finally, in spite of being the two oldest DCL ships, the *Magic* and *Wonder* both boast something singular:

UNIQUE TO THE *MAGIC* **AquaDunk**, a vertical waterslide. (The **AquaDuck** on the *Dream* and *Fantasy* sounds similar—the name is off by just one letter—but it's a horizontal water coaster.)

UNIQUE TO THE *WONDER* A **Concierge-only lounge** on Deck 10 boasts 270-degree views of the sea.

As an additional entry point for comparison, see the following pages for differences among key categories on all five ships.

DECK PLANS

SEE PAGES 171–173 for shared deck plans for the *Magic* and *Wonder,* followed by shared deck plans for the *Dream* and *Fantasy* on pages 174–176. Deck plans for the *Wish* are found on pages 177–180.

RANKING THE SHIPS

IGNORING THE DIFFERENT ITINERARIES that each ship serves, here's how we rank the Disney ships:

1. *Fantasy* **2.** *Dream* **3.** *Wish* **4.** *Wonder* **4.** *Magic*

The *Wish,* of course, is the bright, shiny new star of the DCL fleet. The pool-deck food is yummy, the kids' clubs are second to none, and

continued on page 181

WHAT'S DIFFERENT ACROSS THE SHIPS

FEATURE/CATEGORY

DINING (Adult) *(Note: Eating at these restaurants costs extra.)*

Magic	Wonder	Dream	Fantasy	Wish
Palo	Palo	Palo, Remy	Palo, Remy	Palo Steakhouse, Enchanté

DINING (Counter Service) *(An asterisk* below indicates that menu items cost extra.)*

Magic	Wonder	Dream	Fantasy	Wish
Daisy's De-Lites, Duck-in Diner, Eye Scream Treats, Frozone Treats*, Pinocchio's Pizzeria	Daisy's De-Lites, Eye Scream Treats, Pete's Boiler Bites, Pinocchio's Pizzeria	Eye Scream Treats, Flo's Cafe, Frozone Treats*, Senses Juice Bar*, Vanellope's Sweets & Treats*	Eye Scream Treats, Flo's Cafe, Frozone Treats*, Senses Juice Bar*, Sweet on You*	Daisy's Pizza Pies, Donald's Cantina, Goofy's Grill, Mickey's Smokestack Barbecue, Sweet Minnie's Ice Cream, Inside Out: Joyful Sweets*

DINING (Rotational)

Magic	Wonder	Dream	Fantasy	Wish
Animator's Palate, Lumiere's, Rapunzel's Royal Table	Animator's Palate, Tiana's Place, Triton's	Animator's Palate, Enchanted Garden, Royal Palace	Animator's Palate, Enchanted Garden, Royal Court	Arendelle: A *Frozen* Dining Adventure, 1923, Worlds of Marvel

FAMILY ENTERTAINMENT

Live Stage Shows *(may vary depending on itinerary)*

Magic	Wonder	Dream	Fantasy	Wish
Disney Dreams, Tangled: The Musical, Twice Charmed	Disney Dreams, Frozen: A Musical Spectacular, The Golden Mickeys	Beauty and the Beast, Disney's Believe, The Golden Mickeys	Disney's Aladdin, Disney's Believe, Frozen: A Musical Spectacular	Disney's Aladdin, Seas the Adventure!, The Little Mermaid

FEATURE/CATEGORY	Magic	Wonder	Dream	Fantasy	Wish
NIGHTLIFE AND BARS *(see next page for more)*					
Adult-nightlife area	After Hours	After Hours	The District	Europa	None—the bars and lounges are scattered around the ship.
Champagne bar	None	None	Pink	Ooh La La	None
Dance club	Fathoms	Azure	Evolution	The Tube	None
Live-music venue	Keys, Promenade Lounge	Cadillac Lounge, French Quarter Lounge	District Lounge	La Piazza	The Bayou, Nightingale's
Martini bar	None	None	Meridian	Meridian	None
Pool bars	Signals *(21+)*	Signals *(21+)*	Currents, Waves *(all ages)*	Currents, Waves *(all ages)*	Cove Bar; The Lookout

WHAT'S DIFFERENT ACROSS THE SHIPS *(continued)*

FEATURE/CATEGORY	Magic	Wonder	Dream	Fantasy	Wish
NIGHTLIFE AND BARS *(continued)*					
Pub/sports bar	O'Gills Pub	Crown & Fin	687	O'Gills Pub	Keg & Compass
Craft-cocktail bar	None	None	Skyline	Skyline	The Rose
"Outer-space cantina"	None	None	None	None	*Star Wars* Hyperspace Lounge
POOLS AND WATER PLAY AREAS					
Adult pools	Quiet Cove Pool	Quiet Cove Pool	Quiet Cove Pool, Satellite Falls	Quiet Cove Pool, Satellite Falls	Quiet Cove Pool
Family pool	Goofy's Pool	Goofy's Pool	Donald's Pool	Donald's Pool	Mickey's Pool
Kids' pools and splash areas	AquaLab, Mickey's Pool, Nephews' Pool/Splash Zone	AquaLab, Dory's Reef, Mickey's Pool/Splash Zone	Mickey's Pool, Nemo's Reef	AquaLab, Mickey's Pool, Nemo's Reef	Daisy's Pool, Donald's Pool, Goofy's Pool, Minnie's Pool, Pluto's Pool, *Toy Story* Splash Zone
Teen splash pool *(ages 14-17)*	None	None	Vibe	Vibe	None
Water Rides	AquaDunk *(vertical waterslide)*, Twist 'n' Spout *(kids' waterslide)*	Mickey's Slide, Twist 'n' Spout	AquaDuck *(water coaster)*, Mickey's Slide	AquaDuck, Mickey's Slide	AquaMouse, Slide-a-Saurus Rex
SPORTS AND RECREATION					
Games	Basketball, Foosball, shuffleboard, table tennis	Basketball, Foosball, shuffleboard, table tennis	Basketball, Foosball, minigolf, shuffleboard, table tennis	Basketball, Foosball, minigolf, shuffleboard, table tennis	Basketball, table tennis, foosball, shuffleboard, air hockey, Incredi-Games racecourse
MISCELLANEOUS					
"Enchanted" (Interactive) art	None	None	Yes	Yes	Yes
Interactive game *(played around the ship)*	No	No	Midship Detective Agency	Midship Detective Agency	Disney Uncharted Adventure
Shutters Photo Studio	Yes	Yes	No	Yes	Yes
Virtual portholes in Inside Staterooms	None	None	Yes	Yes	No

Magic/Wonder **DECK PLANS**

continued on next page

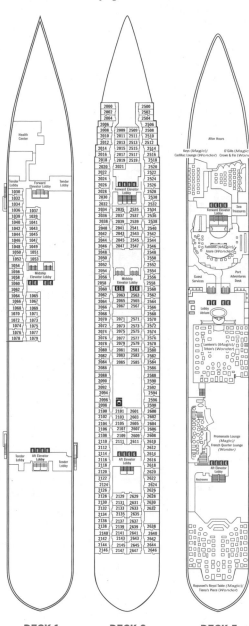
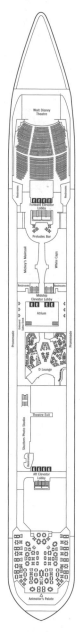

DECK 1   **DECK 2**   **DECK 3**   **DECK 4**

Magic/Wonder
DECK PLANS

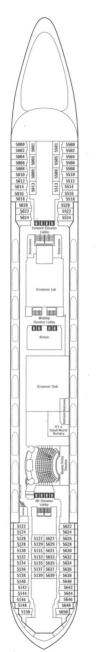

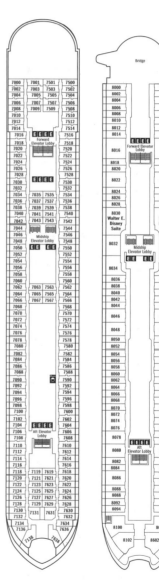

DECK 5 **DECK 6** **DECK 7** **DECK 8**

Magic/Wonder **DECK PLANS**

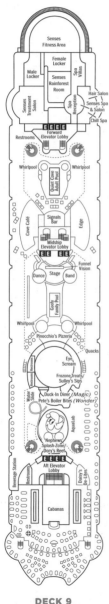

DECK 9

DECK 10

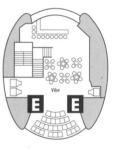

DECK 11

Dream/Fantasy DECK PLANS

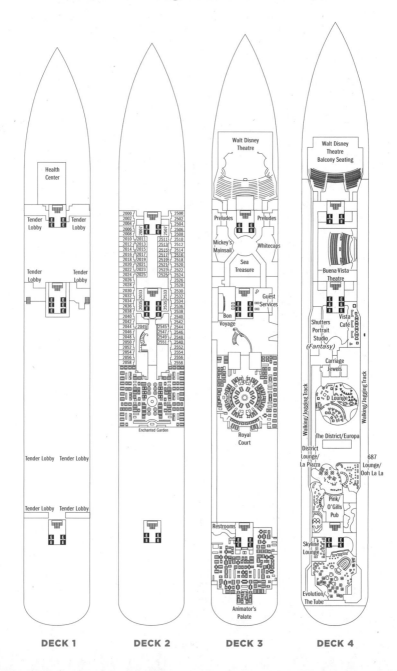

DECK 1

DECK 2

DECK 3

DECK 4

Deck 1 labels: Health Center; Tender Lobby; Tender Lobby; Tender Lobby; Tender Lobby; Tender Lobby Tender Lobby; Tender Lobby Tender Lobby

Deck 2 labels: 2000–2058 cabin numbers; 2500–2558 cabin numbers; Enchanted Garden

Deck 3 labels: Walt Disney Theatre; Preludes; Preludes; Mickey's Mainsail; Whitecaps; Sea Treasure; Guest Services; Bon Voyage; Royal Court; Restrooms; Animator's Palate

Deck 4 labels: Walt Disney Theatre Balcony Seating; Buena Vista Theatre; Vista Café; Shutters Portrait Studio (Fantasy); Carriage Jewels; D Lounge; Walking/Jogging Track; Walking/Jogging Track; The District/Europa; District Lounge/La Piazza; 687 Lounge/Ooh La La; Pink/O'Gills Pub; Skyline Lounge; Evolution/The Tube

Dream/Fantasy **DECK PLANS**

continued on next page

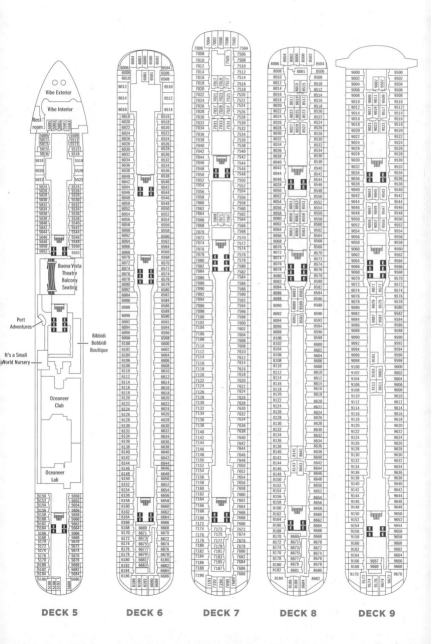

DECK 5　　**DECK 6**　　**DECK 7**　　**DECK 8**　　**DECK 9**

Dream/Fantasy **DECK PLANS**

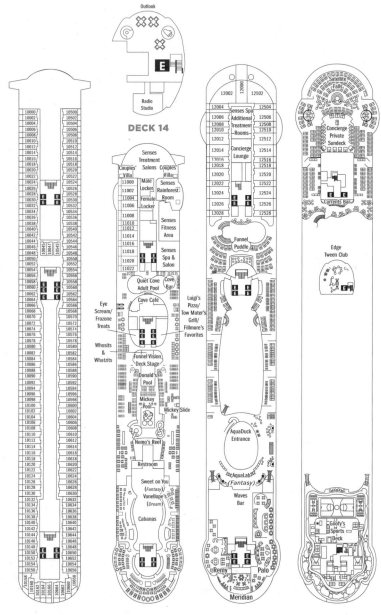

Outlook

E

Radio
Studio

DECK 14

Senses
Treatment
Salons
Couples'
Villa
Couples'
Villa

| 11000 |
| 11002 | Male
Locker |
| 11004 | Senses
Rainforest
Room |
| 11006 | Female
Locker |
| 11008 |
| 11010 |
| 11012 | Senses
Fitness
Area |
| 11014 |
| 11016 |
| 11018 | Senses
Spa &
Salon |
| 11020 |
| 11022 |

Quiet Cove
Adult Pool
Cove
Bar

Eye
Scream/
Frozone
Treats

Cove Café

Luigi's
Pizza/
Tow Mater's
Grill/
Fillmore's
Favorites

Whosits
&
Whatzits

Funnel Vision
Deck Stage

Donald's
Pool

Mickey
Pool

Mickey Slide

Nemo's Reel

Restroom

Sweet on You
(Fantasy)
Vanellope's
(Dream)

Cabanas

E
E

Remy

Palo

Meridian

DECK 11

12002	12000	12502
12004		12504
12006	Senses Spa	12506
12008	Additional
Treatment
Rooms	12508
12010		12510
12012		12512
12014	Concierge
Lounge	12514
12016		12516
12018		12518
12020		12520
12022		12522
12024		12524
12026		12526
12028		12528

Funnel
Puddle

E E

AquaDuck
Entrance

AquaLab
(Fantasy)

Waves
Bar

DECK 12

10000		10500
10002		10502
10004		10504
10006		10506
10008		10508
10010		10510
10012		10512
10014		10514
10016		10516
10018		10518
10020		10520
10022		10522
10024		10524
10026		10526
10028		10528
10030		10530
10032		10532
10034		10534
10036		10536
10038		10538
10040		10540
10042		10542
10044		10544
10046	10045	10045	10546
10048		10548
10050		10550
10052		10552
10054		10554
10056		10556
10058		10558
10060		10560
10062		10562
10064		10564
10066		10566
10068		10568
10070		10570
10072		10572
10074		10574
10076		10576
10078		10578
10080		10580
10082		10582
10084		10584
10086		10586
10088		10588
10090		10590
10092		10592
10094		10594
10096		10596
10098		10598
10100		10600
10102		10602
10104		10604
10106		10606
10108		10608
10110		10610
10112		10612
10114		10614
10116		10616
10118		10618
10120		10620
10122		10622
10124		10624
10126		10626
10128		10628
10130		10630
10132		10632
10134		10634
10136		10636
10138		10638
10140		10640
10142		10642
10144		10644
10146		10646
10148		10648
10150		10650
10152		10652
10154		10654
10156		10656
10158	10160	10161	10164	10165	10664	10665	10660	10662	10658

DECK 10

Satellite
Falls

Concierge
Private
Sundeck

Currents Bar

Edge
Tween Club

E

Goofy's
Sports
Deck

DECK 13

Wish **DECK PLANS**

continued on next page

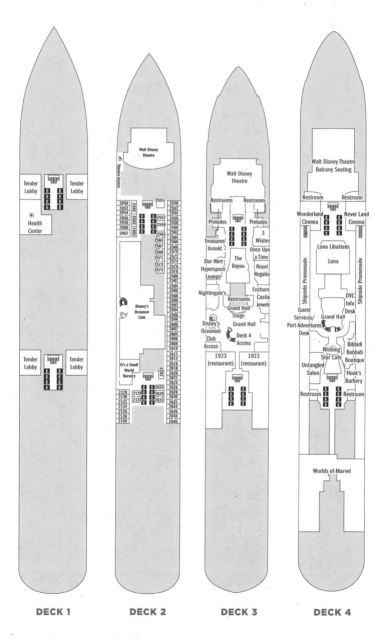

DECK 1

DECK 2

DECK 3

DECK 4

DECK 1

Tender Lobby

Tender Lobby

Health Center

Tender Lobby

Tender Lobby

DECK 2

Walt Disney Theatre

Theatre Access

Disney's Oceaneer Club

It's a Small World Nursery

2050
2052
2954
2956
2958
2960
2962

2551
2550
2552
2554
2556
2557
2558
2559
2560
2562
2563
2564
2565
2566
2567
2568
2569
2570
2571
2572
2573
2574
2575
2576
2578
2580
2582
2584
2586
2588
2590
2592
2594
2596
2598
2600
2602
2604
2606
2608
2610
2612
2614
2616
2618
2620
2622
2623
2624
2626
2627
2628
2629
2630
2631
2632
2634
2636
2638
2640

2128
2130
2132
2134
2136
2138
2140

2129
2130
2131

DECK 3

Walt Disney Theatre

Restrooms

Restrooms

Preludes

Preludes

Treasures Untold

3 Wishes

Star Wars Hyperspace Lounge

Once Upon a Time

The Bayou

Royal Regalia

Nightingale's

Enchanté

Castle Jewels

Restrooms

Grand Hall Stage

Disney's Oceaneer Club Access

Grand Hall

Deck 4 Access

1923 (restaurant)

1923 (restaurant)

DECK 4

Walt Disney Theatre Balcony Seating

Restroom

Restroom

Wonderland Cinema

Never Land Cinema

Shipside Promenade

Luna Libations

Luna

Shipside Promenade

DVC Info Desk

Guest Services/ Port Adventures Desk

Grand Hall

Wishing Star Cafe

Bibbidi Bobbidi Boutique

Untangled Salon

Hook's Barbery

Restroom

Restroom

Worlds of Marvel

Wish
DECK
PLANS

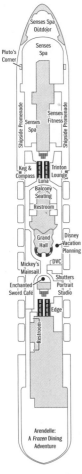

DECK 5 labels: Senses Spa Outdoor, Pluto's Corner, Senses Spa, Shipside Promenade, Senses Fitness Promenade, Keg & Compass, Trinton Lounge, Luna, Balcony Seating, Restroom, Grand Hall, Disney Vacation Planning, Mickey's Mainsail, DVC, Shutters, Enchanted Sword Café, Portrait Studio, Edge, Restroom, Arendelle: A *Frozen* Dining Adventure

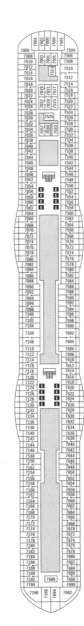

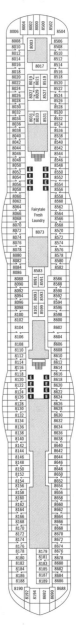

DECK 5   **DECK 6**   **DECK 7**   **DECK 8**

Wish DECK PLANS

continued on next page

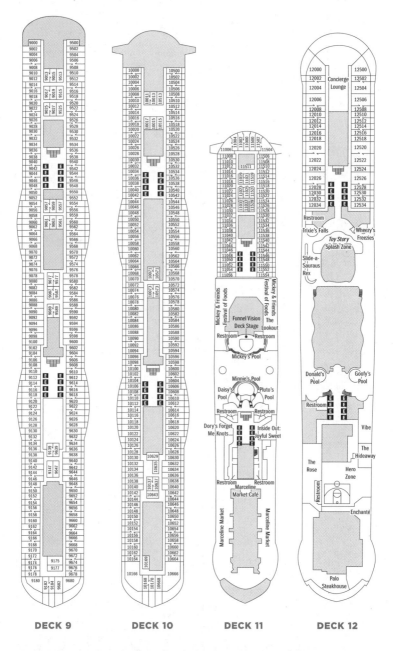

DECK 9 **DECK 10** **DECK 11** **DECK 12**

Wish DECK PLANS

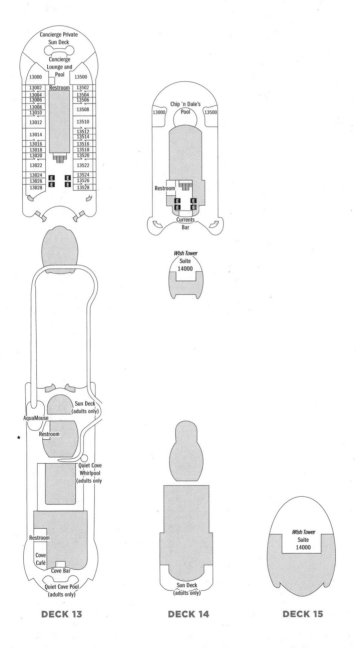

DECK 13

DECK 14

DECK 15

continued from page 170

the stateroom decor is lovely. Nevertheless, we think Disney made a number of missteps with the *Wish*, namely the lack of a walking track around the ship, the dearth of drawer storage and awkward TV placement in the staterooms, and the relatively small scale of the adult lounges—not to mention a few glaring barriers to wheelchair accessibility (see page 158).

Given the premium prices Disney is charging to cruise on the *Wish*, we think you'll have just as lovely a time on the **Dream** and **Fantasy,** which offer significantly better value. These two ships are still in great condition. They have better restaurants, bars, and pools than the two oldest ships, along with more on-deck activities, more space for kids' activities, more deck space for sunbathing, better spas, and more interactive games. These advantages make up for the ships' slightly smaller cabin sizes: non-Concierge staterooms on the *Dream* and *Fantasy,* for example, are 2%–9% (or 5–22 square feet) smaller than corresponding cabins on the *Magic* and *Wonder.*

Of course, some itineraries—basically, any destination that isn't an island—have just one ship as an option. When we want to visit Alaska or Europe, we're happy to be on any of the DCL vessels.

Whichever ship you choose to sail on, you can rest assured that it will be in tip-top shape in 2023. During the 2021 cruise shutdown, the entire Disney fleet underwent dry- and wet-dock updates and deep cleaning at a shipyard in Brest, France. In October 2020, all four existing ships were there at the same time—marking the first time that the entire DCL fleet had ever undergone maintenance simultaneously.

The **Disney Magic**

THE FIRST DCL SHIP, the *Magic* was launched in 1998 and underwent an extensive renovation—or **reimagining,** in Disney-speak—during a two-month dry dock in Cádiz, Spain, during the summer of 2013. This extensive makeover included cosmetic updates to the ship's lobby atrium; **Keys,** the piano bar; **Palo,** the adults-only, fine-dining Italian restaurant; and **Fathoms,** the dance club. In addition, Vista Spa became **Senses Spa.** The *Magic* underwent additional dry-dock tweaking in late 2015. Changes at that time included the addition of a **Bibbidi Bobbidi Boutique** children's makeover salon and a location update for the **Edge** tween club.

The *Magic* underwent yet another dry-dock refresh in 2018. **Vibe** teen club got updated decor; the **Cove Café** coffee bar was spruced up; and, most significantly, the uninspired Carioca's dining room was rethemed as **Rapunzel's Royal Table,** featuring elements from the Disney animated feature *Tangled.*

The **Disney Wonder**

LAUNCHED IN 1999 as the second of DCL's five current ships, the *Wonder* was beginning to show her age by 2016, with visible wear and tear and dated decor in many guest areas. In late 2016 the *Wonder* underwent a dry dock with significant updating and retheming, emerging in much better condition and with amenities, entertainment, and fittings on par with the rest of the fleet.

The *Wonder* continues to have the most in common with its sister the *Magic,* but with slightly different theming. When you board the ship at Deck 3, you're greeted by Ariel instead of Mickey and an Art Nouveau–style atrium rather than Art Deco. In keeping with the *Little Mermaid* theme, one of the standard rotational-dining restaurants on the *Wonder* is **Triton's,** named for Ariel's dad (its counterpart on the *Magic* is the *Beauty and the Beast*–themed **Lumiere's**).

The 2016 dry dock introduced **Cabanas** buffet and a unique restaurant, **Tiana's Place,** inspired by the film *The Princess and the Frog* and serving New Orleans–style cuisine accompanied by live jazz. Additionally, the *Wonder*'s antiquated version of **Animator's Palate** was retrofitted with an interactive show to match its counterparts on the other ships. Following the dry dock, the *Wonder*'s dining is now on par with that of the rest of the DCL fleet.

Len, a cynic whose capacity for scorn would make Ebenezer Scrooge exclaim, "Dude, lighten up!," thinks *Frozen: A Musical Spectacular* (presented on both the *Wonder* and the *Fantasy*) is the best stage show in the DCL fleet. In addition to catchy songs, solid stage design, and a snappy pace, it has special effects that had him literally saying "Wow!" out loud.

The kids' clubs were also reimagined. The **Oceaneer Club** now features **Marvel's Super Hero Academy,** in which young guests train to become superheroes (with help from Spider-Man during live character appearances), and *Frozen* **Adventures,** where a digital Olaf leads kids in games and songs.

A 2019 *Wonder* dry dock saw the addition of a New Orleans–themed family nightclub, the **French Quarter Lounge,** designed to complement Tiana's Place. Also freshened up during this refurb were **Cove Café** coffee bar, **Signals** pool bar, and **Vibe** teen club.

From a bells-and-whistles standpoint, the *Wonder* continues to lag behind its younger sisters. You won't find a headliner waterslide like the AquaDunk (*Magic*) or a water coaster like the AquaDuck (*Dream, Fantasy*) or AquaMouse (*Wish*) on the pool deck, and inside cabins on the *Wonder* lack the "virtual portholes" found in inside rooms on the *Dream* and *Fantasy.*

Nevertheless, the *Wonder* is my (Erin's) sentimental favorite of the DCL fleet. The smaller capacity of the older ships means there are fewer people jockeying for space on Castaway Cay; I also think the older ships have a more cozy, homey atmosphere. By the end of a long sailing on a small ship, the cast members feel like family—something I haven't experienced as often on the *Dream* or *Fantasy,* and something I haven't really experienced yet on the *Wish*.

The *Disney Dream*

FOLLOWING THE SUCCESSES OF THE MAGIC AND WONDER, DCL ordered two new ships that would more than double the number of guests they could serve, allow them to expand the number of itineraries offered, and bring several first-evers to a cruise ship. The new *Dream*-class vessels were built by Meyer Werft in Germany rather than Italy's Fincantieri, which created the *Magic* and *Wonder.*

The *Disney Dream,* the first of these new ships, set sail in 2011. It's 151 feet longer, 35 feet taller, and 15 feet wider than the *Magic* or *Wonder.* With three additional decks, the ship can hold 50% more passengers and crew than her predecessors.

Disney Imagineering had great fun designing the second-generation ships. Inside cabins were given "virtual portholes," which show the view from the bridge on a round screen. This feature proved so popular with kids that on many cruises, interior cabins had fares higher than those of ocean-view cabins. On the top deck, the **AquaDuck**, a waterslide that circles the ship, was added to the usual pools. Between the pool deck and your cabin, you'll find interactive art that reacts when you pass by it, along with the **Midship Detective Agency**, a scavenger hunt–type game that sends families all over the ship collecting clues.

When it came to dining, **Cabanas** buffet improved on both traffic flow and food quality compared with the dire Beach Blanket Buffet on the *Wonder* (which, thankfully, became Cabanas eventually as well). As for the *Dream*'s three standard dining rooms, **Animator's Palate** was improved with new technology as part of the dinner show, **Enchanted Garden** took its place as the prettiest of the three, and **Royal Palace** is a tribute to all things Disney princess, but mostly Cinderella.

Both adults and kids scored big with improvements to the new ship. In addition to the adults-only Palo, **Remy** was added as another upscale-dining option for the 18-and-up crowd. With a subtle *Ratatouille* theme, and not one but two celebrated chefs creating the menus, Remy initially shocked cruisers with its surcharge—now $125 plus alcohol per dinner, among the highest in the industry—but diners were pleased nonetheless. The adult lounges, in the area called **The District** on Deck 4, provide more-intimate, better-themed spaces to take the edge off than **After Hours,** the comparable space on the *Magic* and *Wonder.* **Skyline,** one of The District's bars, showcases a great use of technology, with a cityscape behind the bar that changes every 15 minutes. It's mesmerizing.

Kids got greatly expanded club areas with a Pixar theme. The teen area got a makeover that left it one of the most stylish spaces on board and gave it its own pool (the cast-member pool area from the older ships). Teens also got their own pampering spot, **Chill Spa.**

Though the *Dream* still feels very new, Disney continues to improve the ship. A 2015 dry-dock refresh added a **Bibbidi Bobbidi Boutique** makeover salon for children, on Deck 5; **Vanellope's Sweets & Treats,** a premium-ice-cream shop, on Deck 11 (think of it as Palo for kids); and a *Star Wars*–themed area of the Oceaneer Club where children "pilot" a faux *Millennium Falcon* and participate in a shipboard version of the *Jedi Training* show at Walt Disney World.

After 10 years of being based in Port Canaveral, the *Dream* moved to southern Florida in 2022 to make room for the *Wish* at Port Canaveral. The *Dream* is sailing primarily out of Miami for the first half of 2023 and will make a permanent move to Port Everglades toward the end of the year.

The **Disney Fantasy**

DCL'S THIRD SHIP FIRST SAILED in 2012, one year after the *Dream* came into service. The *Fantasy* is nearly identical to its sister but got some unique tweaks as a result of guest and cast-member feedback. The ship is based in Port Canaveral and sails primarily seven-night itineraries in the Caribbean, with a few shorter or longer sailings that focus on the Bahamas or Bermuda.

Walking into the atrium of the *Fantasy,* you see a bronze statue of Minnie Mouse and a striking peacock-inspired carpet: an indication of the Art Nouveau style of the *Fantasy* as opposed to the *Dream*'s Deco look.

The *Dream*'s technology package got some enhancements on the *Fantasy.* The **Midship Detective Agency** has three different story lines (including the Muppets), surpassing the version on the *Dream,* and the show at **Animator's Palate** got a very cool audience-interaction element that we won't spoil here. Other than this addition, the restaurants are identical to the *Dream*'s, with one subtle name change: Royal Palace is **Royal Court** and includes even more princessy goodness. **Cabanas, Enchanted Garden, Palo,** and **Remy** are the same.

On the pool deck, the **AquaDuck** adds the **AquaLab** splash area.

The *Fantasy*'s nightlife area is **Europa. Skyline** is the one constant between the two bar–nightclub areas on the ships, though it displays different cityscapes in this rendition. **The Tube**'s *Austin Powers*–style decor makes it a very fun place to hang out, but **Ooh La La** is either too high-concept or low-concept for our tastes; we prefer the whimsical look of the *Dream*'s **Pink** for our Champagne needs. **O'Gills Pub** doesn't feel particularly Irish, though it has the same big-screen TVs as **687,** the sports bar on the *Dream.*

The **Disney Wish**

HAVING ENTERED SERVICE IN 2022, a decade after the *Fantasy*, the *Wish* is the first in the third generation (or **Triton class**) of DCL ships. It debuted to near-frenzied levels of excitement, with the first sailing selling out before it even became available to the general public—and during a global pandemic at that.

The *Wish* has a gorgeous exterior that harmonizes with the rest of the fleet's. Inside, the ship has opulent furnishings and visually appealing color schemes. Of particular note, the *Wish* has an even more "Disney" feel than the other ships. We're not sure that's a good thing, however.

What we mean here isn't theming so much as aggressive, in-your-face branding. Whereas, for example, the upscale bars on the *Dream* and *Fantasy* are non-Disney-themed, the *Wish* has the ultra-themed **Star Wars Hyperspace Lounge.** Similarly, the other ships have spas and beauty salons that are tastefully appointed but not specifically Disney-fied. On the *Wish*, however, the women's beauty salon is the **Untangled Salon,** with Rapunzel and *Tangled* imagery throughout, and the barber shop is **Hook's Barbery,** with "narrative details inspired by Captain Hook." And that's just the *adult* spaces.

Don't get us wrong—we love Disney, we write about it for a living, and our combined cruises and visits to the theme parks and other Disney destinations number in the thousands. But there comes a point where "theming" crosses the line into all-consuming.

If you think that's an over-the-top take, consider this: while monitoring guest reports and media accounts of the *Wish*'s first few months of service, we lost count of the number of times we read variations on the phrase "theme park at sea."

For many (if not most) people, the raison d'etre of a cruise vacation is relaxation. "Theme park at sea" is the diametric opposite of relaxation. Yes, it's entertaining—and indeed, it could be exactly what you want for your family—but serene it is not. And while there are a few places on the *Wish* where you can get away from "all Disney, all the time," there are fewer of these than on DCL's four original vessels.

The *Wish* sails primarily three- and four-night Bahamian cruises out of Port Canaveral.

PART SEVEN

DINING

▌ NOSHES, NOSHES *Everywhere*

THE FIRST THING MANY CRUISERS DISCOVER when exploring the ships on embarkation day are the near-endless displays of food at the pool-level restaurants. In the way that some people remember the birth of their first child, we remember our first glimpse of the food stations stretching out as far as the eye can see. (Sorry, kids, it's eatin' time.) On one table sat a pile of crab legs that almost reached eye level, and next to this sat a trawler's worth of peel-and-eat shrimp. Surrounding all this deliciousness was enough cocktail sauce to float the ship itself. On the other side of the aisle, a chef was flash-cooking a steak, the spices, sizzle, and flame making the air smell savory. It was *heavenly.*

unofficial **TIP**

DCL restaurants (except for the adult-dining venues) offer kids' menus for breakfast, lunch, and dinner. Kids (except for infants in the nursery) may also dine in their designated clubs free of charge.

You'll never go hungry on a DCL cruise. The variety of dining options is staggering, with everything from coffee shops and pizza stands to Las Vegas–style buffets to ritzy French and Italian restaurants. That said, we've learned a few ways to increase your chances of enjoying memorable meals on board. This section describes your dining options in detail and includes our advice on how to make the most of them.

ROTATIONAL DINING

ONE OF THE INNOVATIONS that DCL brought to the cruise industry is the concept of **rotational dining,** in which you visit one of three standard restaurants on each different night of your cruise. As you change from restaurant to restaurant, your server team—your waiter, beverage person, and head waiter—all move with you. Your team will quickly learn your dining preferences, including favorite drinks and desserts, and make menu suggestions. Along with your stateroom attendant, you'll almost certainly rely on your dining team more than any other members of the crew during your trip.

11 WAYS TO GET THE MOST FROM DCL DINING

1. Communication is key. If, say, you want your meal served faster or slower, or you don't want your kids eating dessert, let your serving team know.

2. You can order from any part of the menu, in any combination. If you want two main courses or two soups, no problem. If all you want is two appetizers and a salad or just bread and dessert, that's fine too.

3. The main dining rooms are "all you care to eat." If you want more of any dish, let your servers know and they'll bring it to you at no extra charge.

4. Try it—you may like it! Not sure you like scallops? Order some with your favorite steak. Whether you hate the scallops or you love them, you'll have learned something.

5. Don't be afraid to say "when." If you're full, say so politely but firmly.

6. You can order from a main dining room besides the one where you're eating. A full list of menus is available on the DCL Navigator app.

7. Ask your server what's available off-menu. Did you know, for example, that you can order Mickey ice-cream bars for dessert? You can also order some things for free in the main dining rooms that would cost extra elsewhere on board—for example, kiddie "cocktails" like Shirley Temples and "No-Hitos" that you'd have to pay for at an onboard bar.

8. It's OK to skip the main dining room. Honest. You may have any number of perfectly valid reasons for doing this: you want to take advantage of the low crowds at the pool slide while everyone else is eating, your tablemates are getting on your last nerve, or you have an insatiable craving for chicken nuggets from the pool deck. Whatever the case, remember: It's *your* cruise. Do what works for you, and don't feel obligated to do what doesn't.

9. Servers love helping you celebrate (safely). They'll gladly bring you an extra dessert (or extra, *extra* desserts) and a birthday button. (What they *can't* do, however, is put candles on your cake: open flames aren't allowed on the ship.)

10. You can have fancy ice-cream desserts delivered to your main dining room for an extra charge. Early in the day, stop by Vanellope's (*Dream*), Sweet on You (*Fantasy*), or Inside Out: Joyful Sweets (*Wish*) to place an order, tell them your dining time and table number, and they'll make your child's wildest dreams come true.

11. When it comes to ordering, there's an app for that—but you don't have to use it. The restaurant menus are available on the Navigator app and can be accessed on your phone via a QR code you'll find at your table. But if you prefer to use an old-school approach to ordering, your server will be happy to bring you a paper menu.

The rotational restaurants have two dinner seatings, typically around **5:45 p.m.** and **8:15 p.m.** (For sailings originating in Europe, seatings are typically at **6 p.m.** and **8:30 p.m.**) The live stage shows in the theaters are timed to match the dinner hours: if you have the 5:45 dinner seating, you'll be able to watch the 8 o'clock show, and vice versa.

Because Disney sets your schedule, there's no need to make reservations each night. You can request either the earlier or later seating when booking your trip or once aboard the ship. You also can request changes to your rotation, specifying which restaurants you visit each night.

On cruises of four nights or longer, you'll repeat at least one of the three standard restaurants. The menus will change each night, but the decor remains the same. Rather than visit the same restaurant twice on a four-night cruise, we recommend using one of those nights to visit one of the adult-dining venues: **Palo** on the *Magic, Wonder, Dream,* and Fantasy; **Remy** on the *Dream* and *Fantasy;* or **Palo Steakhouse** or **Enchanté** on the *Wish.* You must pay an additional charge to dine at these restaurants, but the food is stellar, the crowds are small, and the service is impeccable. See page 192 for details.

REQUESTING A SEATING You may arrange a specific dining rotation by calling DCL directly at ☎ 800-951-3532. This way, for example, you can pick which restaurant you're assigned to visit twice on a four-night cruise, or three times on a seven-night cruise. Requests aren't guaranteed but are honored whenever possible.

If you can't get the seating you want before you sail, you can join a waiting list on the **My Reservations** section of the DCL website (see page 47). If you don't make it off the list before you sail, check with Guest Services for an opening after you board.

COVID TIP

Cabanas and Marceline Market weren't serving dinner at the time of this writing, but we expect them to in the near future. Check the specifics for your sailing.

DINNER ALTERNATIVES If you'd rather skip the main dining room, you can order room service, eat at one of the counter-service restaurants, or book dinner at one of the adult-dining venues. Another alternative during times of normal operation is eating dinner at the large restaurant on your ship's pool deck: **Marceline Market** on the *Wish* or **Cabanas** on the other four ships. These restaurants—which switch from buffet service to table service at night—are a less formal and less expensive option than eating in the adults-only restaurants: the dress code is the same as in the main dining rooms, and you're not charged for your meal. Plus, they tend to be less crowded at night.

Note that Cabanas and Marceline Market don't serve dinner on the first or last night of most cruises. On days when the ship has an unusually late port departure or an overnight in port (for example, in Bermuda or Reykjavík, Iceland), these restaurants will likely be configured as they are during the day. Check the **DCL Navigator app** (see page 136) for details.

Finally, if you're not in the mood to fight the crowds at Cabanas or Marceline Market during breakfast and lunch, at least one of the rotational restaurants is open during the day. Again, check the Navigator app for more information.

DINNER SHOWS The rotational restaurants feature live entertainment on one night of your sailing. If, for example, you're on a four-night sailing of the *Wish* and are assigned to eat at Arendelle twice, you'll experience the *Frozen* show (see page 219) once. If Anna and Elsa aren't your thing, you can always eat somewhere else on show night.

DINING WITH STRANGERS DCL often seats different families together in the main dining rooms. Of particular note, couples and solo travelers are almost always seated with others. Some cruisers love this—but if, say, you're an introvert (see page 132) or you're a couple on your honeymoon, you'd probably find it awkward and intrusive.

If you'd rather not eat with strangers during your rotational-dining seatings, let DCL know before you sail, or check with your head waiter once you're on board. Again, though, keep in mind that seating changes aren't guaranteed.

HOW TO DINE ON DISNEY CRUISE LINE *by Scott Sanders*

I SUGGEST THAT EVERYONE NEW TO DCL experience the rotational-dining-room menus first. If brunch at the adult-dining venues is offered on your sailing, use that as an opportunity to experience these restaurants. Then, on your next cruise, explore the adults-only dinner options. Alternatively, if your ship features a dinner show and that's not your cup of tea, use this night to dine elsewhere.

Cruising is also a great opportunity to try new foods. For instance, if nothing on the dinner menu strikes your fancy, ask to see the menu for guests with food allergies—it features some delicious dishes that aren't offered on the regular menu.

WHICH DINNER SEATING SHOULD I CHOOSE? The following factors, among others, may influence your decision:

Culture and Customs Early seatings tend to fill up more quickly on US sailings, whereas the late seatings tend to get snapped up faster on European sailings.

Cruise Length You may be able to cope better with a less-than-optimal dining time on a 3-night sailing. Conversely, a 12-night voyage would give you ample time to adapt to either seating.

Time Zone If you live on the West Coast and you're sailing from Port Canaveral or Miami, you may find that the early seating feels more like lunch rather than dinner. On the other hand, East Coast guests sailing out of San Diego or Vancouver may initially have a hard time staying awake during the late seating.

Health Concerns Guests with GI issues such as acid reflux often need to eat their last meal of the day several hours before bedtime. Other guests may be on medications that must be taken on a full (or empty) stomach at a particular time. Here, choose the seating that works best for you.

Your Kids' Sleep Schedules Many young children simply can't stay awake past 7:30 or 8 p.m. If you want them to eat dinner with you in the main dining rooms, then the late seating may be a no-go. If you want to see the early stage show with your kids, skip the main dining room and grab a quick bite from a counter-service restaurant instead.

Seating Preferences for Stage Shows If you're picky about where you sit, a late dinner seating will help you beat the crowds to the early show.

Eating Habits Some guests may need a snack in the late afternoon to ward off the "hangries" before a late seating. (Cheese and crackers, anyone?) Conversely, slow eaters may find the second seating less rushed.

Plans in Port If a shore excursion will have you returning to the ship close to or after the early seating, then choose the late seating.

Noise Tolerance While there will be young kids at both seatings, there are likely to be fewer of them at the late seating, making for a quieter dining experience.

Brunch Plans Brunches at Palo, Remy, and Enchanté are lavish multi-course affairs featuring dishes that are often rich and heavy. A late seating would allow extra time for your meal to digest.

Your Schedule on Your Last Day Aboard The time of your last breakfast is tied to your dinner seating: early diners eat breakfast earlier than late diners. If you don't have an early flight and you want to grab a bit of extra sleep, choose the late seating.

DCL RESTAURANT CATEGORIES

IN GENERAL, FOOD OFFERINGS on Disney Cruise Line are differentiated by freshness, quality, and service:

COUNTER SERVICE Available on each ship's pool deck, the quick-service offerings includes staples such as burgers, chicken strips, pizza, and sandwiches. In *The Unofficial Guide to Walt Disney World*, we equate the quality of the counter-service restaurants in the theme parks with that of McDonald's and Taco Bell. With a few exceptions, the food quality at DCL's counter-service restaurants is more like what you'd find in your local supermarket's frozen-food aisle: if you're hungry, it's fine, but it's not as good as something made from scratch. The best items on board are the fresh sandwiches and wraps. Counter-service restaurants for each ship are listed starting on page 203.

*un*official **TIP**
Note: Cove Café on the *Wish* doesn't serve food.

CAFÉS AND LOUNGES Each ship has a dedicated adults-only coffee bar called **Cove Café** that serves espresso, cappuccino, teas, and smoothies, along with wine, mixed drinks, and spirits. A good alternative to a heavy dinner is Cove Café's small selection of complimentary cold appetizers, available each evening.

Besides Cove Café, a few of the ships' bars and lounges serve appetizers. These venues are described in detail in Part Eight, "Entertainment and Nightlife."

BUFFET DINING Each ship has a large pick-what-you-want eatery, located on the main pool deck. On the *Magic, Wonder, Dream,* and *Fantasy,* this is a buffet called **Cabanas;** on the *Wish,* it's called **Marceline Market.** Both offer a wide array of foods, typically representing a number of themes or cultures, displayed for you to choose from.

Cabanas is self-service: grab a tray, walk up, and help yourself. At Marceline Market, most of your picks are dished up by a cast member. In either case, you may go back as often as you like and eat as much as you desire. Open for breakfast and lunch on most days, the buffets are an easy way to satisfy a group with diverging preferences or appetites; plus, they let picky kids (and adults) to see what the food looks like before taking the plunge.

FULL-SERVICE RESTAURANTS Each DCL ship has four or five restaurants offering full table service. Three of these are part of the standard rotational dinner schedule available to every guest on the ship, with the remaining venues available to guests 18 and older for an additional fee. You may also find that the buffet is configured as a standard menu-based restaurant, with drop-in seating, in the evening. If available on your sailing, this can be a good option for families who prefer a full-service meal but want to skip their assigned main dining room one night.

Virtually all of the food served at the rotational restaurants will be familiar to American palates. Most dishes, especially at dinner, feature cuts of steak, pork, chicken, and fish similar to those you'd find at a decent chain restaurant. DCL's chefs will add some sort of flavor twist to these, such as soy and sesame if it's an Asian-themed menu, but the basic ingredients will be recognizable to almost everyone. If you want your entrée largely unadorned, look for the **Lighter Note** menu offerings—you'll see here that you can always get plain steak or chicken served with plain rice or a baked potato. Those in the mood for mild need not worry.

Although fresher and of higher quality than that of the counter-service restaurants, most of the food served at the full-service restaurants is prepared ahead of time. On the upside, this means you get your meal faster, assuming you don't have a special request. On the downside, not all requests are doable: ordering a different side dish or getting your sauce on the side shouldn't present a problem, but asking the kitchen staff to scrape off a baked-on glaze definitely would.

The main dining rooms' food quality is roughly on par with that of upscale American chain restaurants such as P.F. Chang's and Bonefish Grill, with better presentation. If you've ever cruised on Royal Caribbean or Carnival, we think you'll find DCL's main dining rooms substantially better.

Along with the dining-survey ratings and comments we get, we closely monitor comments about DCL food on social media. A representative sample of recent feedback includes the following:

> We live in Chicago, and we're spoiled by our amazing local restaurants. The food we had on the Magic wasn't amazing, but considering the constraints of preparing food on a big boat, we were pleasantly surprised.

> Compared with other cruise lines, DCL has way better food.

> The food is delightful. They go to the next level to make sure you're satisfied with what you get. We went on our first cruise a year ago, and to this day my daughter still talks about how amazing the food is.

> The food is bland—then again, it has to be to appeal to the masses.

Overall, DCL guests' impressions of the food are highly subjective, but most people like it just fine. Our advice: keep your expectations realistic, and if you aren't enjoying your meal, speak up—your server will be happy to replace your food with something you might like better.

ADULT DINING Each ship features an upscale Italian restaurant, serving only guests ages 18 and up, for which Disney charges an additional fee of at least $45. On the *Magic, Wonder, Dream,* and *Fantasy,* this venue is called **Palo,** while on the *Wish* it's **Palo Steakhouse.** The *Dream* and *Fantasy* have a fifth restaurant, **Remy,** which serves sophisticated French cuisine and levies a $125 surcharge. On the *Wish,* the equivalent restaurant—which also carries a $125 surcharge—is **Enchanté,** with a menu created by acclaimed French chef Arnaud Lallement.

In addition to dinner on most nights, these restaurants serve brunch on select sea days (still adults only). These dining options can be tough to get into, so be sure to make a reservation at your earliest opportunity (see page 200).

In addition to serving food that's superior to what's served in the main dining rooms, the adult-dining restaurants also have a higher level of service. A reader reports:

> *We went to Palo for dinner on our first night. I asked if the chef could make me chicken parmigiana, which wasn't on the menu. One minute later, the chef himself came out and apologized—he didn't have the ingredients on hand to make it. The next day, I got a call in my stateroom. It was my server from Palo; he said he had something special for me and came down to our stateroom with an **entire tray** of chicken parm—the chef had made it for brunch that day and wanted me to try his take on it. Truly amazing!*

Disney often tinkers with its adult-dining offerings, testing special events for specific sailings or individual ships. For example, some sailings of the *Fantasy* have offered an experience at Palo called **Be Our Chef,** providing guests with the opportunity to learn how to prepare four Palo dishes and take home a special keepsake. Other new or limited-time offerings have included dessert-only tasting experiences at Remy or meals themed to a specific style of food. If you're interested in enhanced adult-dining experiences, check your **My Reservations** page online (see page 47) or call DCL at ☎ 800-951-3532.

On some sailings you're limited to just one adult-dining reservation, or one reservation per adult-dining venue, to give as many guests as possible the opportunity to experience these restaurants. If a sailing isn't full or if you elect to dine at one of the adult restaurants on your first night, you may be able to make more than one reservation in advance; check My Reservations online for the specifics of your cruise. Or just stop by the restaurant in person and ask if you can make another reservation—this way, we've been able to eat at the adult restaurants on multiple nights of a single cruise.

ROOM SERVICE

OTHER THAN THE LAST MORNING OF YOUR CRUISE, room service is available on the Disney ships 24 hours a day. Look for the menu on the DCL Navigator app; to order, press the ROOM SERVICE button on your stateroom phone to place an order. To preorder room service breakfast, use the order form in your stateroom's desk drawer.

With the exception of a few packaged snacks and bottled beverages, there's no charge for room service other than a small tip for the person who delivers your meal ($1 or $2 per person or item ordered is appropriate). Typical lunch and dinner offerings include burgers, pizza, sandwiches, chicken fingers, salads, soups, and fresh fruit. The cheese-and-crackers plate is particularly popular with famished guests who need something to tide them over before the late dinner seating. Continental breakfast items are offered in the morning.

*un**official* **TIP**
Need a caffeine hit immediately after you wake up? Order a carafe of coffee from room service at bedtime and it'll still be warm in the morning.

Room service is a great option if you want to eat breakfast quickly before heading out on a port excursion, if you want to dine on your verandah, if you want to eat while enjoying a movie on your stateroom TV, or if you just don't feel like getting dressed for dinner.

If you've brought your own wine on board (see page 74 for guidelines), room service can bring you empty glasses so you can enjoy your beverage in your cabin in style. Room service will also bring you a bucket of ice to chill your wine or bubbly.

The room-service menus always include a selection of warm giant cookies, usually chocolate chip and oatmeal raisin. If you want to be a hero to your kids (or your spouse), have room service bring them surprise cookies and milk as a bedtime snack. Even better, dive into the unadvertised room-service menu and order a round of Mickey ice-cream bars for the room. All you have to do is ask.

THEME NIGHTS

ON CRUISES OF longer than three nights, Disney gets festive with themed dinners. These may include a **Pirates' Menu** (which is somewhat Caribbean-influenced on Pirate Night), **Till We Meet Again** (on the final night of your cruise), the **Captain's Gala,** and **Prince and Princess Menus.** The menus will depend on your itinerary; for example, DCL Alaskan voyages typically include a seafood-focused night featuring local salmon and king crab.

In 2015 Disney began offering *Frozen* **Days** on some Alaskan and Northern European sailings. The movie-themed menu we were served on the *Magic* in Iceland included items such as Sven's Carrot Soup, The Duke of Weselton's Favorite Assorted Meats, Oaken Warm Apple Pudding Cake, and Olaf's White Chocolate Floro Dome. (This menu has some overlap with the regular menu at Arendelle on the *Wish*.)

*un**official* **TIP**
On theme nights, each main dining area serves the same menu, so no one misses out on the fun.

Marvel Days were added to some *Magic* sailings beginning in late 2017. Menu selections include Black Widow's Sliced Smoked Salmon,

Dr. Banner's Greens and Lobster Salad, Bounty Hunter's Pastry, and Ravager's Devil's Food Cake.

Coming to the *Fantasy* in 2023, **Pixar Days** will feature dinner offerings inspired by the commissary at Pixar Animation Studios.

DINING WITH KIDS

*un*official **TIP**

If you want to feed your baby something warm, ask the kitchen staff to puree food that they've prepared, or heat a jar of baby food in very hot water for a few minutes. (A cereal bowl from the buffet and hot water from the coffee/tea dispenser will do the trick.)

ON DISNEY CRUISE LINE, kids are people, too, when it comes to dining. While there are kids' menus with standard fare like corn dogs and mac and cheese (see page 196), kids of all ages are welcome to eat from any part of the upper-deck buffet and order any item in the main dining rooms. If *you* want chicken nuggets for dinner and your 6-year-old wants escargot and prime rib, DCL has you covered.

Your serving team should be your partner in planning a strategy on how to best meet your family's dining needs. Do you want your kids' food brought to the table first so they're not ravenous? Do you want the bread basket left off the table so your kids fill up on more protein and veggies than carbs? Do you want only milk and water offered to your kids, not soda? Tell your serving team those things on the first night, and they'll make notes about your preferences.

If you've been assigned to the second dinner seating, you can even arrange to have staff from the onboard childcare centers pick your kids up in the dining room so that you can linger over dessert while they're off playing. (*Note:* This service may not be available on all post-COVID sailings.) Be aware, however, that there are some special experiences that occur toward the end of the usual dinner hour, some of which your children might not want to miss. For example, at the end of dinner on one night at Animator's Palate on the *Fantasy* and the *Magic,* guests are treated to a short animated film created from diners' drawings. Most kids get a real kick out of seeing their artwork on screen.

In the realm of healthy eating, Disney is taking ongoing positive steps toward offering healthful options at its theme parks and on its ships. **Disney Check** meals are available on the kids' menus at the rotational-dining restaurants and on the menus posted on the DCL Navigator app. (See tinyurl.com/disneycheckmeals for details.) The Disney Check symbol indicates that the meal falls within specific dietary guidelines for calorie count; percentages of sugar, sodium, and fat; and recommended amounts of vitamins and other nutrients.

Baby food is sold in the gift shops, near the over-the-counter medications. The selection is typically limited, however, to two to four flavors of jarred baby food and one brand of single-serving baby formula. If you want to bring your own baby food aboard the ship, it must be prepackaged and sealed—homemade foods and open containers of any type are prohibited—and you must pack it in your carry-on luggage, not in your checked bags.

DCL chefs will also puree any food available on the ship for you. For instance, they can whip up something like pureed peas, carrots, or chicken quite easily. Also keep in mind that many of the soft foods already available on the ship may be fine for older babies and toddlers: mashed potatoes, oatmeal, soups, soft-scrambled eggs, and so on.

If you're planning to bring your own baby food on board, be aware that your child will likely have to eat it cold unless you can improvise; see the Unofficial Tip on the previous page. (At Walt Disney World, by contrast, guests have free use of microwave ovens in the food courts.) Additionally, you may not bring any cooking appliances on board with you: no electric kettles, rice cookers, hot plates, Sterno cans, or anything else that could be a fire hazard. Further complicating matters, DCL kitchens won't heat any food you've brought onto the ship, nor will they heat baby food that you've purchased in the onboard gift shop.

Children are welcome to eat in the main dining rooms on their own or with young siblings, cousins, or friends in their party. If, for example, the grown-ups are having dinner at the adults-only Palo restaurant, the kids can still have a nice meal of their own in their regular rotational restaurant. Parents will have to assess at what age their kids are ready for this, but we've seen many 8- and 9-year-olds dining together in the main dining rooms while their parents were having a date-night meal elsewhere. Let your server know that you're planning to do this, and they'll be sure to take special care of your child's dining needs. Of course, you could also feed your children room service or have them dine in the kids' club if you'd rather not have them eat a full restaurant dinner on their own.

On longer sailings, Disney often served a **character breakfast** in one of the main rotational dining rooms, with Mickey, Goofy, and other Disney favorites stopping by to add merriment to your meal. Pre-pandemic, characters would visit every table to sign autographs and pose for photos; post-pandemic, characters would usually just walk through the dining room and wave.

COVID TIP

At press time, DCL began relaxing social-distancing guidelines for characters, but check the specifics for your sailing—Disney could bring back the policy described here in case of a possible COVID surge in the future.

While kids are the main fans of character meals, parties consisting of adults only are also welcome to partake. There is no additional charge for these meals, but they do typically need to be booked ahead using the My Reservations section of the DCL website. If you can't get a reservation immediately after your booking window opens for other activities, keep checking back.

Kids' Menus 101

As noted earlier, youngsters are welcome to order anything on the main menu at the rotational restaurants, but each dining room also has a separate menu for children. Unless you request otherwise, this will be the menu offered to kids under age 10.

Each kids' menu consists of four sections: **starters, entrées, desserts,** and complete **Mickey Check meals.** Each section offers two or three choices in kid-size portions. (*Note:* You can always get French fries by request.) Here's a sampling:

APPETIZERS Soup (chicken noodle, sweet corn, tomato), garden salad

ENTRÉES Mini burger, breaded fish nuggets, mini pizza, corn dog, breaded turkey breast with tomato sauce, mac and cheese

DESSERTS Mickey ice-cream bar, scoop of ice cream, apple pie, cheesecake with strawberry compote, strawberry shortcake, caramel custard

MICKEY CHECK MEALS Baked salmon with broccoli and rice, strawberry yogurt parfait for dessert; whole wheat pasta with tomato sauce and broccoli, apple slices for dessert; grilled beef tenderloin with green beans and smashed potatoes, fruit cup for dessert; grilled chicken breast with steamed carrots, fresh watermelon for dessert; turkey bolognese served over fettuccine and accompanied by steamed carrots, apple slices for dessert; grilled pork tenderloin with brown rice and green beans, applesauce for dessert

Beyond the Kids' Menu: Options for Adventurous Dining

If, on the other hand, your kids are open to more than just munching on nuggets and fries, we suggest the following:

- **Trying new foods.** Because most of the menu items available to children are included in the price of your cruise, kids can feel free to order something they're not sure about, with no repercussions if they don't like it.

- **Practicing restaurant manners.** The DCL main dining rooms are a terrific place for kids to practice proper table etiquette. At home, teach your children to look waitstaff in the eye while speaking, order in a clear voice, make polite dinner-table conversation, and use napkins and utensils properly. If your kids fumble a bit, rest assured that DCL's servers are exceptionally patient and kind. Be sure to tip them well at the end of your cruise.

- **Learning a new vocabulary.** A restaurant can be a terrific place to teach your kids new words: *satay, bisque, reduction, gravlax, strudel, confit, tamarind, marjoram, fennel, harissa, poached, jerk-marinated, tzatziki, brioche, turbot,* and *chorizo* all appear on the menus in DCL's main dining rooms. Clue your children in on what these words mean, or have them practice their manners by quizzing your server (politely) to find out the definitions.

- **Dining alone for the first time.** This can be a great way to give older kids a taste of independence. If your tweens or younger teens have aced their manners prep, book a meal for the grown-ups at an adult-dining venue and send the kids to your regular dining rotation alone. We recommend doing this toward the end of your sailing, by which time your kids should know the lay of the ship. (Be sure to let your server know what you're doing ahead of time.)

- **Discovering the wonders of room service.** Sometimes being lazy and eating grilled cheese in your PJs on vacation is where it's at.

- **Breaking all the rules!** Mealtimes at home call for sensible stuff like eating your vegetables and watching your portions . . . but who the heck wants to be sensible on a cruise? Eat nothing but ice-cream sundaes for lunch! Order your growing tween a second steak as dessert! Stir some soft-serve into your pool-deck Coke! Wolf down piles of chicken nuggets three times in a single afternoon!

DRESS CODES

SHORTS AND T-SHIRTS are acceptable at the standard restaurants, even for adults. We think most adults will feel more appropriately dressed in pants or dresses at dinner; Bermuda shorts paired with a nice button-down shirt and shoes would probably also work.

A mother of four from Midland, Texas, praises Disney's shorts-tolerant policy:

> No way was I going to pack 8–10 pairs of pants (minimum!) for my kids and my husband for our seven-night cruise. Shorts take up less luggage space and can be worn all day. It's less laundry for me to do when we get home too.

Swimwear and tank tops are prohibited at any time, and frankly you'd be freezing for most of your meal.

Many cruises of four nights or longer have a designated **Formal Night.** The food served in the main dining rooms is essentially the same as on any other night. But while dress-up clothing isn't required—you won't be refused service for being underdressed—you will find that many people enjoy upping their dinnerwear game for the occasion. The definition of *formal* is fluid: if you own a tux or evening gown that fits, go ahead and bring it, but you'll also see guys in khakis and pressed golf shirts. Kids should wear whatever nice clothes seem comfortable and appropriate. For girls, a cute sundress is fine; boys may wear a button-down shirt or a tie to look dapper.

If you want to dress up but don't have any fancy duds handy, you can always rent some. Erin swears by **Rent the Runway** (renttherunway .com) for women's wear; good bets for men include **Men's Wearhouse** (menswearhouse.com), **Jos. A. Bank** (josbank.com), and **The Black Tux** (theblacktux.com). If you need to get professionally measured, check at a clothing store in your hometown that does prom and wedding rentals.

The dress code for DCL's adult-dining restaurants—**Palo, Palo Steakhouse, Remy,** and **Enchanté,** along with their adjacent bars—falls just short of semiformal: think "business casual," "cocktail attire," and "smart casual." Dress pants, slacks, and collared shirts are recommended for men, and a dress, skirt, or pants and a blouse are recommended for women. Jeans are fine provided they're in good condition (that means no holes, intentional or not). Verboten are tank tops, swimsuits and cover-ups, shorts, hats, cutoffs, torn clothing, flip-flops, athletic shoes, and T-shirts with offensive language and/or graphics.

unofficial **TIP**
For women, Erin suggests this mix-and-match wardrobe, which works equally well for the main dining rooms and the adult-dining venues: **(1)** one pair of nice black slacks, **(2)** one pair of nice white slacks, and **(3)** three or four dressy blouses, plus coordinating accessories.

When in doubt about what to wear to the adults-only restaurants, err on the side of caution—but don't be surprised if the rules are fluid on occasion. In 2019 Erin was dining at Palo on the *Dream* with friends,

FAQs: What to Wear to Dinner on DCL

SOME OF THE MOST FREQUENTLY ASKED QUESTIONS we get from new cruisers have to do with what to wear to dinner. There's just something about seeing zillions of movies and TV shows with cruisers gliding around in tuxes and glamorous gowns that makes the average traveler question his or her sartorial IQ. We're here to help, so read on.

- **What is *cruise casual*?** This is DCL's term for acceptable casual attire in the main dining rooms—in short, anything but swimwear and tank tops. We've never seen anyone turned away because of how they were dressed, and the "no tank tops" part seems open to interpretation: Erin has worn slacks or skirts with stylish sleeveless tops without incident. (Tops with sleeves, long or short, are safer bets for Palo, Palo Steakhouse, Remy, and Enchanté.)

  The main dining rooms have additional dress suggestions depending on the specifics of your sailing—these might include formal, semiformal, dress-up, pirate, tropical, *Frozen,* or Marvel attire. **All of these are completely optional.**

- **What does *formal attire* mean?** In the strictest sense, it means tuxedos for men and evening gowns for women. Again, though, it's completely optional. Many guests choose to wear something nicer than cruise casual on Formal Night, but the range of dress is broad. *Very* broad.

  While this isn't strictly a Formal Night thing, we've noticed a fun new trend in the *Wish*'s **1923** restaurant: Roaring Twenties attire. Think flapper ensembles for women and *Great Gatsby/Boardwalk Empire*–inspired looks for guys.

- **What do *semiformal* and *optional dress-up* mean?** For men this often means a business suit, with or without a tie; for women this typically means a cocktail dress of approximately knee length. But as with Formal Night, you're likely to see a wide range of styles.

- **Will I get the side-eye if I don't dress up?** If you feel self-conscious, you could grab something from the pool deck or order room service, but if you want to wear shorts in the main dining room on Semiformal Night, don't worry about being judged. *You do you.*

- **What's the scoop with princess gowns?** As in the Disney theme parks, many girls under age 10 enjoy rocking princess attire while cruising. You can buy dresses on the ship, but we've observed that some of the most charming princess wear is homemade.

- **What do I need to know about themed events?** The most common themed event is **Pirate Night,** which takes place on almost all DCL sailings in the Caribbean and Bahamas, plus a few other destinations. On four of the ships, guests get a pirate-themed bandanna to wear, and the onboard shops have kids' pirate costumes for sale along with related accoutrements such as faux hook hands and eye patches. During *Frozen* **Days** and **Marvel Days** (see page 233), about half the ship dresses up to an extent, even if it's just a Marvel T-shirt.

- **When are the Formal, Semiformal, and themed nights on my cruise?** To find out what will be happening on your sailing, call ☎ 800-951-3532. In general, however:
  - **Three-night cruises** typically have one standard cruise-casual night, one Pirate Night, and one optional dress-up night.
  - **Four-night cruises** typically have two standard cruise-casual nights, one Pirate Night, and one optional dress-up night.
  - **Seven-night cruises** typically have four standard cruise-casual nights, one themed night (Pirate Night or other depending on the destination), one Semiformal Night, and one Formal Night.
  - **Cruises of seven-plus nights** typically have additional cruise-casual dinners.

- **Are there times when the dress code isn't just a suggestion? Yes.** The adult-dining venues strictly enforce their respective dress codes, and we've personally seen guests get turned away for not following the rules.

and one gentleman in her party was asked to put on a pair of shoes from the loaner cabinet because he was wearing dressy-casual leather sandals (*not* flip-flops, which are prohibited in the dress code); meanwhile, several women in the same group were wearing leather flip-flop-style sandals but weren't asked to change. Two days later at Palo brunch, that same gentleman got away with wearing dark-colored sneakers, which technically break the "no athletic shoes" rule. In general, women seem to get a bit more leeway than men.

The dress code for Remy and Enchanté is less restrictive now than it used to be—men were required to wear a jacket at dinner, for example—and is now consistent with the dress codes for Palo and Palo Steakhouse. Nevertheless, make sure to exercise care in selecting an outfit when you dine at an adults-only restaurant. In the worst-case scenario, you could be refused entry.

If you need visual aids, check **Pinterest** and other websites for sample outfits. The **Touring Plans** blog also shows suggested looks for different occasions: see tinyurl.com/WhatToWearOnDCL.

SPECIAL DIETS

IF YOU EAT A SPECIAL DIET—gluten-free, vegan/vegetarian, allergen-free, kosher, and so on—traveling can be a challenge. Disney as a company has a pretty good reputation for handling special diets, but guests should nonetheless be prepared and proactive in their dealings with the DCL dining staff.

unofficial **TIP**
Pizza with gluten-free crust is available upon request on the pool deck.

In addition to noting any food allergies or dietary requests at booking, you'll want to check DCL's **Special Dietary Requests** page (tinyurl.com/DCLSpecialDiets) *and* follow up with a phone call (☎ 407-566-3602). Also review Disney's **FAQs for Guests with Disabilities** (tinyurl.com/DCLGuestsWithDisabilities) and, if needed, complete DCL's **Request Special Services** form (tinyurl.com/DCLRequestSpecialServices). If you've booked your cruise through a travel agent, they may also be able to assist you in your communication with Disney.

Once you're on the ship, your servers will also ask you at the beginning of your cruise about any allergies or special diets. Take advantage of this opportunity to discuss your needs with them.

There are no separate kitchen facilities on board for guests with allergies, nor are there separate dining areas for allergen-free items. Also be aware that you'll need to restate your dining needs to any excursion company or restaurant that will be feeding you while you're not on board. Be especially careful when dining in unfamiliar areas or when communicating in a language other than your own.

If you have a specific brand preference—for instance, a type of soy milk or gluten-free waffle—you'll find that there isn't much in the way of choice. If your child will eat only one brand of something, your best bet is to bring it with you.

Vegetarian and Vegan Dining Strategies

Veteran Disney cruiser **Laurel Stewart** sticks to a vegan diet at home. Below and following are her tips for guests who don't eat meat.

unofficial **TIP**
For more tips on vegan dining in the Disney theme parks and on DCL, check out **Vegan Disney Food** (vegandisneyfood.com).

• **BREAKFAST** *Your best bet is the* **buffet**—*you can see exactly what you're getting. Ask a server for nondairy milk.*

- **LUNCH** *Again, you'll rarely go wrong with the buffet. Also, the pool deck's* **counter-service** *eateries have options like cheeseless pizzas, yummy wraps, veggie burgers (vegans, skip the buns), and fries.*

- **DINNER** *Vegetarian entrées are often vegan as well, but egg- and dairy-free appetizers and sweets can be harder to find. Fresh fruit or sorbet is always a good choice for dessert, though.*

- **ADULT DINING** *If your whole table is vegan, this is a hard pass: it's expensive, and your options are very limited. If you're traveling with an omnivore who wants to dine at one of the adults-only restaurants, be prepared to miss out. Ovo-lacto vegetarians have more and better choices.*

- **CASTAWAY CAY** *You can ask ahead for veggie burgers; plus, many of the sides are vegan, and there's lots and lots of fresh fruit.*

- **MISCELLANEOUS** **Room service** *doesn't have a lot to offer right off the menu, but ask when you call if there's anything that can be modified. The evening antipasti served at* **Cove Café** *and* **Vista Café** *are a good choice as long as you skip the cheeses.*

    Finally, ask if **off-menu** *options are available. During one sailing, we learned that we could order Indian food even though it wasn't on any of the menus. After a chat with our servers, they brought us huge bowls of delicious veggie curries and masalas, which were even tastier than many of the regular entrées.*

Vegetarian and vegan dining on DCL have improved substantially in recent years. In 2020 Disney entered into a partnership with **Impossible Foods** to serve its plant-based meat substitute on Disney Cruise Line and in Disney's US theme parks. When DCL announced the dining options on the *Wish*, the press release stated, "Each and every one of our menus will have vegan offerings. Taking care of allergies and special requirements is extremely important to us. We want families to sail with peace of mind." We're happy to report that Disney was true to their word here when we sailed on the *Wish* in summer 2022.

For further discussion, see "Dietary Restrictions" in Part Five, "Tips for Varied Circumstances" (page 161).

MAKING RESERVATIONS FOR ADULT DINING

NO RESERVATIONS ARE REQUIRED at the rotational-dining restaurants. Reservations *are* required for adult dining and can be made up to 130 days in advance as noted below, after you've paid for your cruise in full. Reserve online at **My Reservations** (see page 47).

Guests in suites or Concierge staterooms can reserve **130 days in advance.**
Platinum Castaway Club members can reserve **120 days in advance.**
Gold Castaway Club members can reserve **105 days in advance.**
Silver Castaway Club members can reserve **90 days in advance.**
All other guests can reserve **75 days in advance.**

PALO PRICE HIKES During the pandemic shutdown, DCL raised the baseline price for dining at Palo from $40 to $45 per person. While this doesn't seem like a huge jump, it doesn't tell the whole story: other aspects of the pricing were tweaked such that dining at Palo will likely take a much larger bite out of your wallet than it did in previous years. The new pricing structure is, in fact, much more in line with what you'd pay to eat at a similarly upscale restaurant in a major US city, rather than the true bargain Palo used to be.

Pre-COVID, you paid a fixed price (excluding alcohol) to order anything on the menu you wanted, in any amount. With the pricing reconfiguration, however, the $45 base price gives you just four courses, with a limited range of choices for each. The starter choices are a calamari-and-shrimp cocktail or a buffalo mozzarella salad; second-course choices are a mesclun or baby arugula salad; main-course options are penne with tomato sauce, pan-seared salmon, roast chicken, or a 6-ounce beef tenderloin; and for dessert you can choose from chocolate soufflé or limoncello tart. That's it.

Other popular dishes are still available, but they're now à la carte. Before 2021, for example, your meal would have cost $40 and might have included the antipasti platter (now $22), *ciuppin* (seafood soup, now $14), grilled asparagus (now $4), Dover sole (now $32), and amaretto soufflé (now $10). That same meal now costs a little more than twice as much per person ($82). Additional Palo favorites that are now à la carte include butternut squash agnolotti ($12); prosciutto di Parma, basil, and burrata pizza ($22); seared jumbo scallops ($28); Parmesan-crusted rack of Niman Ranch lamb ($26); and homemade tiramisu ($8).

As before, Platinum Castaway Club members and other adults in their staterooms will continue to be offered one free meal at Palo, either brunch or dinner; at dinner, the prix fixe ($45) menu is included, but again, anything you want beyond that now costs extra.

Theoretically, you *could* order à la carte instead of prix fixe for a total cost of less than $45, particularly if you're a light eater and/or a vegetarian, but that would be an unusual circumstance. (See pages 199 and 200 for one DCL cruiser's assessments of adult dining for vegetarians and vegans.)

Palo's **brunch** was also raised to $45, but on a positive note, the price at press time still includes everything on the menu (again, sans adult beverages), and you can still eat as much as you want. This makes brunch a *much* better value than dinner.

*un*official **TIP**
Palo's brunch was served buffet-style before the pandemic but moved to family-style, all-you-care-to-eat table service after sailings resumed. We hear that service will remain family-style for the foreseeable future.

PRIVATE DINING Each ship's adult-dining venue has an adjacent private dining room. When not reserved by DCL for onboard activities, they can be reserved by guests for special occasions such as birthday and anniversary parties.

To request a private room at **Palo** or **Remy,** download the form at tinyurl.com/PaloPrivateDiningRequestForm or tinyurl.com/Remy PrivateDiningRequestForm, fill it out, and email it to dcl.cruise.activities @disney.com. Requests should be made at least 30 days in advance. *Note:* At press time, private-dining forms were not yet available for **Palo Steakhouse** or **Enchanté,** so call DCL to reserve (☎ 800-951-3532).

DCL TABLE-SERVICE RESTAURANTS BY CUISINE

RESTAURANT	SHIP	OVERALL RATING	QUALITY RATING
AMERICAN/ASIAN			
Animator's Palate	*Magic, Wonder, Dream, Fantasy*	★★★	★★★
AMERICAN/BUFFET			
Cabanas	*Magic, Wonder, Dream, Fantasy*	★★★	★★★
Marceline Market	*Wish*	★★★	★★★
AMERICAN/CALIFORNIAN			
1923	*Wish*	★★★★	★★★★½
AMERICAN/CONTINENTAL			
Enchanted Garden	*Dream, Fantasy*	★★★	★★★
AMERICAN/ECLECTIC			
Worlds of Marvel	*Wish*	★★★	★★★
AMERICAN/GERMAN			
Rapunzel's Royal Table	*Magic*	★★★	★★★
AMERICAN/FRENCH			
Lumiere's	*Magic*	★★★	★★★
Royal Court	*Fantasy*	★★★	★★★
Royal Palace	*Dream*	★★★	★★★
Triton's	*Wonder*	★★★	★★★
AMERICAN/SCANDINAVIAN			
Arendelle: A *Frozen* Dining Adventure	*Wish*	★★★	★★★
AMERICAN/SOUTHERN			
Tiana's Place	*Wonder*	★★★	★★★

DCL ADULTS-ONLY RESTAURANTS

RESTAURANT/CUISINE/SHIP	OVERALL RATING	QUALITY RATING	VALUE RATING
Enchanté French (*Wish*)	★★★★½	★★★★½	★★★★½
Palo Italian (*Magic, Wonder, Dream, Fantasy*)	★★★½* ★★★★**	★★★½* ★★★★**	★★★½* ★★★★**
Palo Steakhouse Italian/Steak (*Wish*)	★★★★	★★★★½	★★★★½
Remy French (*Dream, Fantasy*)	★★★★½	★★★★½	★★★★½

(* *Magic, Wonder,* ** *Dream, Fantasy*)

DCL RESTAURANT PROFILES

WE TYPICALLY RECEIVE AROUND 150,000 dining surveys per year for Walt Disney World, and we've received nearly 1 million such surveys since 2018. Because DCL serves far fewer guests, we get substantially fewer surveys—in most cases (and especially in 2020–23), they're not enough to provide a reasonable assurance of data accuracy for any single restaurant. The ratings here are therefore based on a combination of reader surveys, conversations with other travel professionals, and our own firsthand experience.

To help you make your dining choices, we've developed profiles of DCL's counter-service and table-service restaurants, grouped by ship and listed alphabetically by restaurant. To keep things simple, we've grouped buffets with restaurants offering full table service.

RATINGS For table-service restaurants, the **overall star rating** represents the entire dining experience: style, service, and ambience, in addition to the taste, presentation, and quality of the food. Five stars is the highest possible rating; four-star restaurants are above average; three-star restaurants offer good, though not necessarily memorable, meals. (No DCL table-service restaurant rates below three stars overall for this edition.)

Quality ratings, on the other hand, focus on the food. The quality of counter-service food is measured on a scale of **A (excellent) to F (poor).** (No DCL counter-service restaurant rates below a C for this edition.) For table-service restaurants, food quality is measured on a scale of **one to five stars,** with five stars being the highest possible rating. Here, the star ratings take into account flavor, freshness of ingredients, preparation, presentation, and creativity.

For the adult-dining venues, where you pay extra to eat, price is not considered in the quality rating. But if you're looking for both quality *and* a good meal deal, check the **value rating,** also expressed as stars.

A REMINDER ABOUT ALCOHOL Wine, beer, and mixed drinks cost extra in the rotational restaurants and aren't included in the cost of meals at the adult-dining venues.

Disney Magic DINING

COUNTER-SERVICE RESTAURANTS

Daisy's De-Lites

QUALITY B   LOCATION DECK 9 AFT

OPEN Morning–midday.

SELECTIONS Breakfast includes pastries and fruit, as well as build-your-own yogurt parfaits and oatmeal or granola bowls. Lunch offerings include sandwiches, soups, and a build-your-own-bowl station with a base of rice or quinoa and toppings such as shredded pork or chicken and a variety of fresh veggies.

COMMENTS Daisy's De-Lites is our favorite quick-service restaurant on the *Magic* and *Wonder.* It's a good alternative to the breakfast buffet if you want something light. The customizable bowls are terrific for vegetarians.

Duck-In Diner

QUALITY B   LOCATION DECK 9 AFT

OPEN Midday–late evening.

SELECTIONS Middle Eastern meats such as chicken and lamb shawarma, served on your choice of pita bread or a tortilla. Burgers and French fries are also available.

COMMENTS There are lots of creative toppings and condiments, such as hummus, pickled veggies, baba ghanoush, chile mayonnaise, *kachumber* (an Indian cucumber salad), garlic-mustard aioli, *sambal* (an Indonesian hot sauce similar to sriracha), tzatziki, or a mint-cilantro sauce.

Pinocchio's Pizzeria

QUALITY C   LOCATION DECK 9 AFT

OPEN Midday–late evening.

SELECTIONS Cheese, pepperoni, and specialty pizzas (including veggie); cheeseless or gluten-free pizza on request. If you're in the mood for fancy pizza, look for offerings labeled "flatbread." This is a more upscale version of pizza, often topped with mushrooms, pancetta, or other items of adult appeal.

COMMENTS About the same quality as store-bought frozen pizza—but hey, there are plenty of times when that's just what you want.

TABLE-SERVICE RESTAURANTS
Animator's Palate ★★★ Deck 4 Aft

AMERICAN/ASIAN   QUALITY ★★★   SERVICE ★★★★   FRIENDLINESS ★★★★

Reservations Not accepted. **Meals served** Dinner. **Alcohol** Red, white, and sparkling wines, plus mixed drinks and spirits.

SETTING AND ATMOSPHERE The idea behind Animator's Palate is that you begin dining inside an old-fashioned black-and-white animated film that slowly colorizes as dinner goes along. The entrance's walls are decorated with black charcoal sketches of various Disney characters. Inside, the entire color scheme starts out in black, white, and gray from floor to ceiling, including checkerboard-tile floor, black chairs, white tablecloths with black napkins, and black-and-white uniforms for the waitstaff. Even the ship's support columns are dressed up—in this case, as white artist's brushes pointed to the ceiling.

Along the outside wall are video monitors that display images and "how to draw" sketches from Disney films. As the evening progresses, you'll notice bits of color being added to the walls and artwork, eventually becoming fully saturated by the end of your meal.

At the beginning of the **Animation Magic** dinner show (typically your second evening at Animator's Palate on a seven-night cruise or your third evening at Animator's Palate on a longer sailing), you're given a sheet of paper and a marker and instructed to draw a self-portrait. (There are guidelines on how to do this.) At the end of the evening, all of the diners' self-portraits are shown in an animated cartoon similar to Disney's 1929 short cartoon *The Skeleton Dance.*

HOUSE SPECIALTIES Pennette Bolognese, grilled tuna steak, ginger teriyaki beef, sesame halloumi parcels (a vegetarian entrée of goat-and-sheep-milk cheese in puff pastry), roasted-garlic dip with bread.

COMMENTS Animator's Palate on the *Magic* (and *Wonder*) is different from the versions on the *Dream* and *Fantasy* (see pages 211 and 216) in terms of the entertainment and technology, although all four serve the same food. Disney characterizes the cuisine as Pacific Rim/American, but it's really just standard chain-restaurant fare, with probably as many Italian selections as Asian dishes.

Cabanas ★★★ Deck 9 Aft

AMERICAN/BUFFET   QUALITY ★★★   SERVICE ★★★★   FRIENDLINESS ★★★★

Reservations Not accepted. **Meals served** Breakfast and lunch; dinner service is temporarily suspended at press time (see below), **Alcohol** Red, white, and sparkling wines, plus mixed drinks and spirits.

SETTING AND ATMOSPHERE Cabanas is entered from either side of Deck 9 Aft. On either side is a line of buffet tables that run the length of the restaurant. Indoor and outdoor seating are arranged around the buffet. The indoor seating is air-conditioned and features floor-to-ceiling windows, affording excellent ocean views. Outdoor seating is great on mornings when the ship is docking because you're sometimes able to watch the port come into view. Coffee, soft drinks, juices, and water are served from dispensers placed throughout the restaurant.

HOUSE SPECIALTIES Made-to-order omelets for breakfast; lunch seafood bar including oysters, clams, crab legs, and peel-and-eat shrimp.

COMMENTS The breakfast and lunch buffets easily compare with those at upscale Las Vegas resorts and serve about as wide a variety of items. Breakfast includes everything from fruit, yogurt, and oatmeal to doughnuts, lox, and custom-made omelets. Even cold cereal has options: besides the usual cornflakes and granola, there's a build-your-own-muesli bar where you can add ingredients ranging from brown sugar to exotic dried fruits. Don't worry if you skipped dessert last night—you can get several at breakfast here.

Lunch is a similarly lavish spread, with everything from chicken tenders, sandwiches, and burgers to salmon steaks and pasta. A big draw at lunch is the peel-and-eat shrimp, sometimes complemented by clams, oysters, and crab legs.

Note: Cabanas is open only for breakfast and lunch at press time. Prepandemic, the buffet switched over to regular table service at night, but dinner hours were suspended after sailings restarted. We expect them to resume as the pandemic wanes; in the meantime, check the specifics for your sailing, or check tinyurl.com/UGDisneyCruise2023 for updates.

Lumiere's ★★★ Deck 3 Midship

AMERICAN/FRENCH   QUALITY ★★★   SERVICE ★★★★   FRIENDLINESS ★★★★

Reservations Not accepted. **Meals served** Dinner; breakfast and lunch available on select days. **Alcohol** Limited selection of red, white, and sparkling wines, plus mixed drinks and spirits.

SETTING AND ATMOSPHERE Despite the name, there are only a few references to *Beauty and the Beast* inside the restaurant. The most notable are the light fixtures, which contain a single red rose. There's also a mural on the back wall that depicts characters from the movie. Besides these touches, most of Lumiere's decor is Art Deco, which makes sense given the restaurant's location, just off the ship's atrium.

HOUSE SPECIALTIES Breaded deep-fried brie, iced lobster and jumbo shrimp, crispy roasted duck breast, rack of lamb.

COMMENTS With 95% thumbs-up among the *Unofficial Guide* readers we've surveyed, Lumiere's is the highest-rated main dining room on any Disney cruise ship.

DCL puts escargot and French onion soup on the menus of its French-themed standard dining rooms. Besides these dishes, however, most of the rest of the menu is decidedly un-*français* and would be equally at home at a so-called neighborhood bistro: grilled meats and chicken, a vegetarian tofu selection, and pasta. A couple of entrées, such as the herb-crusted rack of lamb and the crispy duck breast, stand out. The Grand Marnier soufflé is the most popular dessert, but unlike the authentic soufflé served at Palo (described below), this is more of an airy cake. We're partial to the crème brûlée ourselves.

Palo ★★★½ Deck 10 Aft

ITALIAN   QUALITY ★★★½ VALUE ★★★½ SERVICE ★★★★½ FRIENDLINESS ★★★★

Reservations Required. **Meals served** Brunch on sea days; prix fixe dinner nightly. **Alcohol** Large list of Italian wines, listed by region, plus select wines from around the world; mixed drinks and spirits; limoncello; grappa; ice wine. **Special comments** An additional $45/person charge will be added to your cruise bill for each meal at Palo. If you need to cancel a reservation, you must do so 24 hours in advance, or the full per-person charge may be applied to your bill. Guests must be 18 or older to dine.

Note: Palo's base dinner service now consists of a four-course, prix fixe menu (see page 201). The dinner selections described below—with the exception of the chocolate soufflé—now cost extra. Also note that Palo's brunch transitioned from a serve-yourself buffet to table service post-pandemic, with courses served family-style. We hear that table service will continue to be the norm for the foreseeable future.

SETTING AND ATMOSPHERE Palo sits across the entire Aft section of Deck 10, which means that almost every seat has a spectacular view of the ocean sunset during dinner. On the *Magic,* Palo has contemporary decor, with tan-wood panels, round leather benches, and deep-purple fabric on the wood chairs. A small bar is available for guests waiting for their tables to become available; part of the kitchen is open to the view of guests sitting in the middle of the restaurant. Red-and-white-striped poles near the bar, evocative of those used to steer gondolas, call to mind Palo's roots in Venice (*palo* means "pole").

Because Palo is adults-only, it's much quieter than DCL's main dining rooms. The quietest tables of all are on the port side, aft (left and forward), tucked away behind the curve of the restaurant. If you're looking to do some people-watching with dinner, request a table on the starboard (right) side of the ship, near Palo's entrance. Background music is mostly Italian and ranges from Vivaldi to Sinatra, as the good Lord intended.

HOUSE SPECIALTIES For a first course at dinner, try the *ciuppin,* a soup of fish, mussels, clams, and lobster in a tomato broth. The *antipasto freddo,* a selection of familiar cheeses and cured meats, could be a little more adventurous. Our favorite entrées are the pasta in lobster and tarragon sauce, the Dover sole, and the rack of lamb. The chocolate soufflé, by far the most popular dessert, is served with both dark- and white-chocolate sauces. If you're not in the mood for chocolate, there may be other versions of the soufflé available—it never hurts to ask.

Palo's brunch is excellent. At the time of this writing, it's served family-style: you can have as much or as little of each offering as you like. Starters may include ahi tuna, crab legs, or prosciutto. The main course includes breakfast options such as eggs Benedict and lunch options such as artichoke ravioli and made-to-order pizza. If there's any room left for dessert, small cups of tiramisu or berries with cream will take care of your sweet tooth.

COMMENTS Palo, the *Magic*'s one upscale restaurant, is its own little island of adult serenity and food. Service is very good, and don't be surprised if the maître d' and your server are from Italy.

Dinners at Palo are tasty and relaxing, especially with a glass or two of wine. That being said, we think Palo is better for brunch: besides offering the best selection of midday food anywhere on the ship, the view out of Palo's windows is much better during the day; once the sun sets at dinner, Palo's spectacular windows just reflect the inside of the restaurant. And with the recent changes to Palo's pricing structure—which made many favorite dishes à la carte (see page 201)—we consider brunch a much bigger bang for your buck than dinner, even though both meals now cost $45. Brunch pricing still includes anything you want, in any amount (alcohol excluded).

If we could improve one thing at Palo, it would be the coffee, which is Joffrey's (read: barely drinkable). A restaurant this good can do better.

Finally, note that we rate Palo on the *Dream* and *Fantasy* slightly higher than the versions on the *Magic* and the *Wonder:* the decor is more sophisticated, and the kitchens are larger, allowing for more efficient food preparation. (For the purposes of this comparison, we consider **Palo Steakhouse** on the *Wish* to be its own thing.) Nevertheless, Palo on the *Magic* and the *Wonder* is outstanding and definitely worth the extra cost.

Disney sometimes adds special adult-dining experiences to specific sailings; see page 214 for more information.

Rapunzel's Royal Table ★★★ Deck 3 Aft

AMERICAN/GERMAN QUALITY ★★★ SERVICE ★★★★ FRIENDLINESS ★★★★

Reservations Not accepted. **Meals served** Dinner. **Alcohol** A decent selection of reds, whites, and sparkling wines, plus mixed drinks and spirits.

SETTING AND ATMOSPHERE During the *Magic*'s 2018 dry dock, Carioca's restaurant was transformed into Rapunzel's Royal Table, a nod to the popularity of the 2010 Disney film *Tangled*. Characters such as Rapunzel and Flynn Rider make appearances. Encourage your kids to stick around to the end of the meal to see the procession of floating lanterns.

HOUSE SPECIALTIES Many dishes have a *Tangled* theme, such as the Snuggly Duckling Platter (sliced meats with pumpernickel and mustard); Maximus Salad (potatoes, carrots, and greens); Flynn Rider Platter (smoked pork loin with braised cabbage); Pascal Punch (Odwalla Mango Tango smoothie with coconut and strawberry yogurt); and the pièce de résistance, Tangled Pasta (angel hair tossed with basil pesto and scallops). Gimmicks aside, the food is quite good.

OTHER RECOMMENDATIONS On longer sailings, Rapunzel's serves German-style dishes in honor of the Brothers Grimm (who popularized Rapunzel and other characters in their bestselling *Children's and Household Tales*): pretzel bread, a grilled-knockwurst appetizer, green-and-white asparagus salad, trio of veal (tenderloin, pulled shank, and pasta with veal sauce), and Sacher torte for dessert.

COMMENTS Rapunzel's kids' menu is full of safe bets—macaroni and cheese, mini burgers, baked salmon, whole-wheat pasta—but much of the adult fare successfully straddles the line between kid-friendly and grown-up. It's a great way to introduce your children to more-sophisticated dishes that aren't totally weird or unfamiliar. (At Lumiere's, on the other hand, we've heard a few kids cry with dismay when they learned what escargot is.)

Disney Wonder DINING

COUNTER-SERVICE RESTAURANTS
Daisy's De-Lites

QUALITY B	LOCATION DECK 9 AFT

COMMENTS See the profile of Daisy's De-Lites on the *Magic* (page 203) for details.

Pete's Boiler Bites

QUALITY B	LOCATION DECK 9 AFT

OPEN Midday–early evening.

SELECTIONS Hamburgers, fish burgers, veggie burgers, hot dogs, chicken tenders, fries. The shawarma station offers carved chicken or lamb with optional toppings such as hummus, pickled veggies, baba ghanoush, chili mayo, and mint-cilantro sauce.

COMMENTS A nearby fixin's bar provides standard burger toppings, but if you want to mix things up, ask for a plateful of shawarma toppings instead.

Pinocchio's Pizzeria

QUALITY C	LOCATION DECK 9 AFT

COMMENTS See the profile of Pinocchio's Pizzeria on the *Magic* (page 204) for details.

TABLE-SERVICE RESTAURANTS
Animator's Palate ★★★ Deck 4 Aft

AMERICAN/ASIAN	QUALITY ★★★	SERVICE ★★★★	FRIENDLINESS ★★★★

COMMENTS See the profile of Animator's Palate on the *Magic* (page 204) for details.

Cabanas ★★★ Deck 9 Aft

AMERICAN/BUFFET	QUALITY ★★★	SERVICE ★★★★	FRIENDLINESS ★★★★

COMMENTS See the profile of Cabanas on the *Magic* (page 205) for details.

Palo ★★★½ Deck 10 Aft

ITALIAN	QUALITY ★★★½	VALUE ★★★½	SERVICE ★★★★½
FRIENDLINESS ★★★★			

COMMENTS See the profile of Palo on the *Magic* (page 206) for details.

Tiana's Place ★★★ Deck 3 Aft

AMERICAN/SOUTHERN	QUALITY ★★½	SERVICE ★★★★	FRIENDLINESS ★★★★

Reservations Not accepted. **Meals served** Breakfast, lunch, and dinner. **Alcohol** Limited selection of red, white, and sparkling wines, plus mixed drinks and spirits.

SETTING AND ATMOSPHERE An homage to the restaurant in *The Princess and the Frog,* Tiana's Place evokes a New Orleans supper club, with rustic elements interspersed with purple-and-green fabrics and fixtures of polished gold (think upscale Mardi Gras). Live music, a first for a DCL rotational-dining room, is performed on the main stage and features the jazz, swing, and blues sounds of Louisiana. While the music is fun and usually performed well, it can sometimes be loud, overwhelming dinner-table conversation. If you have a child with sensory-processing issues and you want to enjoy the performances, you may want to consider noise-canceling headphones for your child to wear during sets.

HOUSE SPECIALTIES Look for respectable approximations of New Orleans specialties, including boudin sausage fritters, a shrimp-and-grits appetizer, Cajun-spiced sea bass, and roasted Creole chicken. The buttermilk beignets are delicious, and you can't go wrong with the Bananas Foster sundae.

COMMENTS When Tiana's first opened, there were a few complaints about the food, but it has improved since then. As for us, it's a toss-up: Erin enjoys the food, but Len wishes there were a secret door leading to a quieter restaurant with more-authentic flavor.

Triton's ★★★ Deck 3 Midship

AMERICAN/FRENCH **QUALITY ★★★**   **SERVICE ★★★★**   **FRIENDLINESS ★★★★**

Reservations Not accepted. **Meals served** Breakfast, lunch, and dinner. **Alcohol** Limited selection of red, white, and sparkling wines, plus mixed drinks and spirits.

SETTING AND ATMOSPHERE In case you've forgotten that King Triton is Ariel's father in *The Little Mermaid,* a large tile mosaic of Triton and Ariel sits at the back of this restaurant to remind you. Besides the art, Triton's blue, beige, and gray color scheme lends a vaguely seaworthy theme to the inside.

HOUSE SPECIALTIES Breakfast features the usual suspects: fruit, cereal, eggs, waffles, bacon, sausage, and pastries. Lunch includes soups, salads, sandwiches, and burgers, plus a couple of alternative offerings such as pasta or fish. Dinner appetizers include escargots and French onion soup; order a crispy duck breast for the table if no one is adventurous enough to try it themselves. The Grand Marnier soufflé is the most popular dessert, but unlike the soufflé served at Palo (see page 206), this one is more of an airy cake.

COMMENTS Triton's serves essentially the same menu as **Lumiere's** on the *Magic* (see pages 205 and 206). There's a decent selection of French-inspired entrées, plus enough standard vegetarian, chicken, beef, and pork dishes to satisfy almost anyone.

Disney Dream DINING

COUNTER-SERVICE RESTAURANTS
Fillmore's Favorites

QUALITY C   LOCATION DECK 11 MIDSHIP

OPEN Midday–early evening.

SELECTIONS Sandwiches, wraps, salads, fruit, cookies.

COMMENTS While the menu can change from time to time, it usually includes a roast-beef-and-Cheddar sandwich, a Greek-salad veggie wrap, and a chicken Caesar wrap. Fresh fruit, such as whole bananas, grapes, and oranges, is also available.

Luigi's Pizza

QUALITY C   LOCATION DECK 11 MIDSHIP

OPEN Midday–early evening.

SELECTIONS Cheese, pepperoni, and specialty pizzas (including veggie); cheeseless or gluten-free pizza on request. If you're in the mood for fancy pizza, look for offerings labeled "flatbread."

COMMENTS As with the pizza joints on the *Magic* and *Wonder,* you'd never mistake Luigi's for authentic pizza, but it's fine if you need a quick bite. Occasionally open after dinner, when ordering a whole pie is a convenient alternative to room service or restaurant dining.

Senses Juice Bar

QUALITY B   LOCATION SENSES SPA, DECK 11 FORWARD

OPEN Morning–midday and mid- to late afternoon.

SELECTIONS Fresh-squeezed juices in inventive combinations; fruit smoothies customized with ingredients like spinach leaves; ginger; avocado; basil; protein powder; chia seeds; yogurt; and soy, almond, or coconut milk.

COMMENTS Prices range from about $6 to about $10, depending on the ingredients you select. Suggested smoothie blends are listed on the menu, but feel free to try whatever combination strikes your fancy. A small selection of Champagnes and cordials is also available.

Tow Mater's Grill

QUALITY C   LOCATION DECK 11 MIDSHIP

OPEN Midday–late evening.

SELECTIONS Grilled hot dogs, sausages, burgers, and chicken sandwiches; fried chicken strips; French fries.

COMMENTS The burgers and fries are sustenance for chlorine-addled kids (that is, if they can be pried out of the pool long enough to eat). The chicken strips and hot dogs are the best things on the menu. A nearby fixin's bar provides toppings for burgers and sandwiches.

Vanellope's Sweets & Treats

QUALITY B   LOCATION DECK 11 MIDSHIP

OPEN Midday–late evening, with a 1-hour closure during the late afternoon.

SELECTIONS Named for Vanellope Von Schweetz, the sugar-fueled game character from Disney's *Wreck-It Ralph,* Vanellope's Sweets & Treats serves ice cream and house-made gelato with an extensive array of toppings, along with cupcakes, cookies, candy apples, chocolate truffles, and bulk and packaged candies. Ice cream and gelato flavors vary seasonally. Kick your sugar buzz into high gear with espresso-based drinks.

COMMENTS You can get free soft-serve at the **Eye Scream** self-service machine and smoothies at an extra charge at **Frozone Treats,** both around the corner. The more-upscale treats at Vanellope's start at about $3.50 for a single scoop; toppings and waffle cones are available at a small upcharge. Sundae selections are imaginative, and the serving sizes are generous—even the smallest sundaes, starting at about $5.75, can likely serve two. (*Note:* Prices are subject to change.) If you have a large group, indulge in Ralph's (as in

Wreck-It) Family Challenge: an eight-scoop, eight-topping sundae served in a souvenir trophy cup. Like **Sweet on You** on the *Fantasy* (page 215) and **Inside Out: Joyful Sweets** on the *Wish* (pages 218 and 219), Vanellope's delivers to the main dining rooms.

TABLE-SERVICE RESTAURANTS
Animator's Palate   ★★★   Deck 3 Aft

AMERICAN/ASIAN   QUALITY ★★★   SERVICE ★★★★   FRIENDLINESS ★★★★

Reservations Not accepted. **Meals served** Dinner. **Alcohol** Red, white, and sparkling wines, plus mixed drinks and spirits.

SETTING AND ATMOSPHERE Four DCL ships have a restaurant called Animator's Palate, but the versions on the *Dream* and the *Fantasy* have touches that differentiate them from the ones on the *Magic* and the *Wonder,* as well as from each other. Animator's Palate on the *Dream* (and the *Fantasy*) has red carpeting with silver, gold, and blue stars, and walls that are the color of caramel. The backs of the dining-room chairs are patterned after Mickey Mouse's pants, with red backs, yellow buttons, and a black "belt" at the top.

Shelves along the walls hold small toy versions of Disney and Pixar icons in between video screens displaying animation sketches from popular Disney movies. The more interesting ones will show on one screen how one complete animated cell is drawn, starting from sketches of the main characters to how key background elements are drawn, color samples for walls and floors, and the finished art. The art changes throughout the evening, keeping the view fresh for everyone.

At certain points during your dinner, some of the screens will switch from sketches to an interactive video featuring the surfer-dude turtle Crush from *Finding Nemo.* When we say *interactive,* we mean it—Crush will ask you questions and react to your responses.

Based on the same real-time computer graphics found in EPCOT's *Turtle Talk with Crush* attraction (also found at other Disney parks), the technology behind this minishow allows Crush's mouth to move in the appropriate way as his words are spoken. Parents may be more amazed than kids.

HOUSE SPECIALTIES Penne Bolognese, grilled tuna steak, ginger teriyaki beef, lemon-thyme chicken, roasted-garlic dip served with bread.

COMMENTS The "wow" factor doesn't extend to the food—as is the case at the other Animator's Palates, the cuisine isn't much different from what you might get at your local Applebee's or Chili's.

Cabanas   ★★★   Deck 11 Aft

AMERICAN/BUFFET   QUALITY ★★★   SERVICE ★★★★   FRIENDLINESS ★★★★

COMMENTS See the profile of Cabanas on the *Magic* (page 205) for details.

Enchanted Garden   ★★★   Deck 2 Midship

**AMERICAN/CONTINENTAL   QUALITY ★★★   SERVICE ★★★★
FRIENDLINESS ★★★★**

Reservations Not accepted. **Meals served** Dinner; breakfast and lunch available on select days. **Alcohol** Limited selection of red, white, and sparkling wines, plus mixed drinks and spirits.

SETTING AND ATMOSPHERE Designed to evoke a 19th-century French greenhouse, with patinaed cast-iron arches supporting a spectacular ceiling display of plants, sun, and sky, Enchanted Garden is the prettiest of the *Dream*'s three main rotational restaurants.

During lunch, lights in the ceiling simulate the midday sun, and diners see what appears to be ivy climbing up the side of the ironworks; as the sun sets, the "sky" turns to dusk and eventually to dark. Lights, in the shape of flowers and hung from the ceiling, open their "petals" as night falls.

The centerpiece of Enchanted Garden is a burbling concrete fountain, 7 feet tall, topped by Mickey Mouse. Look for framed Hermès scarves outside the restaurant—a posh touch of France. (Disney says Enchanted Garden is inspired by the gardens at Versailles, but we think it looks more like the hothouse at Paris's Jardin des Plantes.)

HOUSE SPECIALTIES Roast pork tenderloin seasoned with smoked salt; scallops with roasted asparagus; pan-seared sea bass with fava beans and pea risotto; marjoram-scented roast chicken.

COMMENTS The menu is more American bistro than Paris brasserie, despite the French setting. Besides substituting brioche for bread, the Frenchiest thing on the menu is the word *julienne* to describe how the vegetables are cut.

There's usually at least one pork dish, such as roast pork tenderloin; one chicken dish (baked or roasted); and a steak or prime rib available, along with several seafood and vegetarian options. Honestly, you could serve these dishes at Animator's Palate or Royal Court without anyone noticing, but maybe the scenery here makes the food taste a little bit better.

Palo ★★★★ Deck 12 Aft and Starboard

ITALIAN QUALITY ★★★★ VALUE ★★★★ SERVICE ★★★★½ FRIENDLINESS ★★★★

Reservations Required. **Meals served** Brunch on sea days; prix fixe dinner nightly. **Alcohol** Large list of Italian wines, listed by region, plus select wines from around the world; mixed drinks and spirits; limoncello; grappa; ice wine. **Special comments** An additional $45/person charge will be added to your cruise bill for each meal at Palo. If you need to cancel a reservation, you must do so 24 hours in advance, or the full per-person charge may be applied to your bill. Guests must be 18 or older to dine.

Note: Palo's base dinner service now consists of a four-course, prix fixe menu (see page 201). The dinner selections described on the next page—with the exception of the chocolate soufflé—now cost extra. Also note that Palo's brunch transitioned from a serve-yourself buffet to table service post-pandemic, with courses served family-style. We hear that table service will continue to be the norm for the foreseeable future.

SETTING AND ATMOSPHERE Palo is on the starboard side at the back of Deck 12, opposite the adults-only French restaurant Remy (see next profile) and adjacent to Meridian bar. We think Palo on the *Dream* and *Fantasy* has nicer furnishings than the versions on the *Magic* and *Wonder*.

The entrance to Palo on the *Dream* has a pretty, gold-and-ruby-colored glass chandelier, surely one of the most photographed parts of the restaurant. Guests entering Palo walk past a glass-enclosed wine closet and see the main dining room, decorated with deep mahogany wood–paneled walls and columns and rich burgundy carpet. One half of the room features deep-green patterned fabric on the booths and chairs, with paintings of the Italian countryside and seashore along the walls. The other half of Palo uses a saturated red fabric for its seating; illustrations of Italian villas hang on the walls. Also within the *Dream*'s Palo, and unique to Disney's larger ships, are small private dining rooms with custom fabrics, wallpaper, and lighting. Peek inside if one of the rooms is empty, and you'll see how the wealthy merchants of Venice might have lived.

Naturally, tables next to Palo's floor-to-ceiling windows afford the best views, but tables near the back wall sit on an elevated platform, allowing diners there to see over the tables nearest the windows. Our favorite table is to the left of the entrance, tucked by itself in a rounded corner along the inside wall and surrounded by a mural depicting Venice from the water. It's a bit high profile, though; quieter seats are available at the far ends of either side of the restaurant. Brunch offers open seating.

HOUSE SPECIALTIES Start your dinner with the *ciuppin,* a soup of fish, mussels, clams, and lobster in a tomato broth, or the white-bean soup, with prosciutto and perfectly al dente beans. A large selection of pastas is available; the vegetarian mushroom risotto, for example, is so rich you'd swear it had meat in it. Our favorite entrée is the rack of lamb, which comes in a crispy crust of Parmesan cheese and oregano. For seafood, we like the grilled tuna with potato risotto a bit more than the grilled scallops. The chocolate soufflé, by far the most popular dessert, comes with both dark- and white-chocolate sauces. If you're not in the mood for chocolate, there may be other versions of the soufflé available—it never hurts to ask.

As on the other ships, Palo's brunch menu is excellent. At the time of this writing, it's served family-style: your server will bring you as much or as little of each offering as you like. Starters may include ahi tuna, crab legs, or prosciutto. The main course includes breakfast options such as eggs Benedict and lunch options such as artichoke ravioli and made-to-order pizza. If there's any room left for dessert, small cups of tiramisu or berries with cream will take care of your sweet tooth.

COMMENTS With the recent changes to Palo's pricing structure, which made many favorite menu items à la carte (see page 201), we consider brunch a much bigger bang for your buck than dinner, even though both meals now cost $45—brunch pricing includes anything you want in any amount (except, of course, for alcohol).

Remy ★★★★½ Deck 12 Aft

FRENCH QUALITY ★★★★½ VALUE ★★★★½ SERVICE ★★★★½ FRIENDLINESS ★★★★

Reservations Required. **Meals served** Dinner. **Alcohol** An extensive selection of French wines and Champagnes. **Special comments** An additional $75/person charge will be added to your cruise bill for each brunch at Remy and $125/person for each dinner, with à la carte offerings available at an additional charge. See the next page for information about special dining experiences. If you need to cancel a reservation, you must do so by 2 p.m. on the day of your reservation, or the full per-person charge will be applied to your bill. Guests must be age 18 or older to dine.

SETTING AND ATMOSPHERE Remy is remarkably elegant and understated for a Disney restaurant—and one named after a cartoon rat at that. The most prominent features are the floor-to-ceiling windows, which look out over the ocean on the port side of the ship from high on Deck 12, and the Art Nouveau lights, which seem to spring from the floor as thick vines, branching out into yellow lights as they reach the ceiling. Besides those touches, and perhaps the oval mirrors along the wall opposite the windows, the rest is simple and elegant: oval, round, and square tables, all with white-linen tablecloths, and round-backed wood chairs with white upholstery. The olive-green carpet pattern matches the Art Nouveau decor without being distracting. A small teak deck wraps around Remy, allowing you to walk out for a quick breath of fresh air between courses.

HOUSE SPECIALTIES Entrées, such as Australian Wagyu beef and pork from central France, are divine. Splurge on a wine pairing. The tasting menu may be one of the best 3-hour dining experiences you'll ever have, but if that sounds like too much food, you can't go wrong with the regular menu.

Remy also offers an extensive brunch on days when the ship is at sea. Like the brunch at Palo, Remy's has an extensive selection, including fruit, pastries, seafood, beef, pork, pasta, and fish. A Champagne pairing is available for an additional $30 per person. We prefer the dinner experience, but spending the morning at Remy is a lovely way to start a day at sea.

Remy sometimes offers special dining experiences. Recent ones have included **Pompidou's Patisseries Dessert Experience,** which featured a sampling of six premium desserts for $60 per person ($85 per person with a supplementary wine pairing), and **Petites Assiettes de Remy (Remy's Small Plates),** a six-course tasting menu for $50 per person. If you're interested in these or similar experiences, check online at **My Reservations** (see page 47) or call DCL at ☎ 800-951-3532 to see if they'll be offered during your sailing.

COMMENTS What makes a great restaurant such as Remy different from restaurants that are simply very good is that, while the latter usually have a few signature dishes that they do very well, virtually *everything* at Remy is nothing short of exceptional. An appetizer of carrots—yes, the humble root vegetable—will be the most extraordinary carrots you've ever had, probably in varieties and colors you didn't know existed, and with a flavor that is the pure essence of carrot-ness. Now imagine a meal of three to eight courses, all equally as good, ranging from soups, seafood, and beef, to sides, cheese courses, and desserts. That's your average evening at Remy.

If you have the time or the inclination, order the tasting menu, which allows you to savor every bit of creativity and technical mastery that Remy's kitchen can muster.

Pro tip: If you order a wine pairing, be aware that each guest gets a *lot* of wine that could easily be split between two people. Len's first evening at Remy was preceded by a martini at Meridian and continued with a wine pairing at dinner. The first few courses were memorable—both in the sense that they were delicious and the sense that Len remembered them—but as the meal wore on and the wine kept flowing, he was observed applauding a cheese cart as it rolled by for dessert service. That called for another dinner at Remy, minus the booze.

Royal Palace ★★★   Deck 3 Midship

AMERICAN/FRENCH   QUALITY ★★★   SERVICE ★★★★   FRIENDLINESS ★★★★

Reservations Not accepted. **Meals served** Breakfast, lunch, and dinner. **Alcohol** Limited selection of red, white, and sparkling wines, plus mixed drinks and spirits.

SETTING AND ATMOSPHERE The most attractive part of Royal Palace may be its entrance, done in gold-and-white-marble tile below a pretty flower-shaped chandelier accented with blue-glass "diamonds" and red "rubies." Inside the doors, gold-and-white faux-marble columns form a circle just inside one ring of tables; royal-blue carpet with gold trim lines the inner part of the restaurant. Drapes cover the windows lining one side of the room, and mosaic-tile pictures of Disney princesses line another.

HOUSE SPECIALTIES Breakfast is standard buffet fare: fruit, cereal, eggs, waffles, bacon, sausage, and pastries. Lunch includes soups, salads, sandwiches, and burgers, plus a couple of alternative offerings such as pasta or fish. Dinner appetizers include escargots and French onion soup; the crispy roasted duck breast is tasty. The Grand Marnier soufflé is the most popular dessert, but unlike the soufflé served at Palo (see pages 198 and 204), this is more of an airy cake.

COMMENTS You know Disney is serious about the French theme when they put snails on the appetizer menu. There are other Gallic influences on the menu—many of the entrées have sauces made with butter, wine, or spirits—plus enough standard vegetarian, chicken, beef, and pork dishes to make anyone happy.

Disney Fantasy DINING

COUNTER-SERVICE RESTAURANTS
Fillmore's Favorites

QUALITY C   LOCATION DECK 11 MIDSHIP

COMMENTS See the profile of Fillmore's Favorites on the *Dream* (pages 209 and 210) for details.

Luigi's Pizza

QUALITY C   LOCATION DECK 11 MIDSHIP

COMMENTS See the profile of Luigi's Pizza on the *Dream* (page 210) for details.

Senses Juice Bar

QUALITY B   LOCATION SENSES SPA, DECK 11 FORWARD

COMMENTS See the profile of Senses Juice Bar on the *Dream* (page 210) for details.

Sweet on You Ice Cream & Sweets

QUALITY B   LOCATION DECK 11 MIDSHIP

OPEN Midday–late evening, with a 1-hour closure during the late afternoon.

SELECTIONS Choose from chocolate truffles (about $2 each), macarons (French meringue cookies, about $2 each), fancy cupcakes (about $4 each), wrapped candy by the pound, and an array of Mickey-themed pastries. The star attraction is the freezer case, stocked with ice cream, housemade gelato, and toppings aplenty. Ice cream and gelato flavors vary seasonally. Kick your sugar buzz into high gear with espresso-based drinks.

COMMENTS You can get free soft-serve at the machine by the pool and free ice cream at dinner in the main dining rooms. If you need a fancier fix, single scoops at Sweet on You start at about $3.50; toppings and waffle cones are available at a small upcharge. (*Note:* Prices are estimates and subject to change.) Sundae selections are imaginative and portions are generous; even the smallest sundaes, starting at about $5.75, can likely serve two. For a special indulgence, try the create-your-own ice-cream sandwich (about $5): pick any combination of two cookies (white chocolate-macadamia, chocolate chip fudge, M&M's, chocolate chunk, or peanut butter) and any flavor of ice cream or gelato. Like **Vanellope's Sweets & Treats** on the *Dream* (see page 210) and **Inside Out: Joyful Sweets** on the *Wish* (pages 218 and 219), Sweet on You delivers to the main dining rooms.

Tow Mater's Grill

QUALITY C   LOCATION DECK 11 MIDSHIP

COMMENTS See the profile of Tow Mater's Grill on the *Dream* (page 210) for details.

TABLE-SERVICE RESTAURANTS
Animator's Palate   ★★★   Deck 3 Aft

AMERICAN/ASIAN   QUALITY ★★★   SERVICE ★★★★   FRIENDLINESS ★★★★

Reservations Not accepted. **Meals served** Dinner. **Alcohol** Red, white, and sparkling wines, plus mixed drinks and spirits.

SETTING AND ATMOSPHERE Four DCL ships have a restaurant called Animator's Palate, but the versions on the *Dream* and the *Fantasy* have touches that differentiate them from the ones on the *Magic* and the *Wonder,* as well as from each other. Animator's Palate on the *Dream* (and the *Fantasy*) has red carpeting with silver, gold, and blue stars, and walls that are the color of caramel. The backs of the dining-room chairs are patterned after Mickey Mouse's pants, with red backs, yellow buttons, and a black "belt" at the top.

Shelves along the walls hold small toy versions of Disney and Pixar icons in between video screens displaying animation sketches from popular Disney movies. The more interesting ones will show on one screen how one complete animated cell is drawn, starting from sketches of the main characters to how key background elements are drawn, color samples for walls and floors, and the finished art. The art changes throughout the evening, keeping the view fresh for everyone.

Like Animator's Palate on the *Magic* and *Wonder* (see page 204), the version on the *Fantasy* features **Animation Magic,** an impressive dinner show. At the beginning of the second night you dine there, you're given a sheet of paper and crayon and invited to draw a self-portrait. At the end of the evening, the diners' self-portraits are incorporated into a cartoon projected onto a video screen. The presentation is reminiscent of Disney's 1929 animated short *The Skeleton Dance.*

At your first scheduled dinner at Animator's Palate, you get a different show. Some of the screens will switch from sketches to an interactive video featuring the surfer-dude turtle Crush from *Finding Nemo.* When we say *interactive,* we mean it—Crush will ask you questions and react to your responses, allowing you to have an actual conversation with him.

Based on the same real-time computer graphics found in EPCOT's *Turtle Talk with Crush* attraction (also found at other Disney parks), the technology behind this minishow allows Crush's mouth to move in the appropriate way as his words are spoken. Parents may be more amazed than children.

HOUSE SPECIALTIES Ginger-teriyaki beef tenderloin; roasted-garlic or red-pepper dip with bread.

COMMENTS When it comes to the food here, it's a tale as old as time, as is the case at the other three Animator's Palates: the dishes are pedestrian chain-restaurant fare, in spite of the Pacific Rim/American designation. However, the innovative entertainment on the *Fantasy* (and the *Dream*) helps make up for the lackluster cuisine.

Cabanas ★★★ Deck 11 Aft

AMERICAN/BUFFET QUALITY ★★★ SERVICE ★★★★ FRIENDLINESS ★★★★

COMMENTS See the profile of Cabanas on the *Magic* (page 205) for details.

Enchanted Garden ★★★ Deck 2 Midship

AMERICAN/CONTINENTAL QUALITY ★★★ SERVICE ★★★★ FRIENDLINESS ★★★★

COMMENTS See the profile of Enchanted Garden on the *Dream* (pages 211 and 212) for details.

Palo ★★★★ Deck 12 Aft and Starboard

ITALIAN   QUALITY ★★★★   VALUE ★★★★   SERVICE ★★★★½
FRIENDLINESS ★★★★

COMMENTS See the profile of Palo on the *Dream* (page 212) for details.

Remy ★★★★½ Deck 12 Aft

FRENCH   QUALITY ★★★★½   VALUE ★★★★½   SERVICE ★★★★½
FRIENDLINESS ★★★★

COMMENTS See the profile of Remy on the *Dream* (page 213) for details.

Royal Court ★★★ Deck 3 Midship

AMERICAN/FRENCH QUALITY ★★★ SERVICE ★★★★ FRIENDLINESS ★★★★

Reservations Not accepted. **Meals served** Breakfast, lunch, and dinner. **Alcohol** Limited selection of red, white, and sparkling wines, plus mixed drinks and spirits.

SETTING AND ATMOSPHERE The most distinctive design elements of Royal Court are the gold-colored wood columns on the floor, which rise to attach to the ceiling through flared white glass decorated with plant stems and shaped like flower petals. Along with these, white-marble columns and carpet patterned to look like fancy rugs give Royal Court a formal feel, even when it's half-full of kids. Small, round lamps placed around the room are designed to look like Cinderella's pumpkin coach, and some of the walls feature tile murals depicting scenes from *Cinderella* and other Disney-princess films. Tables near the starboard wall sit under portholes that offer ocean views, although these are partially blocked by a privacy wall running along the inside perimeter of the restaurant.

HOUSE SPECIALTIES Breakfast is standard fare: fruit, cereal, eggs, waffles, bacon, sausage, and pastries. Lunch includes soups, salads, sandwiches, and burgers, plus a couple of alternative offerings such as pasta or fish. Dinner appetizers include escargots and French onion soup; the crispy roasted duck breast is tasty. The Grand Marnier soufflé is probably the most popular dessert.

COMMENTS Only differences in decor distinguish Royal Court on the *Fantasy* from **Royal Palace** on the *Dream* (see pages 214 and 215).

▌ *Disney Wish* DINING

COUNTER-SERVICE RESTAURANTS

THE *WISH*'S QUICK-SERVICE EATERIES are housed in a food court called **Mickey and Friends Festival of Foods.** The food is a substantial step up from what you get at the comparable pool-deck venues on the other four ships.

Daisy's Pizza Pies

QUALITY C **LOCATION** DECK 11 AFT

OPEN Mid- to early evening.

SELECTIONS Pizza in various permutations: prosciutto, pepperoni and sausage, four-cheese, and margherita.

COMMENTS Plant-based and gluten-free options are also available.

Donald's Cantina

QUALITY B **LOCATION** DECK 11 AFT

OPEN Mid- to early evening.

SELECTIONS Mexican favorites such as burritos, tacos, and build-your-own bowls similar to what you might get at Chipotle. Start your bowl with a base of rice or lettuce, then add any combination of fajita beef, chicken, pork carnitas, beans, veggies, guacamole, salsa, sour cream, or queso.

COMMENTS We're *obsessed* with the hot-sauce bar.

Goofy's Grill

QUALITY C **LOCATION** DECK 11 AFT

OPEN Mid- to early evening.

SELECTIONS Grilled burgers, Impossible burgers, bratwurst, hot dogs, and plant-based sausages with all the fixin's. You'll also find DCL's famous chicken nuggets here.

COMMENTS Fries are available by request with any entrée—or on their own.

Mickey's Smokestack Barbecue

QUALITY B **LOCATION** DECK 11 AFT

OPEN Mid- to early evening.

SELECTIONS Smoked brisket, St. Louis pork (cuts of smoked pork butt—think a barbecue "steak"), smoked chicken, pulled pork, and smoked kielbasa. Sides include baked mac and cheese, collard greens, sweet potato fries, and cornbread.

COMMENTS There are several different barbecue sauces to choose from. Have a family taste test to see which everyone prefers.

Inside Out: Joyful Sweets

QUALITY B **LOCATION** DECK 11 AFT

OPEN Midday–late evening.

SELECTIONS The signature dessert is the colorful Memory Orb cupcake—a chocolate sphere filled with gummy candies, marshmallows, and other goodies ($4.50)—but most folks are here for the house-made ice creams and gelatos. At press time, prices for one to three scoops are $3.50–$6 (ice cream) and $3.75–$6.25 (gelato). Packaged treats and fresh pastries round out the offerings.

COMMENTS Inside Out: Joyful Sweets is the *Wish*'s equivalent of **Vanellope's Sweets & Treats** on the *Dream* (page 210) and **Sweet on You** on the *Fantasy* (page 216). (Free soft-serve is available at **Sweet Minnie's Ice Cream.**) The theme, in case you haven't guessed, is Disney's *Inside Out:* Memory Orbs decorate the space, and statues of Joy, Sadness, Fear, Anger, and Disgust make for fun photo ops.

TABLE-SERVICE RESTAURANTS
Arendelle: A *Frozen* Dining Adventure   ★★★   Deck 5 Aft

**AMERICAN/SCANDINAVIAN   QUALITY ★★★   SERVICE ★★★★
FRIENDLINESS ★★★★**

Reservations Not accepted. **Meals served** Dinner. **Alcohol** Modest wine selection, plus mixed drinks and spirits.

SETTING AND ATMOSPHERE The restaurant's theming begins before you even step into the dining room—the jewel-toned Nordic decor in the extra-long entry corridor extends into the restaurant.

Not surprisingly, the main draw here isn't the food but the entertainment, provided by the *Frozen* characters. Elsa and an animatronic Olaf play host to a wedding celebration for Anna and Kristoff; Oaken (of Wandering Oaken fame) provides the catering. The main characters sing, accompanied by a small band of troubadours.

HOUSE SPECIALTIES Arendelle serves a mix of standard-issue American fare and Scandinavian-inspired dishes. Appetizers include a smoked-fish plate, baked scallops, chilled-asparagus and field-greens salads, a ham-and-cheese tart, and carrot soup (definitely *not* made from Olaf's nose). The entrées include sea bass with asparagus, roasted rib eye, pork tenderloin, and chicken breast. If, like us, you're a fan of the IKEA food court, you'll love the meatballs with rosemary cream and lingonberry chutney.

For a sweet ending to your meal, try the Norwegian pancake roulade, layered with lingonberry jam and white-chocolate cheesecake, or the Troll Family's Rock Chocolate Bar, made with chocolate cake, pistachio-cookie pieces, and elderflower meringue.

COMMENTS Musical performances take place during more than half of your meal. You'll hear the greatest hits from both *Frozen* films, although they're sometimes performed by characters other than the ones who performed them in the movies.

We think the entertainment is charming—the performers are talented, and their comic patter is delivered with a light touch. As fans of the films, however, we'll admit to a little bias: some guests we've talked to who don't share our enthusiasm for the *Frozen* franchise think the show runs too long and find the volume level intrusive.

Enchanté ★★★★½ Deck 5 Aft

FRENCH **QUALITY** ★★★★½ **VALUE** ★★★★½ **SERVICE** ★★★★
FRIENDLINESS ★★★★

Reservations Required. **Meals served** Dinner. **Alcohol** An extensive selection of French wines and Champagnes. **Special comments** An additional $75/person charge will be added to your cruise bill for each brunch at Enchanté and $125/person for each dinner, with à la carte offerings available at an additional charge. If you need to cancel a reservation, you must do so by 2 p.m. on the day of your reservation, or the full per-person charge will be applied to your bill. Guests must be age 18 or older to dine.

SETTING AND ATMOSPHERE The decor reminds us of a spa—in fact, we think it looks more like a spa than the Senses Spas on the ships. The carpet is ocean blue, with dabs of white and gold echoing the ocean below, while nearly everything else is bedecked in shades of cream and gold. The overall effect is so clean and lovely that we'd be a little nervous to order red wine here, lest we spill it and taint that aura of cleanliness. Each table is decorated with a dark-blue dried rose—a touch that we find slightly macabre.

The centerpiece of the dining room is a floor-to-ceiling gold-toned chandelier festooned with bubble-shaped orbs. The entryway walls are decorated with clever candelabras (Lumiere from *Beauty and the Beast* makes an appearance) and showcase a selection of the ship's finest wines.

HOUSE SPECIALTIES At dinner, Enchanté offers both à la carte and prix fixe options. **Passion,** the prix fixe dinner ($125), consists of six courses: an appetizer of soil-grown tomatoes prepared three ways, John Dory with sea urchin and plankton, wild halibut with onion confit and vermouth sauce, and squab fermière (pigeon in puff pastry) with turnip relish, along with a cheese cart and dessert. The pricier **Collection** menu ($195) includes some of the previous prix fixe offerings, along with à la carte options such as Waygu beef, langoustines, caviar, Maine lobster, and assorted seasonal specialties. The lemon dessert is a particular standout.

Brunch ($75) features tomato pie, braised pork with salad, halibut with creamy scrambled eggs, chicken with gnocchi, and dessert. Wine and Champagne pairings are available for all meals.

COMMENTS We think Enchanté offers one of the finest culinary experiences you can have at sea—it's as much about the ambience, service, and presentation as it is the incredible food. That said, a few DCL guests say they've found the food and service to be less than impressive. If you eat at Enchanté, we'd love to hear from you.

Marceline Market ★★★ Deck 11 Aft

AMERICAN/BUFFET **QUALITY** ★★★ **SERVICE** ★★★★
FRIENDLINESS ★★★★

Reservations Not accepted. **Meals served** Breakfast and lunch; dinner may be offered in the future as the pandemic wanes. **Alcohol** The adjacent **Marceline Market Café** and **The Lookout** pool bar have bar service. **Special comments** This is very much the equivalent of Cabanas on the other ships—so much so, in fact, that we just call it Cabanas among ourselves ("Marceline Market" is a mouthful).

SETTING AND ATMOSPHERE Marceline Market comprises two identical food-service areas, accessible from twin entrances on Deck 11. (*Note:* During slower hours of the day, only one line may be open.) There are both indoor and outdoor seating options. Inside you'll find warm wood tables appropriate for various party sizes, as well as high-top bar-style seating for individuals. Self-service soft drink fountains are located around the restaurant.

HOUSE SPECIALTIES Breakfast stations include areas for bacon and sausage, made-to-order eggs and omelets, pancakes and waffles, grits and oatmeal, cold cereals and yogurt, pastries, and the like. We're particularly fond of the Asian breakfast station, which features a rotating selection of congees (porridges) and a savory-toppings bar.

Lunch options vary daily and include both hot and cold selections such as pasta, rice and veggie dishes, carved meats, soups, curries, fish, salads, sandwich fixings, and peel-and-eat shrimp. The kiddie station (available to adults as well) includes faves like mac and cheese, French fries, and chicken nuggets. We're fans of the mini charcuterie board, which has a small selection of cheeses, meats, and antipasti.

COMMENTS On one hand, Marceline Market is very similar to the Cabanas buffets on the other ships; on the other hand, getting your food isn't as straightforward as it is at Cabanas. Instead of serving yourself, you tell cast members what you want; then they dish it up for you and hand you a plate. But unlike a cafeteria, Marceline Market doesn't provide guests with trays. Depending on what you want to eat and the size of your group, transporting your plates to your table could get really complicated really fast.

Chances are your family will want to eat from several different food stations—each of which will provide you with a plate. So at breakfast, for instance, you may end up with an egg plate, a waffle plate, *and* a fruit plate. And with no trays to put your plates on, this means you'll have to (1) make several trips to the service line, dropping off a plate at your table after each trip, or (2) ask a cast member to help you carry several plates. If you're a single parent or helping care for someone with a mobility issue, we recommend flagging down a cast member for assistance *before* you get in line.

Note: Before the *Wish*'s inaugural sailing, DCL said that Marceline Market would offer regular table service at dinner, but it's open for breakfast and lunch only at press time. Check the specifics for your cruise.

1923 ★★★★ Deck 3 Aft

AMERICAN/CALIFORNIAN   QUALITY ★★★★½   SERVICE ★★★★
FRIENDLINESS ★★★★

Reservations Not accepted. **Meals served** Dinner. **Alcohol** Impressive selection of wines for a rotational dining room, along with mixed drinks and spirits.

SETTING AND ATMOSPHERE The dining room is divided into two separate areas: the **Roy Disney Room** and the **Walt Disney Room.** (The restaurant's name refers to the year the Disney brothers opened their first animation studio in Los Angeles.) The partitioning cuts down on the cavernous feeling—and the accompanying noise—that's endemic to DCL's other main dining rooms. The overall vibe is old-Hollywood glamour: if you're familiar with Carthay Circle at Disneyland, you're in the right ballpark, but 1923 is sleeker and more refined. The decor includes more than 1,000 drawings and props illustrating Walt and Roy's early days in California.

HOUSE SPECIALTIES Starters include duck confit, guinea hen corn chowder, Napa baby romaine salad with Caesar dressing and grape tomatoes, and fennel-and-pear salad with manchego cheese. The entrées are several steps up from the ones in the other rotational-dining rooms: peppered filet mignon; salmon filet with parsnip purée; rosemary-crusted rack of lamb; and roasted chicken with Brussels sprouts, potatoes, and apple chutney. Vegetarians will love the soft-shell tacos stuffed with quinoa, salsa fresca, peppers, and onions. The signature dessert is the blueberry-lemon Bavarian cream; other options include flourless orange-almond cake, Fuji apple cheesecake, spicy churros, and a classic hot-fudge sundae.

COMMENTS You won't find a better rotational-dining venue on the *Wish*—or any other DCL ship. Every dish we've tried at 1923 has been delicious.

Palo Steakhouse ★★★★ Deck 12 Aft

ITALIAN/STEAK   QUALITY ★★★★   VALUE ★★★★½   SERVICE ★★★★ FRIENDLINESS ★★★★

Reservations Required. **Meals served** Brunch on sea days; prix fixe dinner nightly. **Alcohol** Large list of Italian wines, listed by region, plus select wines from around the world; mixed drinks and spirits; limoncello; grappa; ice wine. **Special comments** An additional $45/person charge will be added to your cruise bill for each meal at Palo Steakhouse. If you need to cancel a reservation, you must do so 24 hours in advance, or the full per-person charge may be applied to your bill. Guests must be 18 or older to dine.

SETTING AND ATMOSPHERE The dining room is divided into two main seating areas. The first features booth and banquette seating with plush red-velvet upholstery. The second has tables, mostly for groups of two or four, with beige armchairs. Carpets are a muted rust color, and both rooms have floor-to-ceiling panoramic views of the ocean.

HOUSE SPECIALTIES The Italian portion of the dinner menu is similar to that of Palo on the other four ships. At Palo Steakhouse, however, the bill of fare is beefed up (see what we did there) with a plethora of proteins. Choose from bone-in cowboy rib eye, Angus tenderloin, New York sirloin, porterhouse, Wagyu tenderloin (*tender* being the operative word—you can cut it with a fork), veal rib chops, and Parmesan-crusted rack of lamb.

Brunch is likewise similar to what you'll find at Palo on the other ships—in other words, divine. Choose from seafood or meat antipasti, then move on to frittatas and omelets. The breakfast-y entrées are variations on waffles and pancakes (we're partial to the blueberry pancakes with whipped cream). The lunchier part of the menu includes lasagna, veal saltimbocca, chicken Parmesan, red snapper, mushroom ravioli, and sirloin. The desserts are tempting—chocolate-raspberry tart, limoncello torte, amaretto chocolate cake, and panna cotta—but don't sleep on the warm apple-cinnamon sticky buns, a brunch staple at the other four Palos. We're not ashamed to admit that we've booked cruises solely to sate our cravings for these.

COMMENTS The food is great at dinner, but we prefer brunch for the more economical pricing and the daytime views of the ocean.

Worlds of Marvel ★★★ Deck 4 Aft

AMERICAN/ECLECTIC QUALITY ★★★ SERVICE ★★★★ FRIENDLINESS ★★★★

Reservations Not accepted. **Meals served** Dinner. **Alcohol** Limited selection of wines, plus mixed drinks and spirits.

SETTING AND ATMOSPHERE You're in the world of Pym Tech, with decor coming from the mind of Tony Stark—it's superhero chic bathed in blue light. Even the silverware is marked with the Avengers logo. (Just between us, we wouldn't be surprised if the place settings became a target for sticky-fingered Marvel fans.)

The dining room is encircled by video screens, much as the newer versions of Animators Palate are on the other DCL ships. In this case, however, you're not talking to Crush from *Finding Nemo* but gazing upon the eternally boyish face of Paul Rudd as Ant-Man. Also making on-screen appearances are The Wasp, the new Captain America, and Ms. Marvel, along with various and sundry villains. The "Quantum Core" gadget sitting on your table is nominally interactive: you'll be asked to press some buttons on it to help the superheroes save the world.

HOUSE SPECIALTIES Disney describes Worlds of Marvel's cuisines as "American, Sokovian, and Wakandan," which translates to American with a light smattering of cuisines from around the world. To begin your meal, you can choose from an heirloom-tomato or iceberg-wedge salad (both curiously classified as Wakandan) or appetizers such as steamed bao buns, crispy fried shrimp, and hearts of palm ceviche. The entrées include Delmonico rib eye, seared turbot filet, pork chops, and chicken schnitzel. The Lighter Note offerings include baked salmon filet, grilled sirloin, roasted chicken breast, and lamb shawarma salad.

When it comes to desserts, the "signature" Cheesecake Byte (a basic slice of cheesecake) pales in comparison to the showstopping Pym Doughnut Sundae: dulce de leche ice cream topped with a pecan brownie, caramel fudge sauce, whipped cream, and a chocolate-glazed mini doughnut. This is an over-the-top indulgence on the order of the extra-cost treats at Inside Out: Joyful Sweets—if you're in the mood for a calories-be-damned dessert, skip the premium ice cream during the day if you'll be eating dinner at Worlds of Marvel later on. Rounding out the dessert offerings are sticky date pudding, Key lime pie, Dobos torte (a Hungarian-style layer cake with chocolate filling), and flourless chocolate-beetroot cake.

COMMENTS The video presentation is cute (as is Paul Rudd), but like the live show at Arendelle, it's very loud and hard to ignore—you won't be having much family conversation while it's going on.

Keep in mind as well that the "wow" moments of the show take place at the very end of your meal, much like the revelatory moments during the end credits of a Marvel movie. If your kids grow tired and cranky during late dinner seatings, getting them to bed may be a higher priority than waiting around to be wowed.

A further consideration: if you're not familiar with the Marvel universe, you'll probably find the on-screen action hard to follow. To glean a bit of back story, you can drop by one of the **Oceaneer Club open houses** (see page 216), even if you're not traveling with kids.

Finally, the entertainment is prerecorded—meaning it will be exactly the same at every seating. If you've seen the show before and you don't care to see it again, you may want to consider springing for dinner at Palo Steakhouse or Enchanté on one of your assigned Worlds of Marvel nights.

PART EIGHT

ENTERTAINMENT *and* NIGHTLIFE

▌ LIVE THEATER *on the* SHIPS

LIVE STAGE PERFORMANCES take place at the **Walt Disney Theatre.** The shows are generally either Disney-themed theatrical productions (typically musicals) or variety acts such as comedians, magicians, and ventriloquists. The theatrical presentations are usually of two types: (1) retellings of familiar Disney stories and (2) so-called jukebox musicals.

unofficial **TIP**
If you're sailing on the *Wish* and you're awake at midnight, head to the Grand Hall atrium to see the *Glass Slipper Kiss Goodnight,* a charming little music-and-light show that concludes the day on board.

Disney's Aladdin: A Musical Spectacular, on the *Fantasy* and the *Wish,* is an example of the retelling genre. This is DCL's interpretation of the *Aladdin* story: it's not the same *Aladdin* as the 1992 animated feature or the 2019 live-action film, nor is it exactly the same as the musical that's been playing on Broadway since 2011. The cruise version features live actors and multiple Arabian-themed sets reprising key scenes from the animated film, including the most popular songs, in about half the time of the original movie.

Frozen: A Musical Spectacular, on the *Wonder* and the *Fantasy,* is the best of the retelling shows. The character puppets (Sven and Olaf, naturally) are charming, and the lighting, sets, and costumes are the best we've seen in any show at a Disney property, the theme parks included. We also like the *Magic*'s **Tangled: The Musical,** with songs from beloved composer Alan Menken. **Beauty and the Beast** on the *Dream* draws from both the 1991 and 2017 films; while it breaks no new ground—and yes, "Be Our Guest" is among the musical numbers—it's still entertaining. The *Magic*'s **Twice Charmed: An Original Twist on the Cinderella Story** is a fresh spin on the retelling genre, with surprises aplenty. The *Wish*'s new **Little Mermaid** show, on the other hand, is a letdown.

DCL's jukebox musicals are **Disney Dreams, Disney's Believe, The Golden Mickeys,** and **Disney Seas the Adventure!** Each features songs and characters from a variety of Disney films, with the numbers linked by an original narrative. While we enjoy the jukebox shows for the most part, the weakest of these merely serve to string together unrelated songs. (*The Golden Mickeys,* we're looking at you.) And we'd be remiss if we didn't mention that these shows—even the ones we like—tend to recycle the same handful of characters and songs that permeate virtually every entertainment venue throughout the ship.

A BIT OF ADVICE You'll probably see at least one musical if you're taking small children on your cruise. (Note that not all productions are performed on every sailing.) Along with reading the show profiles that follow, we recommend watching a few minutes of each show on YouTube before your cruise. This will not only help you decide which shows are worth your time, it will also let you know what you're missing in case another entertainment option is available.

Disney describes its theatrical offerings as "Broadway-style." This doesn't mean, however, that you're going to see the touring-company equivalent of a Broadway hit (like the versions of *Cats, Mamma Mia!,* and *Grease* staged on some Royal Caribbean sailings). As devotees of actual New York City theater, we confess that we used to scoff at the notion of "Broadway-style"—we thought it laughable to compare the stripped-down shows on the ships with real Broadway productions such as Disney's own stage version of *The Lion King.*

But in discussing our criticisms with Disney cast members, we've learned that, at least from a technical standpoint, DCL performances actually have much more in common with Times Square than Topeka: the stage mechanics, costuming, special effects, and lighting are as close to state of the art as is practical at sea. If you're watching a show with your kids and you find your eyes glazing over, try paying attention to the technological aspects of the production. They'd be top-notch in most locales—and they're nothing less than remarkable given the constraints of a cruise ship.

Check the **DCL Navigator app** (see page 136) for showtimes on your sailing.

THE *MAGIC*'S SHOWS
Disney Dreams: An Enchanted Classic ★★★★
WALT DISNEY THEATRE DECK 4 FORWARD

PETER PAN SAVES THE DAY

DURATION 55 minutes. **OUR TAKE** Not to be missed.

DESCRIPTION AND COMMENTS Peter Pan must help a girl named Anne Marie "find her own magic" before sunrise, whisking her through settings from *Aladdin, Beauty and the Beast, Cinderella, The Little Mermaid, The Lion King,* and *Frozen.* Each story's main characters appear in key scenes from their respective movies and sing their signature songs. The sets are attractive, the special effects are good (expect Elsa to unleash a minor blizzard in the Walt Disney Theatre), and the script is fast-paced and entertaining. The cast seems to enjoy it, too, and it shows.

Tangled: The Musical ★★★½
WALT DISNEY THEATRE DECK 4 FORWARD

RAPUNZEL LETS DOWN HER HAIR AND SINGS UP A STORM

DURATION 50 minutes. **OUR TAKE** A fresh take on a classic fairy tale.

DESCRIPTION AND COMMENTS This faithful retelling of Disney's *Tangled* features songs by Broadway and film composer–demigod Alan Menken (*Little Shop of Horrors, The Little Mermaid, Beauty and the Beast, Aladdin, Hercules, Pocahontas, Newsies,* and many more). Actors, singers, and dancers—and miles and miles of synthetic hair—wend their way through intricate sets. The Snuggly Duckling tavern is particularly charming, the puppetry for the larger-than-life sidekick horse Maximus is good enough to make you believe its operator is actually equine, and the ending lantern scene is among the most appealing segments of any DCL production. Having seen this show several times, we think the lighting is more moving and affecting if you sit in the center of the theater rather than close to the stage.

Twice Charmed: An Original Twist on the Cinderella Story
★★★½ **WALT DISNEY THEATRE DECK 4 FORWARD**

HAPPILY EVER AFTER? *NOT SO FAST!*

DURATION 55 minutes. **OUR TAKE** An engaging spin on a familiar story.

DESCRIPTION AND COMMENTS If you're familiar with Disney's animated *Cinderella* movie, you'll recall that the wicked stepmother breaks the first glass slipper just as it's about to go on Cinderella's foot. Cinderella, however, produces the second glass slipper, shows that it fits, and goes on to marry the prince.

Twice Charmed begins where the original story ends. As the show opens, Cinderella's stepmother and stepsisters are bemoaning the fact that they didn't know Cinderella had the second slipper. A nefarious fairy godfather sends Cindy's evil kin back in time to destroy her slipper before the prince's foot-fitting team ever arrives. This means Cinderella must figure out a new way to persuade the prince that they're meant to be together.

As is the case with most Disney classics, you can guess in the first 5 minutes how everything is going to end, but *Twice Charmed* is interesting anyway because it has a new narrative. The sets are pretty, the songs aren't bad, and it's an enjoyable way to spend an evening.

THE *WONDER'S* SHOWS
Disney Dreams: An Enchanted Classic ★★★★
WALT DISNEY THEATRE DECK 4 FORWARD

PETER PAN SAVES THE DAY

COMMENTS See profile of this show on the *Magic* (previous page) for details.

Frozen: A Musical Spectacular ★★★★½
WALT DISNEY THEATRE DECK 3 FORWARD

WE DON'T MIND THE COLD . . . OR THE SAME OLD SONGS

DURATION 50 minutes. **OUR TAKE** *Brrr!* Not to be missed.

DESCRIPTION AND COMMENTS You know the music—you've heard it over and over and over and over—but if you haven't seen DCL's take on this modern animated classic, you haven't seen the story performed with more heart or better artistry. The puppetry here is critical to the storytelling, adding warmth to what could be a mere rehash served cold. Life-size reindeer Sven and snowman Olaf are your obvious guesses for which characters are portrayed as puppets, but there are several surprises as well.

Frozen's special effects provide a couple of genuine "Wow!" moments; we count them among our favorites in any Disney venue, and no, we're not talking about soap-bubble snow. The costumes are gorgeous too: if you, like we, are fascinated by theatrical costuming, try to sit up close so you can see the details in the fabrics; otherwise, a middle-of-the-theater view is the best vantage point from which to take it all in.

The Golden Mickeys ★★
WALT DISNEY THEATRE DECK 4 FORWARD

DISNEY DOES AN AWARDS SHOW

DURATION 45 minutes. **OUR TAKE** This is the weakest of DCL's live shows.

DESCRIPTION AND COMMENTS The premise here is that you're at an Oscars-style ceremony (complete with a red carpet outside the theater) honoring Disney characters for their movie performances in various categories. As each award winner is announced, live actors reenact the movie's key scenes, including the songs, as video clips from the movies play in the background.

DCL does many things well, but *The Golden Mickeys* isn't one of them. The meager "plot" is just a device to tie the musical numbers together, and what little story line there is doesn't always make sense. Cruella de Vil, of course, is a natural for Best Villain; on the other hand, the Salute to Friendship award was apparently the only way the writers could think of to get Woody, Buzz, and Jessie together on stage. Unless you just *have* to see yet another rehash of songs from *The Lion King* and *Beauty and the Beast,* skip this one.

THE *DREAM'S* SHOWS
Beauty and the Beast ★★★½
WALT DISNEY THEATRE DECK 3 FORWARD

I'M NOT CRYING, *YOU'RE* CRYING!

DURATION 50 minutes. **OUR TAKE** We love the score—*really,* we do—but even we think "Be Our Guest" is overplayed.

DESCRIPTION AND COMMENTS This is an abridged but otherwise-faithful version of *Beauty and the Beast.* No, not *that* one, the other one: the set design and costuming are inspired by the 2017 live-action/CGI movie starring Emma Watson, not the 1991 animated classic.

DCL's *Beauty and the Beast* includes songs from both films. The actors who play the inanimate-object characters—Mrs. Potts, Cogsworth, and the like—wear regular (that is, human) period clothing rather than full-body character costumes, and they carry puppets of the household items they represent. (Example: Mrs. Potts carries a teapot with a painted face and lips that move.) Disney has made this concept work in other shows, such as *The Lion King* on Broadway; unfortunately, puppets *don't* work well to convey the idea of nonsentient things that have been magically transformed into living beings. Nevertheless, the music soars; Gaston still needs to get his toxic masculinity under control; and true love prevails at the end—perhaps prompting a tear or two, depending on how much of a sentimental sort you are.

Disney's Believe ★★★
WALT DISNEY THEATRE DECK 3 FORWARD

DISNEY MAGIC TRIUMPHS OVER CYNICISM

DURATION 50 minutes. **OUR TAKE** This is a nice change of pace.

DESCRIPTION AND COMMENTS A botanist father who doesn't believe in magic must learn to believe in order to reconnect with his daughter on her birthday. The father's guide is *Aladdin*'s wisecracking Genie, who takes Dad through time, space, and Disney music on his journey to acceptance.

Believe has one of the most sophisticated sets of any Disney stage show at sea, and there are enough visual elements to entertain almost any kid. Although it's not a holiday show, the plot seems like a loose adaptation of Charles Dickens's *A Christmas Carol*, with "ghosts" including Mary Poppins, Peter Pan, Baloo from *The Jungle Book,* and Rafiki from *The Lion King.* Other Disney stars make appearances, but, thankfully, *Believe* includes some less-familiar characters and songs. The final stretch has a hit parade of other princesses and ends with performances by Mickey and Minnie.

The Golden Mickeys ★★
WALT DISNEY THEATRE DECK 4 FORWARD

DISNEY DOES AN AWARDS SHOW

COMMENTS See profile of this show on the *Wonder* (previous page) for details.

THE *FANTASY'S* SHOWS
Disney's Aladdin: A Musical Spectacular ★★★
WALT DISNEY THEATRE DECK 3 FORWARD

CLASSIC SONGS AND A COMEDY CLUNKER

DURATION 45 minutes. **OUR TAKE** Genie needs better material.

DESCRIPTION AND COMMENTS A retelling of Disney's *Aladdin,* this show features stage sets depicting Agrabah, the Cave of Wonders, and the Sultan's palace. It also stars the film's main characters: Aladdin, Princess Jasmine, Jafar, Iago, and Genie. All of the big musical numbers are performed, including "Friend Like Me" and "A Whole New World."

This show is one of five variations on Disney's *Aladdin* story: the original animated film from 1992; a stage show (also called *Disney's Aladdin: A Musical Spectacular*) that ran at Disney California Adventure (DCA) from 2003 to 2016; the current Broadway show, which began its run in 2011; and the 2019 live-action film, starring Will Smith as Genie.

Aladdin is less sweet and sentimental than a show like *Believe.* Nevertheless, it has its shortcomings—take Genie, for instance. In the animated movie, he has the most important role: besides providing narrative and background, he tells jokes to keep the action moving. In the DCA show, Genie likewise ad-libbed topical humor into the act, and he delivered so many fast-and-furious zingers that he inevitably got the biggest ovation at the end. On board, however, Genie's jokes are watered down so much that they don't provide the spark the rest of the script needs.

Incidentally, with Disney's upcoming sixth ship, the *Treasure* (see page 5), being themed to *Aladdin,* we wonder if this show will become exclusive to that ship—it would be lazy of DCL not to make that happen, if you ask us.

Disney's Believe ★★★
WALT DISNEY THEATRE DECK 3 FORWARD

DISNEY MAGIC TRIUMPHS OVER CYNICISM

COMMENTS See previous page for details.

Frozen: A Musical Spectacular ★★★★½
WALT DISNEY THEATRE DECK 3 FORWARD

WE DON'T MIND THE COLD . . . OR THE SAME OLD SONGS

COMMENTS See profile of this show on the *Wonder* (page 226) for details.

THE *WISH*'S SHOWS

Disney's Aladdin: A Musical Spectacular ★★★
WALT DISNEY THEATRE DECK 3 FORWARD

CLASSIC SONGS AND A COMEDY CLUNKER

COMMENTS See previous page for details.

Disney Seas the Adventure! ★★★
WALT DISNEY THEATRE DECK 3 FORWARD

GOOFY TAKES THE HELM

DURATION 35 minutes. **OUR TAKE** A fun spin on the jukebox genre.

DESCRIPTION AND COMMENTS Minnie Mouse, here a ship's captain, hands over navigating duties to Goofy, and gentle chaos ensues. With an assist from Tinker Bell, Goofy sails through scenes that draw from the Disney canon. Among the songs you'll hear are "Go with the Flow" from the *Finding Nemo* stage show, "Into the Unknown" from *Frozen 2,* and "Almost There" from *The Princess and the Frog.* The overall feel is upbeat and silly instead of sentimental, as other DCL shows tend to be. We left the theater in a great mood.

The Little Mermaid ★★½
WALT DISNEY THEATRE DECK 4 FORWARD

A DISAPPOINTING ADAPTATION OF A BELOVED STORY

DURATION 50 minutes. **OUR TAKE** This is the weakest of DCL's retelling musicals. Prepare to be underwhelmed.

DESCRIPTION AND COMMENTS This retelling of the *Little Mermaid* story bears little resemblance to Disney's 1989 animated classic, the Broadway musical that ran from 2007 to 2009, or the production that aired live on ABC in 2019. Cast members enter the stage clad in costumes that would have been equally at home in a 1970s community theater presentation of *Godspell:* lots of flowing harem pants and ombre silk scarves. The production has a "Let's put on a show!" vibe, with cast members pulling additional costume elements, props, and puppets out of a giant treasure chest.

In a puzzling costuming decision, the mermaid characters, including Ariel, wear dresses that stop midcalf, fully exposing their legs and feet. (In the Broadway and TV productions, Ariel wore a floor-length skirt in scenes that required her to stand.) Willing suspension of disbelief is one thing, but we think this design choice feels lazy and asks too much of the audience.

Also, while the performers are talented, the script has some weaknesses. Specifically, the story line has been modified to include messages about climate change, conservation, and consent in romantic relationships. These messages are well intentioned, but they feel forced and heavy-handed in the context of a DIsney musical.

There are some bright moments, however: crabby Sebastian steals the show, and, as with Disney's other live renditions of this tale, bubbles inevitably fall from the sky. The end is happily ever after—but you have to swim through some murky waters to get there.

OTHER LIVE PERFORMANCES

BESIDES LIVE STAGE SHOWS, the Walt Disney Theatre hosts variety acts, including everything from magicians and comedians to jugglers and ventriloquists. Repositioning cruises, with their many sea days, sometimes host guest Broadway artists or other niche celebrities. Many of these acts will do preview shows or short sets at various venues throughout the ship before their major engagement at the theater.

We've seen some incredible onboard acts, and we've also seen a few for whom *mediocre* would be putting it kindly. If there are preview performances on your sailing, we suggest catching a few minutes (or asking other guests who've seen them) to decide whether the act is worth your time. In our experience, the best live acts tend to be the magicians and comics, who can adapt their material on the fly.

If you refresh the DCL Navigator app frequently throughout the day on a longer or specialty sailing (such as a holiday cruise), you may occasionally come across listings for **special performances** not announced ahead of time. For instance, on a New Year's Eve sailing on the *Fantasy* not long after *Frozen 2* was released, Erin and her family got to attend a surprise performance/seminar by Bobby Lopez and Kristen Anderson-Lopez, the husband-and-wife team who wrote the songs for both *Frozen* movies. They described their creative process, played a few pieces cut from the films, accompanied some of the ship's stage actors in song performances, and even passed a microphone around the audience so that selected guests could belt out verses of "Let It Go."

MOVIES

RECENT DISNEY, PIXAR, *Star Wars*, and Marvel movies, including films released during the cruise, are shown on every DCL ship. On all ships except the *Wish*, films are shown primarily in the **Buena Vista Theatre,** on Deck 5 Aft on the *Magic* and *Wonder* and spanning Decks 4 and 5 Midship on the *Dream* and *Fantasy*. The *Wish* has two movie theaters, the **Wonderland Cinema** and **Never Land Cinema,** located across the hall from each other on Deck 4.

Each theater is outfitted with a digital film projector, a state-of-the-art sound system, and 3-D equipment (plus glasses for guests). Padded, upholstered seats are arranged stairlike behind the screen, allowing good views from almost anywhere in the theater. About half a dozen films (more on longer sailings) are shown almost continuously through-out the day, from about 9 a.m. to midnight. Admission is free.

Popcorn and drinks are sold outside the theater before and during each presentation; you can also bring your own snacks and drinks. We've been known to make a quick dash up to the pool deck just before movie time to grab a free order of chicken nuggets and a soda to snack on during the film.

In the case of real blockbusters, films will be shown in the larger **Walt Disney Theatre** in addition to (or sometimes in place of) the live stage shows. We've been on board during the first week of release for several of the newer *Star Wars* films. In each case, the entire theater was packed more than once, and the concession stand was doing a brisk business in Darth Vader–helmet drink holders and popcorn buckets shaped like Han Solo in Carbonite.

The movie schedule for your entire sailing is available on the DCL Navigator app. The same film may be shown three or four times dur-ing your cruise, at different times of day.

Classic Disney films are also shown on a giant 24- by 14-foot LED screen perched high above each ship's family pool: **Goofy's Pool** on Deck 9 of the *Magic* and *Wonder,* **Donald's Pool** on Deck 11 of the *Dream* and *Fantasy,* and **Mickey's Pool** on Deck 11 of the *Wish.*

Deeper cuts from the Disney catalog, including rarely seen films and documentaries, are also shown on the ships' in-room televisions (see next section).

▌ **TELEVISION** *and* **NEWS**

DCL STATEROOM TVS don't broadcast anything approaching the programming you're used to at home. You won't find HBO or Comedy Central, or even NBC or CBS.

The strength of DCL's TV lineup is its film content. Guests have on-demand access to a giant library of films from Disney, DisneyNature, Pixar, the Marvel and *Star Wars* franchises, and other Disney-owned properties.

*un**official* **TIP**
Note: You can't bring TV-streaming boxes or sticks on board.

The modest channel lineup includes several ship-information stations (including a live broadcast of the view from the bridge; the weather fore-cast; port, shopping, and shore-excursion information; and character-appearance schedules); some infomercial-type stations (advertising Dis-ney Vacation Club time-shares, for example); a few channels airing clips of Disney TV shows or playing Radio Disney music; and basic news and sports (BBC News, CNBC, ESPN, ESPN 2, Fox News, and MSNBC).

Live-news and sports stations usually come in fine when you're cruis-ing in the Caribbean, but they may be available only sporadically—or, occasionally, not at all—in other locations, due to international broad-casting rights or (more likely) poor satellite reception. To its credit, DCL is up front about this on its website.

The onboard shops sell a small selection of romance and thriller paperbacks but not newspapers or magazines. We recommend bringing your own reading material or stocking up in port.

LIVE SPORTS

THE DCL SPORTS BARS are **Crown & Fin** on the *Wonder*, **687** on the *Dream*, **O'Gills Pub** on the *Magic* and *Fantasy*, and **Keg & Compass** on the *Wish*. These are your primary venues for watching baseball, basketball, and soccer. NFL games are usually shown here too; some are also shown on the ships' **Funnel Vision** big screen on the pool deck.

Keep in mind that the ships get their TV programming from satellite feeds, which can be affected by weather. If you want to watch a specific game, show up at least 30 minutes beforehand and ask a crew member to find the right station.

If you happen to be sailing during a sporting event of national or worldwide interest, expect that it will be available for viewing in nearly every public space that has seating. During one *Wonder* sailing during the World Cup soccer finals, the Navigator app listed just two viewing venues, but we found screens pulled down from the ceiling in every bar, lounge, and café.

If you want to watch a big game without leaving your stateroom, try looking for **special-event channels** on your TV. Although the ships don't normally carry NBC, CBS, and Fox in the standard shipboard channel lineup, they sometimes turn these networks on during football season or during playoffs for other sports.

THEMED EVENTS *and* HOLIDAY ENTERTAINMENT

PIRATE NIGHT

THIS IS HELD ON ONE NIGHT on virtually all DCL Bahamian and Caribbean cruises. The crew, restaurants, and entertainment take on a buccaneer theme. The ship's transformation begins early in the day, when the usual background music is replaced by songs and audio from the theme parks' Pirates of the Caribbean ride and the spin-off film series. Afternoon craft sessions and family activities are pirate-themed as well. Some time in the afternoon, your stateroom attendant will leave a pirate bandanna for each member of your group, along with booty such as chocolate "coins" covered in gold foil.

On cruises of four-plus nights, each ship's main restaurant will have a special menu for the evening, designed to look like a treasure map. Virtually all of the crew, as well as the ship's officers, will wear special pirate outfits, and families have an opportunity to pose for photos with them before dinner. Many guests pack their own outfits, including black knee-high boots, capri pants, white puffy shirts, and eyeliner (or guyliner, as the case may be).

Pirate Night concludes with a stage show and video on the family pool's Funnel Vision screen, accompanied by a short fireworks display. The fireworks are usually shot from the starboard side, so you'll have a better view from there. The best viewing spots are as follows:

- *Magic* and *Wonder:* Deck 10 Port side. From the port, you can see Mickey on the zip line with the fireworks behind him instead of having to turn back and forth to look at one or the other.

- *Dream* and *Fantasy:* Viewing spots are on Deck 12 Forward, near Currents bar.

- *Wish:* Look for viewing spots on Decks 11, 12, and 13.

Pirate Night on the *Wish* is slightly different than on the other ships. Pirate bandannas are sold in the shops rather than being freely distributed. But more significantly, the entertainment on deck takes the form of the **Pirate's Rockin' Parlay Party,** with a live rock band playing moderately Disneyfied covers of songs by Twisted Sister, the Rolling Stones, and KISS. Jack Sparrow swings onto the stage instead of Mickey ziplining over the deck. If you're in the right age group to know the songs, you'll have an absolute blast; youngsters may be baffled by the headbanging grown-ups around them.

FROZEN DAYS

ADDING TO ITS AVALANCHE of *Frozen* tie-ins, DCL introduced yet another one to its lineup of themed onboard activities in 2015. *Frozen* Days are held on Alaskan sailings on the *Wonder* and Northern European cruises on the *Magic*. The lobby atrium is bedecked with paper icicles; a special themed menu is served at dinner (including a delightful Olaf-inspired carrot cake); a traditional Scandinavian dance lesson is held in the lobby; a chocolate-themed scavenger hunt takes place; and a stage show and dance party called **Freezing the Night Away** is held on the upper deck, with appearances by Anna, Elsa, Kristoff, and an animated Olaf and Sven.

MARVEL DAYS

DCL BEGAN HOSTING MARVEL DAYS in 2017. In 2023, they take place on select five-night sailings of the *Dream*. Expect featured activities to include photo ops with Marvel stars such as Iron Man, Spider-Man, Thor, Black Panther, and Captain Marvel; a superhero-filled stunt show on deck; a **Ravagers Night Club** adult dance party; an interactive show where Dr. Strange tutors guests in the Mystic Arts; Disney characters like Mickey and Minnie dressed up in their own superhero costumes; near-constant showings of Marvel films; trivia games; and character-drawing lessons. The menu items offered are standard DCL fare, with suggestions matched to specific characters—Thor, for example, likes Roasted Cod or Pasta with Meatballs, while Scarlet Witch prefers Gingered Soba Noodles or Ricotta Gnocchi. Who knew?

PIXAR DAYS

REPLACING DCL'S *STAR WARS* DAYS, Pixar Days debut in 2023 on selected seven-night cruises on the *Fantasy*. Themed dining includes a character breakfast with appearances by Woody, Jessie, and Bullseye. The rotational dinner menu will include dishes inspired by the commissary at Pixar Animation Studios.

Other characters you may encounter include Buzz Lightyear and Bo Peep from *Toy Story;* Mike, Sulley, and Boo from *Monsters, Inc.;* Mr. Incredible, Elastigirl, Frozone, and Edna Mode from *The Incredibles;* and more. They'll be part of a Pixar dance party and a new nighttime event in which guests help the Incredibles save the day.

Additionally, a troupe of storytellers will be on board to share the tale of Miguel and his family from the Pixar film *Coco,* using puppetry, video, and live music.

FORMAL NIGHT

MOST CRUISES OF SEVEN NIGHTS or longer have a designated Formal Night. This is a chance for families to put on the ritz. The crew and officers also get into the act by wearing their dress whites. While there are no special meals or activities, you'll see many families getting their photos taken in the ship's atrium before or after dinner.

If you break out in hives at the thought of dressing up, not to worry: you can still come to dinner in your shorts and running shoes, or you can avoid the whole business altogether by ordering room service or grabbing some fast food from the pool deck. As for what *formal* and *dress-up* mean, you'll see a wide range of interpretations, from "audience with the Queen" to "staff meeting at work." For more information, see our FAQs on page 198 in Part Seven.

EASTER

EASTER IS CELEBRATED ON THE DISNEY SHIPS, but in a much more low-key fashion than many of the other holidays. There are no Easter decorations on the ship, and the festivities last for only one day rather than throughout the sailing. Religious services will be offered, typically including a sunrise service, a Catholic Mass, and an interdenominational Protestant service. When we sailed on the *Fantasy* during one recent Easter, secular observations of the holiday included appearances by the White Rabbit from *Alice in Wonderland* (as a stand-in for the Easter Bunny), and Mickey and Minnie wearing what was supposed to be their pastel Easter finery but looked to us like what they'd be sporting on the golf course. Other Easter events include themed craft activities, face painting for children, and the distribution of candy and cookies in the lobby atrium.

INDEPENDENCE DAY

DEPENDING ON YOUR SHIP'S ITINERARY, you'll likely see some special onboard activities on July 4. We recently spent Independence Day on the *Magic*. There was a lobby party that started with a truly inspiring rendition of "The Star-Spangled Banner" sung by a Walt Disney Theatre performer and concluded with a dance party featuring Mickey in an Uncle Sam hat, Minnie dressed like Betsy Ross, and Chip 'n' Dale in tricorne caps, bopping to songs like "Party in the USA," "American Pie," and "Sweet Caroline"(because nothing says the Fourth of July quite like Neil Diamond).

Other activities included themed crafts, American-history trivia contests, and face painting. The breakfast and lunch buffets at Cabanas were heavy on red, white, and blue desserts.

HALLOWEEN ON THE HIGH SEAS

ONE OF THE BEST PLACES TO CELEBRATE HALLOWEEN is on a Disney cruise. The crew and officers dress up, and many families bring special costumes to wear for this one night on board. Even the Disney characters dress up—one of our favorite memories is being "attacked" by Zombie Goofy one Halloween on board the *Magic* while his guide murmured "Brains!" as they shuffled along.

Expect that one afternoon activity will be **Mickey's Mouse-Querade Party,** with music and dancing, and one evening will have a grown-up version, **Halloween Isn't Just for Kids,** with dancing and an adults-only costume party.

DCL ships begin celebrating Halloween in September. Expect to see pumpkins, black cats, and other decor starting around the second week of September and running through October 31. Every ship offers Halloween-themed movies, deck parties, crafts, and more.

Introduce your kids to the audience-participation legacy of *The Rocky Horror Picture Show* at the **Nightmare Before Christmas Sing and Scream.** Sing along with the movie, then meet Jack and Sally after the show. There's also a deck party, **Mickey's Calling All the Monsters Mouse-Querade,** along with storytelling sessions for kids. For the grown-ups, the ship's dance club hosts a costume party.

THANKSGIVING

IF YOUR CRUISE DATES INCLUDE the fourth Thursday in November, you'll be celebrating Thanksgiving aboard your ship. Expect to see Mickey, Minnie, Goofy, and Donald in their Pilgrim costumes, plus many other Disney characters in seasonal outfits. (Don't be surprised, however, to see the rest of the ship already decked out for Christmas.) The main dining rooms on each ship will serve a traditional Thanksgiving menu. And it wouldn't be Turkey Day without (American) football, even on DCL. Games are broadcast on each ship's big Funnel Vision LED screen near the family pool, as well as at the sports bars.

CHRISTMAS, HANUKKAH, AND KWANZAA

DCL BEGINS DECORATING ITS SHIPS for the winter holidays in early–mid-November. Dates vary from year to year: in 2022, for example, the first **Very Merrytime Cruise** began on November 6. (*Merrytime* is a Disneyfied play on the word *maritime*.) Among the many decor elements on board, expect to see the ship's atrium decked out with a massive Christmas tree, a Hanukkah menorah, and a Kwanzaa kinara. A tree-lighting ceremony typically takes place on the first night of each Very Merrytime cruise.

Family activities include making greeting cards, drawing Disney characters in holiday outfits, building gingerbread houses, and so on. As at EPCOT, each ship will have storytellers scheduled throughout the day, along with special holiday-themed merchandise. Expect to see Mickey, Minnie, Goofy, and other characters dressed in winter finery, plus lots of holiday movies on your stateroom TV.

The most interesting decorations, however, are on **Castaway Cay,** where some of the palm trees are decorated with garlands and lights and plastic sandy snowmen provide an amusing photo op. Disney characters wear holiday-themed island outfits, and even the shuttle bus from the dock is decorated with reindeer antlers.

Jewish religious services are typically conducted during each night of Hanukkah. A Catholic Mass is held at midnight on December 24; another Mass and an interdenominational Protestant service are held on December 25. Santa Claus distributes small gifts to children in the atrium on Christmas morning, along with milk and cookies. Should you need a little gift-wrapping help, that service is available on board at no extra charge; consult the DCL Navigator app or check with Guest Services for details.

Finally, the ships' onboard music, piped into the hallways and public areas, switches from standard Disney tunes to Christmas-themed tracks. Some people enjoy it; others prefer the regular Disney music.

What If I Don't Celebrate Christmas?

Don't want to dress up for Formal Night or Pirate Night? Not a fan of the Marvel and Pixar franchises? No problem—you're by no means obligated to participate in anything. If you're content to relax with a good book on the themed days, you'll be good to go.

If, on the other hand, you're an observant Jew who isn't comfortable with Christmas festivities or you're a Christian who has religious reservations about Halloween, then you may want to avoid cruises themed to these holidays, which permeate every aspect of the ships, from decor to music to activities. Granted, we have non-Christian friends and family who love the Very Merrytime Cruises—but during late November and December, it's all Christmas all the time, with a barely audible whisper of "How do you spell *Hanukkah*?"

NEW YEAR'S EVE

DURING THE DAY, video screens on each ship's pool deck display a clock counting down the hours, minutes, and seconds until midnight. The pool deck is also the site for a big family-themed party in the evening, with DJs and live entertainment continuing through midnight. Each ship's dance club also hosts a party, complete with DJ, hats, noise-makers, confetti, and bubbly drinks at midnight. Families will want to see the special fireworks display and the atrium's balloon drop at midnight. The kids' clubs host parties early in the evening, allowing the little ones to get to bed at a reasonable hour.

A word of warning if you're traveling with teenagers: Just before midnight, waiters pass out flutes of Champagne on deck. They do check IDs (offering underage guests something like sparkling cider instead), but be aware that many grown-ups take just a sip or two of their drinks and then set down their glasses on a table or ledge before they retire for the night. On different New Year's Eve sailings, we've seen more than a few teens polishing off the abandoned bubbly—so keep a watchful eye out if your holiday travel party includes young people under 21.

OTHER SPECIAL CRUISE EVENTS

TCM CLASSIC MOVIE CRUISES These cruises aren't themed days per se, but rather buyouts of a DCL ship by Turner Classic Movies (TCM), typically once a year. In 2022, the TCM Classic Movie Cruise took place on the November 12–17 sailing of the *Dream* from Miami, with visits to Grand Cayman and Castaway Cay. See tcmcruise.com for more information.

DVC MEMBER CRUISES Booked through and open exclusively to members of the Disney Vacation Club (DVC), Disney's time-share program, these cruises also take over a ship for an entire sailing. Perks include special stateroom gifts, discussions led by Imagineers and Disney executives, and previews of Disney films that haven't been released yet. These sailings, typically two per year, often sell out quickly. For more information, go to disneyvacationclub.disney.go.com.

NIGHTCLUBS, BARS, CAFÉS, *and* LOUNGES

EACH DISNEY CRUISE LINE SHIP has a collection of places to drink, dance, and listen to music; some are geared more to quiet conversation than partying. Some clubs host family activities during the day but become adults-only at night, usually around 9 p.m. (Guests must generally be age 21 or older to drink; see page 47 for an exception.)

ABOUT THOSE DRINK PRICES . . .

IF IT'S BEEN A WHILE since you last cruised with Disney, you may notice that some signature cocktails cost significantly more than they used to. For example, the **Shipbuilder's Wife**—made with Absolut Pears vodka, limoncello, grappa, agave, and fresh lemon juice—was introduced on the *Fantasy* in 2012 for $5.75. By summer 2016 the price had increased by just a dollar, but by early 2017 the same cocktail showed up on the menu of the *Dream*'s 687 sports bar for a notably higher $8.50. By mid-2019 it was sold at 687 for $11.75, and in early 2022 it was $12—more than double its original price. (On the *Fantasy*, the same drink is sold at the same price but under a different name: the **Mercutio**.)

unofficial **TIP**

If you're trying to keep tabs on costs, stick with domestic beers, grab a Drink of the Day on deck, or BYOB (see page 74 for details on DCL's alcohol carry-on policy).

If you're used to drinking in a major city or at Walt Disney World, $12 for a fancy cocktail might seem like a bargain. Similar drinks are priced at $14–$16 at Jaleo in Disney Springs and $18–$20 at the Gramercy Tavern in New York City. (A few specialty cocktails on the ships are priced in the $20–$25 range, although most cost a bit less.)

You may even find the same or similar drinks at different prices on the same ship. On one sailing of the *Dream*, for instance, we found Bloody Marys priced at both $4.75 (at the bar in Cabanas) and $10 (at Palo brunch).

If you enjoy wine with dinner, ask your server about a multibottle **Wine & Dine package,** available in the main dining rooms and at Palo. You can save as much as 25% compared with buying by the bottle. Likewise, a **beer package** may be a better deal than buying brews individually; choose from six-packs or a refillable mug (you present a token at the bar instead of carrying the mug around with you). You can also preorder these packages online in the **Onboard Gifts** section of the DCL website (see page 302).

The poolside bars and roving waiters on the ships and at Castaway Cay have menus listing fun-in-the-sun drinks like daiquiris and piña coladas. You'll probably order at least one of these, if only to post about it on Instagram, but be aware that the menus don't list prices—and that doesn't mean the drinks are free. They can pack a punch on your final bill if you're not careful, so check before you order. Also check for **Drink of the Day** discounts on specialty cocktails.

Finally, keep an eye out for **Sommelier's Bin** wine and Champagne specials, which are offered in at least one bar or lounge on every ship. The price is right—$11 per glass at the time of this writing—but there's a catch: the bartender randomly pours from whatever bottles are already open and need to be finished. (Think of it as beverage roulette.) We've tried wines this way that ranged from average to extraordinary—including a Champagne that normally costs more than $40 a glass.

DCL BAR AND NIGHTCLUB PROFILES

THE FOLLOWING SECTION focuses on the cafés, clubs, bars, and lounges found across the DCL fleet; we've included the **Cove Café** coffee bar as well, since it also serves alcohol. Check the **DCL Navigator app** (see page 137) for exact hours, menus, and prices on your sailing.

While the primary bars on each ship feature signature cocktails available only at those venues, there's a fair amount of overlap among the other offerings. In particular, you'll find that wine-by-the-glass options are substantially similar throughout each ship.

On the four oldest ships, specialty coffees are served in just one or two locations. Most bars on the *Wish,* on the other hand, have state-of-the-art espresso machines, so you can power up with caffeine almost anywhere.

Also, whereas the bars on the *Magic, Wonder, Dream,* and *Fantasy* are concentrated in so-called adult districts, the *Wish*'s watering holes are scattered around the ship. There are pros and cons to each setup, depending on your proclivities: you can find a drink wherever you are on the *Wish,* while on the other ships, it's easier to avoid alcohol if you're not in the mood to imbibe.

ON THE *MAGIC*

Cove Café   LOCATION Deck 9 Midship

SETTING AND ATMOSPHERE Cove Café on the *Magic* received a complete design overhaul during the ship's 2018 dry dock. The decor now features neutral cushions on dark rattan seating, with green accents on the walls and bar and large potted palms in the corners. There are open areas for socializing, but you can still find nooks and crannies where you can curl up with a book or magazine and a latte to while away the day.

SELECTIONS Cove Café serves just about every kind of java you can think of: espresso, cappuccino, latte, Americano, and cold drip. Cove also serves hot teas and has a good selection of wines, Champagnes, spirits, and mixed drinks. Service is excellent.

> *unofficial* **TIP**
> If you're one of those people who need a coffee or six every day, ask your server for a **Café Fanatic** rewards card; you'll get every sixth specialty coffee free.

In addition to beverages, Cove Café has a self-serve refrigerated case stocked with small bites. Breakfast items usually include plain and chocolate croissants, Danish pastries, and fresh fruit. Afternoon and evening snacks consist of assorted cookies, brownies, cakes, crackers, and fruit.

Served for a couple of hours, the nighttime appetizer selections are our favorite: prosciutto, dried sausages, marinated olives, cheeses, bread, and the like. You can make a light supper out of these, and because most families are either at dinner or preparing for it, there's a chance that you'll have the café all to yourself.

COMMENTS The Wi-Fi signal here is fairly strong, making it a good spot to catch up on email or the latest news. This is a big part of Cove Café's appeal: the ability to sit in a comfy chair, sip coffee, and read in blessed silence, surrounded by $350 million of luxury cruise ship.

ACROSS THE SHIPS All five DCL ships have a Cove Café. The finishes are slightly different across the ships, but all are similarly cozy. Guests at Cove Café must be at least 18 to enter and at least 21 to drink alcohol.

Promenade Lounge   LOCATION Deck 3 Aft

SETTING AND ATMOSPHERE Promenade Lounge hosts family activities during the day and live music at night. It's decorated in the same Art Deco style as the rest of the *Magic,* with cherry-wood finishes, creamy lighting, and brass accents.

SELECTIONS Beer and wine by the glass, spirits, mixed drinks, and coffee. Free snacks are served, starting in the afternoon—mostly chips, salsa, and coffee.

COMMENTS Promenade Lounge is one of the most attractive nightspots on the ship. Unfortunately, it's also noisy: it sits adjacent and open to pedestrian traffic from one of the *Magic*'s main inside walkways. Nighttime entertainment is usually provided by a musical duo, such as a pianist and vocalist, but it's got to be like performing in Grand Central Station due to the din from outside. We recommend the Promenade as a meeting place for groups to get a drink before dinner at Lumiere's (see Part Seven) or to listen to the live music with a nightcap.

ACROSS THE SHIPS The *Wonder* doesn't have a Promenade Lounge; the closest equivalent is the **French Quarter Lounge** (page 244). The similar but much smaller lounge on the *Dream* and *Fantasy* is **Bon Voyage** (see pages 245 and 252). On the *Wish,* the most centrally located bar is **The Bayou** (page 257), with a menu comparable to the French Quarter Lounge's (the theming is different, however).

Signals   LOCATION Deck 9 Midship

SETTING AND ATMOSPHERE Signals is an adults-only outdoor bar next to the adult pool. It has a few seats for those looking to get some shade, but most patrons take their drinks back to their deck chairs to sip in the sun.

SELECTIONS Much of Signals' menu is devoted to beers and frozen drinks, but the bartenders can whip up almost anything you can think of. Signals also serves coffee, juices, and bottled water. Soda machines are nearby.

COMMENTS Signals doesn't offer much in the way of atmosphere, but because it's near the Quiet Cove Pool, it's a little less hectic than other bars.

ACROSS THE SHIPS Only the *Magic* and *Wonder* have Signals. The *Dream* and *Fantasy* each have two poolside equivalents, **Currents** and **Waves** (see pages 246 and 247); the *Wish* also has a Currents, along with **The Lookout** (page 259). Drinks and service are comparable at all of these, but we think Currents has the best views. Of the poolside bars, Waves is the only one that permits guests under age 18.

After Hours

This is DCL's name for the collection of bars on the *Magic*'s Deck 3 Forward: **Fathoms,** a dance club; **Keys,** a piano bar; and **O'Gills Pub,** a sports bar. (These bars get higher reader-satisfaction ratings than those found elsewhere on the ship.) After Hours has a urban-nightclub theme, pulled together by a white-and-silver color scheme.

Some After Hours lounges, such as Fathoms, are home to family-oriented entertainment during the day, but all usually have an adults-only policy (ages 18 and up to enter, 21 and up to drink) after 9 p.m.

After Hours' bars generally carry the same wines and beers, although each serves its own unique line of cocktails. O'Gills Pub also serves a collection of Irish beers not found elsewhere.

Fathoms   LOCATION Deck 3 Forward

SETTING AND ATMOSPHERE Fathoms has an undersea theme: fiber-optic light fixtures shaped like jellyfish, sand-art murals along the bar, and silver-and-black bench seating that evokes undulating ocean waves. Six sets of couches are built into Fathoms' back wall, providing an excellent semiprivate view of the entertainment stage.

The middle of the club holds a dance floor and a raised stage with a professional sound system and lighting. Armchairs upholstered in silver fabric are arranged in groups of two or three around circular cocktail tables. These help control the echo in Fathoms' large, open floor plan.

SELECTIONS Sea-themed cocktails make up most of Fathoms' bar menu, with beer, wine, and spirits also available. Expect to find lots of fruity drinks made with blue curaçao, orange liqueur, and muddled citrus.

COMMENTS Like other DCL nightclubs, Fathoms does double duty during the day by hosting family-oriented activities, such as scavenger hunts, bingo, and talent shows. At night the stage hosts everything from live music and karaoke to performances by comedians and magicians.

ACROSS THE SHIPS Fathoms doesn't have an identical sibling on the other DCL ships, but it's most similar to **Azure** on the *Wonder* (see page 243), **Evolution** on the *Dream* (see page 249), and **The Tube** on the *Fantasy* (see page 256). The *Wish* doesn't have a dedicated dance club, although **Luna** and **Triton Lounge** (see Part Nine, page 264) host game shows and other entertainment for adults at night.

Keys LOCATION Deck 3 Forward

SETTING AND ATMOSPHERE Keys features live piano music nightly. Six large porthole windows run along one of the rectangular room's long walls. The bar is in the middle of the opposite wall, and the piano player is between the two, at the far end of the room from the entrance doors.

Keys' theming is supposed to evoke nightspots of Hollywood's Golden Age, circa the late 1940s–early 1950s. The furnishings include midcentury-modern sofas and chairs with curved, radius-style arms and backs. Carpeting is a crisp silver with geometric sunbursts. Over the bar area is a columned pavilion topped with panels of stylized piano keys.

SELECTIONS The bar menu includes specialty drinks with musically themed names, such as the Moji-Do, a mojito, and the Bloody Mi-Re, a Bloody Mary with vodka, yellow-tomato juice, lime, and whiskey-flavored Worcestershire sauce. Cocktail prices are comparable to those at the other bars on the ship, but a specialty drink is typically offered for several dollars more—for example, a Manhattan made with top-shelf ingredients such as Jack Daniel's Sinatra Select whiskey and Carpano Antica Formula vermouth. Coffee, cappuccino, and espresso are also available, but for those we recommend **Cove Café** (see page 239).

COMMENTS Live entertainment usually begins with a show around 7:30 p.m.; a typical night's schedule will have more performances around 9:30, 10:30, and 11:30 p.m. The pianists, acceptably talented if nondescript, play medleys of well-known songs by familiar artists. Some nights have themes, such as Elvis or Simon and Garfunkel, but you can always submit requests.

During the day, Keys is often used for group seminars on everything from wine and spirits to acupuncture. The bar typically opens anywhere from 5:30 to 6:30 p.m.; check the DCL Navigator app for hours on your sailing. Children are admitted to Keys until 9 p.m., when it becomes an adults-only venue until its midnight closing.

ACROSS THE SHIPS Keys is most similar to the **Cadillac Lounge** on the *Wonder* (see profile starting on the next page). The entertainment is interchangeable between the two, but Cadillac Lounge's decor is on the gimmicky side (albeit well done). **Nightingale's** on the *Wish* (page 259) is DCL's most elegant take on a piano bar.

O'Gills Pub   LOCATION Deck 3 Forward

SETTING AND ATMOSPHERE This bar's name is a nod to the Disney classic and Sean Connery vehicle *Darby O'Gill and the Little People,* which is set in Ireland. That said, O'Gills is an Irish bar in the same way that Lucky Charms is an Irish breakfast: if you've come here expecting Raglan Road at Walt Disney World, you're in for a disappointment.

Nine wall-mounted televisions provide live satellite coverage of whatever sports are being played around the world. Comfortable burgundy leather banquettes are built into the wall, and padded leather armchairs surround the tables set within the banquettes. In the middle of the room, about a dozen bar-height tables and stools provide the best views of the most TVs.

SELECTIONS The bar menu includes a beer flight of 5.5-ounce Irish brews. There's also a selection of Irish whiskeys (and cocktails made with them), as well as standard beers, wines, and a full bar. We like to sip an Irish coffee here after dinner when we're sailing in Northern Europe. Another nice choice is the Gin Tea Tonic (Hendrick's Gin, cherry marzipan–flavored tea, and The King's Ginger liqueur), served from a pretty china teapot, with a macaron on the side. It's like you're drinking with the Queen.

COMMENTS O'Gills is a comfy spot to sit, sip, and watch the game. Complimentary snacks like chips, crudités, small sandwiches, and pigs in a blanket are often available at night—enough for a light dinner. More-substantial items are available at an extra cost (bangers and mash, for example), but we've found that ordering these could take up to an hour.

ACROSS THE SHIPS O'Gills on the *Magic* has a counterpart on the *Fantasy* (see page 253). Along with the *Wonder's* **Crown & Fin** (see page 244), the *Dream's* **687** (see page 250), and the *Wish's* **Keg & Compass** (see page 258), these are the DCL fleet's upscale sports bars. The larger televisions at the *Magic's* O'Gills make it easier to watch events from across the room.

PALO Adults on the *Magic* and *Wonder* also have the option of grabbing a before- or after-dinner drink at Palo (see page 197 for information on the dress code and page 200 for booking information). When Palo is open for dinner, guests may sit at the bar, which is full-service and offers a view of the open kitchen. Because many people don't realize they can do this, you could find yourself with the counter to yourself. We love it because it's quiet and you can talk to the bartender and servers while they bring in drink orders for their tables. Because of the brunch setup during the day, bar service is available only during dinner.

ON THE *WONDER*

After Hours

Like its counterpart on the *Magic* (see page 240), After Hours has a contemporary-nightclub theme. Some After Hours lounges are home to family-oriented entertainment during the day, but all usually have an adults-only policy (ages 18 and up to enter, 21 and up to drink) after 9 p.m. After Hours' bars generally carry the same wines and beers, although each serves a unique line of cocktails.

Azure   LOCATION Deck 3 Forward

SETTING AND ATMOSPHERE This is the *Wonder*'s dance club. The color palette of creams and blues is meant to evoke the sea.

SELECTIONS You'll find beers and wines along with some hard ciders and hard sodas. Cocktails are on the expensive side and include ingredients like sparkling sake, pomegranate puree, and elderflower liqueur.

COMMENTS The small stage will likely be the site of your bingo game during the day and some crew-facilitated partying in the evening.

ACROSS THE SHIPS Azure doesn't have an identical sibling on the other ships, but it's most similar to **Fathoms** on the *Magic* (see page 240), **Evolution** on the *Dream* (see page 249), and **The Tube** on the *Fantasy* (see page 256). The *Wish* doesn't have a dedicated dance club, although **Luna** and **Triton Lounge** (see Part Nine, page 264) host game shows and other entertainment for adults at night.

Cadillac Lounge   LOCATION Deck 3 Forward

SETTING AND ATMOSPHERE This is the *Wonder*'s piano bar. The decor pays tribute to 1950s-era Cadillac cars by way of leather-upholstered barstools and chairs, couches made to look like automobile rear seats, and a bar built into a replica of the front of a 1959 Cadillac Coupe de Ville.

"Designed by General Motors" isn't a concept that we normally associate with bar theming, but it works well in this case. The furnishings—dark woods; carpets in hues of burgundy, gold, and fuchsia; leather-covered walls; chrome accents; and those butter-and-chocolate-colored leather barstools—clearly call to mind a very specific time and place.

The best seats in the house are in the far corner, opposite the main entrance and to the right of the piano player. These include a comfortable leather couch and two leather armchairs, plus a side table to hold drinks. From here you can listen to the music and watch some of the action at the bar, tucked away in your own discreet corner of the lounge.

SELECTIONS The Cadillac Lounge serves beer, wine, spirits, and cocktails, and it's the only bar in After Hours that serves Champagne by the glass. The signature cocktails here are the Twenty One Rob Roy (Johnnie Walker XR 21 Scotch, Carpano Antica Formula vermouth, and bitters) and the Ketel One Experience for Two (Ketel One vodka, jasmine tea, and Cabernet Sauvignon ice wine). Coffee, cappuccino, and espresso are also available, but for those we recommend the **Cove Café** (see page 239).

COMMENTS Live entertainment usually begins with a show around 7:30 p.m.; a typical night's schedule will have more performances around 9:30, 10:30, and 11:30 p.m. The pianists, acceptably talented if nondescript, play medleys of well-known songs by familiar artists. Some nights have themes, such as Elvis or Simon and Garfunkel. Plus, you can always make requests.

During the day, the Cadillac Lounge is often used for group seminars on everything from wine and spirits to acupuncture. The bar typically opens anywhere from 5:30 to 6:30 p.m.; check the Navigator app for hours on your sailing. Children are admitted to the Cadillac Lounge until 9 p.m., when it becomes an adults-only venue until its midnight closing.

ACROSS THE SHIPS The Cadillac Lounge is most similar to the *Magic*'s **Keys** (see page 241). The entertainment is interchangeable between the two, but Keys' retro-Hollywood decor is more restrained **Nightingale's** on the *Wish* (page 259) is DCL's most elegant take on a piano bar.

Cove Café   LOCATION Deck 9 Forward

COMMENTS See the profile of Cove Café on the *Magic* (page 239) for additional details.

Crown & Fin   LOCATION Deck 3 Forward

SETTING AND ATMOSPHERE Crown & Fin is the *Wonder*'s sports bar, modeled after an English tavern. The space is adorned with dark woods, plush leather furniture, and brass accents. Subtle nods to classic Disney films set in London can be found in the artwork and props.

SELECTIONS Cocktails and British craft beers are on tap, and a pub-grub menu is available for an extra charge. In a world with an abundance of free food, we're not sure why you'd want to pay for a German pretzel in a British bar—but sometimes the sea makes you do things you shouldn't.

COMMENTS Given that you're on a large cruise ship, the odds are good that you'll be able to find other fans of your favorite teams here. In addition to televised sports, Crown & Fin hosts family-oriented and adult activities throughout the day, ranging from Disney-character-drawing classes for kids to trivia contests and afternoon beer tastings. Check the DCL Navigator app for the schedule.

ACROSS THE SHIPS Crown & Fin is comparable to the clubby sports-viewing venues on the other DCL ships. We're pretty sure we'd be happy to watch the big game here or just while away a sea day nursing a pint of beer and playing checkers.

French Quarter Lounge   LOCATION Deck 3 Aft

SETTING AND ATMOSPHERE The French Quarter Lounge complements Tiana's Place, the ship's *Princess and the Frog*–inspired dining room (see Part Seven, page 208). Live music is performed on a gazebo stage, and there are themed activities for everyone in the family. The decor incorporates New Orleans–style design cues such as wrought-iron balconies, lampposts evocative of those in the Vieux Carré, and a seating area inside a replica of one of the city's famed green-and-red streetcars.

SELECTIONS Soft drinks, coffees, cocktails, and snacks all have a decidedly New Orleans flavor. From Louisiana-based Abita Brewing Company, Purple Haze Lager, Strawberry Lager, and Big Easy IPA are available on tap, along with Andygator Doppelbock and Hop-On, Maison Blanc, and Turbodog ales in bottles. For kids and teetotalers, there's root beer and vanilla cream soda. If you're in need of caffeine—and maybe some sugar—order a NOLA Café (that is, a regular cup of coffee) or café au lait (hot or frozen) in traditional, caramel, mocha, and vanilla variations. Get in a Mardi Gras mood with a Hurricane, Cajun Bloody Mary, Lillet Cocktail, or Sazerac.

The snack menu features beignets—New Orleans's square, deep-fried, powdered sugar–dusted spin on a doughnut—and for that we couldn't be more thankful. Order them in single, double, or triple batches, or opt for La Bouff Favorite: a coffee of your choice with a shot of Evangeline praline liqueur on the side, plus two beignets, a chocolate truffle, a macaron, and a madeleine, along with chocolate or caramel dipping sauce.

COMMENTS If you're not into jazz, you'll probably have a better time over at the **Cadillac Lounge** (see page 243) or **Crown & Fin** (see previous page).

ACROSS THE SHIPS The approximate equivalent on the *Magic* is **Promenade Lounge** (see pages 239 and 240). The *Dream* and *Fantasy* have **Bon Voyage** (see next page and page 252) in a similar location, but they're much smaller. The menu at **The Bayou** on the *Wish* (page 257) is substantially similar to the French Quarter Lounge's, but the theme is a New Orleans garden.

Signals LOCATION Deck 9 Midship

COMMENTS See the profile of Signals on the *Magic* (page 240) for details.

PALO As on the *Magic*, adults on the *Wonder* have the option of grabbing a before- or after-dinner drink at Palo (see page 197 for information on the dress code and page 200 for booking information). When Palo is open for dinner, guests may sit at the bar, which is full-service and offers a view of the open kitchen. Because many people don't realize they can do this, you could find yourself with the counter to yourself. We love it because it's quiet and you can talk to the bartender and servers while they bring in drink orders for their tables. Because of the brunch setup during the day, bar service is available only during dinner.

ON THE *DREAM*

Bon Voyage LOCATION Deck 3 Midship

SETTING AND ATMOSPHERE Sitting just off the atrium, Bon Voyage is one of the prettiest, if not smallest, of the *Dream*'s bars, with just 10 seats at the counter plus 4 armchairs a few feet away. The two highlights here are the gorgeous Art Deco mural behind the bar and the swirled, maize-yellow, illuminated bar face, which reflects golden light off the beige-marble floors. Unfortunately, the lovely decor doesn't make up for the noisy location: the bar is in a heavily trafficked area that makes quiet conversation difficult.

SELECTIONS Bon Voyage's bar menu is similar to that in The District (see page 248) and includes draft and bottled beer; wines by the glass and bottle; spirits; and mixed drinks, including a few special fruit-flavored martinis. Service is excellent.

COMMENTS Open from midday to late evening, Bon Voyage is a good place for groups to meet up before dinner. However, it's not conducive to much more than a quick cocktail due to the noise outside—which also makes live entertainment a no-go here.

ACROSS THE SHIPS The *Fantasy* also has a Bon Voyage just off the Deck 3 atrium (see page 252). **Promenade Lounge** is the comparable bar on the *Magic* (see pages 239 and 240), and the approximate equivalent on the *Wonder* is the **French Quarter Lounge** (see previous page). On the *Wish,* the most centrally located bar is **The Bayou** (page 257), with a menu comparable to the French Quarter Lounge's (the theming is different, however).

Cove Café   LOCATION   Deck 11 Forward

COMMENTS See the profile of Cove Café on the *Magic* (page 239) for additional details.

Currents   LOCATION   Deck 13 Forward

SETTING AND ATMOSPHERE This outdoor space has the best views of any bar on the *Dream*. Built behind and into the structure supporting the forward stairs and elevators, the curved, glossy white face of the bar mirrors the curve along the opposite deck rail and provides some shade during the day. Currents is lovely at night, when a royal-blue neon sign with CURRENTS rendered in a retro-looking script (think a nameplate on a 1950s car) lights up the bar and bar shelves, accented with matching blue tile.

Ten stationary barstools are spaced far enough apart for easy access to walk-up traffic. Most guests take their drinks back to their lounge chairs, but there's also plenty of (unshaded) armchair seating around Currents.

SELECTIONS Currents serves standard-issue bottled and draft beer, cocktails, and frozen drinks.

COMMENTS The one downside to Currents is that it's next to a smoking section. Depending on the prevailing winds and your tolerance for smoke, this is either not an issue at all or a mild annoyance.

ACROSS THE SHIPS Currents is the same on the *Dream,* the *Fantasy,* and the *Wish*. **Signals** on the *Magic* and *Wonder* is similar (see page 240), but Currents' layout is much more open, with much better views and nicer decor.

Meridian   LOCATION   Deck 12 Aft

SETTING AND ATMOSPHERE Situated between the adults-only restaurants Palo and Remy, Meridian is the *Dream*'s martini bar. It's also one of our very favorite bars on the ship.

Sitting high up on Deck 12 Aft, Meridian has windows on three sides of its relatively small, square room. Panoramic views of the sunset await early diners who stop in around dusk. Antique ship-navigation maps and instruments adorn the walls and shelves. Meridian's furnishings include rich brown leather couches and armchairs, as well as cocoa-colored teak floors with brass inlays. Meridian also has outdoor seating on a teak deck that runs along one wall of Remy. It's lovely on warm summer evenings—and in demand around dusk—so don't be surprised if it's standing-room only.

SELECTIONS Meridian's bar menu emphasizes mixed drinks and spirits over beer and wine, although those are also available, as are coffees. The best thing about Meridian is the bartending staff, who will often offer to make a custom martini for you on the spot. This usually starts with the bartender inquiring whether you like fruit- or herb-based drinks and what kinds of liquors you usually prefer. A couple of minutes of muddling, shaking, and stirring, and you have the first draft of your new drink. And if it's not quite what you expected, they'll be happy to start over.

Meridian on the *Dream* also offers an antipasti tray for a significant upcharge, but we're not sure why guests wouldn't simply choose the free evening appetizers at Cove Café or Vista Café. Meridian also offers a cigar menu, with prices ranging from about $10 to about $50 for individual or small packages of cigars. The smoking area is nearby but outdoors (see page 162 for more information about smoking areas on the ships).

COMMENTS We recommend stopping by Meridian for its martini experience alone, even if you don't have reservations for Remy or Palo (see page 200). If you're dining at Remy, though, beware of the one-two punch of Meridian's martinis and Remy's wine pairings.

Meridian usually opens around 5 p.m. and stays open until midnight. It's one of the few DCL nightspots with a dress code: inside the lounge, men should wear dress shirts and pants, and women should wear dresses, skirts and blouses, or pantsuits. If you're just visiting the outdoor area, jeans and shorts are OK, but swimwear, T-shirts, and tank tops are a no-no.

ACROSS THE SHIPS Both the *Dream* and the *Fantasy* have nearly identical Meridian lounges; the *Magic* and *Wonder* do not. Together with the two Skyline bars (see pages 251 and 255), the two Meridians rate at the top of reader-satisfaction polls across all DCL ships. The similarly swanky bar **The Rose** (see page 260) links the two adult-dining restaurants on the *Wish;* we're sure it will post stellar marks as we get in more reviews.

Vista Café   LOCATION Deck 4 Midship

SETTING AND ATMOSPHERE This small, Art Deco–themed nook is tucked into a corner of Deck 4.

SELECTIONS Vista Café serves everything from coffee and free pastries in the morning to beer, wine, cocktails, and light snacks at night.

COMMENTS With just four seats at the bar, this isn't the place for large groups. It's most useful as a place for a family to get a drink and a bite to eat on their way to one of the day's activities on Decks 3 or 4.

ACROSS THE SHIPS Vista Cafés can be found on both the *Dream* and the *Fantasy* but not the *Magic* or the *Wonder*. Both cafés offer the same food and drink and are about the same size; the only significant difference is the decor—the Vista on the *Fantasy* has that ship's Art Nouveau theme rather than the Art Deco styling of the *Dream*. On the *Wish,* you can grab coffee midship at the **Enchanted Sword Café** (page 258), the **Wishing Star Café** (page 258), and **The Bayou** (page 257).

Waves   LOCATION Deck 12 Aft

SETTING AND ATMOSPHERE Tucked behind the rear smokestack, Waves is an outdoor bar catering primarily to sunbathers on Deck 12. Waves' eight fixed barstools are arranged around an attractive white tile face, and the back of the bar is decorated with small tiles in varying shades of blue. An overhang above the bar provides shade for guests seated or standing at the bar, but most of the seating—upholstered blue cushions on glossy, curved-back teak booths, plus various sets of tables and chairs—is directly in the sun.

SELECTIONS The most popular drinks at Waves are bottled beers, frozen cocktails, and mixed drinks. Nonalcoholic smoothies and fruit juices are available for children and teetotalers.

COMMENTS Waves' hours vary, but it's usually open from late morning to late evening. Most visitors are coming from the lounge chairs or sports activities on Deck 13; some are just looking for a quiet spot away from the crowds.

ACROSS THE SHIPS Both the *Dream* and the *Fantasy* have Waves. **Signals** is the outdoor bar on the *Magic* and *Wonder* (see page 240); Waves, however, is quieter, has nicer decor, and welcomes kids (Signals is 21-and-up only). On the *Wish,* the closest equivalents are **Currents** (see page 258 for our profile of Currents on the *Dream*) and **The Lookout** (see page 259).

The District

This is the designation for the five bars and lounges on the *Dream*'s Deck 4 Aft: **District Lounge,** in a hallway connecting the different venues; **Evolution,** a dance club; **Pink,** a Champagne bar; **687,** an upscale sports bar; and **Skyline,** a cosmopolitan watering hole.

The theming is meant to evoke images of exclusive urban nightlife. Along the faux-brick walls and behind velvet ropes are black-plastic silhouettes of couples "waiting" to get in.

Most of The District's bars open between 5 and 5:30 p.m. and stay open until midnight (check the Navigator app for hours on your sailing). District Lounge usually opens a little earlier; Evolution operates from around 10 p.m. to 2 a.m. Hot appetizers are usually served throughout the evening in one of The District's circular pedestrian walkways.

Evolution, Pink, and Skyline admit guests ages 18 and up only. Families are welcome at District Lounge and 687 until 9 p.m., when the bars become adults-only.

District Lounge   LOCATION Deck 4 Aft

SETTING AND ATMOSPHERE An attractive, contemporary bar and seating area are bisected by a walkway connecting The District's bars. The bar seats six along its curving, white-stone front. Lights hidden beneath the black-marble top point down, creating smoky gray shadows in the stone. Behind the bar is a bronze-colored wall; orange lighting illuminates the bottles and provides this side of District Lounge with its most prominent color.

A lounge with couches and armchairs sits across the walkway opposite the bar; although it's not perfect, it's one of the more stylish places on the *Dream.* While the lounge is completely open to (and exposed to noise from) guests going from club to club, off-white leather couches, Champagne-colored metal poles, and cocoa-colored carpeting provide a visual boundary marking its border. Deeper inside are U-shaped armchairs, covered outside in the same white leather and inside in deep-brown leather, arranged in groups of four around small tables.

SELECTIONS A little bit of everything: draft and bottled beer, cocktails, frozen drinks, whiskeys and tequilas, and wine and Champagne by the glass. The signature drink takes its name from the bar: The District is hyped on the menu as "inspired by the Prohibition era" and "prepared in secret," but in a nutshell, you tell the bartender if you want dark or light alcohol and something fruity, herby, or plain, and they'll concoct a custom cocktail for you. A few nonalcoholic drinks and coffees are available as well.

COMMENTS The best seats are along the lounge's inside wall, where you can relax in those deep armchairs while you watch everyone else shuttle between clubs. This is also the best vantage point from which to watch the District Lounge's entertainment, which includes live singers and pianists later at night. The lounge is also a good meeting place to start out the evening, especially for groups who haven't decided which of The District's bars to visit.

ACROSS THE SHIPS District Lounge roughly corresponds to the Venetian-themed **La Piazza** on the *Fantasy* (see page 254) but has no relative on the *Magic, Wonder,* or *Wish.* We like District Lounge more than La Piazza: its recessed seating allows you to enjoy a drink away from the bustle of club-goers walking to their next destination.

Evolution   LOCATION Deck 4 Aft

SETTING AND ATMOSPHERE The *Dream*'s dance club, Evolution is, according to Disney, designed as "an artistic interpretation of the transformation of a butterfly . . . emerging from a chrysalis." What this entails is a lot of yellow, orange, and red lights arranged in the shape of butterfly wings and hung around the club. Pairs of wings also hang above the dance floor, and we'll forgive you for comparing slightly tipsy dancing tourists to wriggling pupae.

Fortunately, most of the butterfly business is concentrated around the dance floor and along a couple of back walls. Between the two, it's not as noticeable; plastic-shell chairs sit in the dimly lit sections, occasionally along-side high-backed couches. Short barstools line the outside edge of the room, surrounding small, round tables. The circular bar has gold leather seats on one side, allowing guests a view of the dance floor while they drink; the other half of the bar is for walk-up traffic.

SELECTIONS Evolution's drink menu is similar to District Lounge's, offering draft and bottled beer, cocktails, spirits, and wine, and Champagne by the glass and bottle.

COMMENTS Because it's one of the largest venues on the *Dream,* Evolution is the site of family activities throughout the day, holding everything from hands-on crafts-making seminars to tequila tastings to time-share presentations. Evolution's adults-only entertainment usually starts later than at other bars in The District, around 10 or 10:30 p.m.; check the Navigator app for details.

Live entertainment includes magicians, comics, singers, and more. In addition to live acts, Evolution's DJs sometimes dedicate an entire night's music to a specific genre. Common themes include classic rock, disco, and something called urban country.

ACROSS THE SHIPS Evolution is most similar to **The Tube** dance club on the *Fantasy* (page 256), **Fathoms** on the *Magic* (page 240), and **Azure** on the *Wonder* (page 243), although it has no direct equivalent. We rate Evolution as the second-best dance club on DCL, behind The Tube. Theming, lighting, and seating are nicer than at Fathoms and Azure, while The Tube's London Underground ambience is better executed than Evolution's more-conceptual "caterpillar to butterfly" theme. The *Wish* doesn't have a dedicated dance club, although **Luna** and **Triton Lounge** (see Part Nine, page 264) host game shows and other entertainment for adults at night.

Pink   LOCATION Deck 4 Aft

SETTING AND ATMOSPHERE Pink, the *Dream*'s Champagne bar, is our favorite nightspot on the ship. Decorated in silvers, whites, and golds, the space is intended to make you think you're sitting inside a glass of Champagne. In the walls are embedded round lights of white and pink, tiny near the floor and larger near the ceiling, imitating the carbon dioxide fizz inside a flute of bubbly. The silver carpet's starburst pattern calls to mind bubbles rising from below, and the rounded, glossy white ceiling is meant to represent the top of the glass. The light fixtures are upside-down Champagne flutes. Behind the bar are a multitude of glass "bubbles," expanding as they rise from the bar shelf to the ceiling.

Around the bar are half a dozen stools, with silver legs and clear, oval plastic backs that continue the bubble theme. Beyond the bar, a couple of burgundy chairs sit among their silver-velvet siblings. (Our best guess is that burgundy is supposed to evoke rosé Champagne, several varieties of which are served at the bar.) The best seats in the house, though, are on the padded couch inside a dome-shaped cubby in the wall at one end of the lounge. Move a couple of those big chairs in front and you have a private little cocoon, or slide them away for a view of the entire room.

SELECTIONS Pink's Champagne menu includes many recognizable names: Cristal, Moët et Chandon, Taittinger, Veuve Clicquot, and the requisite Dom Pérignon. Champagne-based cocktails are also available; most include fruit juices, such as mango, pomegranate, and peach, while a few include other liquors—the Elderbubble, for example, contains raspberry vodka along with Champagne and elderflower syrup. A small selection of white, red, and dessert wines is available by the glass (more by the bottle), along with a dozen or so whiskeys and Cognacs.

COMMENTS If you love Champagne, Pink is a relative bargain. We estimate that its bottle markup is less than twice the average retail price—and often considerably less than what Disney charges at its theme park resorts.

ACROSS THE SHIPS You can get Champagne and Champagne cocktails on all of the Disney ships; however, only the *Dream* and the *Fantasy* have dedicated Champagne bars. We like Pink's relatively understated theming better than the *très feminine* French-boudoir decor of **Ooh La La** on the *Fantasy* (see pages 253 and 254).

687   LOCATION Deck 4 Aft

SETTING AND ATMOSPHERE Anytime you see a venue with a dozen flat-screen TVs, chances are it's a sports bar. On the *Dream* it's called 687, and the screens are set in rows above the bar, in a cluster at a far end of the room, and individually in some seating areas.

The bar is set in the middle of 687's rectangular floor. Four porthole windows across from the bar let in light during the day, and moss-colored couches beneath them work to separate the wall into group-size partitions. The scarlet, green, and gold carpet and the burgundy-painted, wood-paneled walls give 687 a more masculine feel than the sports bars on the *Fantasy, Magic,* and *Wonder.*

Besides the couches, barstools and tables are arranged around the room to provide good views of either set of televisions. A few leather-covered armchairs are also arranged around the screens and across from the couches. There's plenty of room to stand between these, too, in case you want to just catch up on some scores. Couches arranged in some of the corners provide quieter spots to unwind.

SELECTIONS The menu is similar to those at the sports bars on the other ships. There's a small wine and cocktail selection (though there's also a full bar and they'll make almost anything), but the focus is on beer, with more than a dozen varieties on tap and more available by the bottle.

The signature cocktail list consists of two drinks: the Shipbuilder's Wife (Absolut Pears vodka, limoncello, grappa, agave, and lemon juice) and the Keel (Maker's Mark bourbon, Campari liqueur, limoncello, orange juice, and fresh ginger, with a mint garnish). Among the beers are Lindemans Framboise Lambic and Trappist Ale.

The pub grub includes sliders, wings, loaded potato tots, and chips and dip; you can also get free chicken fingers and fries from the pool deck and order a Bud Light if you want to watch some football the old-fashioned way (and we often do).

COMMENTS We've spent a few evenings watching games at 687. The seating is comfortable, and it's easy to see and hear the action on the screens. Because of the way the seating is arranged, however, we've found it difficult to start conversations with other patrons. Try sitting at the bar if conviviality is important to you. Besides sporting events, 687 hosts family activities during the day, including movie, music, and sports trivia.

ACROSS THE SHIPS We find 687 more upscale than **Crown & Fin** on the *Wonder* (see page 244) or **O'Gills Pub** on the *Magic* and *Fantasy* (see pages 242 and 253, respectively). While its seating isn't as open, it's a posh place to catch up on the day's highlights in relative quiet. The *Wish*'s **Keg & Compass** (see page 258) is similar to the other sports bars, only with a more nautical bent to the decor.

Skyline LOCATION Deck 4 Aft

SETTING AND ATMOSPHERE Along with Pink, Skyline is one of our two favorite bars on the *Dream*. The idea is that you're in a lounge high on the edge of some of the world's most famous cities. Behind the bar are seven "windows"—large HD video screens—affording panoramic views of New York City, Chicago, Rio de Janeiro, Paris, and Hong Kong.

Each city is shown for about 15 minutes across all seven screens; then the scene changes to another locale. The foreground of each view includes close-ups of apartments and offices, while the middle and background show each city's iconic architecture and landscape.

That would be mildly interesting scenery on its own, but Disney has added special effects that make Skyline beautiful. Each view shows the city in motion: cars move along streets, neon signs blink to illuminate sidewalks, and apartment lights go on and off as their residents come and go. (Look closely and you can even see Mickey Mouse waving to you from inside a tiny apartment in Paris.) Another interesting touch is that the scenery changes depending on the time of day you're inside. If you get here in late afternoon, you'll see the sun setting on these towns. Stay long enough—and we have—and dusk turns to evening, then evening to night.

Lastly, Skyline has mirrors on the walls perpendicular to the video screens. Because the mirrors are set at right angles to the screens, they reflect the videos and make the bar look longer than it is. It's a well-known decorating trick for making a small room seem larger, but it's still nice to see it included here.

The rest of the decor is natural surfaces: wood panels, ceiling, and floors, in colors ranging from honey to mahogany; dark marble countertops; and leather chairs.

SELECTIONS The specialty is "around the world" cocktails themed to the featured cities. For example, the 1914, representing Chicago, pairs Absolut Vanilla and Kurant vodkas with fresh blackberries and raspberries; the Zen-Chanted, representing Hong Kong, is made with 3Vodka (distilled from soybeans), Zen green-tea liqueur, Cointreau, and guava and lime juices.

COMMENTS Adding movement to the scenery means the view at Skyline doesn't get boring. It also means that the club doesn't need a television to hold its patrons' attention.

ACROSS THE SHIPS Although there are Skylines on both the *Dream* and the *Fantasy,* their drink menus are mostly different. Drinks at the *Dream*'s Skyline tend more toward the fruity, whereas drinks at the *Fantasy*'s Skyline make more use of herbs and spices, such as basil, coriander, and cilantro.

ON THE *FANTASY*

Bon Voyage   LOCATION Deck 3 Midship

SETTING AND ATMOSPHERE Located just off the atrium and designed in the same Art Nouveau style as the rest of the ship, Bon Voyage is one of the prettiest bars on the *Fantasy.* Behind the bar are two gold-and-white peacocks etched in glass, while the bar's face is a translucent gold marble. Bon Voyage has just 10 seats at the counter, plus 2 fabric-covered couches and 6 armchairs a few feet away.

SELECTIONS The bar menu is similar to that at La Piazza (see page 254) and includes draft and bottled beer, wines by the glass and bottle, spirits, and mixed drinks, including a few special fruit-flavored martinis.

COMMENTS Open from midday to late evening, Bon Voyage is a good place for groups to meet up before dinner. But like its counterpart on the *Dream* (see page 245), it isn't conducive to quiet conversation—or live entertainment—due to its location near a heavily trafficked area.

ACROSS THE SHIPS **Promenade Lounge** is the comparable bar on the *Magic* (see pages 239 and 240). Similarly located are the **French Quarter Lounge** on the *Wonder* (page 244) and **The Bayou** on the *Wish* (page 257), which have a New Orleans theme versus Bon Voyage's geographically nonspecific Art Nouveau (*Fantasy*) and Art Deco (*Dream*) decor.

Cove Café   LOCATION Deck 11 Forward

COMMENTS See the profile of Cove Café on the *Magic* (page 239) for details.

Currents   LOCATION Deck 13 Forward

COMMENTS See the profile of Currents on the *Dream* (page 246) for details.

Meridian   LOCATION Deck 12 Aft

COMMENTS See the profile of Meridian on the *Dream* (page 246) for details.

Vista Café   LOCATION Deck 4 Midship

COMMENTS See the profile of Vista Café on the *Dream* (page 247) for details.

Waves   LOCATION Deck 12 Aft

COMMENTS See the profile of Waves on the *Dream* (page 247) for details.

Europa

This is the designation for the five nightspots on the *Fantasy*'s Deck 4 Aft: **O'Gills Pub,** a sports bar; **Ooh La La,** a Champagne bar; **La Piazza,** an Italian-inspired lounge; **Skyline,** a cosmopolitan watering hole; and **The Tube,** a London subway–themed dance club.

While the nightlife districts on the *Magic, Wonder*, and *Dream* have distinctive theming, Europa has next to none. The ostensible theme is Europe, but the decor consists mostly of just shiny gold walls on which each club's name is illuminated and repeated. That said, one nice touch found only at Europa is the round black-and-white photos on the walls: the images, which feature European icons, including the Eiffel Tower, London's Big Ben, and the Leaning Tower of Pisa, turn into short animated videos.

Most of Europa's bars open between 5 and 5:30 p.m. and stay open until midnight (check the Navigator app for hours on your sailing). La Piazza usually opens a little earlier than that; The Tube operates from around 10 p.m. to 2 a.m. Hot appetizers are usually served throughout the evening in one of La Piazza's circular pedestrian walkways.

Ooh La La, Skyline, and The Tube admit guests ages 18 and up only. Families are welcome at La Piazza and O'Gills Pub until 9 p.m., when they become adults-only.

O'Gills Pub   LOCATION Deck 4 Aft

SETTING AND ATMOSPHERE The *Fantasy*'s sports bar, O'Gills lies just off one side of La Piazza (see next page). It's supposed to be an Irish pub, but it's the least visually interesting bar in Europa. With some paint, antiques-store scavenging, and the right beer-of-the-month subscription, O'Gills would be right at home in Chicago, Dallas, or Green Bay.

A huge video screen in the back corner shows sporting events and sports news all day long. Several other smaller screens are distributed throughout the room, and there's plenty of seating and standing room.

SELECTIONS The bar menu includes bottled and draft beer, including a house draft lager and several Irish brews. Wine is available by the glass and bottle, and the friendly bartenders can mix up virtually any cocktail you want. The specialty is Irish whiskey and Scotch; a private-label Irish cream liqueur is on the menu too.

COMMENTS You wouldn't come here for the Irish ambience, but as a generic sports bar, O'Gills isn't bad.

ACROSS THE SHIPS There's another O'Gills on the *Magic* (see page 242). As a sports bar, however, it's similar to **687** on the *Dream* (see page 250), **Crown & Fin** on the *Wonder* (see page 244), and **Keg & Compass** on the *Wish* (see page 258). We prefer 687, the O'Gills on the *Magic,* and Crown & Fin over the *Fantasy*'s O'Gills—those three sports bars have better sight lines to the TV screens from the seating areas.

Ooh La La   LOCATION Deck 4 Aft

SETTING AND ATMOSPHERE This is the *Fantasy*'s Champagne bar. The French-boudoir theming is enough to make you break out in "Lady

Marmalade" as performed in *Moulin Rouge:* rose-colored upholstery on the walls, purple carpet, and chairs lined with gold fabric. Along one wall is a series of padded couches in ivory and green. Gold-edged mirrors and fleurs-de-lis line the walls. A single red chair and a couple of small, red-topped side tables provide a touch of bold color.

The bar, at the far end of the lounge, seats six around its black marble top. In keeping with the boudoir theme, the mirror behind the bar looks like an oversize version of one you might find on the dressing table of a fashionable Frenchwoman at the *fin de siècle*. And because it's a Champagne bar, hundreds of small glass bubbles fill the mirrors.

SELECTIONS The menu here is virtually identical to the one at Pink on the *Dream*. Bubbly by the glass starts at about $9 and goes up to $60; bottles start at about $80 and go up to $500. If you're in the mood for something more indulgent—and you have the dough—have the staff call upstairs to Remy, which has a few truly special bottles that sell for about $3,000 each.

Several of Ooh La La's offerings are Champagne cocktails, combining bubbly with fruit juices or liqueurs, but remember the Second Law of Champagne: if it needs another ingredient, then you're drinking the wrong Champagne. (The First Law: Champagne goes with everything!) Sparkling wines, along with reds and whites, are available by the glass and bottle, and the fully stocked bar can furnish virtually any cocktail you like.

COMMENTS The best seats in Ooh La La are on the L-shaped silver couch near the main entrance. It's the perfect private place to do some people-watching. Another nice touch is the use of area rugs to mark off sections of seats—it's possible to mingle within that small area, having individual conversations while still being part of the group. The club also has three porthole windows with ocean views and seating below them. If you visit during the late afternoon, the light from outside provides a gentle transition from day to dusk.

ACROSS THE SHIPS You can get Champagne and Champagne cocktails on all of the Disney ships; however, only the *Dream* and the *Fantasy* have dedicated Champagne bars. We like the relatively understated theming of **Pink** on the *Dream* (see page 249) better than the frilly decor of Ooh La La.

La Piazza   LOCATION Deck 4 Aft

SETTING AND ATMOSPHERE This Venetian-themed lounge sits near the front of Europa. Appropriately, La Piazza ("The Plaza") serves as the walkway to O'Gills and Ooh La La, whose entrances sit just off this venue; farther beyond are Skyline and The Tube, so you'll walk by La Piazza on the way.

The bar sits in the middle of a bright, circular room. It's themed to look like an Italian merry-go-round, its ceiling decorated with hundreds of carousel lights. Around the bar are rose-colored barstools; lining the wall are golden, high-backed, upholstered couches with small tables for drinks. The couches are separated, elevated, and set into niches in the walls, making them good vantages from which to watch people walk between the clubs.

SELECTIONS La Piazza's bar menu features Peroni and Moretti, two Italian beers, as well as prosecco (Italian sparkling wine) and limoncello (an Italian lemon-flavored liqueur). These ingredients also make their way into La Piazza's five signature cocktails: the Mercutio, for example, features Absolut

Pears vodka, limoncello, grappa, and fresh lemon juice, with the sweetness of the pear and grappa balancing out the tartness of the citrus.

COMMENTS The couches are good spots for watching La Piazza's live entertainment, which has been an up-tempo jazz trio on our most recent cruises. Our favorite pastime at La Piazza, however, takes place starting at 11 p.m., when we start to wager a round of drinks on the number of couples who will stop to take photos on La Piazza's Vespa motorcycle-and-sidecar prop in the next 10 minutes. The over-under on that bet is usually 2.5, and the rules prohibit shouting encouragement to the *ubriachi*.

ACROSS THE SHIPS Somewhat similar to **District Lounge** on the *Dream* (see page 248), La Piazza has a better drink menu, while District Lounge has a better layout. No comparable bar is found on the *Magic, Wonder,* or *Wish*.

Skyline LOCATION Deck 4 Aft

SETTING AND ATMOSPHERE Skyline is our favorite bar on the *Fantasy*. The concept is that you're in a lounge high on the edge of some of the world's most famous cities. Behind the bar are seven "windows"—large HD video screens—affording panoramic views of seven cities: Athens, Barcelona, Budapest, Florence, London, Paris, and St. Petersburg.

Each city is shown for about 15 minutes across all seven screens; then the scene changes to another locale. The foreground of each view includes close-ups of apartments and offices, while the middle and background show each city's iconic architecture and landscape.

That would be mildly interesting scenery on its own, but Disney has added special effects that make Skyline beautiful. Each view shows the city in motion: cars move along streets, neon signs blink to illuminate sidewalks, and apartment lights go on and off as their residents come and go. (Look closely and you can even see Mickey Mouse waving to you from inside a tiny apartment in Paris.) Another interesting touch is that the scenery changes depending on the time of day you're inside. If you get here in late afternoon, you'll see the sun setting on these towns. Stay long enough—and we have— and dusk turns to evening, then evening to night.

Lastly, Skyline has mirrors on the walls perpendicular to the video screens. Because the mirrors are set at right angles to the screens, they reflect the videos and make the bar look longer than it is. It's a well-known decorating trick for making a small room seem larger, but it's still nice to see it included here.

The rest of the decor is natural surfaces: wood panels, ceiling, and floors; dark marble countertops; and leather chairs.

SELECTIONS The specialty is "around the world" cocktails themed to the featured cities. For example, El Conquistador, representing Barcelona, pairs Tanqueray gin and Absolut Peppar vodka with fresh muddled strawberries, basil, and cracked black pepper; the Aquincum, representing Budapest, is made with Casamigos Reposado tequila, Grand Marnier, paprika, and freshly squeezed lime juice.

COMMENTS Adding movement to the scenery means the view at Skyline doesn't get boring. It also means that the club doesn't need a television to hold its patrons' attention..

ACROSS THE SHIPS Although there are Skylines on both the *Dream* and the *Fantasy,* the latter version features two more cities in its "windows" than

Skyline on the *Dream*. Also, the bars' drink menus are mostly different. Drinks at the *Dream*'s Skyline tend to be flavored with fruits and fruit juices, such as cranberry, pomegranate, lemon, and lime; drinks on the *Fantasy*'s Skyline are made with fruits, too, but also with herbs and spices, such as basil, thyme, coriander, cilantro, and paprika.

The Tube   LOCATION Deck 4 Aft

SETTING AND ATMOSPHERE With its London subway–meets–Austin Powers theme, The Tube is the *Fantasy*'s dance club. Its decor includes leather couches with prints that look like Underground tickets, Sixties-mod egg-shaped chairs, and a floor painted like a subway map. We especially like the upholstered leather couch set deep inside the lounge: it's under a set of lights in the shape of a crown and across from two shiny silver armchairs designed to look like thrones. A couple of red phone booths are set on either side of the dance floor. *Oh, behave!*

SELECTIONS The Tube's circular bar, set under Big Ben's clock face, serves a typical menu of bottled beer, mixed drinks, spirits, and wine and Champagne by the glass. The Tube also serves six signature drinks, our favorite of which is Mind the Gap, a mix of whiskey, Drambuie, and Coke.

COMMENTS The Tube usually opens around 10 p.m. and sometimes gets things going with a quick game of Match Your Mate (think *The Newlywed Game,* only groovier). Dancing usually gets started around 10:30 or 11 p.m. Most of the music is contemporary dance tunes, but there are also themed nights with disco and, of course, British hits. If you want a good view of the stage, particularly if you have a large party, plan to arrive a few minutes early for nondance activities.

ACROSS THE SHIPS The club's closest counterparts are **Fathoms** on the *Magic* (see page 240), **Azure** on the *Wonder* (see page 243), and **Evolution** on the *Dream* (see page 249). The Tube, though, is our favorite dance club on any of the ships. The *Wish* doesn't have a dedicated dance club, although **Luna** and **Triton Lounge** (see Part Nine, page 264) host game shows and other entertainment for adults at night.

ON THE *WISH*

THE *WISH*'S BARS AND LOUNGES, profiled in the next section, are distributed around the ship—there's no dedicated "adult district" as is the case on the other four Disney ships. Adults have plenty of spaces for relaxing with a cocktail, listening to live music, or watching sports. Curiously, however, the *Wish* doesn't have a nightclub comparable to Azure on the *Wonder,* The Tube on the *Fantasy,* and so on.

*un**official* **TIP**
A DCL ship isn't a party barge. That said, some adults may find the nightlife on the *Wish* more sedate than on the other ships.

Luna and **Triton Lounge** serve first and foremost as daytime hubs for family activities and group seminars, similar to **D Lounge** on the other ships. Both venues serve alcohol at night, but to call them *nightclubs* is a stretch: they host some evening events for adults (including karaoke, game shows, and trivia contests), but neither has a dance floor, unless you count moving a few tables and chairs out of the way. (For more information, see Part Nine, page 264.)

Unique to the *Wish* is **Star Wars Hyperspace Lounge** (see page 260), a smaller-scale version of Oga's Cantina at Walt Disney World and Disneyland. The drinks are pricey—one, in fact, costs a jaw-dropping $5,000—and depending on when you sail, you may need a reservation to get in. Plus, if you've already experienced the *Star Wars* nightclub at the theme parks, DCL's rendition will probably seem redundant.

The Bayou LOCATION Deck 3 Midship

SETTING AND ATMOSPHERE You're in a New Orleans garden with flower-laden trees above. The velvet upholstery, in shades of green and burgundy, is elegant and indulgent. The Bayou is centrally located and open to foot traffic on two sides, making it the best place on the ship for people-watching.

SELECTIONS The Bayou's cocktails have a decidedly New Orleans twist. Options include an Absinthe Frappe (Pernod absinthe, anisette, and vanilla cream soda); the Cajun Michelada (Abita Amber Lager beer, Clamato, and Cajun spices); and a take on the classic Hurricane (Bayou Reserve rum, passion fruit, and lime). The nonalcoholic choices include sodas from Covington, Louisiana–based Abita Brewing Company. The King Cake Soda, for example, re-creates the flavors of the traditional Mardi Gras confection—think a coffee cake or a cinnamon roll—in soft drink form. The specialty coffees and fresh juices sold here are also available at other locations around the ship.

Speaking of sweet treats, don't sleep on the freshly made beignets. We like Mama's Special: three beignets served with Valrhona chocolate sauce. In the mood for a morning pick-me-up? The Bayou has carts serving custom Bloody Marys and mimosas made with fresh-squeezed juices.

COMMENTS The flowers hanging from the ceiling are lovely, but they're bound to get dusty after several months of sailing.

ACROSS THE SHIPS From a theming perspective, The Bayou, with its *Princess and the Frog*–inspired decor and menu items, is most similar to the **French Quarter Lounge** on the *Wonder* (see page 244), although the latter emphasizes the urban aspects of the Big Easy rather than nature and the outdoors. From a location perspective, its closest equivalent is **Bon Voyage** on the *Dream* and the *Fantasy* (see pages 245 and 252): each has a prominent position directly adjacent to the main atrium of its respective ship.

Cove Bar LOCATION Deck 13 Aft

SETTING AND ATMOSPHERE The Cove Bar serves the Quiet Cove adults-only pool area. Tables, chairs, and chaise longues are located adjacent to the walk-up bar, which has a *Moana* theme

SELECTIONS The menu is heavy on tropical drinks, with updated riffs on the Mai Tai, piña colada, mojito, and Blue Hawaiian. The signature cocktail is the Amazonia Fizz: Hendricks Amazonia gin, pineapple juice, lime, agave nectar, and Fever Tree tonic water. The Infinity Swirl (named after the nearby infinity pool) combines layers of SelvaRey white rum, strawberry puree, Dole Whip soft-serve, Dos Maderas PX 5+5 dark rum, and frozen piña colada.

COMMENTS The same drink menu is offered at **Currents** on the *Wish*. (See page 246 for our profile of Currents on the *Dream*.)

ACROSS THE SHIPS Aside from the Hawaiian-style theming, Cove Bar is more or less the same as the adult pool bars on the other ships.

Cove Café LOCATION Deck 13 Aft

SETTING AND ATMOSPHERE Seating areas for small groups have upholstery in muted shades of beige and seafoam.

SELECTIONS This 18-and-up venue serves specialty coffees and teas (hot or cold). The baristas can top your latte's steamed milk with images of Disney characters. If you're not a coffee person, try the Hot Cocoa Magic or the Cornetto Caffé—a blend of milk chocolate, dark chocolate, and white chocolate. Wines by the glass and cold-brew coffee cocktails are also available.

COMMENTS Cove Café is an oasis of quiet on this bustling cruise ship.

ACROSS THE SHIPS All five ships have Cove Cafés. This one, however, doesn't serve food.

Currents LOCATION Deck 14 Forward

COMMENTS See the profile of Currents on the *Dream* (page 246) for details.

Enchanted Sword Café LOCATION Deck 5 Midship

SETTING AND ATMOSPHERE This is a grab-and-go spot with a few stools to sit on while you wait for the barista to pull your brew.

SELECTIONS Like Cove Café, Enchanted Sword serves specialty coffees and teas and wines by the glass. Also on offer are such healthful juice blends as the Booster (orange, carrot, lemon, and ginger), the Rejuvenate (beet, carrot, and apple), and the Detox (kale, spinach, cucumber, and spirulina). Add vanilla or chocolate protein powder for an extra hit of nutrition.

COMMENTS This is a great place to grab your morning latte if you don't feel like trekking all the way upstairs to Cove Café. A basically identical venue, the **Wishing Star Café,** is located on Deck 4 Midship.

ACROSS THE SHIPS When it comes to the beverages served, Enchanted Sword combines elements of **Cove Café** on all five ships (see page 243), **Vista Café** on the *Dream* and *Fantasy* (see page 247), and **Senses Juice Bar,** also on the *Dream* and *Fantasy* (see page 210).

Keg & Compass LOCATION Deck 5 Forward

SETTING AND ATMOSPHERE Eight large TV screens cover the walls. Tables with cozy leather chairs line the sides of the room, while the central area has two long common tables and stools that seat a few dozen guests. DCL uses this area for trivia games—seating is at a premium, so arrive early if you want to sit here. Be sure to check out the map artwork on the ceiling.

SELECTIONS This is primarily a brewpub, with menu selections divided into Lagers & Ales, Stouts & IPAs, Wheats & Ciders, Meads, and Specialty Beers. You'll also find wines by the glass and a few cocktails that pay homage to the bar's seafaring theme, including Northern Lights (aquavit, mead, Lillet Blanc aperitif, Cointreau orange liqueur, and Uncharted Lager) and Old-Fashioned Glogg (port, bourbon, and "Viking spices," whatever those are).

COMMENTS Like DCL's other sports bars, Keg & Compass serves late-night pub grub at an extra cost. Options include Buffalo wings, fish and chips, loaded potato tots, plant-based "chicken" nuggets, a charcuterie board, fried coconut shrimp, and a giant German soft pretzel served with mustard and beer cheese for dipping. For dessert, try the brioche bread-and-butter pudding with marmalade glaze and vanilla sauce.

ACROSS THE SHIPS Aside from differences in theming and menus, Keg & Compass is comparable to the other DCL sports bars.

The Lookout   LOCATION **Deck 11 Forward**

SETTING AND ATMOSPHERE This is the bar window for Mickey's Festival of Foods, the quick-service food court on the main pool deck. There are plenty of lounge chairs nearby.

SELECTIONS A little bit of everything: grab a beer, wine by the glass, a can of Truly, an iced tea, or a tropical cocktail.

COMMENTS You're not going here for the ambience, but to tank up before the kiddos make you ride the AquaMouse with them for the hundredth time.

ACROSS THE SHIPS All the ships have poolside bars. This one just happens to have a name.

Marceline Market Café   LOCATION **Deck 11 Aft**

SETTING AND ATMOSPHERE The café bridges the two halves of the Marceline Market buffet. The decor is upscale Starbucks, with plenty of seating for small groups.

SELECTIONS Similar to Cove Café and Enchanted Sword Café, Marceline Market Café serves coffee, tea, and cocoa, as well as wines by the glass, cold-brew coffee cocktails, and a few of the tropical-themed drinks also available at the Cove Bar.

COMMENTS This is another convenient place to grab a fancy coffee. The café's proximity to Marceline Market, however, means it'll be hopping in the morning, so if you don't feel like waiting in line, swing by Enchanted Sword Café or Wishing Sword Café before you head up to breakfast.

ACROSS THE SHIPS Marceline Market Café is unique to the *Wish*.

Nightingale's   LOCATION **Deck 3 Midship**

SETTING AND ATMOSPHERE Nightingale's gets its name from "Sing, Sweet Nightingale," a song performed by Cinderella in the Disney animated film from 1950. A grand piano and an ornate chandelier, featuring elements of a musical staff and glass-orb "bubbles," anchor the far end of the room. The walls are covered with navy upholstery and the ceiling limned with a crystal border. The combined effect is elegant and intimate.

SELECTIONS The signature cocktail is the Sweet Nightingale (Hendricks Amazonia gin, passion fruit juice, rosemary, and mint), served in a bird-shaped sipper. Other featured drinks fall into three categories: Air Bubbles, Smoke Bubbles, and Frozen Bubbles. For the first two, the bartender uses an air gun to "blow" a large bubble—filled with smoke in the second case—on the surface of the liquid; the bubble pops within seconds. (Frozen Bubble drinks contain spheres made of ice.) Gimmicky, yes, but fun.

The Butterfly, a Smoke Bubble drink, is made with citrus juices, butterfly-pea tea, and Bombay Sapphire gin; Dreams Come True, an Air Bubble cocktail, combines Empress gin with elderflower liqueur, white cranberry juice, and rosé Champagne. Also available are wines by the glass and Champagne by the glass or bottle.

COMMENTS The evening entertainment consists of piano renditions of everything from classical music to Broadway to Elton John.

ACROSS THE SHIPS Nightingale's combines the piano-bar ambience of **Keys** on the *Magic* (see page 241) and **Cadillac Lounge** on the *Wonder* (see page 243) with the bubbly beverages and decor of **Pink** and **Ooh La La,** the Champagne bars on the *Dream* and *Fantasy* (see pages 249 and 254).

The Rose   LOCATION Deck 12 Aft
(at the entrance to Enchanté and Palo Steakhouse)

SETTING AND ATMOSPHERE One entire wall of this space is floor-to-ceiling windows facing the sea. Mirrors on the opposite wall make the ocean feel even more present. The ceiling is dominated by a raised rose motif. The seating around the room is plush green and beige upholstered chairs and settees. The barstools are crimson velvet.

SELECTIONS The specialty concoctions here are named for aspects of the *Beauty and the Beast* story: The Rose (Komos Reposado Rosa tequila, Grand Marnier Cuvée Louis-Alexandre liqueur, and Perrier-Jouet Belle Époque Rosé Champagne); Mrs. Tea (SelvaRey white rum, Belvedere Pear & Ginger vodka, Pique Passion Fruit green tea, and Moët et Chandon Impérial Rosé Champagne); and the Royal Wedding (Buckingham Palace Dry Gin, Hangar One Fog Point vodka, and Lillet Blanc aperitif). There's also a full bar and a selection of wines by the glass and Champagne by the glass or bottle.

COMMENTS The Rose is restricted to guests ages 18 and older. The dress code for Palo Steakhouse and Enchanté applies here as well.

ACROSS THE SHIPS The Rose is similar to **Meridian** on the *Dream* and *Fantasy* (see page 246), both in terms of location and atmosphere. You'll also find the atmosphere familiar if you've been to the **Enchanted Rose Lounge** at the Grand Floridian Hotel & Spa in Walt Disney World.

Star Wars Hyperspace Lounge   LOCATION Deck 3 Midship

SETTING AND ATMOSPHERE You're in a bar, in space. The room itself—which seats just 60 people—is rather blandly industrial, with clean metallic lines and not much else in the way of embellishment. One side of the bar is home to a collection of drink dispensers that would be right at home in a science lab. The key theming element is the central giant screen that functions as a porthole on this "spaceship." Via the screen, hyperspace drive kicks in, and you're virtually transported to locations throughout the *Star Wars* universe. You may see familiar ships such as X-Wings and Star Destroyers, but you won't see any characters—for those, you'll have to visit **Star Wars: Cargo Bay** at the Oceaneer Club during open-house hours for the kids' clubs (see page 278).

The jump to hyperspace can be intense for guests who are prone to sensory overstimulation: the banquette seats vibrate, and the entire space becomes engulfed in noise for several seconds.

SELECTIONS The drinks are "exotic, otherworldly concoctions" made with ingredients that exist both in the *Star Wars* universe and on the earthly plane. The Golden One from the Moons of Endor, for example, is made with a mix of herbs and berries from the Forest Moon surface. Here on Earth, that translates to Belvedere Blackberry & Lemongrass vodka and Disaronno Velvet cream liqueur, with a glow-in-the-dark stamp floating in the liquid. The Freetown Reserve from Tatooine, meanwhile, is made of Bantha hides mashed with fermented grains (aka Woodford Reserve Double Oaked bourbon). And the Spire Sunset from Batuu is made from substances gathered from the sides of the planet's petrified spires (in other words, Saigon Bagur gin, kumquat, lychee, and coconut).

Teetotalers and kids can choose from nonalcoholic drinks such as the Cloud City (oat milk, blue raspberry syrup, and ice cream) and the Temple Twist (apple, pineapple, and kiwi juices, with mint and ginger beer). For $12, you can add a souvenir Hyperspace Lounge glass to any of the primary cocktail offerings; for $17, you can have your mocktail served in a souvenir Porg-shaped glass. (After 9 p.m., guests must be 18 to enter and 21 to drink.)

The drink with the biggest buzz, however, is the **Kaiburr Crystal,** which costs an eye-popping **$5,000**—as much as a small used car. Disney PR is reluctant to disclose the ingredients, but travel blogger Arthur Levine and *Orlando Sentinel* reporter Scott Gustin verified them with Disney insiders.

The Kaiburr Crystal is actually a beverage flight consisting of a cocktail and three shots. The cocktail is made with Camus Cuvée 4.160 Cognac and Grand Marnier Grande Cuvée Quintessence liqueur, plus yuzu and kumquat juices. The shots are made with Pappy Van Winkle's Family Reserve 23-Year-Old bourbon, Taylor Fladgate Kingsman Edition Very Old Tawny Port, and Watenshi gin.

Retail prices for the individual liquors range from around $2,700 a bottle for the gin to around $7,000 a bottle for the Cognac. As for the bourbon, Pappy Van Winkle—known among aficionados as "the unicorn of whiskeys"—*officially* retails for $299 a bottle, but because the distillery releases just 7,000–8,000 cases each year, distributors sell it at ridiculous markups—often into the five figures. (Many retailers sell it by lottery only.)

The drinks are served in a multichambered containment cooler. The cups are silver-plated, and you get to keep them. Guests who buy the Kaiburr Crystal package also get a *Star Wars* backpack and water bottle, plus a Hyperspace-themed stateroom decoration. *But wait, there's more!*

Also part of the package is a bottle of sparkling wine from George Lucas's Skywalker Ranch in Marin County, California, along with a voucher good for one visit to the ranch, which isn't open to the public otherwise. The pièce de résistance: a special escort off the ship. (Gustin and Levine couldn't confirm exactly what this entails, however.) At least three packages were sold on the *Wish*'s maiden voyage.

*un**official* **TIP**
The cooler used to serve the Kaiburr Crystal drink package—aka the **Camtono Safe**—isn't included in the $5,000 price, but it retails for about $45 at shopDisney (shopdisney.com).

COMMENTS According to Disney Imagineers, the Hyperspace Lounge isn't tied to any particular aspect of the franchise—rather, it's a celebration of all things *Star Wars.* So many *Wish* guests want to experience it that some sailings have instituted a reservation system. If you'd like to visit, check with DCL to see if you'll need reservations for your sailing; if so, make them *immediately* after you board the ship. *Note:* Your visit may be limited to 45 minutes, depending on how many other guests have booked a seating.

ACROSS THE SHIPS There's nothing like the Hyperspace Lounge on the other DCL ships. The most similar watering hole in the Disney theme parks is **Oga's Cantina,** part of *Star Wars:* Galaxy's Edge at Walt Disney World and Disneyland. This is a far more immersive experience than Hyperspace Lounge, however—if you've already been to Oga's, then you won't be missing much if you skip the lounge on board.

PART NINE

ACTIVITIES, RECREATION, *and* SHOPPING

BESIDES EAT, DRINK, BE ENTERTAINED, and tour ports, you'll find lots of things to do on every Disney Cruise Line itinerary:

- **Family activities,** held throughout the day, include trivia contests, bingo, deck parties, and more.
- **Children's programs,** the strength of Disney Cruise Line, begin early in the morning and end after midnight on most days.
- **Pools and water-play areas** are usually the center of activity during the day.
- **Onboard seminars** (some of them free) and cover everything from cooking demonstrations to wine tastings.
- **Sports and fitness amenities** include a measured track on four of the ships, plus, a full gym, fitness classes, a half-size basketball court, and more.
- **Senses Spa** is a great place to relax after a tough day on shore.
- **Character appearances** include Mickey, Minnie, the Disney princesses, and many others, often wearing special costumes themed to the cruise destination
- **Shopping opportunities** are available on board and in port.

FAMILY ACTIVITIES

BINGO

DCL IS ONE OF THE FEW CRUISE LINES that have no casino gambling on board. What it does have is bingo, played most days on most ships, in one or two hour-long sessions per day. The cost to play is about $30 per paper card per game, with four games played per hour. Prizes range from DCL swag to actual cash jackpots of several thousand dollars. On one sailing, we watched a young guy win nearly $9,000 at bingo—enough to pay for his entire vacation and then some.

With that much money potentially at stake, it's no surprise that many people take Disney bingo quite seriously. Games are fast-paced, and players are expected to keep up. Additionally, DCL interjects sound effects, music, dance, and random chatter into the number calling. (*Pro tip:* The reason the bingo crew members do a wacky dance every time the B-11 ball is called is that when the machine is in Spanish-language mode, *B-11* is *B once,* pronounced more or less like "Beyoncé.")

Children may play but must be accompanied at all times by a guest age 18 or older, who will officially be the winner of any cash prize. The cost to play varies; pricing is typically higher at the end of a sailing, when payouts are larger. Buy-ins start at around $30 for one set of paper bingo cards per session. Many guests, however, opt to rent electronic bingo machines, often priced at $40 or $50 for 24 cards per session. Because the machines keep track of which numbers have been called, you don't have to be on high alert every second.

If you think you're going to be playing frequently, be sure to stick around at the end of each session. The caller will often give out a special one-day-only password that's good for free bingo cards if you mention it at the next session. On longer sailings, the caller will sometimes offer free cards to guests who present personal items such as a child's drawing of the ship or a photo they took of a specific thing in port. Frequent-player discounts may also be available—be sure to ask.

IS THIS WORTH YOUR TIME? Len rarely plays bingo—he doesn't like to gamble—but Erin's family plays several rounds on every sailing. If you you're OK with risking relatively small amounts of money, it could be worth the $30 buy-in just once to see if it's your cup of tea. But be aware that once you get hooked, costs can add up quickly.

DECK PARTIES

FEATURING DISNEY CHARACTERS, deck parties are usually held several times per cruise, typically near the family pool or in the ship's main lobby. The first party, known as the **Sail-Away Celebration** or **Sail-A-Wave Party** depending on the ship, happens as you leave port on embarkation day. Additional deck parties will happen any time there is a themed day/evening on the ship (Pirate Night, Marvel and Pixar Days, New Year's Eve, and so on).

Outdoor parties are high-energy affairs, with loud music, dancing, games, and other activities, plus videos displayed on the ship's giant LED screen. The indoor versions of these parties are virtually identical except for the giant video screen. Check the **DCL Navigator app** (page 136) for event dates and times.

IS THIS WORTH YOUR TIME? If you're a fan of classic TV, *The Love Boat* in particular, deck parties are a virtual must-do for the kitsch/pop culture factor. Little kids typically love the show if they can see the stage. If you're an adult who's cruising for relaxation, feel free to skip it.

FAMILY NIGHTCLUBS

IN ADDITION TO ITS MYRIAD entertainment offerings for adults (see Part Eight), DCL has what would be an oxymoron in any other context: family nightclubs. Set up like grown-up nightspots, with their own bars, tables and chairs, and dance floors, these

*un*official **TIP**
Check the Navigator app for club hours and available activities on your sailing.

lounges offer daytime and nighttime entertainment, including stand-up comedy, talent shows, trivia contests, cooking demos, karaoke, line dancing, and more. (Many of the same activities are also offered during the day at some adult clubs; see "Nightclubs, Bars, Cafés, and Lounges," page 237.) Refreshments are served, including cocktails for Mom and Dad and smoothies and sodas for the kids, all at an extra charge.

On the *Dream, Fantasy, Magic,* and *Wonder,* most family-nightclub activities take place in **D Lounge,** on Deck 4 Midship. On the *Wish,* **Luna** is the primary family nightclub, with the adjacent **Triton Lounge** providing space for additional events.

Luna is a two-level space, with entrances on Decks 4 and 5 Midship. There is no internal staircase between the levels, so if you want to go from one level to another, you'll have to walk down a long hallway, take the stairs or elevator, and then walk down another long hallway. Many of the events that take place here involve audience participation, which is effectively impossible from the upper level. If you want to be part of the action, enter on Deck 4; if you just want to observe, enter on Deck 5.

The activities in the family nightclubs (and sometimes in the lobby atrium) vary considerably depending on the length of the sailing, the itinerary, whether it's a special-events sailing (Marvel Days, holidays, and so on), and other factors. Days at sea will have a wider range of programming than days in port, when many guests will be off enjoying the sights on land.

There are, however, a number of activities that show up with some frequency. Among them are the following:

- **Disney Trivia, Cruise Trivia, Sports Trivia, Movie Trivia, Pirate Trivia, Holiday Trivia, Tunes Trivia, and so on** Trivia is big on longer sailings. It often helps to have team members from different generations, because the questions may come from current topics or ancient times (like, you know, the 1980s). Tunes Trivia uses a live pianist rather than prerecorded music snippets. Though the prizes are typically things like plastic medals and keychains, the gameplay can get cutthroat. Keep an eye out for Disney know-it-alls who study in advance with the specific aim of wiping the floor with their onboard competition.

- **Game Shows** may include any of the following: **Who Wants to Be a Mouse-keteer?,** a simplified version of *Who Wants to Be a Millionaire?;* **So You Think You Know Your Family,** a spin on *The Newlywed Game* where parent-child pairs try to guess how the other generation will answer various questions; **The Feud** (think *Family Feud* with Disneyfied questions); and **Mickey Mania,** in which four parent-child teams have to be quick on the buzzer for a chance to answer moderately challenging trivia questions.

- **Crafts** These are usually low-mess, cut-and-paste projects geared to younger kids. Teens will likely find them boring.

- **Family Karaoke** Guests choose from a list of preselected songs. Obviously, songs from Disney films number among the possibilities, but you'll also find classic and contemporary pop and rock tunes, country hits, American Songbook standards, and a few Spanish-language hits. As you might expect, any song with even a hint of profanity is a no-go. If you want to sing, arrive promptly at starting time; available time slots often fill quickly.

- **Animation Lessons** If you're familiar with the Animation Experience at Disney's Animal Kingdom (or a similar experience that once took place at Disney's Hollywood Studios), then you have an idea of what to expect here. If you have a child who's a perfectionist, this could be a trouble spot—we once had a little one melt down when her drawing came out less than identical to the instructor's.

- **Dance Lessons** Longer sailings may offer instruction in some locally flavored dance—Irish step dancing on a Northern European cruise, for example, or tango on a Mediterranean cruise.

- **Cooking Lessons** These are observational rather than hands-on—you'll be watching someone else do the cooking. Printed recipes are usually distributed at the end; we've had good luck re-creating dishes at home.

- **Art of the Ship Tour** DCL cast members lead guests around the ship, pointing out noteworthy construction and design elements along the way.

- **Family Talent Shows** Some cruises of seven nights or longer will have one of these. If you're interested in performing, sign up at Guest Services early in your trip, and make sure to pack whatever costumes, recordings, or sheet music you might need to perform. While you're not allowed to bring your own musical instruments onto the ship, you can usually borrow a guitar or keyboard that's kept on hand.

- **Diaper Dash** Babies old enough to crawl participate in a "race" along a padded mat. The cruise staff livens things up by "interviewing" the contestants. There are likely to be few Diaper Dash "competitors" on extended European and repositioning sailings, but the spectacle can be fierce—and highly entertaining—on short Caribbean hops. Beware, however, of having your baby participate if he or she is sensitive to loud noises, as the cheering can get intense.

IS THIS WORTH YOUR TIME? Your enjoyment of any of these activities may be affected by your mood, the personalities of the other participating guests, and your perception of the staff who are running the event. While the staff who run the family activities are enthusiastic and engaging, it's always possible that someone could be having a bad day. Also, while it's usually good to arrive on time at the beginning of an activity (so you can hear the instructions for a game, for example), you're not required to stick around if you find it doesn't interest you.

SPORTS AND FITNESS

THE DISNEY SHIPS have several sports options available for families, covered later in this chapter, beginning on page 295.

CHILDREN'S PROGRAMS *and* ACTIVITIES

KIDS' CLUBS AT A GLANCE

WHEN IT COMES TO ENTERTAINING CHILDREN, Disney Cruise Line has no equal. The kids' clubs (Disney officially calls them **youth clubs**), for infants to 17-year-olds, open as early as 7:30 a.m. for babies and close as late as 2 a.m. for teens.

Kids can participate in organized activities ranging from craft-making to trivia contests and dance parties, or they can play individually with computer games, board games, books, and crafts materials. Most of the organized activities last 60–90 minutes, so a new event will likely start soon after your child arrives; this means kids become part of the group quickly.

Reservations are required at the nurseries, but they're not needed at the kids' clubs for children ages 3 and up. Once you've registered your kids at the club, you can drop them off there as little or as often as you like, with no need to let anyone know in advance. It's an incredibly flexible system that allows for a great deal of vacation spontaneity.

Much like the Disney theme parks, the DCL ships offer a contained environment that gives tweens and teens some autonomy to roam on their own. The texting function of the DCL Navigator app means you'll always be able to reach your children, and the free food on the pool deck and at the buffet means there's no worrying about finding something to eat or how to pay for it.

Children with separation-anxiety issues may resist going to the clubs, but based on our reader surveys, most kids love them and don't want to leave. That said, there's plenty for children and families to do away from the clubs. Activities from karaoke to character appearances are scheduled throughout the day (see the previous section); check the Navigator app for times and locations. Other recreational opportunities include minigolf (*Dream* and *Fantasy*) and the sports areas, all topside.

We provide profiles of DCL's nurseries and kids' clubs starting on page 272, organized by ship and ordered from the youngest to oldest age groups.

DCL YOUTH CLUBS IN BRIEF

IT'S A SMALL WORLD NURSERY

- **LOCATION** Deck 5 Aft (all ships except the *Wish*), Deck 2 Midship (*Wish*)
- **AGES** 6 or 12 months (depends on itinerary)-3 years
- **FEE** $9/hour for first child, $8/hour for each additional child
- **MEALS** Bring your own food, milk, and formula

OCEANEER CLUB/OCEANEER LAB

- **LOCATION** Deck 5 Midship (all ships except the *Wish*). On the *Wish,* the Oceaneer Club is on Deck 2 Midship. The check-in desk is on Deck 3—kids can access the main club from here via a secret slide.
- **AGES** 3-12 years • **FEE** None • **MEALS** Lunch and dinner

EDGE

- **LOCATION** Deck 9 Midship (*Magic, Wonder*), Deck 13 Forward (*Dream, Fantasy*), Deck 2 Midship (*Wish*)
- **AGES** 11-14 years • **FEE** None • **MEALS** None

VIBE

- **LOCATION** Deck 11 Midship (*Magic, Wonder*), Deck 5 Forward (*Dream, Fantasy*), Deck 12 Aft (*Wish*)
- **AGES** 14-17 years • **FEE** None
- **REFRESHMENTS** Sodas (free), smoothies (extra charge)
- **EXTRAS** Sun deck with splash pools (*Dream, Fantasy*)

Kids' Club Open Houses

The kids' clubs hold several open-house sessions during each sailing. During open houses, families may use the clubs' facilities together, making this the perfect time to, say, dance on the Magic Floor with your son or play some PS5 Mario Kart with your daughter.

unofficial **TIP**
Parents aren't allowed in the kids' clubs during regular hours.

Open houses are especially good for kids who aren't ready to separate from their parents, kids who are slightly too young or too old for a particular club, and children with special needs that make them ineligible to go to the clubs alone.

Special Considerations

INFANTS Babies must be 6 months of age or older to sail on most Alaskan, Bahamian, Caribbean, and other cruises of seven nights or fewer. On some longer cruises, often those with multiple consecutive sea days (such as the Transatlantic crossings), DCL requires that children be at least 1 year old to sail.

TWEENS AND TEENS Based on both our own experiences and those of other parents, teens will practically forget you exist once they get a feel for the clubs and activities. In fact, before you even set foot on the ship, you should set some ground rules for how often your teen needs to check in with you. Our rule was that everyone had to eat two meals per day together during sea days and stay together during shore excursions. On Castaway Cay, we reserved morning activities for family time, and the teens were allowed to explore the island on their own after lunch.

ONLY-CHILD SITUATIONS The clubs for middle school/high school–age kids are seamless for tweens and teens who are traveling with similarly aged siblings, cousins, or friends: they have built-in companions for activities and can sample the club offerings at will, with no fear of being the odd kid out. But for a middle-schooler or teen who's an only child—or, as in the following instance, the only sibling on the cruise—the clubs can be more challenging.

One of Erin's teen daughters was completely fine joining in the introductory games during the Sail-Away Celebration, where the fun was orchestrated by a counselor. Several other times, however, she dropped in at Vibe and found just a few kids who had already formed friend groups. Thus, Erin's normally outgoing daughter had trouble breaking into the onboard teen social scene.

More recently, Erin traveled with a party that included a teen girl named Willow King, who ran into a similar situation at Vibe, with the kids seeming to have found their tribes already. In this case, Willow took the bold step of introducing herself and saying, "Hey, I don't know anybody here yet—can I hang out with you guys?"

Huge props to Willow for putting herself out there: as it turned out, most of the kids she met hadn't known each other either before the cruise, and they were happy to add her to their newly formed squad.

The only times Erin and her family saw Willow after that (except for family dinners) were when she was hanging with a group of six or seven other teens at the pool, the movie theater, and so on.

Many teens who've sailed on DCL observe that the so-called single kids who do best at Vibe are the ones who take the initiative to participate in as many activities as possible, increasing their opportunities for bonding with the group. On previous cruises when Erin's teen daughter had sailed without her sister, she had preferred activities geared to families, stepping into the club only sporadically—and that made it harder for her to click with the other kids.

ACTIVE KIDS As a parent, you're the best judge of how much physical activity your child needs. We've rarely seen truly bad behavior on the DCL ships, but when we have, it's usually been an active child running wild after sitting in passive activities all day.

To ensure that your kids burn off their excess energy in a positive way, keep an eye out for ways to add physical activity to their day, particularly if you're spending several consecutive days at sea. The pool and

A TEEN CRUISER'S TAKE ON KIDS' CLUBS

SEVENTEEN-YEAR-OLD CRUISE BLOGGER **Kieran Sweeney** shares his thoughts on DCL's youth clubs.

THE YOUTH CLUBS have always been among my favorite features of the DCL ships. The combination of exciting activities and excellent counselors makes the clubs a great place to be.

The clubs have a variety of scheduled recreation that appeals to many interests. Check the Navigator app to find card tournaments, trivia competitions, improv games, art activities, video game challenges, and more. There's a nice balance between diversions that are team-based and those you can engage in on your own. At Edge and Vibe, some activities, such as scavenger hunts, even allow teams to leave the clubs to explore the ship together.

While the counselors are normally the only adults in the clubs, they're not babysitters. They're companions in the fun, starting conversations and playing games with us. It often feels like they're just other kids.

Most of the kids' club counselors I've encountered have learned my name very early in the cruise and greeted me whenever I entered, making me feel welcome in a place where I know almost nobody. That feeling of knowing nobody doesn't last for long, though—the clubs make it very easy to meet new people and make new friends. Icebreaker events are typically held at the start of a cruise, and they're a great way to get to know the peers you'll be seeing throughout the trip. Also, by participating in activities that appeal to you, you'll meet others who share the same interests.

The end of a cruise is always sad, but the friendships you make can continue long after the cruise ends!

sports deck are obvious solutions, but these may sometimes be unavailable due to weather or temporary maintenance issues. Speak with the kids' club counselors about which activities have the most opportunity for movement—for example, onboard dance parties that are happening during your sailing.

USING THE KIDS' CLUBS WHEN YOU'RE OFF THE SHIP Guests are welcome to use the kids' clubs whenever they're open, including when the ship is in port. Using the clubs in this situation can play out in a number of ways. You might, for example, choose to leave your sand-phobic 6-year-old on the ship for an hour while you're a 10-minute walk away on Castaway Cay.

At the other end of the spectrum, Erin met another cruiser during an 11-hour-long excursion in Rome while the ship was docked in Civitavecchia, Italy, a 90-minute drive away. The guest had left her 7-year-old daughter at the kids' club because she knew the girl would be bored with the long ride and sightseeing. Since this mom had been saving for years to make her cruise happen and visiting Rome was a lifelong dream for her, letting her daughter hang out at the kids' club was a win–win for them.

If you do decide to leave your child on the ship for an extended period of time, communicate your plans to the counselors at the club and possibly also to Guest Relations. Let them know where you'll be, when you'll return, your cell number, and any pertinent medical information, along with contact information for the child's home medical providers and other emergency contacts.

> *unofficial* **TIP**
> Keep your passport with you at all times. In the unlikely event that you get left behind at the port, having your passport handy will help expedite your reunion with your child.

The kids' club could be a real boon if you're traveling with an unvaccinated child and you want to explore a country where unvaxxed cruise-ship passengers aren't allowed to debark. Keep in mind, though, that you may be better served by taking a Disney port adventure than by booking your own shore excursion (see Part Twelve). In the event that you encounter delays in getting back to the ship, chances are that the crew will wait a few extra minutes for a large group on a DCL port adventure versus a lone guest on a third-party excursion.

KIDS' CLUBS IN DEPTH

Nurseries

All Disney ships have **It's a Small World Nursery,** which operates by reservation and charges an hourly rate for services. Rates are $9 an hour for the first child and $8 an hour for each additional child in the same family, with a 1-hour minimum. Parents should bring their own milk, formula, and baby food, along with diapers and wipes, a change of clothes, and a blanket and pacifier (if their child needs those to nap).

Space is typically limited at each nursery; reservations are required and are first come, first served, as detailed on the following page:

- **Concierge guests** (page 105) can make reservations **130 days** in advance.
- **Platinum Castaway Club members** (page 85) can make reservations **120 days** in advance.
- **Gold Castaway Club members** can make reservations **105 days** in advance.
- **Silver Castaway Club members** can make reservations **90 days** in advance.
- **All other guests** can make reservations **75 days** out.

unofficial **TIP**
A fee of 50% of the cost of your nursery booking applies if you cancel a reservation less than 4 hours before your scheduled time to drop off your child. No-showing or arriving more than 30 minutes late will result in both a cancellation charge and losing the reservation.

If you haven't made reservations by the time you board the ship, either stop by before dinner or call from your stateroom: ☎ **7-5864** on the *Magic, Dream,* and *Fantasy;* ☎ **7-18500** on the *Wonder;* and ☎ **7-1439** on the *Wish.*

Hours vary, especially when the ship is in port, but on most sea days the nurseries are open 9 a.m.–11 p.m.; they sometimes open during late afternoon/early evening on the first day of a cruise.

Note that the nurseries take child health very seriously. Kids who show signs of a contagious illness—fever, a runny nose, or the like—must be picked up by their parents immediately and may not return to the nursery unless cleared to do so by the ship's medical staff.

Youth Clubs

Most of DCL's children's activities take place at the youth clubs (aka kids' clubs) on the ships. They're organized by age group, as follows:

- **Oceaneer Club** and **Oceaneer Lab** for children ages 3–12
- **Edge** for kids ages 11–14 • **Vibe** for kids ages 14–17

Children in the following age groups may choose which club they wish to participate in: 3-year-olds may choose the nursery or (as long as they're potty-trained) the Oceaneer Club/Lab; 11- and 12-year-olds may choose between the Oceaneer Club/Lab and Edge; and 14-year-olds may choose between Edge and Vibe. This flexibility is helpful when siblings who are close in age want to be in the same club.

unofficial **TIP**
If you forget to return your child's wristband to the kids' club at the end of your sailing, a $12.95-per-band charge will be added to your final stateroom bill. You'll be issued a receipt when you return the wristband, so hang on to this in case you get charged for a missing band by mistake.

Once a choice is made, however, it may not be changed. Disney is also strict about making sure that kids stick to the club for their age group—that means, for example, no sneaking into Vibe if they're not old enough or if they're even slightly too old.

Kids in the nurseries, the Oceaneer Club, and the Oceaneer Lab are required to wear a wristband while they're on the premises, and their parents' contact information is recorded. The wristbands look like the MagicBands in use at Walt Disney World, but they work differently. When a child enters the kids' club, the band is secured to his or her wrist or ankle. The fastener mechanism, easily visible to the staff, is color-coded: a red fastener, for instance, alerts counselors to a food or other allergy.

Door sensors at each club trigger an alarm if a child tries to leave without a parent on hand to deactivate the wristband. If the staff needs to contact you, they'll text you on the Navigator app. Kids ages 8–12 may check themselves out of the clubs with a parent's permission.

Tweens and teens registered at Edge and Vibe (ages 11–17) are free to come and go as they please—no check-in or checkout is necessary. If your kids get bored, they may leave to visit a character greeting, go to the pool, grab a snack, go back to the room, or just roam around. (They *won't* be allowed to leave the ship without a supervising adult, unless you've specifically completed a special form allowing them to do so.)

*un*official **TIP**
My Disney Cruise Adventure is a printable guide for kids (see tinyurl.com/MyDCL Adventure). Simple language helps explain what happens during the boarding process and on the ship. Parties traveling with some special-needs teens or adults may also find this helpful.

For some kids, this is an unprecedented amount of freedom, which may cause discomfort for the parent or child. Other children relish the opportunity to have a little more ownership of their time on the ship. In either circumstance, it's a good idea to set ground rules for your kids about notifying you where they are. This might mean periodic texts or leaving a note in your stateroom.

Parents can sign up their children either before boarding and after completing online check-in (see page 69) or on embarkation day during one of the clubs' open houses (see page 271). Once a child is registered for a club, he or she may use its facilities for the entire cruise.

Some activities, such as video games and crafts, are generally available anytime. Throughout each day there are also planned themed activities, which will be noted in the Navigator app (also see "What Goes On in a Kids' Club?," page 280). Most of the listed activities are self-explanatory; others, however, are more cryptic.

Case in point: we'd been wondering for years what "4th Pig's Pasta Palace" at the Oceaneer Club/Lab was until we were finally clued in by *Unofficial Guide* reader Lori Ketcherside:

> In the 4th Pig's Pasta Palace, the fourth pig (in addition to the original Three Little Pigs) uses science to test different options for building his home. This involves using macaroni to create houses that will withstand damage when bumped, hit, or dropped.

This sounds awesome, but there's no way we would have figured out what it was from the title alone. Lori adds:

> My daughter loves it, but when my son was on a gluten-free diet, he couldn't participate for fear that he would put one of the pasta pieces in his mouth. He never felt left out, though, because they always had other special projects for kids with food allergies.

Her comments here are a good reminder for families with special diets to double-check what's happening with food during all activities on the ship. (See Part Five, page 153, and Part Seven, page 194, for more information.)

Additionally, parents of older children with food allergies will want to make sure they're adept at advocating for their own needs. Ben Lawrence-Comerford, a tween friend of ours who's a veteran of several DCL sailings, tells us that one of the main things he liked about making the transition from the Oceaneer Club to Edge was that in the latter club, kids are allowed to bring in their own food and beverages to consume while they're hanging out—this is forbidden in the younger childrens' spaces.

The *Magic*'s Youth Clubs

It's a Small World Nursery   LOCATION   Deck 5 Aft

OVERVIEW This is the *Magic*'s onboard nursery for infants and toddlers ages 6 months–3 years. (On some longer sailings, DCL requires children to be 12 months of age or older.) Trained staff play with the children throughout the day. Unlike the activities at the clubs for older kids and teens, activities at the nursery are unstructured but may include movies, story time, crafts, and occasional visits from Disney characters.

DESCRIPTION AND COMMENTS Too cute. Decorated with brilliantly colored murals inspired by the art of Mary Blair, the Disney animator who designed It's a Small World at Disneyland and Walt Disney World, the nursery is cleverly divided into three sections. Up front is the "acclimation zone," a welcome area where kids can get used to their surroundings; this leads to a long, narrow, rectangular, brightly lit play area, off of which is a darkened, quiet room for naps. The play area is stocked with pint-size activities, including a playground slide on a padded floor, a small basketball hoop, plenty of leg-powered riding vehicles, play mats with large toys, and adorable miniature crafts tables that you'd swear came from the Lilliput IKEA. A one-way mirror lets parents check up on their tots discreetly. (*Tip:* If your little one has a known fear of costumed characters, alert the nursery staff so they can take your child to a different room in case any characters stop by.)

At the far end of the nursery is the resting room, with several cribs and glider chairs. Murals in soothing blues and golds adorn the walls. This room is kept dark most of the day, and the staff ensures that activities in the main room happen far enough away that noise isn't a problem. Just outside are a sink and changing area.

ACROSS THE SHIPS All DCL ships have It's a Small World Nurseries. With only slight differences in configuration, they're substantially the same.

Oceaneer Club and Oceaneer Lab   LOCATION   Deck 5 Midship

OVERVIEW The Oceaneer Club and Oceaneer Lab are connected spaces that host the 3- to 12-year-old set. Activities for older kids usually take place in the Lab and are often educational or participatory in nature (such as cooking demonstrations or science experiments). Younger children's programs are generally held in the Club and include story time, character appearances, and movement activities. Disney designates 7 as the border age for the Club and Lab and provides details in the Navigator app about each area's different activity tracks. During open houses, one side remains open for activities while the other side is open to the public. Lunch and dinner are provided during times of normal operation.

Parents must check kids up to age 7 in and out of the club. With their parents' permission, 8- to 12-year-olds may check themselves in and out—just designate your preference when you register your kids.

DESCRIPTION AND COMMENTS The Oceaneer Club and Lab are separate areas connected by a short private hallway, allowing children to go from Lab to Club and back. Besides providing kids twice as much space, this arrangement separates younger and older children while giving siblings of different ages the chance to stay in contact.

The Oceaneer Club consists of four distinct sections branching off from a central "library" decorated with oversize children's books and outfitted with a huge high-definition TV for movie screenings. **Andy's Room** is *Toy Story*–themed and is for smaller children. Its main feature is a tall, circular, gentle playground slide in the shape of Slinky Dog. There's also a large pink Hamm (the piggy bank) sitting in the middle of the play floor, and a giant Mr. Potato Head with equally large plug-in pieces, all scattered about.

Club Disney Junior, the second themed room, serves as the Oceaneer Club's primary activity center. The grass-green carpet is surrounded by sky-blue walls painted with clouds. The room has a large video screen on one wall and sturdy kid-size furniture in bold colors.

Club Disney Junior connects to both Andy's Room and **Marvel Avengers Academy,** where you'll find Thor's hammer, Captain America's shield, and a life-size Iron Man suit, as well as another video screen and computer collection. Avengers Academy activities follow a multiday story in which kids embark on a recruitment experience that has them team up with various Avengers, meet Captain America, and suit up like Iron Man to battle the evil Red Skull.

Opposite Marvel Avengers Academy is **Pixie Hollow,** a Tinker Bell–themed dress-up and play area with costumes, an activity table, and a few computer terminals with themed games.

The Oceaneer Lab is done in a 19th-century nautical theme, with lots of exposed woods, red leather chairs, navigation maps, and sailors' tools. More than a third of the space consists of one long room, filled with kid-size tables and stools, which serves as the primary area for arts and crafts. At the far end of this space is a set of computer terminals.

Next to the crafts space, in the middle of the Lab, is a large screen for watching movies. Facing the screen is a collection of comfortable beanbags. Finally, the left side of the Lab is a set of small rooms. A couple have computer terminals or video-game consoles; one is a smaller crafts room, and another is an animation studio where kids can learn to draw Disney characters and create their own computer animations.

ACROSS THE SHIPS All DCL ships have an Oceaneer Club/Lab. On the *Dream* and the *Fantasy,* the Club is also subdivided into themed areas, but they differ somewhat from those on the *Magic.* The Lab has a similar nautical theme and layout but is distinguished by a central **Magic Floor,** composed of individual video screens surrounded by foot-operated touch pads and used to play different interactive games.

The *Wonder* Club/Lab's play areas are **Marvel Super Hero Academy** (which is slightly different from the *Magic's* Avengers Academy), **Andy's Room, Club Disney Junior** (here an area for storytelling and games), and *Frozen* **Adventures** (for play related to everybody's favorite fake Scandinavian country, Arendelle).

The Oceaneer Club on the *Wish* consists of several zones: **Fairytale Hall** for story time and crafts, the **Imagineering Lab** for educational games and science experiments (plus a roller-coaster simulation machine), *Star Wars* **Cargo Bay** and the **Marvel Super Hero Academy** for play related to these entertainment franchises, and **Mickey & Minnie Captain's Deck** play space for young children. There is no distinction between Club and Lab on the *Wish:* each space can be configured for any age group.

Edge   LOCATION Deck 9 Midship

OVERVIEW Tweens and early teens rule at Edge. Unlike at the Oceaneer Club/Lab, kids can come and go as they please. Activities range from drawing and cooking classes to scavenger hunts and computer games. Parents may be surprised to see things scheduled past midnight on some nights.

DESCRIPTION AND COMMENTS The Edge is the rec room of your kids' dreams. There are sections for electronic gaming, active play, and lounging. You'll see both a high-tech zone and comfy couches. Kids can move freely between both.

Edge is likely to be the first of the youth clubs in which the staff will treat your kids as peers to interact with rather than as children to be supervised. The staff generally does a great job of getting to know each child and will even compete in games alongside the kids. If you ever want to feel old and slow, watch the cup-stacking competition, where the object is to stack and unstack a pyramid of 15 plastic cups as quickly as possible. Some kids can do both in less than 10 seconds total.

ACROSS THE SHIPS All DCL ships have an Edge. The amenities, layout, and decor of Edge on the *Magic* are more or less the same as those of Edge on the *Wonder.* On the *Dream* and the *Fantasy,* Edge is inside the ships' (nonfunctioning) smokestack. The design and atmosphere are ultramodern and high-tech, compared with the homier feel of Edge on the *Magic* and the *Wonder.* Edge on the *Wish* on is an eclectic mix of stylized country comfort (a carpet depicting grass and daisies) and big kids' playhouse (books about Imagineering, displays of vintage Vinylmations and Pez dispensers).

Vibe   LOCATION Deck 11 Midship

OVERVIEW Vibe is one of the coolest spots on the *Magic.* Counselors lead the activities—dance parties, karaoke, group games, and the like—but teens are given plenty of autonomy. Parents should note that the only curfew for teens on board is whatever one they impose themselves. One rule of note that's strictly enforced: no public displays of affection.

DESCRIPTION AND COMMENTS Vibe sits up a flight of stairs in the ship's forward smokestack, but your teens probably won't mind the climb. Inside is a two-story-tall lounge with exposed brick walls, leather furniture, and a smoothie bar. We think there should be a Vibe for adults.

ACROSS THE SHIPS Amenities are comparable in the four Vibes across the DCL fleet, though Vibe on the *Dream* and *Fantasy* is larger and has a truly special outdoor pool area just for teens. The *Wonder*'s Vibe was updated just before the pandemic shutdown, so everything there is fresh and spiffy.

Vibe on the *Wish* features pillars decorated with travel posters, lots of abstract art on the walls, video games and movie stations, Foosball, couches for conversation, a soda cooler, and a coffee machine. The back third of the room can be closed and separated from the main space to become **The Hideaway,** a dedicated hangout for guests ages 18–20.

The *Wonder*'s Youth Clubs

It's a Small World Nursery   LOCATION   Deck 5 Aft

COMMENTS See the profile of It's a Small World Nursery on the *Magic* (page 272) for details.

Oceaneer Club and Oceaneer Lab   LOCATION   Deck 5 Midship

OVERVIEW See the profile of Oceaneer Club and Oceaneer Lab on the *Magic* (page 272) for details.

DESCRIPTION AND COMMENTS **Marvel Super Hero Academy** is an interactive play area where children can train to be superheroes and interact with current stars of the Marvel family; Spider-Man makes regular appearances. Artifacts on display in this area include Captain America's World War II shield, Iron Man's helmet, Spider-Man's web shooters, and Black Widow's gauntlets.

Other Oceaneer spaces include the *Frozen* **Adventures** area for creative and interactive play. A key feature of the *Frozen* zone is a digital screen where an animated Olaf leads games and songs; character experiences include the requisite visits by Anna and Elsa. **Club Disney Junior** offers storytelling and games featuring *Disney Junior* characters, including Doc McStuffins. **Andy's Room** is a *Toy Story*–themed play zone with larger-than-life toys to romp on.

ACROSS THE SHIPS All DCL ships have an Oceaneer Club/Lab. On the *Dream* and the *Fantasy,* the Club is also subdivided into themed areas, but they differ somewhat from those on the *Magic* and *Wonder.* In addition, the Lab on the two newer ships has a central **Magic Floor,** composed of individual video screens surrounded by foot-operated touch pads and used to play different interactive games.

The Oceaneer Club on the *Wish* consists of several zones: **Fairytale Hall** for story time and crafts, the **Imagineering Lab** for educational games and science experiments (plus a roller-coaster simulation machine), *Star Wars* **Cargo Bay** and the **Marvel Super Hero Academy** for play related to these entertainment franchises, and **Mickey & Minnie Captain's Deck** play space for young children. There is no distinction between Club and Lab on the *Wish:* each space can be configured for any age group.

Edge   LOCATION   Deck 9 Midship

COMMENTS See previous page for details.

Vibe   LOCATION   Deck 11 Midship

COMMENTS See previous page for details.

The *Dream's* and *Fantasy's* Youth Clubs

It's a Small World Nursery   LOCATION Deck 5 Aft

COMMENTS See the profile of It's a Small World Nursery on the *Magic* (see page 272) for details.

Oceaneer Club and Oceaneer Lab   LOCATION Deck 5 Midship

OVERVIEW See the profile of Oceaneer Club and Oceaneer Lab on the *Magic* (page 272) for details.

DESCRIPTION AND COMMENTS The Oceaneer Lab and Club are separate areas connected by a short private hallway, allowing children to go from Lab to Club and back. Besides providing kids twice as much space, this arrangement separates younger and older children while giving siblings of different ages the chance to stay in contact.

The Oceaneer Club consists of four distinct sections branching off from a central rotunda painted royal blue; on the ceiling are "constellations" of Disney characters made up of small, twinkling electric lights. **Andy's Room** is *Toy Story*–themed and intended for smaller children. There's a crawl-through tube—think a Habitrail for humans—in the shape of Slinky Dog, along with a giant pink Hamm (the piggy bank) sitting in the middle of the play floor, and a large Mr. Potato Head with equally large plug-in pieces, all invariably scattered about.

The next area is **Pixie Hollow,** a Tinker Bell–themed dress-up and play area with costumes, an activity table, and a few computer terminals with themed games. The *Dream* and *Fantasy* Oceaneer Clubs both have **Star Wars–themed immersive play areas;** on the *Dream,* it's a life-size *Millennium Falcon,* and on the *Fantasy* it's a "Command Post" holo-table where kids can train with X-Wing pilots. The *Falcon* on the *Dream* lets kids pilot a remarkably well-done simulator (yep, it goes into hyperspeed) and participate in a shipboard version of the **Jedi Training** audience-participation show at Walt Disney World's Hollywood Studios. Adult guests can take a turn in the captain's seat of the *Falcon* during regular club open-house times (check the Navigator app for details). Wearing a black vest and knee-high boots is completely optional.

The Oceaneer Lab is done in a 19th-century nautical theme, with lots of exposed woods, red leather chairs, navigation maps, sailors' tools, and inlaid images of sea horses and compasses on the floor. The main hall features a celestial map on the ceiling and a huge **Magic Floor,** composed of 16 high-definition video screens surrounded by foot-powered touch pads and used to play interactive games. (If you remember the giant piano from the movie *Big,* you get the idea.)

Surrounding the main hall are the **Media Lounge,** for relaxing and watching movies; the **Animator's Studio,** where kids can learn to draw Disney characters and create digital animations; **The Wheelhouse,** with computer stations and interactive games; the **Explorer's Room,** where kids can learn about ships and the sea; and the **Craft Studio.**

ACROSS THE SHIPS All DCL ships have an Oceaneer Club/Lab. On the *Magic* and *Wonder,* the Club is subdivided into themed areas, but they differ somewhat from those on the *Dream* and *Fantasy;* also, the Lab on the two older ships is missing the nifty interactive floor.

The Oceaneer Club on the *Wish* consists of several zones: **Fairytale Hall** for story time and crafts, the **Imagineering Lab** for educational games and science experiments (plus a roller-coaster simulation machine), ***Star Wars Cargo Bay*** and the **Marvel Super Hero Academy** for play related to these entertainment franchises, and **Mickey & Minnie Captain's Deck** play space for young children. There is no distinction between Club and Lab on the *Wish:* each space can be configured for any age group.

Edge   LOCATION Deck 13 Forward

OVERVIEW See the profile of Edge on the *Magic* (see page 274) for details.
DESCRIPTION AND COMMENTS Built into the *Dream*'s and *Fantasy*'s forward (nonfunctioning) smokestack, Edge has an open layout and a clean 21st-century feel. The walls are papered in a geometric Mickey-head design. The centerpiece of the space is a huge video wall, more than 18 feet wide and nearly 5 feet tall. Across from it are tables with built-in screens for playing interactive games, surrounded by bright-red seating that looks like something out of *The Jetsons;* behind those are cubbyholes outfitted with flat-screen TVs and Wii consoles. Next to the game tables are an illuminated dance floor (think *Saturday Night Fever*) and a lounge area with beanbags arranged next to floor-to-ceiling windows. On the other side of the video wall are laptop stations loaded with video games and an onboard social media app.

Edge is likely to be the first of the youth clubs in which the staff will treat your kids as peers to interact with rather than as children to be supervised. The staff generally does a great job of getting to know each child and getting in on the fun.
ACROSS THE SHIPS All DCL ships have an Edge. On the *Magic* and *Wonder,* it has a totally different layout and atmosphere—more like a cozy family rec room than a high-tech hangout. Edge on the *Wish* on is an eclectic mix of stylized country comfort (a carpet depicting grass and daisies) and big kids' playhouse (books about Imagineering, displays of vintage Vinylmations and Pez dispensers).

Vibe   LOCATION Deck 5 Forward

OVERVIEW See the profile of Vibe on the *Magic* (see page 274) for details.
DESCRIPTION AND COMMENTS Up a flight of stairs from Deck 4 to Deck 5 Forward and accessed through a neon-lit hallway, Vibe has a decidedly adult look and feel—if you didn't know better, you'd think you were in a trendy urban nightspot. The central indoor gathering spot is the theater-cum–TV lounge, accented with soft pink neon lighting and featuring a 103-inch television. Two rows of couches are arranged in a semicircle in front of the screen; giant throw pillows scattered on the floor make for additional places to lounge. Behind the couches and built into the rear wall are a row of pod-like, porthole-shaped nooks for playing video games, watching videos, or hooking up an electronic device. Just off the row of pods is a smoothie bar; ultramodern stools with low, curved backs; and white banquette seating.

Off the TV lounge is another sleek space for socializing. The walls are covered in alternating black-and-silver horizontal bars. Black leather-look benches line the walls; next to those are retro-mod tables and chairs arranged nightclub-style. Video-game booths stand nearby. Across from the seating area are a dance floor and DJ booth, a karaoke stage, and another large video screen.

The main attraction, though, lies outside. The **Vibe Splash Zone** is a private deck with two splash pools, chaise longues, sets of tables and chairs, and recessed seating. Furnishings and decor share the same ultramod style as the indoor spaces.

ACROSS THE SHIPS All DCL ships have a Vibe. On the *Magic* and the *Wonder,* Vibe is dramatically different but just as cool. Built into the ships' forward smokestack, the two-story-tall lounge features brick walls and leather furniture. It looks more like the lounge at a college student center than something you'd find on a cruise ship

Vibe on the *Wish* features pillars decorated with travel posters, lots of abstract art on the walls, video games and movie stations, Foosball, couches for conversation, a soda cooler, and a coffee machine. The back third of the room can be closed and separated from the main space to become **The Hideaway,** a dedicated hangout for guests ages 18–20

The *Wish*'s Youth Clubs
It's a Small World Nursery   LOCATION Deck 5 Aft

COMMENTS See the profile of It's a Small World Nursery on the *Magic* (see page 272) for details.

Oceaneer Club   LOCATION Deck 2 Midship (club), Deck 3 Midship (check-in)

OVERVIEW Disney calls the largest youth space on the *Wish* "Oceaneer Club" rather than breaking it out into a Club and a Lab. The fun starts right at the entry: kids access the club via a secret slide located in the Grand Hall atrium. (Adults can use the slide, too, during open-house hours. Be careful, though: the trip down is faster than it looks.)

The Oceaneer Club is the crown jewel of the *Wish*'s kids' spaces. Its massive size and attention to detail, are breathtaking. Our only criticism is that a significant number of the interactive elements involve complicated technology that could be prone to downtime. (A roller-coaster simulator we loved on the ship's maiden voyage, for example, was glitchy on the very next sailing.)

DESCRIPTION AND COMMENTS The Oceaneer Club on the *Wish* consists of five areas. At **Marvel Super Hero Academy,** young "recruits" will train to be the next generation of superheroes with help from Marvel favorites like Spider-Man, Black Panther, Ant-Man, and The Wasp. **Fairytale Hall** is a trio of Disney princess–themed activity rooms. Kids can explore their creativity in Rapunzel's Art Studio, read and act out stories at Belle's Library, or test their icy princess powers at Anna & Elsa's Sommerhus. **Walt Disney Imagineering Lab** is a first-of-its-kind opportunity for kids to discover the secrets of world-renowned Disney Imagineers—the creative masterminds behind Disney's theme parks, resorts, and cruise ships—with hands-on activities and experiments.

Star Wars: **Cargo Bay** teaches kids to be "creature handlers" as they manage and care for exotic beings from all corners of the galaxy, including Porgs, Loth-cats, and Worrts. During this experience, kids use augmented-reality datapads and also participate in a mission involving Rey and Chewbacca. The fifth area, **Mickey and Minnie's Captain's Deck,** is a playground-like area designed for the youngest Oceaneer guests. The space includes nautically themed slides, crawl-throughs, busy boxes, and other interactive and physical activities. Offered here on some days, Minnie's Captain Academy includes a series of age-appropriate STEAM learning challenges and visits from Captain Minnie.

Cast members have the ability to open up and close off any room to segregate groups by age or interest as needed. In addition, some adult character greetings take place in the Marvel and *Star Wars* rooms when these spaces aren't being used by kids.

ACROSS THE SHIPS The Oceaneer Club and Lab on Disney's first four ships have close equivalents to the Marvel and Fairytale spaces on the *Wish*. We're excited to see the Imagineering Lab raise kids' clubs to a new level.

Edge   LOCATION Deck 13 Forward

OVERVIEW See the profile of Edge on the *Magic* (see page 274) for details.

DESCRIPTION AND COMMENTS Edge's design aesthetic on the *Wish* is "eclectic treehouse." Finishes on the walls simulate exposed brick, weathered steel, and poured concrete—sometimes within the space of a few feet. Side tables are built to resemble tree trunks; carpets feature neon checkerboards and fields of daisies.

One side room is dedicated to video games; the central area has a soda and smoothie bar, as well as a giant movie screen. The far end of the room has more game consoles, as well as tables for crafts and board games. The bookshelves are stocked with books on the art behind Disney and Pixar films, including *The Art of Encanto.* Tchotchkes on the shelves include vintage Disney Pez dispensers and an assortment of 9-inch Vinylmation figurines.

ACROSS THE SHIPS All DCL ships have an Edge. On the *Magic* and *Wonder,* it feels like a cozy family rec room; on the *Dream* and *Fantasy,* it's a high-tech hangout.

Vibe   LOCATION Deck 5 Forward

OVERVIEW See the profile of Vibe on the *Magic* (see page 274) for details.

DESCRIPTION AND COMMENTS Vibe on the *Wish* evokes a modern-art collective. Pillars are decorated with posters of Parisian landmarks and splashes of dripping paint. Several walls are adorned with graphic art or painted in bold colors that make excellent backdrops for selfies. Much like Edge, Vibe has areas for video games, movies, board games, crafts, and snacking. One third of the room can be closed off to become **The Hideaway** (see below).

ACROSS THE SHIPS All DCL ships have a Vibe. A key difference between the Vibe on the *Dream* and *Fantasy* versus the *Magic* and *Wonder* is that the former two boast an entire pool deck just for teens.

The Hideaway   LOCATION Deck 12 Aft

OVERVIEW Unique to the *Wish,* The Hideaway is an area of Vibe that can be configured just for young adults.

DESCRIPTION AND COMMENTS This hangout offers a place for young people to relax, listen to music, and more in a stylish setting, complete with a dance floor and DJ booth. The Hideaway is decorated in a vibrant color palette with retro-inspired design details. Configured as a multipurpose space, this flexible venue can be opened to expand Vibe's footprint, closed off for tween activities, or reserved exclusively for the use of guests ages 18–20.

ACROSS THE SHIPS The Hideaway is unique to the *Wish.*

WHAT GOES ON IN A KIDS' CLUB?

IN ADDITION TO FREE PLAY, the kids' clubs offer a range of age-appropriate structured activities, from the creative to the competitive. If your kids prefer directed activity to self-initiated play, keep a careful eye on the DCL Navigator app, which lists the times and short descriptions of planned activities at the Oceaneer Club/Lab, Edge, and Vibe. Here's a small sampling of what may be available on your sailing.

OCEANEER CLUB/LAB (Ages 3–12)

- **Animation Antics** Discover the history of animation, draw Disney characters and create a flipbook to take home.
- **Anyone Can Cook: Cookies** Inspired by the film *Ratatouille,* kids will learn how to mix and measure ingredients before baking up a batch of chocolate chip cookies.
- **Craft Corner** It's time to get creative and put your crafty skills to use!
- **Get the Hook!** Join Detective Clue for a search that leads kids from one "crime scene" to the next—catch the culprit and collect a reward from the captain.
- *Monsters, Inc.* **Open "Mike" Night** Help Mike Wazowski and the gang rescue Monstropolis by putting on a comedy show and collecting enough laughter to power the town.
- **Piston Cup Challenge** Build race cars from bars of soap. (Based on Disney's *Cars.*)
- **Super Sloppy Science** Join Professor Make-O-Mess in some of the most extreme experiments you'll ever see.
- **Wacky Relays** Show off your wacky skills in some of the wackiest races at sea.

EDGE (Ages 11–14)

- **Animation Cels** Learn what it takes to be a Disney animator, then put your skills to the test as you create your very own animation cel.
- **Crowning of the Couch Potato** Do you think you know your movies, TV, and commercials? Well, it's time to test your knowledge.
- **Foosball Tournament** Show us your Foosball skills and see who's the best of the best.
- **Heroes and Villains** Put your athleticism and intellect to the test. Teams compete to solve clues, complete challenges, and win a final prize.
- **Pathfinders** A path has been chosen for you. Can you find it?
- **A Pirate's Life for Me** Compete in physical challenges, and answer trivia questions about scalawags and buccaneers of yore.
- **Scattergories** See who can think of the most creative answers.
- **That's Hilarious** Ever wanted to show off your comedy skills? Then be a part of the cast for this crazy improv show.

VIBE (Ages 14–17)

- **Dream Now! Sea How!: Animal, Science, and Environment** In an interactive session, you'll dive into the background, education, and mentors that sent animal-care workers into their profession.
- **Gotcha!** Armed with a code name and an arsenal of "gotcha" methods, teens spend the day tagging out their competition throughout the ship in creative and cunning ways.
- **Ice Cream Social** Make your own frosty treat with your counselors.
- **Teen Download** Using media technology, interact with other teens and counselors to design your dream vacation—filled with activities, games, Port Adventures, and downtime.
- **Vibe Movie Makers** Learn moviemaking skills to create a film to show your family at the end of the cruise.

Additionally, counselors at Edge and Vibe may take kids in groups to the all-ages performances, game shows, or other events on board.

OTHER KIDS' ACTIVITIES ON BOARD

On the *Magic* and *Wonder*

Many activities take place in **Promenade Lounge** (*Magic*) or **French Quarter Lounge** (*Wonder*) on Deck 3 Aft, including the following:

• *Playhouse Disney* Dance Party	• Pirate Scavenger Maps
• Pirate Trivia Quest • Pop Decades Dance • Wildcat Bingo	

On the *Dream, Fantasy,* and *Wish*

Midship Detective Agency is a self-guided interactive game in which kids help Disney characters solve a mystery. You begin by signing up on Deck 5 Midship, where you'll obtain a small, numbered cardboard game piece. One side of the game piece holds a 2-D bar code and your agent number; the other side displays a detective's badge icon. There are three different games: **The Case of the Plundered Paintings** and **The Case of the Missing Puppies,** both featuring Mickey and friends, and our favorite, **The Case of the Stolen Show,** starring the Muppets.

Along with your badge card, you'll receive a pamphlet describing each of the agency's suspects behind the mystery. The pamphlet also includes a map of the ship that shows where to find clues to solve the mystery. Once you've signed up and obtained your game gear, you'll watch a short video that explains the mystery you're solving. You'll also be told where to go to find your first clue.

Each clue is presented on an "Enchanted Art" video screen somewhere on the ship. The screens look like ordinary wall art to anyone not playing the game—it's only when you hold up your badge that the screen comes alive with video and sound. To obtain the clue, you'll first have to solve a simple puzzle or win a simple game. You do this by using your badge as a sort of game controller while you're playing, tilting and moving the badge to guide the action on the screen. It takes a little practice, but you can repeat the action as often as needed. Once you've obtained the clue, you can eliminate one of the suspects from the mystery; then it's off to another section of the ship to get another clue.

Make no mistake: playing this game involves climbing a lot of stairs. However, you get to see a lot of the ship, and it's good exercise. You'll see kids playing at all times of the day and night, and lines often form in front of each video screen, especially on sea days.

The *Wish* is kicking this concept up a notch with **Disney Uncharted Adventure.** This new game takes place via the Play Disney Parks app, which will transform your phone or tablet into an "enchanted spyglass" that allows you to interact with favorite Disney characters. Using the "spyglass," you'll unlock adventures, solve puzzles, and embark on quests. Uncharted Adventure will also have an outdoor component, in which guests can use the app to have augmented-reality interactions with the stars in the night sky. Families can play together on up to six devices at once or team up on only one or two devices at a time. (*Note:* Disney Uncharted Adventure was not yet operating at press time.)

Bibbidi Bobbidi Boutique

Like the Disney parks, all DCL ships have varying incarnations of this wildly popular makeover spot for kids ages 3–12. Makeovers take about 45 minutes and start at about $100 for the **Deluxe Carriage Package,** which includes hairstyling (but not shampooing or cutting), nail polish, makeup, a princess sash, and a BBB-branded T-shirt. The *Frozen* **Package** (about $180) includes your princess's choice of Anna or Elsa hairstyling and costume, snowflake hair accessories, and a plush Olaf doll. The **Castle Package** (currently about $200) includes much of the same stuff as the Deluxe Carriage Package but swaps the T-shirt for a choice of princess gown, plus some coordinating accessories.

For the princess who has everything, BBB offers luxury options—with prices to match. The **Princess Signature Package** (about $450) starts with the standard hair, makeup, and nail treatments but adds a crystal tiara in a keepsake box, along with an heirloom-quality princess gown (and an organza garment bag and satin hanger to keep it pristine on the way home). The **Royal Sea Package,** priced at about $500–$1,100 (yes, you read that right, *$1,100*) depending on the options you choose, includes multiple variations on the Castle or Princess Signature Package, plus a rolling trunk, a fancy picture frame, a ribbon necklace, and a glass slipper.

Pirates' League packages are available for both kids and adults on Pirate Night (see page 232). The basic **Swashbuckle** package for grown-ups (about $70) includes pirate makeup plus a bandanna, an eye patch, an earring, a vest, and a sash. The deluxe **Pirate Costume** for kids (about $200) adds a full outfit, a drawstring bag for holding plundered booty, a telescope, a coin necklace, and a parrot (not a real one!) for your li'l buccaneer's shoulder.

Parents of 2-year-olds should note that the Bibbidi Bobbidi Boutique age requirement on the ship is nonnegotiable. While a kind Fairy Godmother at Walt Disney World might look the other way and agree to do a makeover on a child who's not quite in the stated age range, the cast members on the DCL ships won't cut you a break, because they know exactly how old your child is.

But while BBB holds a hard line regarding the minimum age for makeovers, they don't discriminate when it comes to gender—boys can get princess makeovers, and girls can get gussied up like pirates.

Children's Performance Opportunities

During most sailings of seven days or more, the Oceaneer Club and Lab invite kids ages 3–12 to participate in a show performed on stage in the Walt Disney Theatre. The show, often called *Friendship Rocks!,* mostly involves having the little ones sit on stage and sing along with a few Disney classics. Mickey will make an appearance. Many younger kids (and their parents) think that being on stage with Mickey makes them rock stars, while others will be completely overwhelmed by the experience—use your best judgment.

Kids with a real yen to perform can check out **karaoke** on most sailings or **talent show** opportunities on many longer sailings (see "Family Nightclubs," page 263). There may also be a few performance opportunities for teens and preteens enrolled in Edge and Vibe.

CHILDREN'S ACTIVITIES IN PORT

WHEN BOOKING PORT EXCURSIONS, look for activities that are specified for families. Some tours will be specially designated for those traveling with kids. All excursion descriptions (see Part Twelve, "Port Adventures") include a recommendation for ages (or a requirement, depending on the type of activity) and an indication of the amount of stamina needed to participate. Another option for days when you're in port is to stay aboard the ship and enjoy the smaller crowds at the pools and waterslides.

CHILDREN'S ACTIVITIES AT CASTAWAY CAY

DCL'S PRIVATE ISLAND (see Part Ten) has designated areas just for children and families. The teen area, **The Hide Out,** is tucked away, though not on the beach, and offers sports, such as volleyball and table tennis, and scheduled activities. **Scuttle's Cove,** a play area for young children, has youth-club counselors on hand to direct activities. Both The Hide Out and Scuttle's Cove are monitored by Disney cast members to ensure that only children and their parents enter.

CHARACTER APPEARANCES

Note: *During the post-pandemic return to sailing, DCL curtailed or modified its character experiences—instead of meet and greets, for example, characters did "appear and waves," standing at a distance (approximately 3 feet) from guests and posing for photos but not touching or hugging anyone. At press time, characters had begun to resume interacting with guests as described below, but check the specifics for your sailing in case the more-restrictive protocols rules are in force. (The cast members who play the characters have other job duties on the ships, and a COVID outbreak among them could throw a wrench into onboard activities.)*

DISNEY CHARACTERS are available for photos and autographs several times per day at various locations on the ships; they also make occasional visits to the It's a Small World Nursery and the kids' clubs. A complete schedule is usually posted on the **Character Information Board** in your ship's atrium; it's also listed in the Character Appearances section of the DCL Navigator app and available by calling ☎ **7-PALS** (7257) from your stateroom phone.

Disney may offer reservation times for meeting the hugely popular *Frozen* characters Anna, Elsa, and Olaf; a selection of Marvel superheroes; and what we call the Princess Bomb: a group of four or five Disney princesses who appear in the atrium at once. (Disney officially calls this the **Royal Gathering,** but we like our moniker better.)

If your sailing offers advance character greetings (and character-dining experiences), they'll appear in the **My Reservations** section for your sailing at the DCL website (see page 47). Character encounters may not become available until days or weeks after your standard port-adventure and adult-dining selections appear, so if you're interested in these keep checking back. If your specific cruise doesn't offer prebooking, check the Navigator app to find out if character-greeting reservations are in effect for your specific sailing.

If reservations *are* being used on your voyage, it's essential that you get them. Some princesses may greet guests on the spur of the moment, with no ticket required, but be aware that the A-list stars—namely, Anna, Elsa, Olaf, and the Marvel gang—are unlikely to make such impromptu appearances.

unofficial **TIP**

You'll have better interactions with "face" characters (that is, those who can speak) if you're familiar with their film franchises and the things they're known for. Ask Thor about shawarma, Elsa about chocolate, Jack Sparrow about sailing, and so on.

There may also be some character greetings for which guests will start lining up well before the posted start times. Unique characters will have long lines—we once had quite a wait to see the White Rabbit from *Alice in Wonderland*, who was serving as the de facto Easter Bunny on the *Fantasy*. Likewise, Captain Jack Sparrow is always a big draw on Pirate Night.

Most onboard character greetings are limited to 15 minutes or half an hour; the line will be closed once it's been determined that no more guests can be accommodated in the allotted time. If your child is intent on meeting a specific character, your best bet is to get in line **15–30 minutes** before that character is scheduled to appear. (We've arrived as much as 45 minutes ahead to get a spot for our kids to meet Belle—and we weren't even the first people in line.)

You can also expect longer waits for common characters in unusual costumes for special circumstances: Mickey Mouse wearing red, white, and blue on the Fourth of July, for example, or Goofy wearing a parka during an Alaskan voyage.

On longer cruises, classic Disney characters such as Mickey, Minnie, Donald, Goofy, and Pluto may make onboard appearances many times throughout the voyage. The lines for these favorites are typically shorter later in the trip, when most folks have already had their fill of photos with Mickey and company.

On **Castaway Cay,** photo ops featuring the Disney gang in beach attire take place near the ship's dock, weather permitting.

In 2019 Disney added character greetings with **Minnie Mouse** decked out in a ship captain's uniform, with the intent of inspiring girls to pursue maritime careers. Concurrent with Captain Minnie's addition to the meet-and-greet lineup, DCL has begun funding scholarships to **LJM Maritime Academy** in the Bahamas for female cadets seeking to become ship captains and other onboard leaders. Scholarships include tuition to the three-year program: two years at the academy and one year working on a Disney ship.

ROYAL COURT ROYAL TEA PARTY (*FANTASY*) This character experience allows kids and their adults to meet Lady Chamomile (the hostess), Chef Bule (the pastry chef), and a cadre of Disney princesses for lavish attention and a tea-time meal of savory and sweet courses. Reserve in advance on the DCL website. The cost is $220 per child and $69 per adult. Kids leave with a plethora of gifts: a doll, jewelry, autograph book, and tiara for girls; a plush Duffy bear, a sword and shield, and an autograph book for boys.

OLAF'S ROYAL PICNIC (*WISH*) Priced at the same $220 per child and $69 per adult as the Royal Court Royal Tea, the Olaf's Royal Picnic features appearances by Olaf, Anna, Elsa, and Kristoff, who will lead guests in celebrating a fictional Nordic midsummer festival, including songs and stories. Kids in attendance receive an assortment of gifts, including Olaf headwear, a cinch bag, a mandolin, a plush troll doll, a water bottle, a picnic blanket, a troll necklace, and an activity book.

PRIVATE CHARACTER GREETINGS If you have a special event taking place on your cruise—a small wedding, a large family reunion, or a big birthday party—you may want to consider booking a private character greeting. For about $500–$600 for a "fur" character (like Mickey or Minnie) or about $1,000 for a "face" character (like a princess), you can book a private room with 30 minutes of character time. While it's pricey, a private character greeting could be an attractive option because it lets you get every family combination in a photo without the possibility of inconveniencing other guests. For the latest pricing and details, check the Navigator app for your sailing, or call DCL at ☎ 800-951-3532.

A Note About Autographs

A significant subset of guests at the Disney parks and on Disney cruises collect character autographs as souvenirs. Guests often have characters sign things other than autograph books: photo mats, pillowcases, T-shirts, and the like. (One of Erin's favorite signature-collecting mediums is a pair of canvas shoes; see this blog post for details: tinyurl.com /AutographShoes.) After waiting in line, you present the character with whatever you want signed, then pose for a photo if you like.

Be aware, however, that DCL imposes a number of restrictions on the kinds of items that characters may sign, as noted on the following page:

- Any autograph book
- Disney-branded items, provided they're appropriate to the character doing the signing. For example, Cinderella would be unable to sign a Buzz Lightyear item.
- A Disney-approved photo. Only characters in the photo can sign the photo.
- Disney note cards
- Disney Dollars—once signed, however, they can no longer be used as currency. (*Note:* Disney Dollars were discontinued in 2016 but are still redeemable.)
- Clothing (may not be worn while being signed)

Characters will *not* sign the following items:

• Flags of any nation	• Receipts or banking slips
• Money other than Disney Dollars	• Skin
• Non-Disney merchandise	• Non-family-friendly or sexually explicit items

POOLS *and* WATER-PLAY AREAS

EACH SHIP HAS SEPARATE FRESHWATER POOLS designed for small children, families, and adults. All are heated to a minimum temperature of 75°F.

During the COVID era, DCL implemented an array of tools, from timed reservations to lifeguard proctors, to limit the number of guests allowed in each pool simultaneously. As the pandemic has evolved, however, most of these interventions have been removed, and the pools are well on their way to returning to what one Ohio reader calls "pool soup."

If you've never been on a cruise ship before, you may have been duped by creative photography into thinking you'll be able to swim laps in DCL's pools. In reality, however, not only is it impossible to exercise in the pools, you can barely even splash in them.

unofficial **TIP**
Disney has lifeguards at the family pools, but you still need to keep a watchful eye on your children around water.

Even during non-COVID times, no DCL pool had a capacity of more than 80 guests (and most pools' capacities are much smaller than this)—even on the *Dream, Fantasy,* and *Wish,* which carry about 4,000 guests each. In a highly unscientific study, we've shown photos of the pools, with varying numbers of guests in the water, to several noncruising acquaintances. The consensus seems to be that the pools start to look uncomfortably crowded when they're filled to about half capacity.

A North Carolina mom comments:

For our cruise on the Dream, *the pool was my only semi-complaint. The pools were PACKED with kids, I couldn't have gotten in if I wanted to, and it was just myself and my then-6-year-old. We love Disney, but the crowds at the pools will definitely be a turnoff for my husband, and I'm not sure I'll be able to persuade him to book another cruise with all of us if they're that crowded.*

POOLS FROM A KID'S PERSPECTIVE

TWELVE-YEAR-OLD veteran DCL cruiser **Lily Mascardo** offers a tween's take on DCL's water activities.

THERE ARE MANY WAYS to have fun in the water on a Disney cruise.

All of the ships have some sort of slide. My favorite is **Mickey's Slide** because it's not too long but not too short. On the *Magic* and the *Wonder,* there's also the **Twist 'n' Spout** slide, and on the *Wish* there's **Slide-a-Saurus Rex**. These are much longer and may be a little scary for young kids. Speaking of scary, the **AquaDunk** (*Magic*) drops people from high up—make your mom or dad ride it first so they can tell you what it's like.

The three coolest water experiences on the ships are the **AquaLab, AquaDuck,** and **AquaMouse.** The AquaLab is a splash zone with pop jets, buckets of water that fall on your head, and water *everywhere.* There's a smaller version of the AquaLab on the *Wonder* and *Magic,* and it isn't on the *Dream,* but the best one is on the *Fantasy.*

You'll get extremely wet! On the *Dream* and *Fantasy,* the AquaDuck (which isn't the Aqua*Dunk*) is basically a slide that you ride in a raft around the ship. At first it seems scary, and the water is *cold,* but as I've gotten older I enjoy it more, and now I can even ride it by myself. While you ride, the people on the deck can see you and you can see them. Make sure someone sees you so they can take your picture!

The AquaMouse on the *Wish* is similar to the AquaDuck, but there are video screens playing cartoons during the first section of the ride.

For younger kids, there's an area called **Nemo's Reef** (*Dream* and *Fantasy*), **Dory's Reef** (*Wonder*), the **Nephews' Splash Zone** (*Magic*), or the **Toy Story Splash Zone** (*Wish*). It's like the AquaLab, but for younger kids. The slide in Nemo's Reef is small, but you can go really fast—have an adult ready to catch you!

The ships aren't the only places that have water activities—there are also many on **Castaway Cay.** There's a splash pad called **Spring-a-Leak** near the Family Beach; it's kind of hidden, but it's a great place to splash around. Inside the **Scuttle's Cove** kid's club, there's another splash pad that only kids and youth counselors can use. For older kids, there are waterslides in the ocean at **Pelican Plunge,** but I don't think I'm ready for that yet!

And a Virginia cruiser says:

We just left the Magic *in Dover [UK] for the Norway and Iceland cruise. There were folks in the pools on days warm enough to swim, but it was nothing at all like the crowding in the pools in the Caribbean.*

The good news for grown-ups is that the adult pools are rarely raucous. In general, all of the pools are more relaxed during cold weather itineraries. You'll can also find less competition for pool space if you visit on port days or during evening showtimes.

RULES ABOUT POOLS

DCL HAS A FEW STRICT REGULATIONS designed to protect the health and safety of guests using its pools. Anyone under age 12 must be supervised at the pools at all times, height and weight restrictions for the waterslides are strictly observed, and snorkels and full-face masks are prohibited (though they are welcome at Castaway Cay). Water wings and other US Coast Guard–approved flotation devices are allowed, but rafts, floats, and foam noodles are not.

DCL's swim-diaper policy states: "The US Public Health Service requires that only children who are toilet-trained are permitted to enter swimming pools and spas aboard cruise ships. Swim diapers are not permitted in hot tubs, spas, or any Disney Cruise Line pools or waterslides, including the AquaDuck, AquaDunk, and AquaLab." Little ones wearing swim diapers *are* permitted at **Nemo's Reef** on the *Dream* and *Fantasy*, at the **Nephews' Splash Zone** on the *Magic*, **Dory's Reef** on the *Wonder*, and *Toy Story* **Splash Zone** and the **AquaMouse** on the *Wish*.

If poop happens in the pool, all guests must evacuate and the pool must then be drained, cleaned, refilled, and tested for bacteria and chemical balance. The entire procedure takes about 4–5 hours depending on the size of the pool—so don't be *that* parent who let your almost-but-not-quite-potty-trained child into the water and ended up spoiling an afternoon for hundreds of other families. Remember, too, that on a cruise even potty-trained kids may get distracted or overwhelmed; plus, unfamiliar foods may make new digestive demands.

THE POOLS ON THE *MAGIC* AND *WONDER*

A VARIATION ON THE AQUADUCK water coaster found on the *Dream* and *Fantasy* (see page 291), the *Magic*'s **AquaDunk** is short and mildly fast, with a vertical start. It starts with your entering a vertical tube. You lean against one side of the tube while a clear plexiglass door closes opposite you to seal the tube. Suddenly, the floor drops away and you plunge nearly vertically down the tube, through a quick 270-degree turn and into a braking pool of water. The entire experience takes perhaps 7 or 8 seconds, but the initial sensation of falling is fun enough to make it worth repeating. Depending on when you sail, the AquaDunk opens at around 9 a.m. and closes around 11 p.m.

unofficial **TIP**
Unlike the other ships, the *Wonder* doesn't have a headliner water attraction.

Because the AquaDunk has an hourly capacity of only around 120 riders, long lines develop quickly; we've seen 80-minute waits posted. If you're not there first thing in the morning, try during lunchtime or the first dinner seating.

Parents of kids with sensitive eyes should be aware that while swim goggles may be worn in the ships' pools and on the smaller slides, goggles and face masks are prohibited on the AquaDunk—the force of the drop all but guarantees that you'd lose the goggles/mask.

AquaLab, the *Magic*'s and *Wonder*'s water-play area for children ages 3 and up, is on Deck 9 Aft. It consists of four areas: AquaLab proper, the Twist 'n' Spout slide (ages 4 and up and over 38 inches tall), the Nephews' Pool, and the Nephews' Splash Zone.

Every inch of AquaLab is covered in water, which comes out from both vertical and horizontal surfaces. Overhead buckets, slowly filling with water, will dump their contents periodically on anyone standing below, while sprays from faux ship-plumbing will drench anyone walking within 10 feet. Your kids will probably want to spend hours here, so it's a good thing that both covered seating and refreshments are available nearby.

Next to the main AquaLab area on the *Magic* is the **Nephews' Splash Zone,** a water-play area for children up to 3 years old. This plexiglass-enclosed area has water spouting from pint-size figures of Donald Duck's three nephews, Huey, Dewey, and Louie. Padding on the ground allows kids to jump and run around safely, and you'll find parents sitting and relaxing nearby while their little ones get soaked. The equivalent area on the *Wonder* is **Mickey's Splash Zone.**

A three-story spiral waterslide, **Twist 'n' Spout** is a lot longer and slower than AquaDunk, making it perfect for kids not quite tall enough for the big slide. Twist 'n' Spout starts above Deck 11 and ends on Deck 9 next to AquaLab. The top part of the slide isn't usually staffed, but a camera system there allows the attendant at the bottom of the slide to monitor both the start and the end simultaneously. Kids must be 4–14 years old and 38–64 inches tall to ride. There's plenty of nearby seating for parents to get some sun while watching the little ones splash around.

The **Nephews' Pool** is a shallow, circular pool in the middle of the deck, touching both AquaLab and the Nephews' Splash Zone. Small children can splash around to their hearts' content while parents sit on ledge seating. Adjacent to AquaLab are three counter-service eateries: just past the forward end is **Pete's Boiler Bites** (*Wonder*) or **Duck-in Diner** (*Magic*), and just past the aft end is **Daisy's De-Lites.**

Goofy's Pool, the *Magic*'s and *Wonder*'s family pool, is on Deck 9 Midship. It's the focal point of outdoor activity on the ship. The pool is 4 feet deep at every point, and deck chairs and lounges are arranged on both sides along its length. At the forward end of the pool is the **Funnel Vision** LED screen, which plays movies, TV shows, and videos almost constantly. At the aft end are **Pinocchio's Pizzeria** and two covered whirlpools. Both Goofy's and the Nephews' Pools are typically open 8 a.m.–10 p.m. every day; check the Navigator app for specific hours.

The adults-only **Quiet Cove Pool** is on Deck 9 Forward. Like Goofy's Pool, it's 4 feet deep throughout, and two adults-only whirlpools are nearby. Teak lounge chairs are provided for relaxing. Just past the aft end of the pool are **Signals** bar and **Cove Café.**

While the *Wonder* lacks a thrill-style feature slide, the ship does have a spiral **Twist 'n' Spout** waterslide. As on the *Magic,* the slide starts above Deck 11; it ends next to a new **AquaLab** children's play area on Deck 9.

On both the *Wonder* and the *Magic* you'll find **Mickey's Pool,** for children ages 3 and up, toward Deck 9 Aft. Divided into three smaller pools corresponding to Mickey's face and ears, the pool has a maximum depth of 2 feet, and the bright-yellow spiral **Mickey's Slide** rises about one deck high (about the same level as Deck 10). Kids must be 4–14 years old and 38–64 inches tall to use the waterslide. There's plenty of nearby seating for parents to get some sun while watching the little ones splash around.

Children who don't meet the requirements for Mickey's Pool on the *Wonder* can play in nearby **Dory's Reef,** on the port side of the pool. Surrounded by short walls and themed to *Finding Nemo,* this water-play area for kids ages 3 and younger features gurgling sprays, jets, and sprinkles of water bubbling up from fountains in the floor. Best of all, there's plenty of covered seating nearby. Kids playing in Dory's Reef must be supervised.

THE POOLS ON THE *DREAM* AND *FANTASY*

LIKE THE WONDER, the *Dream* and the *Fantasy* have **Mickey's Pool** for children ages 3 and up, roughly Midship on Deck 11. Divided into three smaller pools corresponding to Mickey's face and ears, the pool has a maximum depth of 2 feet, and the bright-yellow spiral **Mickey's Slide** rises about one deck high. Kids must be 4–14 years old and 38–64 inches tall to use the slide. There's plenty of nearby seating for parents to get some sun while watching the little ones splash around.

Children who don't meet the requirements for Mickey's Pool can play in the nearby **Nemo's Reef,** toward the aft end of the pool. Larger and wetter than the Nephews' Splash Zone on the *Magic* and Mickey's Splash Zone on the *Wonder,* this *Finding Nemo*–themed water-play area for kids ages 3 and younger features gurgling sprays, jets, and sprinkles of water bubbling up from fountains in the floor and from kid-size replicas of some of the movie's characters. A set of restrooms is just behind Nemo's Reef.

Found on Deck 11 Midship is the *Dream*'s family pool, **Donald's Pool.** Like Goofy's Pool on the *Magic* and *Wonder,* it's the center of outdoor activity on the ship. The rectangular pool is about a foot deep close to its edges; in the middle is a roughly circular section that drops to a maximum depth of around 5 feet. The different depths allow younger swimmers to relax in the shallows without having to get out of the pool.

Deck chairs and chaise longues line both sides of Donald's Pool. At the forward end of the pool is the **Funnel Vision** LED screen, which plays movies, TV shows, and videos almost constantly. At the aft end is the Mickey Pool. Just beyond the Funnel Vision stage are the counter-service restaurants: **Fillmore's Favorites, Luigi's Pizza,** and **Tow Mater's Grill** on the starboard side, and the **Eye Scream** ice-cream station and **Frozone Treats** smoothie station on the port side. Both Donald's and

Mickey's Pools are typically open 8 a.m.–10 p.m. every day; check the Navigator app for specific hours.

Like the *Magic* and *Wonder,* the *Fantasy* (but not the *Dream*) has an **AquaLab** water-play area. On Deck 12 Aft, it's similar to Nemo's Reef in that its entertainment is provided by splashing water, but whereas the water comes up from the floor at Nemo's Reef, it comes down from above at AquaLab. High above your head are pipes filling buckets and buckets of water, which are counterbalanced so that they spill down on unsuspecting (and suspecting) kids below. In fact, water comes at you from every angle in AquaLab, and that's exactly the appeal. AquaLab is for kids too old or too large to play in Nemo's Reef.

unofficial **TIP**
The best time to visit the AquaDuck is between 5 and 7 p.m., when most families are either at dinner or getting ready to go (check hours during your sailing). You'll also find smaller crowds on days when the ship is in port.

The adults-only **Quiet Cove Pool** is on Deck 11 Forward on both the *Dream* and the *Fantasy.* This pool is 4 feet deep throughout. Rather than wasting space on whirlpools, the *Dream*'s designers wisely placed an outdoor bar, **Cove Bar,** at one end of the Quiet Cove Pool. The area around the bar is a splash-friendly nonslip surface, with white bench seating and a round, ottoman-like seat in the middle; there are also a few seats directly at the bar. Behind the pool is the lovely **Cove Café;** on either side is covered seating with chaise longues and chairs.

Both the *Dream* and the *Fantasy* have an **AquaDuck** waterslide, a 765-foot-long, clear-plastic tube that's almost as popular as the Disney princesses. Riders board an inflatable plastic raft at the aft end of Deck 12. The raft is shot forward through the plastic tube by high-pressure water faucets below and to the sides, making the AquaDuck a water-powered miniature roller coaster. There's enough water pressure here to propel your raft up two full decks' worth of height, followed by a descent of four decks into a landing pool. Guests must be at least 42 inches tall to ride, and children under age 7 must ride with someone age 14 or older who also meets the height requirement.

The AquaDuck's track sits at the outside edge of Deck 12 and goes as high as one of the ship's smokestacks. If you can keep your eyes open (and your wits about you), it offers some awesome views of the surrounding ocean and any nearby islands.

The *Dream* and the *Fantasy* also have **Satellite Falls,** an adults-only splash pool and sundeck on Deck 13 Forward. Covered with long, vertical tiles in different shades of blue and green, the pool looks great at night. In the center, a structure that looks like a giant Doppler radar receiver (and mimics a pair of actual satellite receivers on either side of the pool) pours a gentle stream of water into the pool below.

THE POOLS ON THE *WISH*

Unlike the pools on the other ships, which are all on one level, most of the *Wish*'s pools are staggered on several levels, stadium-style, between

Decks 11 and 12. Stairs connect the various pool tiers; guests with mobility issues may need to head back indoors and take the elevator to access some of the water areas. All of the main deck's pools can be covered to become stages for outdoor events such as the Sail-Away Celebration and Pirate Night.

The six family pools vary in size and depth. **Mickey's Pool,** closest to the FunnelVision screen, is most similar in size and design to the main pools on the other DCL ships. The nearby **Minnie's Pool** is just 2 feet deep; you'd think this would be the perfect spot for toddlers to splash, but no children in diapers are allowed here. What's more, we stepped in this pool a few times to cool our feet on an exceptionally hot day, but we found that the water had become uncomfortably warm in the sun.

One level up from these larger pools are **Daisy's** and **Pluto's Pools.** These are just 6 inches deep, ideal for smaller (and potty-trained) children and their caregivers. On the highest tier are **Donald's** and **Goofy's Pools,** the deepest of the family pools at 4 feet 6 inches. They're nowhere near large enough for laps, but they're the only places where adults can fully submerge themselves the main pool deck.

The panoply of pools could be an issue for single adults in charge of monitoring multiple children. If you think your kids will want to sample lots of pools and water-play areas, set some ground rules about whether they need to stick together or how they'll let you know which pool they're visiting.

The *Toy Story* **Splash Zone** (Deck 12 Forward) is the *Wish*'s version of a splash pad for toddlers. Two small slides and several water spouts squirt gentle sprays from the floor or from giant *Toy Story*–character heads. (We'll admit that we found these heads kind of creepy, but the youngsters we saw using the splash pad seemed unfazed.)

There is one entrance/exit to the Splash Zone. **Trixie's Falls,** located near this entrance, is just 6 inches deep, but a waterfall-style shower spans the length of the pool's back wall, adding entertainment and an extra element of cooling.

The **AquaMouse** slide, with its 42-inch height requirement to ride (48 inches to ride alone), is similar to the AquaDuck on the *Dream* and *Fantasy.* You experience the slide on a double raft, which you're welcome to use solo. During the first half of the ride, you're in an enclosed tunnel. The tunnel walls are fitted with video screens showing one of two cartoons in the same style as Mickey & Minnie's Runaway Railway at Walt Disney World. Disney's promotional materials made a big deal about watching movies on a slide, but we were too distracted by the water nozzles spraying us to pay much attention. Overall, we prefer the non-movie-themed versions on the other ships because they provide more-panoramic views of the ocean.

The bright-yellow **Slide-A-Saurus Rex** slide is for guests 38 inches tall or taller. It's a quick ride, but it's fun for elementary school–age kids who might be intimidated by the AquaMouse.

The **Chip 'n' Dale Quiet Pool** is on Deck 14 is a shallow wading pool with views of the front of the ship. This pool is away from the noise and frenetic activity on the main pool deck, making it the best water spot for guests with sensory-processing issues.

On the other hand, the **Quiet Cove** adults-only pool area on Deck 12 is one of our biggest disappointments regarding the *Wish*. On the plus side, the location is far removed from the rest of the ship, so you won't find noisy kids accidentally walking through. On the minus side:

1. No food is available in the adult pool area. Cove Café on the other DCL ships has a refrigerated case stocked with goodies, but not the version on the *Wish*. If you're hungry, you'll have to walk downstairs and wait in line at Mickey's Festival of Foods to grab a bite.

2. Some of the lounge seating is directly under the AquaMouse loading zone, meaning the slide's music is omnipresent. This is not ideal if you want a quiet adult space to read or nap.

3. Some of the adult pool area is adjacent to the ship's main smoking areas, so you may catch whiffs of cigarette smoke, depending on the prevailing winds.

4. The infinity pool—DCL's first—is beautiful but small. It's so small, in fact, that it feels crowded when occupied by even half a dozen guests. It's also accessible only via steep stairs, which could pose a problem for guests with mobility issues.

One reader says:

> *The Quiet Cove area is my biggest complaint about the* Wish. *The overall area is small, and the pool is extremely small and hard to get into and out of; plus, it's flanked by these silly half-circle "pools" that only go to your ankles. Also, the only chairs in the shade are right in front of the bar, so it gets hot there.*

ONBOARD SEMINARS

LED BY CREW MEMBERS and attended by a limited number of passengers, onboard seminars are 30- to 60-minute interactive talks. Topics vary, but most involve food, wine, shopping, fitness activities, or how the ship is run. A fee is charged for seminars involving alcohol (see below) and some fitness activities.

Several **wine-tasting sessions,** led by sommeliers or experienced bartenders, are usually held on most cruises, especially those of more than four nights. The first session is typically an introduction to wine and covers the basics: grape varietals, flavor characteristics, vocabulary, and such. Subsequent sessions may concentrate on a particular style of wine, or those from a particular region. Most tastings serve 2- or 3-ounce pours from four or five varieties. The Champagne bars on the *Dream* and *Fantasy* hold tastings too. In addition to wine, Champagne, and tequila, cruises may offer Cognac, whiskey, martini, mojito, and beer tastings as well as general classes on mixology.

The **cooking demonstrations** are some of the best presentations on board. Like the wine sessions, cooking demos often follow a theme: the first day, for example, may show how to prepare an appetizer; the second involves an entrée; and the third will be dessert. Each demo is led by a member of the kitchen staff, usually a chef. These presentations are typically held in one of the ship's nightclubs so that more people can attend. To make it easy for everyone to see what the chef is doing, several video cameras are often mounted above the chef's work table, providing a view of the preparations.

Cooking demos where wine is served, along with fitness activities, are restricted to guests ages 18 and up. Wine and spirits tastings are for guests ages 21 and up only, except during cruises that sail solely in Europe, where participants may be 18 if a parent or guardian (1) is traveling with them, (2) has provided written permission for them to drink, and (3) is present when they do so.

If you're looking for exercise instead of food, the **walking tours** of the ships are a great way to keep moving and see the inner workings of your vessel. Most tours begin somewhere on the pool deck and wind their way down and back up the ship. The cast members who lead these tours are fonts of knowledge about the ships and can answer most questions you may have. If you want to know what it takes to prepare 800 appetizers at the same time, your tour leader can tell you.

Shopping seminars are usually held on sea days when the ship will be docked at a port the following day. (The seminars are also video-taped and available on your stateroom's television 24 hours a day.) Most seminars last 60–90 minutes, with multiple sessions held per day. Each session usually covers one kind of item, such as watches or a particular kind of gemstone sold at an upcoming port stop.

Frankly, shopping seminars aren't our bag (pardon the pun). You won't hear much—if anything—that's negative about the products being shilled: the seminar leaders are nearly always representatives of local retail associations, *not* Disney cast members, so they have a personal stake in persuading you to buy stuff, even if it's of questionable quality.

If you're considering splashing out big bucks on, say, expensive jewelry, you're almost certainly better off postponing your purchase until you're back at home and you can do your own research. Not to mention most items you'll find for sale in port can easily be found online for much less money. (See "Shopping," page 302, for more information.)

Senses Spa and the ship's Fitness Center host **wellness seminars** most mornings. Activities include everything from stretching exercises and acupuncture to group cycling and Pilates. Many of the sessions, such as stretching and cycling, are free, although space is limited and you're strongly encouraged to sign up well in advance to guarantee a spot. Personal-training sessions cost about $90 per hour, before tip; nutritional consultations are also about $90 per hour; and an hour-long body-composition analysis is about $40.

The **Disney Vacation Club** (**DVC**) also hosts presentations about its time-share program. They're peppy affairs that frequently involve free booze, giveaways of swag like DVC baseball caps, and the opportunity to win a $200 stateroom credit. If you have time to kill and you want a free cocktail, head on over—you don't even have to pay attention to the presentation. (Canadian residents should be aware that there may be legal restrictions that prevent them from winning onboard credit.)

SPORTS *and* FITNESS

EACH SHIP OFFERS AN ARRAY of outdoor and indoor sports and fitness options. While it's no substitute for your local mega-gym, there's enough equipment and variety on board for almost everyone to maintain muscle tone and cardio conditioning during the cruise.

Each DCL ship has a comprehensive **Fitness Center** outfitted with weight machines, free weights, treadmills, stair-climbers, elliptical machines, stationary bikes, and more. Guests ages 14–17 are welcome to used the facilities if accompanied by a parent; the exception is guests on sailings originating in the UK, who must be 18 or older.

The gyms provide yoga mats, step-aerobics benches, exercise balls, and elastic stretching bands. Also provided are a water fountain, complimentary fresh fruit, cloth towels, paper towels, and spray bottles of sanitizer to clean the equipment when you're done. Locker rooms have showers, a sauna, sinks, robes, towels, grooming items, and lockers with electric locks. There is no charge to use these facilities.

Nautilus-style weight machines are available for working every muscle group. Virtually all of the electric cardio machines have video monitors, allowing you to watch the ship's TV programming while you work out, along with plugs for your headphones.

The Fitness Center is generally open from around 6 a.m. to 11 p.m.; check the Navigator app for the exact schedule. It tends to be most crowded in the morning between 8 and 11 a.m. and least crowded between 5 and 11 p.m. Group- and personal-training sessions are available, including weight training, Pilates, and other courses, for an additional fee. Individual training sessions cost about $90 (minus tip) for a 1-hour session. To arrange personal training, stop by the Fitness Center on embarkation day.

One thing we find disconcerting in the gyms is that the treadmills on the *Dream, Fantasy,* and *Wish* face the port (left) side of the ship, not the bow. If the ship is moving while you're running on one of these treadmills, the scenery in front of you will be passing from left to right, but your brain expects to see the scenery moving toward you. Some people—including Len—instinctively twist their bodies left in an attempt to line up the scenery with the way their minds think they should be going. This makes for awkward running (walking doesn't seem to be much of an issue). If you find yourself unable to run correctly on the treadmill and you're not on the *Wish,* try the outdoor course described next.

Runners and walkers will appreciate the **0.3-mile track** circling Deck 4 of the *Magic* and *Wonder* and the **0.4-mile track** on Deck 4 of the *Dream* and *Fantasy.* One of the great things about running laps on the ship is the amazing scenery, which (almost) makes you forget that you're exercising while you're seeing it. We've run a few laps on four of the ships, and the track is certainly good enough to get in a few miles to start your day. Some sections take you through some relatively narrow corridors, and there's a good chance that you'll be running past groups of other tourists who are out enjoying the deck too. Finally, keep an eye open for water on the deck, which can make the track slick.

Of our numerous quibbles with the *Wish*, the biggest is that it lacks a deck that fully circles the ship. Color us disappointed that one of the great joys of a cruise—a leisurely stroll around the deck after dinner—is not available on this vessel. Sets of steep stairs ostensibly take you around the ship via multiple levels, but we found that these were often blocked by locked gates. Runners trying to train would find the steps to be treacherous on rolling seas; plus, the stairs present an obstacle to wheelchair users. A cynical friend muses that since shipboard strolling doesn't generate revenue, Disney didn't think it was important—sadly, we're not sure they're wrong.

If running isn't your thing, every DCL ship has **basketball courts,** surrounded by woven rope fencing to keep errant balls from leaving the ship. The courts are popular with kids and parents looking to shoot a few hoops—we've never seen a competitive game played at one. A basketball court can also be converted to a miniature soccer field or volleyball court if you can find enough people to play. (See the next section for information about basketball on the *Wish*.)

Each ship also has **shuffleboard courts,** located near Deck 4 Midship. Because the only time we ever play shuffleboard is on a cruise, we tend to forget the rules between sailings, and then we make them up as we go along while we're on the ship. There are no official rules posted near the courts, so if you're looking to play a regulation game and you need a refresher, take a peek here before you sail: tinyurl.com /RulesForShuffleboard.

If you're up for a challenge, **Ping-Pong** tables are available as well (Deck 9 Forward on the *Magic* and *Wonder;* Deck 13 Aft on the *Dream* and *Fantasy*). Readers report that the windy conditions on deck make it difficult to play, but perhaps your table-tennis game will benefit from a bit of unpredictability. Ping-Pong is located indoors in the *Wish*'s Hero Zone (see next section).

The *Dream* and *Fantasy* both have Disney-themed **miniature-golf courses** outdoors on Deck 13 Aft; these are a lot of fun for the entire family. The *Dream* and *Fantasy* also have outdoor **Foosball** tables; the *Wish* has Foosball in the Hero Zone and in the Vibe teen club.

If you're looking to get in some individual practice time on the *Dream* and *Fantasy*, **virtual sports simulators** are available on Deck 13 Aft for golf, basketball, soccer, football, hockey, and baseball. These indoor facilities have a large movie screen set up in a dedicated room; a computer projects a simulated soccer field, basketball court, or other appropriate venue on the screen. You're given actual sports equipment to kick, throw, or swing. Your movements, and the movements of the ball, are tracked by computers and displayed on screen—there's a slight lag in the display, but it's not enough to be distracting. Half-hour sessions cost about $28 for golf and about $13 for other sports; hour-long sessions are about $49 for golf and about $22 for other sports. A penalty charge (50% of your simulator session fee) applies if you cancel on the day of your session; you may cancel without penalty up to the day before.

Guests ages 13 and younger must be accompanied by an adult (age 18+) when playing at the simulator; guests ages 14–17 must be accompanied by at least one other guest who's the same age or older.

HERO ZONE (*WISH*) This multipurpose indoor space (Deck 12 Aft) is sports central on the *Wish*. The top level holds games like Ping-Pong, air hockey, and Foosball tables and also serves as a viewing loft for activities taking place on the main floor below. The large, open space can be configured for free play, half-court basketball, chip-it golf, or **Jack-Jack's Incredible Diaper Dash,** an *Incredibles*-themed variation on a popular event for babies old enough to crawl (see page 265).

The showcase element of the Hero Zone is an inflatable obstacle course called **Incredi-Games** (guests must be at least 40 inches tall to participate). The Incredi-Games course will be inflated for 5 or 6 hours during some sea days, with various time slots open to free use, teens only, or timed family competitions. *Note:* You must wear socks to use the course—no bare feet or shoes allowed. To avoid a trip back to your stateroom, bring a pair of socks with you.

SPAS

THIS SECTION SUMMARIZES the major spa and salon services offered on each ship, but note that many more are available. We recommend visiting the spa on your first afternoon aboard to sign up for any last-minute treatments and check for specials. *Note:* Prices listed are approximate and do not include a tip, which is typically 18%–25% of the cost of your treatment. There's a 50% cancellation charge if you cancel within 24 hours of your appointment.

unofficial **TIP**
The best time to visit the spa is during dinner or when the ship is in port.

Some salon services, such as manicures and massages, may be booked on the **My Reservations** section of the DCL website before you sail. If you want to book a hair appointment online, you can reserve the time slot, but you'll have to stop by the spa after you board to specify what kind of service you want (styling, coloring, etc).

If you're trying to book spa services before your cruise, Disney's website may not let you book some services, such as facials, for two people at the same time of day. (We think the website assumes that only one person per ship is qualified to do these tasks, and that this person is unavailable once the first service is booked.) If you run into this problem, try booking the services online one after the other, then visit the spa in person when you board to explain what you want.

One thing that's different about spa treatments on the Disney ships versus on land is that the same person is likely to be your masseuse, facialist, and manicurist—on a confined space like a cruise ship, roles have to be combined. Some readers like the familiarity, but others think a jack of all beauty trades can't provide the same level of service as a team of individuals with particular expertise in one area.

NOT-SO-RELAXING STUFF ABOUT THE SPA We've found two aspects of the DCL spa experience to be not very serene. First, you have to fill out a lengthy intake form and medical waiver before any spa service. This makes sense if you're getting Restylane injections, but not if you're getting your hair cut. (We exaggerate only slightly when we say we were asked about our latest blood work before we sat down for a manicure.)

Second, the spa staff will invariably rope you into a post-treatment upsell spiel: you can never *possibly* look or feel your best unless you buy this $75 bottle of shampoo or that $125 bottle of aromatherapy oil. Be prepared to just say "no," and often.

SERVICES AVAILABLE AT SENSES SPA AND SALON

THE DCL SHIPS offer an extensive array of spa services for men, women, teens, and couples. On the *Magic, Wonder, Dream,* and *Fantasy,* the spas look more or less like their counterparts at a high-end resort.

On the *Wish,* some of these areas have a subtle Disney theme. The women's hair salon is called **Untangled,** with design elements inspired by Rapunzel and *Tangled,* including purple-and-gold floating-lantern light fixtures and cut-metal privacy screens that replicate Rapunzel's paintings. For the guys, there's **Hook's Barbery.** The dark wood-and-leather decor features narrative details inspired by Captain Hook. In addition to offering styling and barbering services, the Barbery has a hidden bar specializing in vintage whiskeys, ports, and aged rums. (Who says hard liquor and sharp objects don't go together?)

Men's salon services include basic haircuts ($29); facials, such as the **Biotec Supercharger for Men** ($169) and the tongue-twisty **Elemis Pro-Collagen Grooming Treatment with Shave** ($109). Touted as "the shave of all shaves," the almost-hour-long Grooming Treatment includes a hot-towel wrap; a shave; a mini facial; and massages of your face, scalp, and hands. (If you normally use an electric shaver, be aware that a straight razor shaves much closer than an electric blade and can cause razor burn. Your face will be as smooth as a baby's bottom, though.)

Women can get a literal head-to-toe makeover, starting with hair-styling. A basic shampoo and blow-out starts at $39, depending on the length and thickness of your hair. A shampoo, cut, and style starts at $79; a formal updo starts at $59. If you want deep conditioning, the **Kérastase Elixir Ultime 24-Carat Treatment** ($59) entails a scalp massage and the application of "precious oils" to your hair.

Manicures ($69) and pedicures ($79) include a heated-stone massage of your various digits. *Note:* You have to book these separately—you can't get a mani–pedi. We've had onboard manicures and pedicures several times. The hand massage is nice, but we've found that the polish invariably chips within hours. *Every time.*

Facials and massages for guests of any gender are administered in private treatment rooms or in one of the dedicated Spa Villas for singles or couples. Facials include the **Biotec Radiance Renew Facial** ($169; includes an ultrasonic peel), the **Biotec Skin Resurfacer** ($199; includes an ultrasonic peel and light therapy), the **Biotec Firm-a-Lift Facial** ($199; includes facial massage and treatment with galvanic technology), and several others. Most facial treatments last 50 or 55 minutes.

Body massages include the traditional deep-tissue kind ($179 for 50 minutes, $209 for 75 minutes), as well as those with aromatherapy and seaweed wraps ($229), aromatherapy and hot stones ($179 or $209), or bamboo shoots ($179 or $209); the **Elemis Couture Touch** treatment combines a facial with Swedish massage ($299). Most of these can be configured as couples' massages, which start at $279 for a basic 50-minute session. *Couple* need not mean "romantic"—it can also mean a sibling, a friend, or even an adult parent or child.

The *Wish* advertises spa experiences in a **Zero Gravity Suite** and a **Hydration Suite** (both $499 for 130 minutes or $599 for 155 minutes), but neither was yet open at press time. If you have a chance to book a treatment in one of the suites, please let us know what you think.

Massages may also be arranged at **Castaway Cay.** The massage hut is located on the adult beach, **Serenity Bay.**

SPA VILLA SERVICES AND TREATMENTS Each Senses Spa has a handful of private Spa Villa rooms. Amenities include special treatments, a private verandah, an in-room whirlpool tub, an open-air shower, a Roman bed with canopy, a tea ceremony, a foot-cleansing ceremony, and the bathing ritual of your choice.

A Spa Villa reservation is typically about 2 hours long and includes your choice of couples' massage, plus private time in the room. Expect to pay about $450–$500, depending on the options you select.

OUTDOOR OASIS (*WISH*) The only fully outdoor adult spa area in the DCL fleet, the Outdoor Oasis features canopy-covered whirlpools, plush lounge chairs, swing-style lounge beds, and spaces for open-air yoga. The only thing that would make it better would be if you could actually see the ocean: though technically outdoors, the Oasis is enclosed, blocking all views of the sea.

REJUVENATION SPA This is DCL's umbrella term for medically supervised beauty treatments (some of which aren't offered on the *Magic* or *Wonder.*) If you book an appointment, you'll be required to participate in a 30-minute consultation with the aesthetic doctor beforehand. Pricing information is revealed only after the consultation. (To paraphrase that quote attributed to J. P. Morgan: if you have to ask, you can't afford it.)

Some Rejuvenation services are noninvasive, including **Thermage** (a radiofrequency skin-tightening treatment) and **CoolSculpting** (which uses freezing temperatures to break down fat cells—allegedly). **GoSmile** teeth whitening and **acupuncture** are semi-invasive.

The most invasive treatments of all are **Dysport** and **Restylane,** temporary fillers that are injected into your face to smooth wrinkles and plump lips. Speaking for ourselves, if we were going to have anything injected into our faces, it wouldn't be with an unfamiliar practitioner in the middle of the ocean, with no possibility of follow-up down the road.

CHILL SPA This is what DCL calls its spa for teens. On the *Dream* and *Fantasy,* it's a dedicated spa-within-a-spa, with several teen-only rooms. On the *Magic* and *Wonder,* it's a single room tucked behind the beauty salon. There is no designated Chill area on the *Wish,* though teens may be able to book some spa experiences with their parents' permission.

Spa services for teens must be booked on board; you can't reserve them in advance as you can most spa services for adults. If you have a stressed-out teenager who needs a massage, you'll probably incur a bit of stress yourself high-tailing it to the spa to score a reservation before they all get snapped up.

At Chill Spa, guests ages 13–17 can partake of a special menu of services, including facials, massage, skin-exfoliating treatments, and manicure–pedicure packages. Prices start at about $29 for a manicure. Parent–child massage sessions cost about $99 for a half-body treatment and $195 for a full-body one.

While your teen may cringe at the thought of a side-by-side massage with Mom, officially a parent or guardian must be present during all Chill Spa appointments. In practice, however, this varies depending on the ship. During one cruise on the the *Dream,* Erin was asked to stay in the treatment room with her teen daughter while she was getting a massage. When the same daughter got a massage on the *Magic* a few months later, Erin was told to wait in the nearby spa lounge because the *Magic's* treatment room is too small. If you have a strong preference for staying in the same room with your child at all times, ask about the spa's policy when you book the appointment.

Finally, if you don't want your teen to be offered additional services or extra-cost lotions and potions, also note that at the time of booking.

THE RAINFOREST (Each DCL ship has a Rainforest, a suite of saunas, specialty showers, and relaxation areas. The Rainforests on the *Dream* and the *Fantasy* are significantly larger and better appointed than those on the *Magic* and *Wonder;* the Rainforest on the *Wish* is a significant step up from the other four iterations. The newer ships have outdoor whirlpools (available to guests with a Rainforest pass), while the older ships' whirlpools are indoors.

*un**official* **TIP**
Bring a towel to sit on in the saunas, and wear sandals—the seats and floors are very hot.

Sauna selections include the **Laconium,** which has mild heat and low humidity; the **Caldarium,** with moderate heat and humidity; and the **Hamam,** a full-on steam bath with the hottest temperatures. Unique to the *Wish* is the **Frigidarium,** an ice lounge that allows guests to combine cold therapies with warm therapies. Each sauna zone also has its own scent and music.

As this guest found, not everyone goes to the Rainforest with peace and quiet in mind:

Some guests enter the Rainforest thinking it's Blizzard Beach [a water park at Walt Disney World], screeching and laughing. I wish Disney would spend 45 seconds educating them on what to expect and explaining that this is a relaxation/quiet area for adults.

We haven't experienced this ourselves, but speak to a cast member if you encounter rowdy behavior in the spa.

We enjoy hopping between these saunas and the nearby Rainforest showers—tiled circular cutouts hidden behind the walls along the path leading to the saunas. Each shower has different options for water temperature, pressure, and spray pattern, each of which you select by pushing a button. For example, one option might be a light, cool mist, perfect for when you've just jumped out of the sauna. Another is like a warm, steady downpour in a tropical jungle.

The best thing about the Rainforest is that DCL sells only a limited number of packages per cruise. We hear that number can be as low as 40 people—as in on the entire ship—on the *Dream* and *Fantasy*. While we haven't actually fact-checked that claim, we can tell you that we've never seen more than two other people in this part of the spa on any cruise. It's the single most relaxing thing you can do on board.

On the *Magic, Wonder, Dream,* and *Fantasy,* expect to pay about $30 per day to use the Rainforest, with possible discounts for multiday/length-of-sail passes or couples' passes. At press time, however, pricing on the *Wish* is significantly higher: $180 per person for a three-night sailing, with no discounts for couples. Granted, the *Wish*'s Rainforest is larger than the other four, and it has an outdoor lounge and whirlpool area, but we're not sure these upgrades are worth paying twice as much for on a three-day sailing.

Shower scrubs in various scents (we like orange) are offered for an additional fee, though sometimes we skip those because it seems like washing money down the drain (literally). An 18% gratuity is added to all spa services.

When it comes to booking the Rainforest, you may be able to make a reservation during your pre-trip activity window, or you may have to call (☎ 800-601-8455); passes can also be purchased at the spa once you're on the ship, depending on availability. If you weren't able to snag a reservation before your sailing, we encourage you to buy your passes as soon as you set foot on the ship.

SENSES JUICE BAR Senses on the *Dream* and *Fantasy* offers freshly blended juices and smoothies for about $7–$10. See the profile in Part Seven, "Dining" (page 210), for more information.

Note that you don't have to use the spa to partake of the juice bar. Also keep an eye out for special juice-tasting menus, typically offered on embarkation day. The same types of juices are available at several of the coffee bars on the *Wish*.

IS IT A REAL BARGAIN?

YOU PROBABLY REALIZE that the "Louis Vuitton" bag you saw on sale for $25 at the Straw Market in Nassau is a fake, but you may not know that perfume and sunglasses are frequently counterfeited as well. Happily, many luxury brands (such as Gucci and the aforementioned Louis Vuitton) have stores in Caribbean and European ports, letting you buy with confidence. (See page 307 for more on shopping in port.)

Another thing to look out for is out-of-season merchandise being sold at full price: on one trip to Nassau, we found an authentic Kate Spade bag being sold at MSRP, but it could be found at 30%–50% off stateside because it was from the previous season.

When it comes to making any purchase, you need to do your due diligence ahead of time to know what a fair price is. In our experience, though, haggling with vendors isn't worth the potential savings.

SHOPPING

SHOPPING DOESN'T HAVE TO BE part of your cruise experience, but, like most cruise lines, DCL makes it hard to avoid. Shops on the ships sell everything from infant T-shirts to engagement rings; there are also shops in every port, both reputable and sketchy, along with opportunities to shop for DCL merchandise before and after your cruise.

STATEROOM GIFTS AND GOODIES

ONCE YOU'VE PAID IN FULL for your Disney cruise, you'll have access to the **Onboard Gifts** section of the DCL website: at the top of the homepage, go to the "Already Booked" tab and choose "Onboard Gifts" from the pull-down menu. This is where you can arrange to have treats and surprises waiting for you when you arrive at your stateroom; you can also have gifts delivered to someone else's room as long as you have his or her reservation number.

The options include stateroom decorations for birthdays and holidays (about $50–$70), floral bouquets (about $50–$100), Champagne and chocolates (about $130), and a selection of deluxe Rocky Patel cigars ($85). You can also preorder a birthday cake (regular or food-allergy-friendly; about $55), along with more-prosaic items like eco-friendly cans of bottled water ($14 for 6, $28 for 12, or $55 for 24) or a six-pack of Bud Light (about $34). Note, however, that you may bring aboard as much bottled water like and up to a six-pack of beer per adult in your carry-on luggage (see page 74), making that a much more economical option.

unofficial **TIP**
You need a reservation number to buy but not to browse—to see what's available, choose "Browse by Departure Port" on the Onboard Gifts landing page at the DCL website.

Cake orders must be placed no later than seven days before you sail; all other orders must be placed no later than three days before.

For more information, call ☎ 800-601-8455 Monday–Friday, 8 a.m.–10 p.m. Eastern time; Saturday and Sunday, 9 a.m.–8 p.m. Note that cake orders have a strict cancellation policy, so read the fine print.

SHOP DCL AT HOME

MANY DISNEY-BRANDED ITEMS sold in the shipboard gift shops are also available at **shopDisney** (shopdisney.com); to find DCL merchandise, type "cruise" into the search bar. This is the place to order personalized DCL family T-shirts before your trip (about $30 each) or pick up that souvenir you forgot to buy. The sale prices at shopDisney are sometimes lower than those on the ships, and they almost always list a free-shipping code for orders over $75.

ONBOARD SHOPS

EACH DCL SHIP has several shops that stock everything from diapers to designer watches. Most shops are located on **Deck 4** of the *Magic* and *Wonder,* **Deck 3** of the *Dream* and *Fantasy,* and **Decks 3 and 4** of the *Wish.* If you think you're going to run out of something critical, stock up while the shops are open (for hours, check the Navigator app); note that the shops close whenever the ship is in port.

unofficial **TIP**
The onboard shops sell colorful pins themed to Disney characters or elements of the ships (most are priced in the $12–$15 range). Much as in the Disney theme parks, you can buy these pins and then trade them onboard with crew members and other guests.

Souvenirs

Expect to see many of the same items you'd find in the Disney theme parks: T-shirts, trading pins, picture frames, ball caps, and plush toys. Some of our favorite DCL-specific souvenirs are brush-shaped butter knives like the ones at Animator's Palate and trading pins with a specific sailing or a specific year.

The souvenir shops may also stock location-specific items. During one Alaskan cruise, for example, the shops carried mittens, knit caps, binoculars, and books about local wildlife. In case you forgot to pack your eye patch for Pirate Night (see page 232), the shops can outfit your entire family from head to toe, buccaneer-style.

Disney-branded merchandise sold through DCL is priced the same as the equivalent souvenirs sold at Disney's US theme parks—a Mickey Mouse T-shirt sold on the *Dream* or *Fantasy* costs the same as if you bought it at EPCOT. To get a feel for what you might spend, approximate prices for typical Disney souvenirs sold on the ships or online are as follows:

• Adult T-shirt: $35	• Disney coffee mug: $20
• Autograph book: $15	• Disney trading pin: $10–$18
• Baseball cap: $30	• Plush Mickey or Minnie: $30
• Beach towel: $25	• Spirit jersey: $75

Note: In the post-pandemic era, Disney, like many other companies, has faced intermittent supply-chain issues. This has resulted in problems keeping souvenir merchandise in stock, particularly on the DCL. If you see something you want on the ship, our advice is to buy it immediately; they're unlikely to have extra stock "in the back." If you change your mind, you can always return items later in your sailing.

Drugstore Items

Each ship also has a sundries shop that sells basics similar to those you'd find at your local CVS or Target. The stock is consistent across the ships, with only minor variations (different flavors of baby food, for example). Here's a sampling of what's typically available.

BABY CARE Baby food and formula; baby oil, body wash, powder, and shampoo; bottles and pacifiers; diapers (including swim diapers), diaper rash cream, and wipes; nursing pads

FIRST AID Adhesive bandages; antibiotic ointment; anti-itch creams and sticks; jellyfish-sting-relief lotion; sunburn spray and gel

FIX-IT GEAR Eyeglass-repair kits; sewing kits

FOR THE POOL DECK AND IN PORT Cooling towels; ear and nose plugs; insect repellent; sunscreen; swim goggles

OVER THE COUNTER Antacids; antihistamine tablets and gel caps; cold remedies (cold-and-flu liquids and tablets, cough drops, decongestants); eye drops; laxatives; pain relievers (aspirin and nonaspirin); seasickness tablets and bands; sleep aids; thermometers

PERSONAL CARE Antiperspirant; body lotion; body wash; contact lens cases; cotton swabs; disposable razors and shaving cream; menstrual products; hair-care products (brushes and combs, hair bands and clips, hairspray/gel, shampoo and conditioner); hand sanitizer; lip balm; nail-care products (clippers and files, polish-remover pads); oral-care products (breath strips, dental floss, mouthwash, toothbrushes, toothpaste); petroleum jelly; tissues; tweezers

TRAVEL-SPECIFIC Electrical adapters; luggage locks

MISCELLANEOUS Condoms; detergent pens; dish soap; pantyhose

When it comes to selection, what's on the shelves is all there is to choose from. The takeaway here—particularly for baby supplies—is to bring your own favorite products if you insist on a particular brand that may not be in stock on board.

Of particular note regarding OTC medications, you *won't* find remedies for gastrointestinal woes, such as Imodium or Pepto-Bismol. (See page 60 for more on treating gastric distress.)

You also won't find much in the way of cosmetics. Depending on the sailing, the duty-free-fragrance section in one of the other shops may also stock a few high-end beauty products. But if you forgot to pack eyeliner, you're probably out of luck until you can buy more in port.

All of these items are sold at a considerable markup in the sundries shop versus your local drugstore, supermarket, discount store, or online retailer. Here are a few products whose prices we spot-checked aboard DCL and at Amazon Fresh:

PRODUCT	PRICE (DCL)	PRICE (Amazon Fresh)
Benadryl Liqui-Gels (24 gel caps)	$7.49	$4.19
Colgate Total Clean Mint Toothpaste (0.75 oz.)	$1.95	$1.10
Coppertone UltraGuard Sunscreen Lotion SPF 70 (8 oz.)	$13.99	$12.83
Degree Men Cool Rush Antiperspirant (0.5 oz.)	$3.29	70¢
Gillette Foamy Shave Foam (2 oz.)	$2.99	$1.19

If you have a sudden personal-care need when the sundries shop is closed—you're feeling seasick and you desperately need a Dramamine, or you don't have a tampon handy—stop by **Guest Services,** which is always open and has a free "single serving" stash of many basics. On rough sea days, we've also seen a basket of free motion-sickness meds placed just outside of the **Health Center** (see page 140).

Accessories, Clothing, Fragrances, and Jewelry

In addition to the souvenir and sundries shops, each DCL ship also has a few stores that sell prestige fragrances (such as Chanel, Hermès, and Prada), along with name-brand clothing (such as Tommy Bahama and Vineyard Vines); handbags (Dooney & Bourke, Kate Spade, and the like); sunglasses (Michael Kors, Prada, Ray-Ban, etc.); jewelry (such as Gucci and Pandora); and wristwatches (including Citizen, TAG Heuer, and Tissot). Aside from a few shipboard exclusives, most of these items can be found at any nice mall or reputable online store.

The full prices for brand-name clothing, accessories, and the like on the ships generally square up with the full prices on land, but you can generally get better deals online than on board. For example, a Vineyard Vines blouse we found on the *Dream* cost $88, the same as on the Vineyard Vines website, but it was eventually marked down to $62.99 during an end-of-season sale online. On the ship, a Platinum Castaway Club discount, along with a lack of onboard sales tax, would bring the price down some, but not as much as if you bought directly from Vineyard Vines.

You'll also find pricey skin- and hair-care products (such as Bliss, Elemis, and Phyto) for sale at **Senses Spa.** If you're having a spa treatment and you don't want these products foisted on you by the staff, be prepared to say "no" early and often (see page 298).

Disney-Themed Art

All ships but the *Wish* have a **Vista Gallery** that sells Disney-themed prints and original art. The prices are the same as what you'd pay at, for instance,

DOING YOUR DUTY

YOU'LL LIKELY ENCOUNTER the words *duty* and *duty-free* when you shop on your cruise, but many international travelers have no idea what they mean. Simply put, duty is a customs tax or tariff that's levied when you bring certain purchases across international borders.

Under certain conditions, US residents may bring back up to $800 in merchandise bought outside of the country without having to pay duty on it. In general, these conditions are as follows: (1) your trip outside of the United States lasted at least 48 hours, (2) you haven't traveled outside of the US more than once within a 30-day period, and (3) the merchandise in question is in your possession and is either for your personal use or a gift for someone else.

You may bring up to 1 liter (33.8 ounces) of alcohol, 200 cigarettes, and/or 100 non-Cuban cigars into the US without having to pay duty on them.

Found primarily in airports, **duty-free shops** sell products to international travelers (you'll be asked for proof of travel, such as an airline boarding pass), but you could still have to pay duty in the US on such purchases if they fall outside of your exemption allowance. If, for instance, you bought 2 liters of wine at the duty-free shop at Charles de Gaulle Airport in Paris, the 1-liter exemption limit on alcohol means you'd still have to pay duty on 1 of those 2 liters even if your overall purchases totaled less than $800.

If your purchases total more than $800, you'll be charged a flat 3% rate on the portion in excess of your $800 exemption, up to $1,000; thus, if you're bringing $1,500 worth of merchandise into the US, you'll pay 3% duty on $700 of your total purchases, or $21. Again, the previously listed limits on alcohol and tobacco apply.

If your purchases exceed $1,800, the remaining duty is calculated based on US tariff rates for the country from which you're importing the goods and the types of goods you're importing.

Note: You must pay any duty that you owe before you clear customs. US currency, checks drawn on US banks, and US money orders are accepted; some (but not all) customs checkpoints also take credit and debit cards.

A great resource for information on duty-free shopping is the **US Customs and Border Protection** website: see tinyurl.com/CBPCustomsDutyInfo. For more on clearing customs, see page 147.

the Art of Disney store at EPCOT. The pieces are nice enough if Disney art is your thing—but if you decide to buy a sofa-size painting, have a game plan for getting it home before you commit to the purchase.

On the *Wish*, art sales take place at a stand-alone kiosk near the Guest Services desk. The kiosk offers the same **Disney Art On Demand** service available at several locations in the Disney theme parks. Select an artwork, the size you'd like it to be, whether you want the print on paper or canvas, and if you want your art framed or matted. Your piece will be delivered to your home within a few weeks

CASTAWAY CAY

THE SHOPS SELL SOME ITEMS that are exclusive to the island, such as T-shirts and beach towels. We've purchased cords for our sunglasses, water-resistant pouches for our phones, and other beach supplies here. No sales tax is charged on Castaway Cay or on board, which makes purchases cheaper than if you bought them at a Disney park.

IN PORT

MANY TRAVELERS FIND SHOPPING IN PORT as essential to cruising as gambling is to Las Vegas. If you approach buying things with this attitude, you won't be disappointed. You'll be surrounded by shopping opportunities at each port from the moment you step off the ship; bargaining is expected, so assume that the first price you're quoted isn't the final one. If you need cheap souvenirs, you'll have no trouble finding T-shirts and tchotchkes within a few hundred yards of the ship.

Northern European ports are the exception to the schlock-shopping onslaught. As in every port, though, you need to ask pointed questions about the things you want to buy. If it's mittens in Norway, for instance, ask not only if they're made from local wool but also whether they were hand- or machine-knit, as well as whether they were knit in Norway or in a factory in China.

JEWELRY Buying jewelry in port can be tricky. Because fair prices vary greatly with the quality of gems available for sale, you need to be an informed shopper to know just what a fair price is. Our recommendation is to pre-shop online—**Amazon** and **Blue Nile** (bluenile.com) are great places to start—to know the going rates for gems of the weight and quality you're interested in. One common brand **Effy,** is sold on Amazon and at its own website (effyjewelry.com); **Diamonds International,** which is ubiquitous in the Caribbean, has an online presence as well (diamondsinternational.com).

ALCOHOL Duty-free alcohol is available in most ports. If you're thinking about purchasing spirits during your cruise, be sure to do a little pricing research before you travel. Depending on your place of residence and its tax situation, the duty-free pricing may not differ much from what you'd pay at home. Look at the *per-ounce* price to make sure you're comparing apples to apples, or rather tequila to tequila. Further, be aware of price differences between different grades of liquor (*añejo* versus *reposado* tequila, for example).

*un*official **TIP**
If you decide to buy alcohol during your trip, remember to review DCL's rules for bringing it on board (see page 74). In many cases, you won't have access to your purchase until the last night of your cruise.

On the other hand, cost may not be a major concern if you're considering a sentimental purchase (that bottle of wine you learned about during a port-adventure vineyard tour) or you want to buy something that you can't get anywhere else (say, a liqueur made from a flower that grows only in the part of the world you're visiting on your cruise).

ONBOARD PHOTOGRAPHY

MANY DISNEY CRUISERS consider pictures taken by shipboard photographers to be an integral part of their experience (although you're certainly under no obligation to buy photos or have your picture taken). You can buy an all-inclusive onboard photo package before your trip by visiting the **My Reservations** section of the DCL website (see page 47) and selecting "Onboard Fun"; your cruise must be paid in full, and you must be within your window for booking activities. Advance purchases may be completed up to two days before you sail. Photos are provided to you either on a USB flash drive or via digital download.

*un*official **TIP**
To pre-purchase a photo package, you must select a specific day and time. We're not sure of the reasoning behind this, though: your photo package remains in effect from the moment you board the ship untll the photographers stop taking pictures on the last day of your cruise.

Pre-purchasing a photo package is often less expensive than buying one on the ship. For example, on a five-night, summer 2022 sailing of the *Wish,* the onboard price for an unlimited photo package was $249.95, while the pre-cruise price was $211.95. The main disadvantages to pre-purchasing photos are that (1) you may not be happy with the photos or (2) something unforeseen may happen—onboard quarantine, for example—that prevents you from taking as many photos as you might otherwise.

Because there's no limit to the number of pictures in an all-inclusive package, you want to put your face in front of the cameras as often as you can to get the biggest bang for your buck. You can also buy smaller quantities of photos, but you can do this only on board, and smaller packages aren't discounted. Typically, if you think you'll want more than 15 onboard photos, it makes better economic sense to buy the unlimited package in advance.

*un*official **TIP**
Photos must be downloaded within 45 days of the day the photo was taken, **not** from the end of your cruise. Thus, you'll lose access to pictures taken at the beginning of your trip sooner than for those taken at the end of your trip.

Photo packages are sold by stateroom, *not* by passenger or party. If you pre-purchase a package, you'll need to designate one person in your stateroom as the purchaser—all guests in your cabin may use the package, but the transaction won't go through if you select more than one purchaser. If your party includes more than one stateroom, check with DCL regarding discounts or bulk rates.

Photos take on board come with a decorative custom border that includes such details as the ship's name—this border can't be removed. Note as well that DCL photos are taken in nonstandard aspect ratios, so if you want to get them printed on your own, you may need to crop or resize them to print on standard 4 × 6, 5 × 7, or 8 × 10 paper.

Finally, all ships have a **Shutters Portrait Studio.** The pictures taken here are artistic black-and-white shots that aren't included in the price of regular onboard photography. Packages range from $550 for 5 digital images to $2,500 for a USB drive containing up to 100. If you're also vacationing at Walt Disney World, we think Disney's **Capture Your Moment** portrait sessions (tinyurl.com/wdwcaptureyourmoment) are a much better value.

RELIGIOUS SERVICES

CRUISES OF SEVEN NIGHTS or longer hold a nondenominational Christian service on Sunday mornings and a Shabbat service on Friday evenings. Worship times depend on when the ship is in port or, in the case of Jewish services, when sunset occurs. There are no dedicated chapels on the ships—services are typically held in a lounge or theater, depending on the number of guests on board and the ship's other offerings. **Guest Services** can recommend houses of worship in port.

Additional services take place during religious holidays. Check the DCL Navigator app for details.

Many DCL ports have houses of worship as key points of interest. If you'd like to attend services while in port, check the institution's website in advance to view hours of operation or check whether a dress code applies (as is common in many European churches).

WHAT TO DO
During A DAY AT SEA

SOME OF THE MOST FREQUENTLY ASKED QUESTIONS we hear from new cruisers are variations on, "What happens during a day at sea?" and "Won't I be bored staying on a ship all day?" To that we say, "There are zillions of things to do for all ages and interests" and "You'll only be bored if you want to be." Below is just a handful of the things we've done on sea days. (Note that not all DCL-organized activities are available on all sailings—the longer your sailing and the more sea days you have, the more options you'll have.)

On a Day at Sea, You Can . . .

▪ Meet characters. ▪ Get a manicure or pedicure. ▪ Sleep. ▪ Watch old Disney films. ▪ Watch new Disney films. ▪ Read a novel. ▪ Write a short story. ▪ Shop for souvenirs. ▪ Play a round of minigolf. ▪ Play shuffleboard. ▪ Learn to mix drinks. ▪ Enjoy the drinks you mixed. ▪ Savor fine cuisine. ▪ Learn to draw Disney characters. ▪ Watch a stage show. ▪ Meet a Broadway performer. ▪ Learn the fine art of towel folding. ▪ Play cards. ▪ Take a cooking class. ▪ Lift weights. ▪ Go for a swim. ▪ Go for a run. ▪ Take a tour of the ship. ▪ Attend a religious service. ▪ Whoop it up at a deck party. ▪ Play Foosball. ▪ Play video games. ▪ Hang out at a piano bar. ▪ Get an acupuncture treatment. ▪ Stare at the sea. ▪ Attend a history class. ▪ Dance in a nightclub. ▪ Take a ballroom dance class. ▪ Sit in a sauna. ▪ Soak in a hot tub. ▪ Have a family portrait taken. ▪ Go on a waterslide. ▪ Order room service. ▪ Buy jewelry. ▪ Trade Disney pins. ▪ Watch for wildlife. ▪ Sing karaoke. ▪ Get a massage. ▪ Sample a food you've never tried before. ▪ Do the entire *New York Times* Sunday crossword puzzle in one sitting. ▪ Play in a trivia competition. ▪ Chat with other guests. ▪ Chat with your family.

PART TEN

CASTAWAY CAY

COVID TIP
Appropriate face coverings are required on Castaway Cay for guests ages 2 and up—regardless of vaccination status—in queues, on trams, in areas that sell merchandise, in restrooms and in dining pavilions when they're not actively eating or drinking.

CASTAWAY CAY (*cay* is pronounced "key") is likely to be your favorite island on your Bahamian or Caribbean cruise. The weather is almost always gorgeous; the shore excursions are reasonably priced (mostly); and, as is the case with Walt Disney World, there's little of the real world to get in the way of a relaxing day. And that's before the free food and (non-alcoholic) drinks. We provide additional coverage of Castaway Cay in Part Twelve, "Port Adventures."

 ## WHAT *to* BRING

THE SUN AND HEAT ARE INTENSE, so bring plenty of high-SPF sunscreen and water. Insulated sports bottles are a great idea. Other solar protection you may need includes light-colored, long-sleeved, lightweight shirts; sweatpants; swimsuit cover-ups; hats; lip balm; and sunglasses. See the next page for additional items that you may want to bring along.

Disney will provide you with medium-size towels for use while on Castaway Cay—as many as you can carry. If you'd rather use a full-size beach towel, bring one of your own or buy one while you're on the island. Disney also provides free life jackets to use on Castaway Cay, with strollers, wagons, and sand-capable wheelchairs available for rent on a first-come, first-served basis.

 ## WHAT *to* DO

THERE ARE MORE THINGS TO DO than you'll have time for in a single day or even two. A list of our favorite Castaway Cay shore activities follows; see Part Twelve for details.

OTHER ITEMS TO BRING TO CASTAWAY CAY

- **Face coverings.** In the immediate post-COVID era, masks are required in certain areas of Castaway Cay (see Unofficial Tip on the previous page).

- **Sunglasses.** The light reflecting off the sand and water can be a problem if you or someone in your party has sensitive eyes.

- **A watch or cell phone** for checking how long everyone has been in the sun and when it's time to reapply sunscreen. Also useful for knowing whether the island's restaurants are open (usually 11 a.m.–2 p.m.).

- **An underwater/waterproof camera** for taking photos while swimming, snorkeling, etc.

- **A small cooler** to keep medicine, baby formula, and other perishables cool. Fill it with ice before you leave the ship, and refill it from the restaurants' ice machines on the island. The cooler must be soft-sided and no larger than 12 x 12 x 12 inches.

- **Water shoes** will protect your feet from sharp rocks and coral and provide some insulation from hot sand and pavement.

- **Small beach toys**, such as a shovel and pail, though pails might present some packing issues. Toys are also available for purchase on the island.

- **Your own snorkeling gear** if you already have it, or if the idea of sharing a snorkel tube just grosses you out. DCL provides flotation vests for free.

- **Swim diapers**, if you have little ones who like the water.

- **A hairbrush or comb.** It's windy on Castaway Cay, and you'll want to look good in your vacation photos.

- **Insect repellent.** Disney does a good job of keeping bugs at bay, but with heightened concerns about Zika virus, it's still a good idea to bring something like Off or Repel. Disney now provides insect repellent at many ports, but if you're sensitive to certain ingredients or you prefer a particular brand, bring your own.

- **Something to read—a book or e-reader.** Be careful, however, about leaving expensive electronics unattended on the island.

- **A portable music player and headphones,** which are especially useful if you're going for a jog around the island's 5K course. Don't bring external speakers.

- **Athletic shoes and socks.** If you want to play basketball, you'll also want proper footwear.

- **A change of clothes.** While Castaway Cay's sun will dry your swimsuit in a hurry, you may want dry clothes to wear while you're walking around the island, sitting down for meals, or riding bikes. You can also return to the ship to change, but going through security takes time.

OUR FAVORITE FUN STUFF ON CASTAWAY CAY

- **Castaway Ray's Stingray Adventure** affords you the opportunity to pet and feed small and medium-size stingrays in a dedicated lagoon.

- The **snorkeling lagoon** features underwater sights, such as a replica of the *Nautilus* submarine from *20,000 Leagues Under the Sea* and statues of Minnie and Mickey. Common marine life seen in the snorkeling lagoon includes stingrays, blue tang, and yellowtail snapper (plus the occasional barracuda).

- Rent **sailboats or paddleboats, personal watercraft,** or **inflatable floats and tubes.**

- Runners may want to start their day with the **Castaway Cay 5K,** a free (as in no-cost) jog through the developed parts of the island.

- Single-speed **bicycle rentals** allow you to fully explore the island, including its observation tower and trails, which can be accessed only on foot or bike.

Castaway Cay's lagoons are shallow, with small, gentle waves. Anchored within a short swim from shore is **Pelican Plunge,** a floating platform with two waterslides and a water-play area. The waterslides begin on the platform's second story (accessed by stairs) and end with a splash back into the lagoon. Each slide offers a different experience:

continued on page 314

Castaway Cay

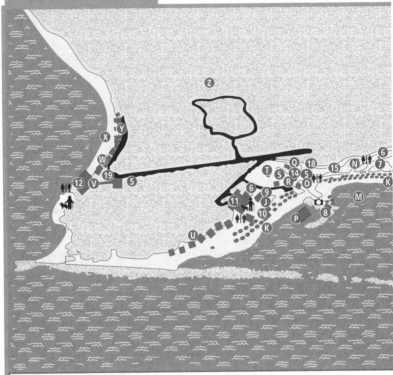

ATTRACTIONS

A. Arrival Plaza
B. Post Office
C. Marge's Barges and
     Sea Charters Dock
D. Boating Harbor
E. Scuttle's Cove
F. Boat Beach
G. Monstro Point
H. Castaway Ray's
     Stingray Adventure
I. Gil's Fins and Boats
J. Gazebos
K. Castaway Family Beaches
L. Snorkeling Lagoon
M. Swimming Lagoon
N. In-Da-Shade Games
O. Flippers and Floats
P. Pelican Plunge

ATTRACTIONS

Q. The Hide Out (teens only)
R. Bike Rentals
S. Beach Sports
T. Spring-a-Leak
U. Family Cabanas 1–21
V. The Windsock Hut
W. Massage Cabanas
X. Serenity Bay Adult Beach
Y. Adult Cabanas 22–27
Z. Observation Tower

FOOD AND DRINK

1. Pop's Props and Boat Repair
     (Covered Seating)
2. Dig In (Covered Seating)
3. Cookie's BBQ
4. Conched Out Bar

FOOD AND DRINK

5. Summertime Freeze
6. Outdoor Seating
7. Gumbo Limbo (Covered Seating)
8. Heads Up Bar
9. Grouper (Covered Seating)
10. Sand Bar
11. Cookie's Too BBQ
12. Castaway Air Bar

SHOPPING

13. She Sells Sea Shells . . .
    and Everything Else
14. Buy the Seashore
15. Bahamian Retail

MISCELLANEOUS

16. Kargo Handling Tram Stop
17. Scuttle's Cove Tram Stop
18. Pelican Point Tram Stop
19. Serenity Bay Tram Stop

Animal-Relief Area
Bike/Nature Trail
First Aid
Photo Opportunities
Restrooms and
    Outdoor Showers

continued from page 311

one is a long, open slide with moderate turns, while the other is a shorter, enclosed slide with plenty of tight turns and twists.

Along with the slides, Pelican Plunge's water-play area includes pipes, nozzles, and plumes of water spraying out from every direction. The main feature is a giant overhead bucket, which is constantly being filled with water from the lagoon. The bucket is counterbalanced so that when the water reaches a certain level, the bucket tilts over suddenly, pouring gallons of water on anything nearby.

If you have small children who enjoy water but you're concerned about ocean currents, consider letting the little ones run around at the inland **Spring-a-Leak** water-play area, just beyond the Pelican Point tram stop, near the middle of the family beaches. Like Pelican Plunge, Spring-a-Leak has plenty of burbling, spraying, misting water to keep kids wet and happy all day long.

Scuttle's Cove, an additional area for the little ones, offers supervised activities, yet another water-play area, and a giant-whale-bone excavation site. Teens have their own dedicated area inland: **The Hide Out,** with volleyball, tetherball, and other activities. Some teens, however, may not like the fact that The Hide Out is located away from the beach and has no water features or water-play areas. Note that kids and teens must be registered at their respective youth clubs on board (see page 265) to play at Scuttle's Cove and hang out at The Hide Out.

HEIGHT AND AGE REQUIREMENTS AT CASTAWAY CAY

- **Pelican Plunge waterslide:** No official height or age requirement listed, but life jackets are encouraged. Tweens (ages 11–13) have scheduled time to hang out (supervised by youth counselors) at both Pelican Plunge and the **In-Da-Shade Games pavilion.**
- **The Hide Out:** Ages 13–17; must be registered for Vibe on board
- **Scuttle's Cove:** Ages 3–12; children must be registered for the Oceaneer Club/Oceaneer Lab on board

---

WHERE *to* **RELAX**

CASTAWAY CAY IS ALSO a great place to sit back, listen to the ocean, and feel the sea breeze on your face. Two family beaches are available, while adults ages 18 and up have **Serenity Bay,** a private beach with its own outdoor barbecue, bar, rental cabanas, and more.

FAMILY BEACHES Most of Castaway Cay's developed beachfront is reserved for families. If you're taking the tram from the dock, get off at the first stop, **Pelican Point,** and you'll find yourself in the middle of both family beaches.

A small, hook-shaped peninsula juts into the lagoon and effectively separates the family beaches. If you're going to rent floats or boats or

CASTAWAY CAY DONE RIGHT *by Scott Sanders*

DISNEY'S PRIVATE ISLAND is an extension of the cruise ship experience, because the ship's crew works in various roles on Castaway Cay. You may, for instance, see your serving team barbecuing at Cookie's BBQ or your favorite bartender at Heads Up Bar on Pelican Point.

On the island, there are plenty of loungers and beach chairs for everyone, even if you sleep in and get a late start on the island. Hammocks are more scarce, so arrive early (or look for one around 3 p.m.) if that's part of your island dream.

My favorite time to explore the snorkeling lagoon is in the morning before it gets crowded. As for seeing the rest of the island, the bike rental is a relatively inexpensive way to cover the trails and quickly get to the observation tower.

Not interested in going ashore? No problem. While most guests are on the island, that leaves plenty of loungers around the pool and makes lines for the waterslides much shorter—sometimes nonexistent.

do some snorkeling, you'll want to head to the left of the peninsula once you're off the tram. If you're going to play in the water, especially at the Pelican Plunge waterslide, bear right.

CABANAS The Pelican Plunge side of the beach has 21 private cabanas for rent. The base price is $599 or $649, plus tax, depending on the season, for up to six guests. Up to four additional guests may be added for $50 each, plus tax. One Grand Cabana on the family beach can accommodate up to 16 guests at $949, plus tax, for the first 10 guests, plus an additional $50, plus tax, for up to 6 more.

At Serenity Bay adult beach, six cabanas are available for $399, plus tax, for the first four guests. Up to two additional guests may be added for $50, plus tax, each.

Cabana rentals also include free use of snorkeling equipment, floats, and bikes. Those three things total $46 a person. If you have six people in your cabana, that's a $276 value. If you'd normally spring for that equipment and several soft drinks, the price of some private shade and comfort seems a lot more reasonable. (*Note:* Snorkeling equipment is currently not included with the Serenity Bay cabanas.)

The cabanas are so popular that they're often fully booked in advance by Concierge and Platinum Castaway Club members before the general public gets a crack at them; however, cancellations do happen. If you're interested, ask at the Port Adventures desk as soon as you board the ship, and periodically check back a few times before the ship docks at Castaway Cay.

PART ELEVEN

ITINERARIES *at a* GLANCE

OVERVIEW

THE FOLLOWING SECTION provides a broad, general overview of the geographic areas visited by Disney Cruise Line: the pros and cons of cruising in each area, the ports from which the cruises sail, the ships that serve these itineraries, how long most cruises run, and the time of year for most itineraries. We've also included advice and suggestions about what to pack and things to see and do.

FURTHER INFORMATION

FOR THE LATEST INFORMATION ABOUT specific ports and itineraries in these regions for 2023–24, visit the DCL website (disney cruise.disney.go.com) and click the "Destinations" menu at the top of the page; then select a specific geographic area, and click "View Prices" to see a list of cruises for that region.

*un*official **TIP**
Disney Cruise Line cast members hail from more than 80 different countries. In addition to exploring the ports, you and your kids can learn a lot about the world by chatting with the crew.

Scott Sanders's **Disney Cruise Line Blog** lists all currently scheduled itineraries on one convenient page that's updated regularly: see tinyurl .com/DCLBlogItineraries. Each itinerary includes a sketch map showing the route and ports of call. Pull-down menus on the left side of each page let you access itinerary information by port, ship, month, and year.

For tips on researching the weather in the ports that your itinerary visits, see page 77.

ITINERARIES IN THE COVID ERA

IF YOUR PRIMARY REASON for choosing a cruise itinerary is that you want to visit a specific, once-in-a-lifetime attraction, it may make sense for you to postpone your trip until COVID fully dissipates. Otherwise, you should be prepared for tourist access to a particular port or a particular venue to be curtailed or restricted at any time. See Part Two, pages 50–55, for further discussion.

ALASKA

PROS	CONS
▪ **Vancouver,** one of the most beautiful cities in North America, is a noteworthy destination in its own right, one that we recommend visiting for a few days before or after your cruise.	▪ The weather can range from chilly to downright cold—and it *will* rain at some point during your cruise.
▪ Breathtaking scenery.	▪ If shopping is a big part of your cruise experience, you'll be disappointed.
▪ If you've ever wanted to see a glacier from a hot tub, here's your chance!	▪ The length of the cruise plus travel time to and from Vancouver may be more than you can schedule (at least 9 days).
▪ West Coasters, this is an easy and convenient trip for you.	▪ Only one DCL ship, the *Wonder,* cruises Alaska, and then only during the summer.

CRUISES SAIL FROM Vancouver | **SHIP** *Wonder*

CRUISE LENGTHS Mostly 7 nights, occasionally 5 or 9

SEASON Summer

SPECIAL TOUCHES A naturalist on board who talks about the glaciers and wildlife you'll see, mulled wine on the bar menu, blankets to keep warm on the upper decks, hot soup at the counter-service food venues. A **Taste of Alaska** menu with Alaskan seafood is a big hit.

WHAT TO PACK Warm clothing, including gloves, hats, and scarves; waterproof shoes (that you can hike in); binoculars; sunscreen

SIGNATURE PORT ADVENTURE **Dogsledding.** It's pricey, but you'll *love* it.

COMMENTS We realize that Caribbean-cruise fatigue is the ultimate in first-world problems, so if you're rolling your eyes at us when we say that an Alaskan cruise is the cure for too many trips to Nassau, we hear you. That said, for the opposite of the Caribbean experience without leaving the United States, we heartily recommend seeing the 49th state by ship.

ATLANTIC CANADA

PROS	CONS
▪ Nice change from beach-based cruises.	▪ Not much shopping in the smaller ports.
▪ Canada residents: no need for currency exchange. US residents: remember to pick up some "loonies" (Canadian dollar coins) before you embark.	▪ Just a couple of ports.
	▪ Your kids may not be keen on a cruise where a highlight is looking at lighthouses.
▪ Good deals are available on transportation to New York City.	▪ Itinerary is offered only on the *Magic*, and then not every year.

CRUISES SAIL FROM New York City | **SHIP** *Magic*

CRUISE LENGTHS 4–7 nights | **SEASON** Early fall

continued on next page

WHAT TO PACK Rain jacket, umbrella

SIGNATURE PORT ADVENTURE Boat trip plus a lobster dinner

COMMENTS A DCL cruise along Canada's Atlantic coast is a great option for anyone who can easily get to New York City. (Disney confusingly designates this geographic area as the **Canadian Coastline**—as if Canada had just one coast.) Because the ports aren't primarily tourist destinations, there's much less focus on buying souvenirs; plus, your ship is often the only one in port, which makes for a relaxing day ashore. This cruise is a perfect fall-break vacation if you just want to get away for less than a week.

CARIBBEAN, BAHAMAS, *and* BERMUDA

PROS	CONS
■ Ports are easy to get to.	■ The port experience (except at Castaway Cay) is *very* commercial.
■ The US dollar is accepted in all ports, and English is spoken nearly everywhere.	■ Your ship will most likely be one of many others in port.
■ Castaway Cay is on nearly every Caribbean itinerary.	■ If you're not at least a little creative, DCL's Caribbean port stops tend to blend into one big duty-free-jewelry/hair-braiding/ frozen-cocktail blur.
■ A cruise can be combined with a Walt Disney World vacation.	
■ You have your choice of five ships and many cruise lengths.	■ The summer heat can be oppressive.

(Please see our Mexico travel advisory on page 320 and our Nassau travel advisory on page 333.)

CRUISES SAIL FROM Port Canaveral, Miami, Galveston, New Orleans, San Juan

SHIPS *Dream, Fantasy,* and *Wish* (year-round), *Magic* and *Wonder* (fall, winter, spring)

CRUISE LENGTHS 3-7 nights, occasionally 8, 10, and 11

SEASON Year-round | **WHAT TO PACK** Sunscreen, shorts, swimsuits, and shoes that you don't mind getting sandy

SIGNATURE PORT ADVENTURE **Castaway Cay**

CLASSIC DISNEY ADD-ON **Walt Disney World, Disney's Vero Beach Resort**

COMMENTS With more than 200 annual DCL sailings to these ports, the numbers are in your favor if you're looking for sun and fun. In case you're wondering why the Bahamas is singled out from the rest of the Caribbean, it's because the *Dream* and the *Wish* cruise almost exclusively to Nassau and Castaway Cay, which are Bahamian ports.

HAWAII/TRANSPACIFIC

CRUISES SAIL FROM Vancouver, Honolulu, or Sydney | **SHIP** *Wonder*

SEASONS Spring and fall | **CRUISE LENGTH** 10, 13, or 15 nights

PROS	CONS
▪ Cruises stop at 4 Hawaiian islands as well as Polynesian islands such as Fiji and American Samoa.	▪ If you're sailing from Hawaii or Sydney, prepare for jet lag that ranges from heavy-duty (if you're traveling from the West Coast) to crushing (if you're traveling from the East Coast).
▪ In the South Pacific, you can see everything from blue oceans to rain-forests and volcanoes.	▪ These cruises aren't cheap; plus, they're a major time commitment. If you're on a budget, be aware that an inside cabin isn't the best choice for a 10- to 15-night sailing.
▪ Weather is mild (but often rainy).	
▪ Sailing from **Vancouver** eases you into the time difference.	▪ To really experience Hawaii, you're better off flying to one island and staying there.
▪ **Sydney** is a world-class city with plenty of sightseeing and shopping opportunities.	▪ Because everything has to be shipped into Hawaii, food and other necessities are very expensive here.
▪ These new itineraries afford the chance to see places you may have never experienced before.	▪ Your only ship choice is the *Wonder*, and only during limited dates throughout the year.

SPECIAL TOUCHES Onboard cultural ambassadors who give seminars on lei-making, hula, and ukulele; Hawaiian food, music, and dance.

SIGNATURE PORT ADVENTURE Renting a car and seeing the islands for yourself, on your own time

DEFINITELY VISIT Volcanoes National Park, on the Big Island of Hawaii; **Mount 'Alava** in Pago Pago; the **Sydney Opera House**

CLASSIC DISNEY ADD-ON Disney's Aulani Resort & Spa on Oahu

WHAT TO PACK A variety of clothing for warm to chilly weather; suitable shoes for hiking if you plan to venture beyond the beaches

COMMENTS These cruises are expensive, but they could be well worth it if you've never been to the South Pacific or Australia before.

SOUTHERN EUROPE *and* MEDITERRANEAN

PROS	CONS
▪ A Mediterranean cruise is a good way to sample lots of ports without having to move your luggage.	▪ If you're coming from North America, round-trip airfare may put a serious dent in your budget.
▪ Shopping opportunities abound.	▪ You're only scratching the surface of all there is to see in this part of Europe.
▪ You have lots of family-friendly port adventures from which to choose.	▪ Your budget will likely be affected by currency-exchange rates.

Note: *The US Department of State currently advises travelers to this region to "exercise increased caution due to terrorism." No specific threats are mentioned in the advisory, but countries mentioned include Spain, France, and Italy, among others. Consult the country-specific information at travel.state.gov as you make decisions related to your family's travels.*

continued on next page

CRUISES SAIL FROM Barcelona | **SHIP** *Dream*

CRUISE LENGTHS 5, 7, 9, or 12 nights | **SEASON** Summer

WHAT TO PACK Good walking shoes, lots of euros

SIGNATURE PORT ADVENTURE City tour

CLASSIC DISNEY ADD-ON An **Adventures by Disney** tour or a side trip to **Disneyland Paris**

COMMENTS Mediterranean cruises are popular with families who want to see southern Europe with minimal hassle. Dining has an international flair. For many years, DCL used the *Magic* for its European itineraries; in 2023, they switched to the larger *Dream.*

MEXICO

Note: *In 2022 the US Department of State reaffirmed ongoing warnings about travel to Mexico. In a nutshell: US citizens traveling in certain parts of Mexico have been the victims of violent crimes, including homicide, kidnapping, carjacking, and robbery. Most of the homicides appear to have been targeted hits related to organized crime, but turf battles between rival criminal groups have resulted in shootings during daylight hours, injuring innocent bystanders.*

PROS	CONS
▪ Cruises can be affordable, particularly if you live on the West Coast.	▪ These cruises are marketed to families, but the fact that they take place while school is in session could make scheduling a problem.
▪ Short sailings are easy on your schedule.	▪ There's really nothing that sets these itineraries apart from comparable ones on any other cruise line.

CRUISES SAIL FROM San Diego | **SHIP** *Wonder*

CRUISE LENGTH 2, 3, 5, and 7 nights | **SEASONS** Year-round

WHAT TO PACK Sunscreen and sturdy walking shoes if you plan to visit the Maya ruins

SIGNATURE PORT ADVENTURES The usual suspects: sightseeing, dolphin excursions, beach pursuits, shopping, partying

CLASSIC DISNEY ADD-ON **Disneyland**

COMMENTS These ports are standard stops for most cruise lines—the selling point for the autumn sail dates is Disney's onboard Halloween decor. For the spring sail dates, there's little to differentiate these cruises from those offered by other lines.

NORTHERN EUROPE, BRITISH ISLES, *and* NORWAY

CRUISES SAIL FROM Copenhagen, Southampton | **SHIP** *Dream*

CRUISE LENGTHS 7–12 nights | **SEASON** Summer

WHAT TO PACK Binoculars, warm clothing

SIGNATURE PORT ADVENTURE It's all about the fjords.

PROS	CONS
■ The scenery is spectacular.	■ We really hope you enjoyed *Frozen*.
■ This is a very family-friendly way to see Northern Europe.	■ Food in port can be quite expensive.
■ Most of your meals are included in what are some very expensive places to visit.	■ These are among the most costly cruises that DCL offers—and that doesn't include your airfare.

CLASSIC DISNEY ADD-ON If you have any money left after your cruise, **Adventures by Disney** will gladly snap it up (see page 340).

COMMENTS There was this movie called *Frozen* that was mildly popular a few years ago. We're not saying that Disney decided the best way for DCL to take advantage of this was to sail to Arendelle—sorry, *Norway*—but there are definitely a lot of tie-ins on the cruise. But there's also scenery that can be appreciated only from a cruise ship.

PACIFIC COAST

PROS	CONS
■ These cruises are among DCL's shortest and can therefore be very affordable, particularly if you already live on the West Coast.	■ Because they visit only a few of the many worthwhile destinations along the Pacific Coast, we don't think these cruises are the best way to see California.
■ Short cruises are easy on your schedule.	

CRUISES SAIL FROM San Diego or Vancouver | **SHIP** *Wonder*

CRUISE LENGTHS 7 days or fewer **SEASON** Before and after the Alaskan runs

WHAT TO PACK Walking shoes, sunscreen

SIGNATURE PORT ADVENTURE City tour—but you're better off exploring on your own.

CLASSIC DISNEY ADD-ON Disneyland

COMMENTS Although marijuana is legal in many ports visited on these cruises, it is not permitted on the ships. Bringing marijuana on board in any form may result in expulsion from the ship or legal action.

PANAMA CANAL

Please see our Mexico travel advisory on the previous page.)

PROS	CONS
■ On a per-night basis, longer cruises are less expensive than shorter ones.	■ With just one trip each way per year, this itinerary can be hard to schedule.
■ Two weeks gives you lots of time to get to know the crew.	■ Other than the canal itself and the city of **Cartagena, Colombia,** the ports are kind of a snooze—they're the same ones visited by every other line.
■ This is a great way to experience the Panama Canal.	

continued on next page

CRUISES SAIL FROM Miami, San Diego | **SHIP** *Wonder*

CRUISE LENGTH 14 nights | **SEASONS** Spring and fall as the ship heads to Alaska from Florida; westward in the spring and eastbound in the fall

WHAT TO PACK Your formalwear—14-night cruises give you lots of chances to dress up.

SIGNATURE PORT ADVENTURE It's all about going through the canal.

CLASSIC DISNEY ADD-ON Disneyland

COMMENTS Going through the Panama Canal is a classic itinerary for cruising, and you can let your friends and family know when they can see the ship in one of the great engineering achievements of the world by sending them to pancanal.com/eng/photo/camera-java.html. Be sure to wave to the camera!

TRANSATLANTIC

PROS	CONS
▪ A Transatlantic cruise can be a cost-effective way to travel to Europe if you have the time to spare.	▪ You may not have 2 weeks to dedicate to a Transatlantic cruise.
▪ A Transatlantic crossing is on many cruisers' bucket lists.	▪ This is one-way transportation. Even if you end up getting a great deal on the cruise itself, remember that you'll have to make room in your budget for your airfare home.
▪ You can sometimes score excellent last-minute deals on these cruises.	

CRUISES SAIL FROM Barcelona, New York City, | **SHIP** *Dream*
Southampton

CRUISE LENGTHS 10 or 12 nights

DATES Spring and fall as the ship heads to Europe from Florida; eastward in the spring and westbound in the fall

WHAT TO PACK Your formalwear—you'll have plenty of opportunities to dress up—and a steamer trunk, if you have one.

SIGNATURE PORT ADVENTURE When it comes to Transatlantic cruises, it's all about the journey rather than the destination.

CLASSIC DISNEY ADD-ON Disneyland Paris

COMMENTS Wanna travel to or from Europe without jet lag *and* pretend that you've gone back in time? Crossing the Atlantic by ship is the old-school way to do it, harking back to the era of the grand ocean liner.

PART TWELVE

PORT ADVENTURES

PRECAUTIONS TO PONDER

BEFORE CRUISING WAS PAUSED IN 2020, DCL guests could leave the ship at any time while in port on their own, for as little or as long as they liked, as long as they were back on the ship in time for departure. Post-pandemic, things have bounced around a bit.

During the initial return to sailing, DCL prohibited unvaccinated children from leaving the ship unless their parents had booked a port adventure with Disney. That requirement has since been dropped, as have mask requirements in most cases; nevertheless, a family with unvaxxed kids could run into unexpected problems if they're cruising outside the US and the country they're visiting in port doesn't allow unvaxxed visitors to debark. Of course, the kids could always stay on the ship while their parents explore (see the discussion on page 269 of Part Nine), but if the kids were hoping to join their parents in port, this could create some family drama.

Though the myriad rules and protocols surrounding COVID are more relaxed in general at the time of this writing than they were in 2021, and though DCL, Royal Caribbean, and other cruise lines have been gradually loosening their own rules—or, in some cases, ditching them altogether—be aware that restrictions could tighten again in response to a future COVID surge or other public health emergency. And if you're planning a cruise originating in a port outside the US, such as a DCL European sailing, it pays to stay on top of the entry requirements for the countries you'll be visiting. (See the discussion on pages 54 and 55.)

Finally, we'd like to reiterate that if you decide to book a shore excursion independent of Disney (see page 327), you should pay close attention to the vendor's cancellation and refund policies.

OVERVIEW

DISNEY CRUISE LINE OFFERS more than 600 shore excursions— or **port adventures,** in Disney-speak—for guests to experience while their ship is docked. While it's impossible for us to have tried them all, we have embarked on quite a few. We've also interviewed scores of families and DCL employees to learn which are the most popular and which ones they'd recommend to friends.

Because most Disney cruises stop at **Castaway Cay** (see Part Ten), this section includes detailed reviews of its port adventures. These generally last 1–3½ hours; others, such as snorkeling or biking, are self-guided.

Beyond Castaway Cay, most port adventures last about 3–6 hours, including transportation time, and all are designed to fit comfortably into the ship's schedule. Third-party companies based near the port run virtually all of the port adventures.

DEBARKING THE SHIP

IF YOU WANT TO LEAVE THE SHIP, whether you've booked a port adventure or not, you and everyone in your party must first join a virtual queue in the **DCL Navigator app** (see page 136); you'll then receive debarkation tickets in the app. If you've booked a port adventure, whether before your trip or on board, you and your party will also receive those tickets in the app. (*Note:* If you've booked a non-Disney excursion, you may receive paper tickets instead; check with the vendor for specifics.)

COVID TIP
At press time, unvaxxed kids under age 12 on back-to-back cruises (see page 41) must take a COVID test after they leave the ship and again before reboarding.

When it's time to leave, the app will notify you when and where to gather on the ship; have your masks at the ready. *Make sure you know where your meeting place is;* DCL won't delay a port adventure for stragglers, and you're unlikely to get a refund if you no-show for a reserved excursion. Before you can exit the ship, you and your party must show your debarkation tickets (and port adventure tickets, if applicable); your Key to the World Cards (see pages 133 and 134); your photo ID (if you're 18 or older); and your passports, depending on the country you're visiting. You'll also need your KTTW Cards and ID to reboard.

Disney cast members will escort everyone signed up for a port adventure off the ship to a meeting point on the port's docks. There, representatives of the company running the port adventure will meet you; they may also ask you to sign a liability waiver to participate in a particular activity. You'll be in their care until you're returned to the port after your activity.

FINDING PORT ADVENTURES

IF YOU'VE BOOKED A CRUISE, you can see your port-adventure options on the DCL website in the **My Reservations** section for your voyage (see page 47). But before you book, you can also see full lists of options that may help you choose a specific itinerary.

Your typical starting point for researching port adventures is **Disney Cruise.com;** at the top of the homepage, click "Destinations," then choose "Port Adventures" from the pull-down menu. On the next

---

PLANNING YOUR PORT ADVENTURE *by Scott Sanders*

I'M A BIG PROPONENT of putting together my own port adventures, either with just my family or a small group. It's easy to plan a walking tour with public transportation, and not much more difficult to book a private tour—also significantly cheaper than those offered by Disney.

No matter how you explore a port, it's a good idea to take a portable USB battery charger, water, and snacks ashore. (In a pinch, you can grab some boxed cereal from the breakfast buffet.) If you're traveling with kids and the tour involves riding in a bus or van for long periods, consider bringing an activity for them to do during the trip to help them pass the time. We've been on excursions where the total travel time was pushing 4 hours—and not all of it was scenic.

Finally, take some cash to tip your tour guides if appropriate for the excursion; US dollars are almost always welcome worldwide.

---

page, scroll down until you see "Port Adventures by Destination." From there, select a region—"Caribbean Port Adventures," for example. From here you can further sort excursions by specific port and by using the "Experience Type" tab (active, cultural, nature, and so on), the "Activity Level" tab (athletic, moderate, or mild), the "Accessibility" tab (wheelchair accessible and the like), and the "Price Range" tab. Clicking on any individual port adventure lets you drill down to specifics like price, age/clothing requirements, length of the adventure, and so on. Some ports offer dozens of choices in a wide range of activity levels and price points.

You can also check out specialized port adventures in the "Premium Experiences" section, in the center of the main port adventures page. Options here include "Private Adventures," which are typically expensive but may hold appeal if you're interested in an off-the-beaten-path experience or you want to tour in the lap of luxury; "Port Adventures by Accessible Travel Solutions," which list excursions designed for guests who use wheelchairs or have other mobility issues (see page 160); or "Culinary Adventures," which feature cooking classes or wine and dessert tastings.

Of course, you're not limited to Disney's offerings: you can explore on your own (see Part Eleven for general suggestions in the profile for each port), or you can book an alternative excursion through another vendor. If you don't see something that strikes your fancy on the DCL website, check the shore-excursion information for other cruise lines. There will likely be overlap, but Norwegian or Carnival, for instance, may have identified a third-party vendor that better suits what you're looking for.

If you're not up for a full port adventure but you don't want to hang out on the ship all day, you can also book a day pass to a hotel or resort in port. A safe and convenient alternative to finding a beach on your own, a resort pass gives you access to amenities such as pools,

20 QUESTIONS TO ASK WHEN CHOOSING A PORT ADVENTURE
1. Have I looked at all the physical requirements of the excursion?
2. Does this excursion's price make sense to me?
3. Are there hidden fees that increase the cost of the excursion—for example, add-on photo packages or meals?
4. How does the price of this individual excursion fit into my overall excursion budget?
5. What percentage of the excursion will be spent in transportation?
6. What percentage of the excursion will be spent with a guide versus on my own?
7. Is there an adults-only or teens-only version of this excursion? Do those variations make more sense for me?
8. Does the excursion's mode of transportation make sense for me? (If you are prone to motion sickness or afraid of heights, for example, then you'll probably want to avoid helicopter excursions.)
9. Is a meal or snack provided as part of the excursion? Do I want there to be?
10. Will adverse weather conditions drastically affect my enjoyment of the excursion?
11. Does the excursion take place in a port where guests tender to shore? (Tender excursions are more likely to be canceled.)
12. Are there similar excursions at other ports during my itinerary? (For example, numerous ports have dolphin encounters—is this particular port the best for such an excursion?)
13. Are there similar excursions at the same port? (For example, several dogsledding variations are available in Juneau—consider which one appeals to you the most.)
14. How long is the excursion? What percentage of my day will it encompass? Are there other things I'd rather do in port?
15. Is a similar experience available close to home or at another frequently visited vacation spot? (Think zip line and go-kart experiences.)
16. Does this excursion appeal to everyone in my party, or might we be better off choosing different excursions on different port days?
17. Is this excursion too similar to something I'm doing in another port?
18. Will the timing of the excursion interfere with my child's dining or nap schedule?
19. Can I bring a stroller on the excursion?
20. Are there elements of the excursion specifically designed with children in mind?

beaches, and spas; some packages include transfers and meal vouchers as well. Good sources for partial-day hotel access are **Resort for a Day** (resortforaday.com) and **Daycation** (daycationapp.com).

Finally, remember that you're under no obligation to participate in *any* organized activities. Feel free to hang out on the ship or just amble aimlessly around the port city. Your vacation, your call.

EVALUATING A PORT ADVENTURE

THE PORT ADVENTURES OFFERED through Disney Cruise Line have all been vetted by its staff for quality and reliability. When you book your excursion through DCL, it's unlikely that you'll end up with an experience that's *completely* without merit. That said, just because an excursion is right for one person doesn't mean it's right for you. If you ask yourself the questions in the chart above, you should increase your odds of choosing the best option for your needs.

Our research shows that two of the most important factors that affect a guest's enjoyment of a shore excursion are the weather in port and the expertise of the guide. Even with the best planning, you may find that a sudden storm or an inexperienced guide dims the quality of the port adventure. Of course, if the excursion turns out to be a total wash or the guide is a jerk, you should speak to the tour provider and to Disney, but try not to let normal ups and downs derail your enjoyment of the experience.

BOOKING EXCURSIONS ON YOUR OWN VS. THROUGH DISNEY

AS WE'VE MENTIONED, YOU CAN BOOK port adventures on your own or through Disney. Some advantages to booking through Disney include the following:

unofficial **TIP**
Port adventures booked on your own or through non-Disney vendors may have different cancellation policies, so always ask when booking.

- **CONVENIENCE OF SELECTION** To book through Disney, just head over to the DCL website (see page 324). If you find an excursion appealing, you can book it with just a few clicks. Booking excursions through other vendors may or may not offer the same convenience as the DCL site.

- **CONVENIENCE OF BILLING** When you book through Disney, the fee appears on your stateroom bill, which you can pay using any of the acceptable DCL methods, or in US dollars, British pounds, or euros. As a bonus, you don't pay a deposit, and you're not charged until you sail. If you're booking an excursion in another country on your own, you may have to pay a large deposit, you may have to pay in another currency, or you may be limited to a particular credit card or other form of payment.

- **SAFETY** Of course, you'll want to exercise an abundance of caution on *any* port adventure, but if you book a Disney-vetted excursion, you can rest assured that they've done some of the work for you. Disney verifies that the excursions they offer are through legitimate businesses. They make sure that the transportation used is safe and that the guides are accountable for your whereabouts. If you book an excursion on your own, the onus is on you to do that research.

- **COMMUNICATION WITH THE SHIP** When you book an excursion through Disney, they know where you are. If something unforeseen happens, they have representatives who can contact your group and vice versa. If you book your own excursion, cast members on the ship will likely have no idea where you are. And they're not going to wait up for you if you're not back by sail-away time.

- **LANGUAGE ISSUES** Booking your excursion through Disney means that the transaction will take place in English. If you're booking an excursion on your own for a port in another country, the website or phone representative may use another language or speak limited English.

- **CANCELLATION POLICIES** DCL's port-adventure cancellation policy is clearly stated on its website (also see the next page). If you book on your own, you may be subject to an entirely different set of policies, which may or may not be clearly outlined—or fair.

On the other hand, some advantages to booking your port adventures through an outside vendor are as follows:

- **PRICE** Many guests have found that they can save money by booking excursions similar to Disney's on their own.

- **MORE OPTIONS** While Disney offers a wide range of excursions at each port, the list of options is certainly finite. If you book on your own, there's no limit to the number of choices you might have.

- **CUSTOMIZATION** When you book on your own, you can often work with a vendor to put together an excursion custom-tailored to your interests or hobbies. You might be able to combine visits to two disparate sites in one excursion. You might be able to skip part of a standard tour that doesn't interest you. You might be able to linger longer at a favorite venue. Or you might be able to arrange for transportation that accommodates a physical need, such as wheelchair use.

- **BOOKING WINDOW** On the DCL website, your ability to access excursion booking is based on your Castaway Club status (see page 85). First-time cruisers booking through Disney might be locked out of some popular activities because they were already fully booked by Castaway Club members. When planning excursions on your own, your ability to book isn't tied to how many times you've cruised before.

CANCELING A DCL PORT ADVENTURE

DEPENDING ON YOUR CASTAWAY CLUB level, you may make port-adventure reservations up to 120 days in advance. Once you make a reservation, you may cancel it with no penalty up to three days before you sail—no refunds after that. Of course, you're not charged if Disney or the tour provider has to cancel the excursion due to weather or other unforeseen circumstances.

The only other exception to the cancellation penalty occurs if you decide to upgrade your excursion. You may change a previously booked port adventure to one that's more expensive; you'll simply pay the difference in excursion fees without any penalty. To upgrade on board, visit Guest Services or the Port Adventures desk.

PORT ADVENTURES
on CASTAWAY CAY

WE CONSIDER CASTAWAY CAY'S SHORE EXCURSIONS among the best values of any that DCL has to offer. Here's a quick rundown of what's available.

BICYCLE RENTALS

THESE SINGLE-SPEED ROAD BIKES with plump tires are good for getting some exercise while exploring the island. Men's and women's models are available, and the seats are designed for comfort. The seats can be adjusted up and down to suit your leg length, although years spent on the island have rusted many of the metal cams used to loosen the seats. Ask a cast member to help (they have wrenches!) if yours won't budge.

Pick up your bicycles just past the **Pelican Point** tram stop, near the middle of the family beaches. You can also rent bikes next to the **Serenity Bay** adult beach, just behind the Castaway Air Bar. Cost is $13 for a one-day rental or $16 for two days.

BOAT RENTALS

VARIOUS WATERCRAFT, including one- and two-seat kayaks, sail-boats, and paddleboats, are available for rent in half-hour increments. Costs range from $18 for a single-seat kayak to $32 for a Hobie Cat catamaran. The paddleboats require an extraordinary amount of leg power to get anywhere, and 30 minutes is going to be plenty for most people. Previous sailing experience is required to rent a sailboat.

CASTAWAY CAY 5K RUN

Note: *The Castaway 5K has been decidedly informal in the COVID era. Guests are welcome to run the course as they wish, without an official start/end time. You'll still get access to water and a fun plastic medal, but a bit of the hoopla is currently missing. As the pandemic further wanes, we expect the race procedures to return to those discussed below.*

ONE OF THE BEST PORT ADVENTURES to start your day on Castaway Cay is fun, well organized, and totally free. Check the Navigator app for current race start procedures and whether preregistration is required (this has varied during the pandemic era).

Runners and walkers who wish to participate in the 5K typically meet at 8:15 on the morning the ship arrives at the island. Cast members will give you a runner's bib (a nice touch for this unchipped race) and safety pins; then you'll walk off the ship with the rest of the runners toward the start of the race, by the Pelican Point tram stop. Parents who need to drop their kids off at Scuttle's Cove will be given time to do so on the way.

Once you arrive at the start, everyone is given a chance to hit the restroom and drop anything they don't want to run with in the storage area by the bike rentals. This is unsecured, so don't leave your gold doubloons, but other stuff is fine.

Once everyone is ready, you're off and running. The route includes a trip up and down the airstrip and two loops out to the viewpoint. You'll be sharing the road with the trams as well as folks on bicycles, so be aware of your surroundings. One cast member will be at the entrance to the loop with water—take advantage of it, because this run is *hot*.

There is a digital timer at the end of the race loop, but there's no imperative to pay it heed—the only person concerned with your time is you. Pre-pandemic, plastic race medals were distributed to all participants at the end of the run; at press time, you could pick up your medal at the Bike Rental booth or at Guest Services on the ship.

On select sailings, **runDisney** offers the **Disney Castaway Cay Challenge,** a more-competitive event combining the 5K on the island with a marathon or half-marathon at Walt Disney World a few days earlier; the signup fee in 2023 was $95. The only things that distinguish the Castaway Cay Challenge from the free version of the 5K are that you get a fancier medal and the runners actually, you know, run. See rundisney.com for details (under the "Events" tab, choose "Walt Disney World Marathon Weekend").

BOTTOM FISHING

A 3-HOUR CATCH-AND-RELEASE fishing excursion ($164 per person) takes place in the waters around Castaway Cay, with DCL-provided fishing rods and bait. Your boat's captain will take you into the waters around the island; the most commonly caught species are yellow jack, grouper, various porgies, and snapper. It's not unheard of to hook a barracuda or small shark too. Most charters leave around 9 a.m. and are back in time for lunch. Cruisers who are prone to seasickness shouldn't take this excursion; kids must be age 8 or older to participate.

CASTAWAY RAY'S STINGRAY ADVENTURE

THIS IS YOUR CHANCE TO PET AND FEED small and medium-size stingrays in a supervised, structured setting on the shore of the Stingray Lagoon. Disney keeps dozens of these stingrays in a sectioned-off part of Castaway Cay's lagoon; the stingrays are trained to use a special feeding platform at mealtimes. The cost is $56 for guests ages 10 and up, $45 for kids ages 5–9.

Holding a specially formulated pellet of food between two fingers, you'll place your hand, palm down, on the platform. A stingray will swim up to the platform, glide over your hand, and grab the food in its mouth. You'll also have the chance to pet each ray as it swims by. There's plenty of food for the stingrays, and there are plenty of stingrays to feed. Besides the feeding, you'll get a brief introduction to stingrays, skates, and sharks before you begin, when a cast member reviews rules and procedures.

Many children are worried about being bitten by the stingrays, and let's face it: the word *sting* in their name doesn't exactly make rays seem cuddly. But rays don't have teeth, and the only thing that seems to get them excited is the prospect of feeding time. Calling them rays may help your kids find these animals more approachable (their fears might also be assuaged by a mention of the friendly Mr. Ray in *Finding Nemo*). Be aware that the stingray adventure is prone to cancellation in windy conditions.

FLOAT AND TUBE RENTALS

INNER TUBES AND RECTANGULAR FLOATS are available for $13 for one day or $16 for two days. You can swap out one type for the other during the day.

GLASS BOTTOM BOAT EXCURSION

GUESTS BOARD A SMALL MOTORIZED WATERCRAFT that holds about 25 people and ventures about 15 minutes out into the ocean. You can observe sea life below through several "windows" in the floor of the boat. During the trip, you're accompanied by a local guide who discusses the fish and other natural elements you'll encounter.

The highlight of the tour takes place at approximately the midpoint of the journey: guests are given a cup filled with about 1 ounce of oatmeal, which they toss overboard to attract fish. During the feeding portion of the tour, several hundred tropical fish of various species surround the boat, and the guide points out the characteristics of as many fish as possible. The feeding lasts about 5 minutes, after which the fish disappear quickly. Sightings of fish at other points of the tour are sporadic.

The trip takes about 45 minutes to an hour (about 15 minutes out, 15 minutes back, and around 15 minutes parked at viewing spots along the reef adjacent to Castaway Cay). Cost is $59 for adults and $39 for kids ages 9 and younger, including infants and toddlers. Guests must be able to climb five steps to board and debark, and they must also stand aboard the boat for the duration of the excursion.

PARASAILING

GUESTS LOOKING FOR A BIRD'S-EYE VIEW of paradise should check out this excursion. Floating hundreds of feet in the air, you're master of all you survey, or at least it seems that way for several minutes.

You board a speedboat and travel several hundred yards away from land. Then, in singles or pairs, you stand at the back of the boat and are harnessed to a line-bound parachute that is slowly let out until you and the parachute are 600–1,000 feet above the water. Enjoy panoramic views of your ship, Castaway Cay, and beyond.

Each excursion takes about 10 people onto the boat. There are no ride-alongs—every guest on the boat must pay. Your actual parasail event will last about 5–7 minutes. Depending on the number of other guests, the entire experience lasts 45 minutes–1 hour.

Open to guests ages 8 and up, parasailing excursions cost $129 for both adults and kids. Guests must weigh between 90 and 375 pounds; those who weigh less than 90 pounds may be able to ride if they fly in tandem with another guest, but their combined weight may not exceed 375 pounds. Determination of single or tandem rides is at the discretion of the staff.

Kids under age 13 must be accompanied by a paying adult age 18 or older. Guests ages 13–17 may go on the excursion unaccompanied but must be escorted to the Marge's Barges meeting area by an adult age 18 or older. All guests must sign a safety waiver.

You must leave your shoes on the dock and are strongly discouraged from wearing a hat or glasses during your sail; a storage area is provided on the boat for your personal belongings. Wheelchairs and other wheeled mobility devices cannot be accommodated.

No photography service is provided during the excursion—you're welcome to bring your phone or a camera along, but you assume all liability if you lose it in the ocean.

SNORKELING

THIS IS ONE OF THE LEAST EXPENSIVE, most rewarding shore excursions offered on a Disney cruise. We recommend it for every family. Cost is $18 for kids ages 5–9 for one day, $23 for two days; guests ages 10 and up pay $34 for one day, $45 for two days.

First, find some chairs on the family beach, where you can store your stuff while you're in the water. If possible, choose something near a vertical landmark such as a tree; it will be easier to find when you come back to shore.

Next, pick up your snorkeling gear at **Gil's Fins and Boats,** a short walk from Scuttle's Cove, the island's first tram stop. You'll be given a mask, snorkel, fins, and an inflatable buoyancy vest to make swimming easier. Also pick up a blue-mesh gear bag, which makes it easier to haul your stuff back to your beach chairs.

Put on your vest before you get in the water, but don't inflate it just yet. Wait until you're in hip-high water to put on your flippers, because it's impossible to walk in them on shore (and they'll get sandy). Don't put your mask on until you get into the water.

If you're snorkeling with younger children, plan on spending 10–15 minutes adjusting the fit of masks and vests. Inflate a kid's vest by blowing into the vertical tube on the left side of the vest, adding just enough air to keep the top of the child's head above water. (If you over-inflate the vests, kids will have trouble getting their masks below the surface.) Also, practice using the flippers, which work best with slow, deliberate leg movements.

Once everyone's gear is working, take one last look at the lagoon to get your bearings. Disney has placed orange-and-white buoys above the underwater sites, so head for those.

There usually aren't a lot of fish in the first 30–40 yards nearest the shore, though it's possible to see almost anything once you're in the water. Fish species in the lagoon include yellowtail snapper, sergeant major, banded butterfly fish, blue tang, and barracuda.

WALKING AND KAYAK NATURE ADVENTURE

THIS PORT ADVENTURE BEGINS at **Marge's Barges,** where everyone boards a tram to the Serenity Bay adult beach. Next you walk behind the adult beach cabanas to a nature trail, which leads to the beach beyond. During the walk, your guide will point out interesting plants and animals and talk about the history of the Bahamas.

Upon reaching the beach, participants don their life jackets and head out in their kayaks. This is the part where you're at Mother Nature's whim. We took this tour after a friend raved about it. She headed out in the morning and was able to kayak to the interior of the island; our own tour was later in the afternoon as the tide was going out. The interior of the island was inaccessible by kayak, and the tides made piloting our single kayak very difficult. We wouldn't book this adventure in the afternoon again, even if it were the only time available.

Even if you're able to book this in the morning, note that the tour is 3–3½ hours long—time you could spend snorkeling, biking, or lazing on the beach. Ideally, you would book this on the morning of the second stop of a five-night Castaway Cay cruise.

Be sure to bring walking shoes, sunglasses, a hat, sunscreen, and a waterproof or water-resistant smartphone/camera; consider gloves for paddling to avoid blisters. Wear a swimsuit under your clothes for swimming. You must stow your belongings on the beach for the kayaking, so leave the doubloons in the cabin. Water is provided. Cost is $73 for guests ages 10 and up.

NASSAU

A NOTE ABOUT NASSAU SAFETY

WE'VE NEVER HAD A BAD EXPERIENCE in Nassau. We acknowledge, however, that we've been lucky: crime is a significant problem here—more so than it is in other Caribbean cruise ports.

A 2022 report by the **US Overseas Security Advisory Council** (osac.gov), a division of the US Department of State, doesn't mince words:

> *The US Department of State has assessed Nassau as being a CRITICAL-threat location for crime. . . . Armed robbery, property crime, purse snatching, theft, fraud, and sexual assault remain the most common crimes perpetrated against tourists. . . . If someone confronts you demanding valuables, comply and make the encounter as brief as possible. Remain calm, be observant, clearly display your hands, and do not make any sudden moves that criminals could interpret as resistance. To help replace lost or stolen documents, make a copy of your driver's license/passport photo page, and keep the originals in a separate, secure location. Instead of carrying large amounts of cash, use a debit/credit card for payments when possible. Avoid using ATMs in isolated areas. ATM skimmers are active throughout Nassau. . . . The Bahamian government only loosely regulates the water sports rental industry. US citizens have reported sexual assaults by Jet-Ski operators for a number of years. According to the criminal complaints, the majority of these sexual assaults occurred on relatively "safe" beaches on Paradise Island and along Cable Beach, which tourists frequent heavily.*

A recent security notice about the Bahamas from the **UK government** states:

> *There have been incidents of violent crime including robbery, which is often armed and sometimes fatal,* in residential and tourist areas. Be vigilant at all times, and don't walk alone away from the main hotels, tourist areas, beaches, and downtown Nassau.

unofficial TIP
If you want to explore Nassau on your own, **exercise the utmost vigilance about your surroundings,** and let family remaining on board (or DCL Guest Services staff) know of your on-shore plans.

unofficial TIP
Don't book watercraft excursions in Nassau.

The **Canadian government** offers these warnings:

Never leave food or drinks unattended or in the care of strangers. Be wary of accepting snacks, beverages, gum, or cigarettes from new acquaintances, as the items may contain drugs that could put you at risk of sexual assault or robbery.

Her Own Way: A Woman's Safe-Travel Guide, a government publication, is available at Canada's official travel and tourism website: travel.gc.ca /travelling/publications/her-own-way. The information in this guide is useful for folks of all genders from any country.

If you're participating in a port adventure at **Atlantis** (see next section), which has its own security staff, or another Disney-vetted excursion, your odds of trouble are quite low. If, however, you haven't signed up for any port adventures and relaxation is your number-one vacation priority, **we recommend that you stay on the ship if your cruise stops at Nassau.**

Remaining on board lets you experience more of the ship's amenities than you'd have time to otherwise during a brief sailing: you can get pampered at the spa, stuff yourself at the buffet, or have your kids participate in activities at the youth clubs. If nothing else, staying put can be an easy way to save some money you might otherwise spend on tacky souvenirs.

NASSAU PORT ADVENTURES

AFTER CASTAWAY CAY, the port most visited by DCL is Nassau. Virtually all sailings of the *Dream* and *Wish* stop here, as do many sailings of the *Magic, Wonder,* and *Fantasy.*

The DCL website currently lists about 50 port adventures in Nassau, with 15 of them taking place at **Atlantis,** a Las Vegas–style resort about a 25-minute drive from the port (☎ 888-877-7525; atlantisbahamas .com). In addition to Disney cruisers, you'll encounter guests of other

unofficial **TIP**
Many websites track the number of ships that will be docked in a given port on a specific date. For Nassau, check vesselfinder .com/ports/BSNAS001. The more ships in port on a given day, the more crowded Atlantis will be.

cruise lines, Atlantis guests, and guests of other area hotels—it's a high-volume operation. The resort generally does things well, but due to the sheer number of people who cycle through every day, it can feel a bit like a factory for fun. We're fans of the Disney parks, so we don't necessarily think that's a *bad* thing, but if you're in the market for privacy or quiet, look elsewhere.

Crowd levels vary substantially at Atlantis, depending on how many cruise ships are in port on a specific day. If your ship is the only one in port, you'll find plenty of open lounge chairs and short lines for the slides; if there are eight large ships in port, you'll be fighting for a place just to lay your towel on the sand.

Most Atlantis-based excursions are variations on a theme: spend time with a dolphin, visit the beach, visit the water park–like **Aquaventure,** go shopping, or some combination thereof. The animal encounters receive generally moderate-to-high marks from guests, with almost all of the variations in opinion based on whether guests thought their specific guide was funny, what the weather was like, whether they knew in advance that the actual amount of time spent interacting with the animals was limited, and if they were aware in advance of upcharges for photos and video of their experience. (You may *not* use your own phone/camera.) The weather and your rapport with your guide are the luck of the draw; if you adjust your expectations accordingly, you're likely to have a good time.

Here's a rundown of the port adventures available at Atlantis. (**Note:** In order to enter the Bahamas at press time, unvaccinated travelers ages 2 and older must present proof of a negative PCR or rapid-antigen test taken **no more than 72 hours** before leaving home.)

- **Discover Atlantis Tour** Free for kids ages 3 and younger, $56 ages 4–9, $68 ages 10 and up. Includes transportation, an aquarium tour, and access to the casino and shopping. Does not include access to the beach, pools, or Aquaventure.

- **Atlantis Beach Day and Discover Atlantis** Free for kids ages 3 and younger, $83 ages 4–9, $98 ages 10 and up. Includes everything on the Discover Atlantis tour, plus beach access. Does not include access to the pools or Aquaventure.

- **Atlantis Aquaventure** Free for kids ages 3 and younger, $124 ages 4–9, $239 ages 10 and up. Some sailings may offer a half-day version of Atlantis Aquaventure priced at $161 for ages 10 and up, $111 for ages 4–9, and free for kids 3 and younger. Includes everything on the previous two tours, plus access to Aquaventure—a mini-waterpark with 11 pools, several waterslides, and a lazy river, as well as a voucher for a fast food–style lunch.

- **Atlantis Aquaventure and Kayak with Dolphins** Guests ages 10 and up only, $289. Includes an education segment about dolphin life and 30 minutes in a glass-bottom kayak in the dolphin habitat, plus access to Aquaventure.

- **Atlantis Aquaventure and Paddleboard with Dolphins** Guests ages 10 and up only, $289. Includes an educational segment about dolphin life and a paddleboard lesson in the dolphin habitat, plus Aquaventure.

- **Atlantis Aquaventure and Snorkel with Dolphins** Guests ages 10 and up only, $309. Includes transportation and lunch, plus access to Aquaventure, the beach, the casino, and shopping. Start with an educational segment about dolphin life; then swim in Dolphin Cay with the bottlenose dolphins. A similar experience in deep water, **Atlantis Dolphin Cay Swim in Wonder and Aquaventure,** costs $317 for kids ages 6–9 (*note:* must wear a life vest) and $344 for ages 10 and up.

- **Atlantis Dolphin Cay Dip 'N Discover Interaction and Discover Atlantis** Free for kids ages 3 and younger, $200 ages 4–9, $213 ages 10 and up. Includes transportation; a self-guided tour of the Ruins Lagoon, a marine habitat (like a giant fish tank) with rays, sharks, and tropical fish designed to evoke the lost city of Atlantis; and access to the aquarium, casino, and shopping. Start with an educational segment about dolphin life; then stand in waist-deep water for a 30-minute face-to-face interaction with a dolphin.

- **Atlantis Dolphin Cay Dip 'N Discover and Aquaventure** Free for kids ages 3 and younger, $275 ages 4–9, $306 ages 10 and up. Includes everything in the Atlantis Dolphin Cay Dip 'N Discover Interaction and Discover Atlantis excursion, plus access to Aquaventure and the beach.

- **Atlantis Snorkel the Ruins and Aquaventure** Cost is $244 for kids ages 8 and 9, $282 ages 10 and up. Spend 30 minutes on a guided snorkel experience in the Ruins Lagoon. Includes transportation, access to the casino and shopping, a voucher for a fast food–style lunch, and access to Aquaventure.

- **Observer at Dolphin Cay and Discover Atlantis** Kids under age 4 admitted free but not permitted in the dolphin experience; $56 ages 4–9, $68 ages 10 and up. Includes transportation, an aquarium tour, and access to the casino and shopping; does *not* include access to the beach, pools, or Aquaventure. This can be booked only if other members of your party are doing the Atlantis Dolphin Cay Dip 'N Discover Interaction and Discover Atlantis. The observer is allowed to stand at the edge of the dolphin facility and take photos but may not interact with the animals. This is a good choice for parents who don't want to swim with the dolphins but whose kids do.

- **Observer at Dolphin Cay and Aquaventure** Kids under age 4 admitted free but not permitted in the dolphin experience; $149 ages 4–9, $215 ages 10 and up. Includes transportation, an aquarium tour, and access to the casino and shopping, plus access to Aquaventure and a voucher for a fast food–style lunch. Again, the observer is allowed to stand at the edge of the dolphin facility and take photos but may not interact with the animals.

- **Private Cabana at Atlantis** For $344, up to six guests have one-day use of a private poolside cabana with a guest host, personal safe, fan, refrigerator, electrical outlets, and private changing area. Note that food is not included in the price; also, each cabana guest must be booked on one of the following tours: Atlantis Aquaventure; Atlantis Aquaventure and Kayak, Paddleboard, or Snorkel with Dolphins; Atlantis Dolphin Cay Dip 'N Discover and Aquaventure; Atlantis Dolphin Cay Swim in Wonder and Aquaventure; or Observer at Dolphin Cay and Aquaventure.

- **Ultimate Trainer for a Day** Cost is $564 for guests ages 10 and up. Take a behind-the-scenes tour of the veterinary hospital and lab for the dolphins and sea lions. Swim in deep water with the dolphins, and do a double dorsal tow and "foot push." Feed predatory nurse sharks and cow-nosed stingrays; then snorkel with them and hundreds of other tropical fish. Includes lunch and photos.

If you want to use the beach, pools, or Aquaventure without adding a dolphin experience, you may end up saving money, depending on the size of your party, if you actually book a hotel room for the day at Atlantis (the **Beach Tower** is the least expensive part of the resort) or at the nearby **Comfort Suites** (comfortsuitespi.com), a 5-minute walk away. Atlantis requires a two-night minimum booking, with rates starting at about $150 per night; rates start at about $275 per night at the Comfort Suites, depending on the time of year.

On the face of it, you may think it's wasteful to pay for a hotel room that you won't be staying in overnight. But consider the convenience: for a few hours, you get a quiet place to relax or nap, free Wi-Fi, a place to store your valuables, and a private shower, among other perks. And you'll note that $300 is still cheaper than a less-well-equipped private cabana at Castaway Cay. On the downside, you'll spend valuable time walking from the pools to your room—Atlantis is *huge*, so this is a real consideration.

unofficial **TIP**

The Atlantis website misleadingly states in a few places that Aquaventure Day Passes must be purchased in person at the resort—actually, advance booking is available at atlantisbahamas.com/daybooking.

If you don't want to book a room, consider an **Aquaventure Day Pass,** available through Atlantis and **Resort for a Day** (see page 326). In 2022 passes were priced at $150–$250, depending on the season, for guests ages 13 and up; passes for kids ages 4–12 cost $75–$125. Guests for whom kids' passes could be particularly appealing are those with 10- to 12-year-olds: Disney considers them adults for monetary purposes, but Atlantis still gives them a discount.

If all you want to do is eat and browse the shops without using the pools, beach, or water park, you can do so at no charge. Taxis from the port to Atlantis typically run in the ballpark of $10 per person.

The Atlantis website lists a few variations on activities that don't appear on the DCL site. For example, Atlantis offers a junior version of its Ultimate Trainer package for 6- to 10-year-olds, along with a sea lion encounter, but the DCL site doesn't mention either. In addition, DCL offers a port adventure at Atlantis's golf course ($599)— it's open to ages 10 and up, but we're pretty sure that several hours on the links wouldn't appeal to kids unless you have another Tiger Woods on your hands.

Also note that Atlantis's pricing for most of its dolphin encounters is significantly less than booking through Disney. DCL includes transportation and a few other items in its packages, but for many guests, booking directly through Atlantis and using a cab makes more sense. See atlantisbahamas.com/daybooking for more information.

After Atlantis, the next largest block of Nassau excursions takes place at **Blue Lagoon,** a beach area about 40 minutes away from the port by catamaran. You can spend your day at the beach, have a dolphin or sea lion experience, or enjoy some combination thereof. Prices are quite a bit less than the Atlantis equivalents. If you don't mind a longer transit time or the lack of a water park, then you'll probably be happier at Blue Lagoon than Atlantis. Again, the animal encounters are typically well rated, with most of the variation coming from rapport with a specific guide, the weather, and the guest's awareness of extra costs.

Other Nassau excursions that receive high marks from cruisers include the following:

- **Catamaran Sail and Reef Snorkeling** A well-priced ocean-snorkeling experience.

- **Graycliff Chocolatier** Take a short tour of the factory, then create your own chocolate treats in the test kitchen.

- **Nassau Forts and Junkanoo Discovery** A relatively painless history lesson for kids.

Nassau excursions that garner less-than-stellar reviews include the following:

- **Ardastra Gardens and Wildlife Conservation Centre** A small, underwhelming "zoo." Avoid this tour if birds weird you out.

- **SeaWorld Explorer Semi-Submarine** The windows of the sub are often so dirty that you can't see the animals.

- **Sunshine Glass Bottom Boat Tour** In addition to guests having to stand the whole time, there's not much viewing space on the boat, and you get to see the fish for just a few minutes while they're being fed. We recommend the Castaway Cay tour instead (see pages 330 and 331).

If you're looking for a safe place to relax in Nassau minus the hubbub of Atlantis, try booking a day pass at **Sandals Royal Bahamian** (sandals.com/royal-bahamian). another safe place to chill is the **Margaritaville Beach Resort Nassau** (margaritavilleresorts.com/margaritaville-beach-resort-nassau), featuring a mini water park with slides and a lazy river; there's also a beach, bowling alley, and movie theater, along with additional entertainment options.

Beyond CASTAWAY CAY *and* NASSAU

DOLPHIN ENCOUNTERS

THESE ARE THE MOST POPULAR shore excursions for families. Every port in Mexico offers dolphin encounters, along with Nassau; Falmouth, Jamaica; and Grand Cayman, Cayman Islands. If your Caribbean or Bahamian cruise includes a port besides Castaway Cay, you'll almost certainly have a chance to book one.

Because of the dolphins' popularity, these port adventures aren't cheap, generally starting at around $180 for adults and $160 for children, or roughly $700 for a family of four.

Most dolphin-related port adventures last 4–7 hours, roughly a half hour of which is actually spent in the water with a dolphin and 10–20 other tourists. During our visits, we took turns with the rest of the group in petting, feeding, and taking photos with the dolphin.

*un*official **TIP**
If you're spending time in the Orlando theme parks area before or after your cruise, dolphin encounters are also available at **EPCOT**'s Seas Pavilion and at **SeaWorld**.

In hindsight, the remarkable thing is that we spent perhaps 1 minute each in direct contact with the animal. The rest of your time is taken up by transportation to and from the port, a background class and instruction on how to interact with the dolphin, a short show during which the dolphins demonstrate their jumping skills and tricks, and some beach or pool time once your encounter is done.

MAYAN PYRAMIDS

DCL TOURS OF THE **Chichén Itzá** Maya ruins take place in **Cozumel, Mexico.** Be aware that the trip involves considerable transportation time: 4 of its 8½ hours are spent on ferries or buses. Prices are $149 for guests ages 10 and up, $119 ages 8 and 9.

ALASKA

Juneau

Alaska Shore Excursions (☎ 888-586-8489, alaskashoreexcursions.com) is a great place to look for port adventures in Alaska if you don't want to book through DCL—they have more options than Disney, often at cheaper prices. Excursions visit Icy Strait, Juneau, Ketchikan, and Skagway; search for "Disney," then "*Disney Wonder,*" and then your sail date to see what's available.

Skagway

Long-winded name aside, the **Liarsville Gold Rush Trail Camp and Salmon Bake Featuring Exclusive Disney Character Experience** is a fun port adventure for families (2½–3 hours; $124 ages 10 and up; $73 ages 3–9). Guests board a bright-yellow school bus and take a 15-minute drive through downtown Skagway to Liarsville, a re-created mining camp at the foot of White Pass. When you arrive, you're greeted by "locals" dressed in period attire and escorted to the Hippodrome, a covered pavilion where you'll see a puppet show that highlights the history of the Gold Rush in Alaska, including how Liarsville came to receive its name.

After the show, you'll receive instructions on how to pan for gold— *scoop, swirl, spill*—before you're released to your very own "handler" and set out to seek your fortune. The pans are prepared and handed out as you approach the mining troughs. Getting the hang of the technique isn't as easy at it looks, but your handler is there to help. While you're panning, Chip 'n' Dale stop by to steal some gold, and Donald, dressed in flannel and a hunting cap, pays a visit. Gold in every pan is guaranteed, but even the most successful panning won't make you rich, or even earn you enough to help pay off your stateroom balance.

The salmon bake is set up across the way. Guests trickle over to the food after they strike it not-so-rich, so crowds aren't a problem. Choose from rotisserie chicken, baked beans, rice pilaf, coleslaw, and salads, plus bread and blueberry cake. Wild-caught salmon is served from an open-air grill; the fish is tasty, but be aware that it contains small bones—we guess that's what makes it wild.

This reader liked (but didn't love) the experience:

The Liarsville gold panning was fun, and it was a huge hit with my stepson (age 8). I felt the price could have been a bit more affordable, the puppet show a bit shorter, and the gold panning a bit longer and more involved. For us it was a one-time experience, but an enjoyable one.

PART THIRTEEN

RIVER *and* EXPEDITION CRUISING

Note: *Like Disney Cruise Line, Adventures by Disney (AbD), including its river cruises, took an extended hiatus in 2020, returned to modified guest experiences in 2021, and resumed near-normal operations in 2022. However, as with all international travel during the COVID era, be aware that things like vaccination requirements, pre-cruise testing, masking requirements, and the intermingling of unrelated parties are subject to change as conditions warrant. Visit the Guest Health and Safety page on the AbD website to verify the protocols in place for your travel dates and destinations: .adventuresbydisney.com/important-updates.*

OVERVIEW

DISNEY OFFERS RIVER CRUISES through **Adventures by Disney** (**AbD**), the world-travel arm of Disney Destinations LLC. Although these are Disney-branded experiences, they don't have anything to do with Disney Cruise Line. And because AbD deemphasizes "all Disney all the time" in favor of bringing Disney-caliber service and quality to exploring the world, you won't be having Mickey moments on a river cruise.

unofficial **TIP**
When AbD is running a river cruise, it charters the entire ship: all guests follow an AbD group itinerary, booked through and organized by AbD. At other times of year, AmaWaterways books its own guests on its ships, but at no point are Disney and non-Disney guests on board at the same time.

Instead of starting its own river-cruise operation from scratch, AbD worked with cruise line **AmaWaterways** to build two brand-new ships: the *AmaViola,* which debuted in 2016, and the *AmaKristina,* which went into service in 2017. These newer ships are similar to existing AmaWaterways ships (see next page), but Disney requested family-friendly touches, such as additional cabins with connecting doors and cabins with pull-out sleeper chairs.

Adventures by Disney also uses several river-cruise ships from the AmaWaterways fleet. Some of these ships that have been in the AbD rotation recently include the *AmaCello, AmaLea, AmaLyra, AmaMore, AmaSerena,* and *AmaStella.*

To check out the deck plans of AmaWaterways ships, go to ama
waterways.com; click on "Ships" and the name of the ship your AbD
trip is using (this will be noted on the AbD website). The deck layouts
and amenities are very similar across the ships. You can find a full
photo tour of the *AmaViola* at tinyurl.com/amaviola—the other ships
are comparable to this one.

Each ship has a spacious sundeck, a walking track, a bar, a plush
lounge and sitting areas, a small gift shop, a fitness room, a soaking
pool, and two restaurants. Most staterooms are configured so that the
main sleep surface can be converted from one queen-size bed to two
twin-size beds, according to guests' needs.

Because Disney doesn't own these ships, there is no Disney theming in
the decor or finishes, such as hidden Mickeys in the upholstery or iron-
work. Further, there are no Disney characters on board, nor are there
dozens of Disney-owned channels on your stateroom TV or Disney-
themed items for sale in the gift shop. Instead of live-performance variations of Disney films, the onboard evening entertainment is provided
by local performers—a light-opera concert in Vienna or a Hungarian
dance lesson in Budapest, for example.

In 2016 the initial series of AbD river cruises had five **Danube River**
departures; demand was so high that AbD added two more sailings
that year. Ports included **Budapest** in Hungary and **Vienna** in Austria.
In 2017 Disney added seven sailings on the **Rhine River** in addition to
eight sailings on the Danube route. The 2018 offerings were expanded
even further, including four regular Danube sailings, one Oktoberfest-
themed sailing, two winter holiday sailings, eight regular Rhine sailings, and three adults-only food-and-wine sailings.

Seine River cruises were added to the AbD roster for 2019, and
Rhône River cruises were added for 2020. The current count of river-
cruise sailings offered by AbD is about three dozen. While this is still
a far cry from the hundreds of sail dates offered by DCL, the steady
growth in the popularity of river cruising over the past several years
indicates that this is a market of interest to Disney. And for the right
traveler, it can be a terrific alternative to ocean cruising.

Unlike DCL cruises, for which your booking price includes just your
stateroom and most meals, AbD river cruises are all-inclusive: excursions; tips; airport and hotel transfers; adult dining; Wi-Fi; and free-
flowing beer and wine at lunch, dinner, and various receptions. It can
be much easier to anticipate your total costs on an AbD river cruise
versus a DCL sailing. On the other hand, if you just want a bare-bones,
budget-friendly trip, that's significantly easier to achieve with DCL (see
"Saving Money," page 34).

RIVER CRUISING *for* FAMILIES

THE STEREOTYPICAL RIVER-CRUISE GUEST IS A RETIREE.
(We've had 60-year-old friends returning from other river cruises tell

us they were the youngest people on board.) Moreover, some river-cruise lines, notably Viking, prohibit guests under age 18. In contrast, Adventures by Disney is one of the first river-cruise operators to cater to families and offer primarily family-friendly activities. Kids will be occupied and entertained throughout their vacation.

Also expect adults on board to be younger than those on the other river cruises. Our AbD river cruises, with a guest population of about 150, have all included two or three children ages 4 and 5, about 20 kids ages 6–12, and about a dozen teens. Many of the adults, the parents of the children on the ship, were in their late 30s to late 50s. Also in the mix were a number of small groups of adults in their 20s to 50s, some vacationing couples, and some adult parent–child pairs. The number of senior citizens we saw on board was small, with most of those being grandparents of children on board.

While AbD river cruises welcome kids, there are three main differences between traveling with children on AbD versus DCL:

AGE TO TRAVEL On most DCL voyages, children may be as young as 6 months old (see page 153). Nurseries and other facilities are available to accommodate their needs. On AbD river cruises, children must be at least 4 years old, and age 8 is recommended. There are no cribs, high chairs, baby food, or the like.

DEDICATED CHILDREN'S SPACES For many families, the big draw of DCL is its kids' clubs (see the section starting on page 265). In contrast, there are no corresponding spaces on the river-cruise ships—kids mix with adults virtually everywhere on the ship.

STATEROOM CAPACITY Most DCL staterooms sleep four guests, meaning that a family of four could stay together in one stateroom. The maximum number of guests allowed in any AbD river-cruise stateroom is three, meaning that a family of four would be obligated to book two staterooms.

While no drop-off childcare is available, there are nonetheless plenty of opportunities for kids and parents to get a break from each other. Every night, AbD guides invite "Junior Adventurers" (kids ages 4–12) to the lounge while their parents eat dinner in the dining room. In the lounge, kids watch movies, work on crafts, and play games. While they're welcome to dine with the grown-ups, the fun—and the piles of chicken nuggets and fries—makes this a rarity. Teens are typically invited to have their evening meal in their own space on the ship.

Additionally, child-specific activities are offered during the "boring" excursions. For example, at many museum stops, kids are invited to play outdoor games with guides in the garden or participate in hands-on activities like baking a regional dessert. That said, if your child doesn't like being separated from you, you have a particularly rambunctious youngster, or your child doesn't enjoy group activities, an AbD river cruise may not be for you.

ADULTS-ONLY ABD RIVER CRUISES

IN 2023 ABD IS OFFERING a handful of river cruises for adults only (ages 18 and older). These typically take place in early May or in the fall, when most children are in school. Some of these sailings have a nominally adult theme like "Food and Wine Tour" or "Oktoberfest Sailing" (see page 345). This means that AbD has done something like swap a child-centric excursion option for a winery tour and changed an evening entertainer from a magician to a musician. Other than that, though, you can expect much the same thing from the family river cruises and the adults-only river cruises: a younger crowd than on most other lines, an all-inclusive luxury product, and fantastic Disney service.

EXCURSIONS *on* *an* ABD RIVER CRUISE

A NUMBER OF DIFFERENCES EXIST between DCL port adventures (see Part Twelve) and AbD river-cruise excursions. On DCL, there is typically a menu of at least a dozen, usually many more, port activities at a range of price points for an additional fee; a penalty fee may be charged if you make a last-minute change or cancellation. Plus, DCL contracts its port adventures to outside companies, which take over once you're off the ship.

Many DCL cruisers elect to book excursions on their own or forgo them altogether. Guests have access to excursion booking at different points depending on their Castaway Club status (see page 85), and some port adventures may become fully booked many weeks prior to sailing.

In contrast, the price of all AbD port excursions is included in your cruise fee. Every morning or afternoon, one to four excursions are offered, and nearly every guest on board participates. Depending on your sailing, you may be asked to choose your excursions in advance, or you may work with an Adventure Guide on embarkation day to discuss your options. Check with AdD or your travel agent to see how port excursions are being handled for your trip.

On our Rhine River cruise, we prebooked our excursions, but after an onboard presentation about the various adventures, we and nearly everyone else on the ship made a few modifications. Even if you're told before a sailing that a particular excursion is overbooked and unavailable, chances are this can be sorted out on board. Changes can even happen even during the middle of an excursion. For example, two families who were booked for the Van Gogh Museum's supplemental painting experience decided they'd rather explore Amsterdam on their own during the museum tour, so two other families stepped in to take their painting slots. Plus, there are no fees to cancel or modify plans, even at the last minute.

As with DCL, AbD contracts with local guides for some excursions; however, Disney guides, with access to Disney resources, accompany you at all times.

Also as with DCL, families on AbD river cruises are welcome to choose their port excursions together or separately according to their interests. If Dad wants to go on the *Sound of Music* tour (singing "Lonely Goatherd" all the way) and Mom wants to tour the Hallein Salt Mines, that's not a problem.

SAMPLE ABD RIVER-CRUISE EXCURSIONS

Note: *Itineraries are subject to change.*

Danube Cruises

VILSHOFEN, GERMANY Oktoberfest party

PASSAU, GERMANY Visit to an aerial tree path and adventure playground; exploration on your own with recommendations from your tour guides

LINZ (SALZBURG), AUSTRIA Walking tour of Salzburg; visit to the **Basilica of Mondsee** (where Georg and Maria von Trapp's wedding was filmed for the movie version of *The Sound of Music*); tour of the **Hallein Salt Mines and Underground Slides**

MELK (KREMS), AUSTRIA Tour of **Melk Benedictine Abbey;** lesson in preparing local foods; hike to **Dürnstein Castle;** bike trip along the Danube; visit to a family-run apricot farm

VIENNA, AUSTRIA Coach tour of Vienna; tour of **Schönbrunn Palace;** marionette show and strudel-making class; bike trip to **Klosterneuburg Monastery;** visit to a traditional wine bar; concert featuring the music of Mozart and Strauss

BRATISLAVA, SLOVAKIA Walking tour of Bratislava, including a scavenger hunt; tours of the **Schloss Hof Palace,** along with lunch and a schnapps tasting

BUDAPEST, HUNGARY Tour of **Lazar Equestrian Park;** visit to **Budapest Central Market Hall;** walking food tour; nighttime tour of Budapest

Rhine Cruises

BASEL, SWITZERLAND Wine-and-cheese party

MANNHEIM, GERMANY Walking tour of **Heidelberg** and **Heidelberg Castle;** walking or biking tour of local villages

STRASBOURG, FRANCE Tour of the **Black Forest** with an alpine toboggan run or zip line adventure; instruction in making whistles with wooden cuckoo-clock components; walk through the medieval town of **Riquewihr;** private organ concert of Mozart music; canal boat trip to the **Cathédrale de Notre-Dame** in Strasbourg; canoe through town; macaron-baking class; tour of the historic wine cellars of the **Cave Historique des Hospices de Strasbourg**

RÜDESHEIM, GERMANY Bike tour of wine country; gondola ride to **Niederwald Monument;** visit to **Siegfried's Mechanical Music Cabinet**

Museum; coffee and hot-chocolate tasting at **Rüdesheim Schloss;** cruise through the **Rhine River Gorge**

KÖLN (COLOGNE), GERMANY Curling, zip lining, and snow biking in an indoor winter park; walking tour of Köln; chocolate-making classes; chocolate tasting; pub tour

AMSTERDAM, THE NETHERLANDS Canal cruise; tour of the **Rijks-museum** or the **Van Gogh Museum;** visit to the fishing village of **Volen-dam** and its **Zaanse Schans** neighborhood (a re-created 18th-century village) to see active windmills, watch cheesemaking demonstrations, and decorate wooden clogs

Seine Cruises

PARIS, FRANCE Nighttime river tour of Paris

VERNON AND GIVERNY, FRANCE Visit to painter **Claude Monet's** house and gardens; painting class at the **Giverny Museum of Impressionisms;** bicycle ride through the town of Vernon; tour the **Chateau de Bizy**

LE HAVRE, FRANCE Excursion to the **Normandy Beaches,** including **Omaha Beach,** site of the World War II D-Day Invasion and the **Nor-mandy American Cemetery;** hike of the **Etretat Cliffs** overlooking the **English Channel**

LES ANDELYS, FRANCE Exploration of the Normandy countryside by bus, bike, or on foot; visit to **Château Gaillard,** a ruined medieval castle; macaron-making demonstration; French cheese seminar and tasting

ROUEN, FRANCE Walking tour with visits to historical sites and cheese and chocolate tastings; kayaking through the countryside

CONFLANS, FRANCE Visit to **Château Malmaison,** former home of Napoléon and Joséphine Bonaparte; visit **Auvers-Sur-Oise,** a 19th-century artists' compound

SPECIALTY RIVER CRUISES

THESE CRUISES INCLUDE many of the same activities and excursions as standard AbD river cruises, but with some targeted tweaks:

- **Food & Wine Rhine Cruise** Enjoy a variety of wine, cheese, and coffee tastings; take a food tour of Riquewihr, France; explore the wine caves of Des Hospices in Strasbourg, France; learn to make "spaghetti" ice cream in an onboard cooking demo; take a pub tour and visit a chocolate museum in Köln, Germany; tour the Heineken Brewery in Amsterdam. (Adults only.)

- **Holiday Danube Cruise** Shop at the Christmas market in Passau, Germany; tour the parks and gardens of Salzburg, Austria; visit Schönbrunn Palace in Vienna; see the sights of Budapest.

- *National Geographic* **Photography Cruise** Travel with *National Geographic* photographers, who offer seminars and provide personal photography tips throughout your sailing. Includes photography scavenger hunt designed for Junior Adventurers.

- **Oktoberfest Danube Cruise** Explore the beer culture of Central Europe. (Adults only.)

ABD PRE- AND POST-CRUISE ESCAPES

IN ADDITION TO ITS CRUISES, AbD offers what it calls **Escapes**—three- to five-day intensive explorations of one city or region. These take place immediately before or after a cruise, typically in the city of a cruise's embarkation or debarkation. See adventuresbydisney.com for more information.

Escapes offered in 2023 include intensive tours of Amsterdam, Budapest, or Paris for AbD river cruises and Barcelona, Copenhagen, London, Rome, or Disneyland and Southern California for DCL cruises. Escapes for AbD's **Expedition Cruises** (see page 354) include in-depth tours of Buenos Aires, Argentina, or the Amazon rainforest, including Quito, Ecuador, and the Napo River.

MORE DIFFERENCES
Between **ABD** *and* **DCL CRUISES**

SIZE OF THE SHIPS The DCL ships are large, ranging from 964 feet long and 11 decks tall (*Magic* and *Wonder)* to 1,119 feet long and 15 decks tall (*Wish*). Because of size constraints related to rivers and river-lock systems, however, the river ships are necessarily much smaller—the *AmaViola* and her sister ships are just 443 feet long and three decks high. The river ships' petite footprint also allows them to maneuver quickly and dock in tight spaces.

PASSENGER CAPACITY While the *Magic* and *Wonder,* the smallest of the five DCL ships, have a maximum capacity of about 2,700 passengers each, the river ships can carry a total of just 158 guests.

DISTANCES TRAVELED Some DCL voyages cover many thousands of miles. In contrast, the entire AbD Danube River cruise is just 650 miles, and the Rhine River cruise is an even shorter 460 miles. Some guests choose to bike between port stops. If you were to miss the all-aboard time on a DCL cruise, you might have to catch a plane to your next port; with an AbD river cruise, on the other hand, you could call an Uber. On our most recent Danube sailing, the ship took just 10 minutes to pull over at a dock to drop off a local entertainer near his home in town.

PRICING VARIABILITY DCL cruise prices may vary hundreds or even thousands of dollars depending on when you book (see "Saving Money," page 34, for pricing trends). AbD river-cruise pricing remains relatively steady, with minimal fluctuations. However, there are sometimes modest discounts for early booking or other promotions.

CABIN TYPES There are nearly 30 different stateroom configurations on the DCL ships. On the river-cruise ships, there are just 9, with only minor differences among them, making it easy to figure out which type of cabin is best for you.

BED CONFIGURATION Most DCL rooms have regular queen-size beds. On AbD river cruises they're split twins, which can be set up as a queen bed or two twin beds. This may be useful for traveling companions who are fine sharing a room but don't want to sleep together.

RELATIONSHIPS The river ships' smaller scale means that you'll see the same guests all the time, giving you an opportunity to really get to know them. The ship's officers and crew are also close at hand at all times. The AbD guides are extremely friendly and strive to foster personal relationships with all guests.

PRIVACY On DCL, how much you interact with other guests is largely up to you: you can request your own table in the dining rooms, skip group excursions, and just generally keep to yourself. On a river cruise, it's all but inevitable that you'll be interacting with other guests throughout the day. There are no private or assigned dining tables. Excursions are group affairs in which nearly everyone participates. And the AbD guides work to engage guests in conversation. A river cruise might not be the ideal way to spend, say, a honeymoon.

FLEXIBILITY DCL is a huge operation that must enforce strict rules to maintain order. On the other hand, AbD river ships are smaller, making it easier to focus on guests' needs and wants. For example, a child who is nearly but not quite old enough for a particular kids' club on DCL will be denied admission, whereas kids on AbD cruises can participate in activities geared to them as they desire. For example, our well-behaved 16-year-olds were invited to dine at the Chef's Table on the river cruise, but DCL insists that guests be 18 and up to dine in its ships' adult spaces.

MOTION OF THE SHIPS During even the calmest of ocean voyages, you'll feel the ship moving, and on open seas during turbulent weather, you may find yourself overcome by motion sickness (see page 60 for more on the subject). On a river cruise, however, you may be entirely unaware that the ship is moving at all.

THE JOURNEY VS. THE DESTINATION Many DCL guests book a cruise without a particular destination in mind: they want someplace, *anyplace* warm on the right dates, at the right price. They care more about stuffing themselves with free food or getting pampered at the spa than experiencing the attractions in port. But on a river cruise, it's all about where you're going. Instead of playing bingo and watching shows on sea days, you'll be exploring historical sites, seeing magnificent artwork, and taking in lush landscapes. The draw is off the ship rather than on it.

WHERE THE SHIPS DOCK Depending on the DCL destination, your ship may dock at a forlorn industrial port several miles from town. This is less common with a river cruise, where much of the time the ship can dock right next to a city sidewalk. Hopping off for a walk around town can take less than a minute.

TIME IN PORT On DCL, most sailings leave port by dinnertime. On AbD river cruises, early all-aboard times are often around 8 p.m.—and sometimes well after midnight.

FOOD AVAILABILITY On DCL, there are two rotational dinner seatings, an all-you-care-to eat venue that's open most of the day, a multitude of quick-bite windows, and 24-hour room service. While there's certainly plenty of food on board a river cruise, mealtimes are more condensed, with just one seating for the three main meals. Limited snacks are available at other times, but there's nothing comparable to full room service. On the other hand, you're likely to dock literally steps away from a quaint café with amazing food.

FOOD QUALITY We find the quality of AbD river-cruise food superior to that of DCL cruise food overall—daily port stops and smaller guest loads make it easy for a river ship to acquire fresh (versus frozen and prepackaged) produce, meats, and dairy. AbD also takes great care to accommodate cruisers with food allergies and special diets. (See tinyurl.com/abdrivercruisefood for a look at some of the food we got to try during a Danube AbD trip.)

ALCOHOL Booze of all sorts is plentiful on both DCL and AbD cruises. The difference is that all alcohol costs extra on DCL, while beer and wine are included with both lunch and dinner on river cruises. Plus, many AbD river excursions offer wine, beer, and schnapps tastings—again included in the cost of your cruise.

INTERNET Wi-Fi generally costs extra on DCL (see page 137), and the connection quality can be spotty, particularly when you're at sea. In contrast, AbD river ships have free Wi-Fi, plus a full-size desktop computer in every stateroom (it doubles as your TV). The Wi-Fi quality is good enough for email and posting to social media, but, like DCL's, it's not quite up to the task of streaming video.

GUESTS WITH DISABILITIES Here, AbD lags behind DCL. For example, while a river ship has an elevator, it serves just part of the ship. This means that a guest who uses a wheelchair can't access the sundeck. Additionally, AbD river ships sometimes double-park at a dock, meaning that guests may have to walk through another ship, or possibly over its sundeck, to get to shore. Exiting this way is all but impossible for someone with restricted mobility.

SOLO TRAVEL Guests traveling alone on DCL and some river cruises have to pay a so-called single supplement, meaning they're essentially paying for a second, nonexistent person in their stateroom. That said, some (but not all) AbD river-cruise ships have a few small cabins specifically designed for one person. If you're lucky enough to snag one of these as a solo traveler, you won't have to pay a single supplement—a potentially huge savings.

CANCELLATION POLICY AbD's cancellation policy is more restrictive than DCL's. If you're booking an AbD river cruise or an AbD Escape (see page 345), it may be costly to cancel your trip early. See adventures bydisney.com/terms-and-conditions for details.

TRAVELING *with* ADVENTURES BY DISNEY

ADVENTURES BY DISNEY TRIPS, including river cruises, are overseen by **Disney Adventure Guides.** Part tour guide, part cheerleader, part therapist, part photographer, part medic, part waiter, and part teacher, they're the best camp counselors you've ever had. Many Adventure Guides work for DCL or the Disney parks in the off-season; one of our recent river cruises, for example, was staffed by an Adventure Guide who had previously been a counselor at the Oceaneer Lab on the *Dream*. Other Adventure Guides are Disney-trained travel experts who are fluent in the languages and well versed in the history and customs of the regions visited. One guest writes:

> *Of all the Disney cast members I've encountered, the Disney Adventure Guides are my favorites. Every one of them is fabulous, fun, and incredibly competent. Their energy level is off the charts—which is impressive because they never seem to sleep!*

Typical land-based AbD trips have two guides for 30–40 guests, yielding a guide-to-guest ratio of about 1–20 or better. AbD river cruises are staffed by seven or eight Adventure Guides who attend to 135–150 guests, which comes out to more or less the same guide-to-guest ratio above.

On a standard AbD trip, you'll have the same 40 or so guests and the same two guides for the entire trip. On river cruises, however, the guides rotate among the 140 or so guests as needed—you won't be assigned your own pair of guides. You'll also be touring with different subsets of the guest pool, depending on which excursions you and they choose. If you're a veteran of AbD land-based trips, it may take you a day or two to get the hang of things. While river cruises certainly have a strong AbD feel, the shifting groups and guides make for slightly less continuity than on a land-based trip. If, however, your only cruising experience is on DCL, a river cruise will feel significantly more welcoming and personal than your previous experiences. Novice cruisers will also feel right at home on the AbD river ships.

COST CONSIDERATIONS

ABD VS. DCL

WHILE IT'S A BIT OF AN APPLES-TO-ORANGES COMPARISON, here's a detailed breakdown of potential costs for a DCL European sailing and an AbD European river-cruise sailing. All pricing is for two adults. We found the prices for these examples in midsummer 2022; DCL pricing typically varies considerably depending on when you do your search.

Our points of comparison are two cruises in spring 2023: the June 11, 2023, **7-Night Danube River Cruise** on an AmaWaterways vessel, sailing from Vilshofen, Germany, and the May 27, 2023, **7-Night Mediterranean Cruise** on the *Disney Dream,* departing from Barcelona, Spain. Both trips include stops in major European cities, with similar opportunities for sightseeing. We'll assume that flight prices to/from your home to Germany or Spain would be similar, as would the price for a pre-cruise hotel night near the port you'd be sailing from.

The lowest listed price for the DCL trip is **$4,660** for a bare-bones Category 11B Inside Stateroom. Beyond this base price, you'd also have to factor in money for gratuities and transfers, but if you did absolutely nothing else except sail, two adults could take the DCL Mediterranean cruise for slightly south of $5,000. That cruise would be considerably more Spartan than an AbD river cruise, however.

To even things up, we have to look at more-expensive cabin categories on DCL. But first, be aware that **staterooms** on DCL and AbD ships are not directly comparable.

Going by square footage alone, the closest matches are (1) a 204-square-foot **Category 9C Oceanview Stateroom** on Deck 7 of the *Dream* for **$5,065** and (2) a 210-square-foot **Category BB Stateroom** on the Ama ship for **$13,598.** On its face, the AbD stateroom costs nearly three times as much as the DCL room; again, though, we're strictly comparing the size of the rooms. When it comes to the size and feel of the rooms, however, it makes more sense to compare the AbD room with two slightly larger and more-expensive options on the Dream: (1) a **Category 5A Deluxe Oceanview Stateroom with Verandah** (246 square feet) on Deck 10 for **$5,905** or (2) a **Category 4A Deluxe Family Oceanview Stateroom** (299 square feet) on Deck 10 for **$6,605.**

While the AbD stateroom has a smaller footprint than either DCL room, its full wall of windows, plus its balcony, makes it feel much more like DCL's Category 5 Verandah room than the cheaper Category 9 Oceanview room mentioned earlier. And because AbD's staterooms have less square footage allotted to closet space than DCL's, the AbD room also compares favorably with the considerably larger Category 4 room on the *Dream.*

There are other considerations, though. **Gratuities** are included in AbD's price but not DCL's. The minimum suggested tip for two people on a seven-night DCL cruise is $189 (see page 160); we usually add a bit more and also tip some of the other crew members, so we'll allocate $250. We'll also add approximately $300 for a DCL **Wi-Fi** package (two devices for seven days; Premium Surf package). For DCL, you also have to add about $250 for two people for a shared **transfer** from the Port of Barcelona to El Prat Airport; similar transfers are included in your AbD price. These necessities raise of the cost of the DCL trip to **$5,905** for the smaller DCL room or **$7,405** for the larger DCL room.

Adding **excursions** on DCL also adds expense. In this example, let's look at full-day excursions that cover the highlights of a particular destination. For the four Mediterranean ports on the DCL sailing, these might include Pompeii, Sorrento, and Capri ($285 per adult); Best of Rome ($399 per adult); Florence and Michelangelo ($204 per adult); or Monaco, Monte Carlo, and Èze ($112 per adult). In addition, we'll allocate $125 per adult for activities in Barcelona (AbD includes some touring in the embarkation or debarkation city). This adds up to **$2,250** in excursion fees for two adults.

To approximate a Chef's Table **premium-dining experience** that's included in the cost of the AbD cruise, we'll add $150 for a meal at Palo on the *Dream,* including alcohol, à la carte items, and tip on top of the $45-per-person minimum price. (Another AbD advantage: well-behaved cruisers younger than age 18 are sometimes welcome to dine at the Chef's Table; at Palo, no one under 18 may dine *period.*) We'll also add a $200 **bar tab,** assuming two adults are going to have two moderately priced drinks per day; again, beer and wine are included with meals on the river cruise.

The real cost of the DCL trip has now risen to **$8,505** for the Category 4 cabin or **$10,005** for the Category 5 cabin. You can see that the second price is still less than the $13,598 price of the river cruise, but when you include the real costs associated with DCL, you're starting to approach the same ballpark. On the AbD side of the equation, you may have options for narrowing the price difference even further. For example, AbD frequently offers a $500-per-person discount for booking early. If you were to take advantage of a discount such as this, the cost of the AbD cruise might come down $1,000, to **$12,598.** We could have also priced a smaller stateroom on AbD: the 160-square-foot Category D cabin, at a base price of $10,798, which might have been reduced by $500 per person with early booking, for a total of **$9,798,** making it just under the DCL price. Every decision has an impact on the bottom line.

Also consider that some of the pluses of AbD include intangibles such as greater flexibility, more personal attention, and more time in port. Other pros are perhaps quantifiable: additional port stops/excursions and higher-quality food, for example. To get the same level of personal attention on DCL that you'd get on the AbD river cruise, you'd have to upgrade to a Concierge-level stateroom, which would push DCL's price well above AbD's.

ABD VS. OTHER RIVER-CRUISE LINES

WHILE COMPARING AbD river-cruise prices with DCL's is an apples-to-oranges proposition, you can compare apples to apples if you look at the cost of an AbD cruise versus one on a competing river-cruise line.

Because **AmaWaterways** and AbD use similar (and sometimes the same) ships for their respective cruises sailing the same itineraries, we can easily compare prices between the two lines. As our AbD example, let's use the same cruise from the previous comparison: two adults in a Category BB Stateroom on AbD's **7-Night Danube River Cruise** on the *AmaLea,* sailing from Vilshofen, Germany, on June 22, 2022. Our Ama Waterways example is a seven-night cruise on the *AmaMagna* in the same stateroom category, sailing the same Danube route, on June 19, 2022. The AbD cruise is **$13,378,** versus **$9,336** for the AmaWaterways cruise—a difference of about $4,000. The AmaWaterways price, however, excludes transfers to and from your pre- and post-cruise hotel or the airport, which can easily reach $400. Thus, the real difference in the price between AbD's Danube sailing and the corresponding AmaWaterways sailing is about $3,600.

Of course, transfers aren't the only thing accounting for the price difference. When AbD charters the ship, it includes additional excursions, along with excursions that are geared to families. For example, on the Rhine River cruise to Köln, Germany, AbD guests are offered a visit to an indoor ski hall in Neuss for sledding and tubing—a real treat for many kids—but nothing similar is offered on AmaWaterways' Rhine River cruises that visit Köln. On most AbD stops, excursion options are available for both the morning and afternoon, but with Ama, it's usually just one or the other.

unofficial **TIP**

The price difference between AbD-chartered river cruises and AmaWaterways river cruises was much less pre-COVID. Expect these prices to become more similar as the European travel industry recovers.

Another key difference with the AbD version of the cruise is that there are children on board. Standard AmaWaterways river cruises have children on board only rarely—typically just during the odd Christmas cruise—and almost never during the summer. The presence of kids also brings down the average age of adult guests on board considerably. If you're a pre-retirement adult sailing with AbD, you're likely to find many more contemporaries on your ship, even if you don't have kids, than on AmaWaterways.

The biggest difference, of course, is that when AbD charters the ship, you enjoy the services of the eight Disney Adventure Guides. They run activities for kids, both on the ship and during excursions. They make sure every birthday and anniversary is acknowledged. They make us laugh on boring bus rides. (Shout-out to Adventure Guide Michaela, whose improv-comedy routine was a highlight of our Rhine sailing.) They distribute special Disney collector pins acquirable only on the ship. One guide on our trip—an actor who's a veteran of several Broadway musicals—even took song requests.

Are extra excursions and extra attention worth about $1,300 more per person than an equivalent non-Disney river cruise? As with most things, that depends. If you're a retiree and you don't mind vacationing with your peers, then probably not. Many older adults won't need some of the Disney bells and whistles, and they'll likely appreciate the more serene atmosphere on board without kids around. On the other hand, if you have kids with you, or even if you don't and you're younger than 55–60, then the Disney version of the cruise will probably be more to your liking.

Many other river-cruise lines operate in the same European waters as AbD and AmaWaterways. **Tauck River Cruises,** for example, have a similar feel to AmaWaterways cruises. When we spot-checked pricing for 2022–23 Danube cruises, Tauck's were typically within a few hundred dollars of Ama's. **Smithsonian Journeys** (affiliated with the

Smithsonian Institution) offers guided river cruises, many with an educational twist. Other reputable lines include **Avalon Waterways, Crystal River Cruises,** and **Scenic River Cruises.** If you want to go adults-only during the summer, try **Viking River Cruises,** which restricts guests to ages 18 and older.

Competing lines include or don't include various AbD components such as transfers, tips, excursions, and alcohol, but none have the real family focus of AbD; consider this when comparing prices. For a deep dive into the nuances of river-cruise pricing, **River Cruise Advisor** (river cruiseadvisor.com) is a good place to start, but make sure that you're looking at prices for the same type of stateroom.

The Bottom Line

AbD river cruises are a luxury product with a luxury feel. Everything is included, all the details are taken care of, and you get fantastic personal service and gourmet food. It's possible to pay less than half the price of an AbD river cruise for a DCL Mediterranean cruise if you select the smallest Inside Stateroom, skip adult dining and alcohol, and don't go on any excursions. You'll have to stick with DCL if you have children younger than 4 years old or if you strongly prefer to be immersed in Disney-themed entertainment and decor.

While the price for an AbD river cruise is about double the cost of the bare-minimum DCL European cruise, it's in the same ballpark as other river-cruise lines with the same itineraries. The extra service and children's activities may make the premium pricing worthwhile, particularly if you have kids who might not otherwise be interested in a river-cruise vacation.

EXPEDITION CRUISING

DISNEY FINALIZED ITS PURCHASE of *National Geographic*'s travel arm in 2019. The first public evidence of this merger has been the introduction of *National Geographic*–branded photography lessons on some of the AbD river cruises—and, more significantly, the introduction of what AbD calls Expedition Cruising. (For more information, see adventuresbydisney.com/expedition-cruising-with-disney.)

The initial Expedition itineraries included a 12-day trip to **Antarctica** and **Patagonia** and a 9-day trip to the **Galápagos Islands.** For 2023, AbD added a 10-day **Arctic Expedition Cruise** to the previous offerings. These cruises feature Disney-trained guides plus shipboard naturalists and experts on these regions. The Expedition trips are more outdoors-oriented than the European river cruises, which focus on museums and local culture versus animal habitats and the natural world.

Your vessel for the Expedition trips will be a small ocean ship, with access to smaller Zodiac boats for excursions and exploration. Pricing for these cruises is even steeper than for DCL's cruises and AbD's river cruises: the Antarctic cruise, for example, starts at **$13,899** per adult.

That eye-popping price includes things like a catamaran tour through the Beagle Channel, a Drake Passage crossing, kayaking through icebergs, a walk in a penguin colony, whale-watching, and a train ride through Tierra del Fuego National Park in Argentina.

AbD's Expedition Cruises had their first sailings during winter 2022, and reviews of these trips were off-the-charts fantastic. Several of our former AbD river cruise guides led Expedition trips and shared social media posts of themselves and guests (with their permission) standing on icebergs and cuddling with penguins. Color us jealous.

If you have a thirst for adventure, love the great outdoors, have money to burn, and aren't overly sensitive to motion sickness (we've heard the Drake Passage crossing in Antarctica can be rough), then we say Expedition away. And if you do try one of these special sailings, please tell us about your experiences.

WHAT'S NEXT FOR DISNEY *and* SMALL-SHIP CRUISING?

AT THE TIME OF THIS WRITING, AbD's Expedition Cruises were Disney's sparkly new offering in the small-ship category, just as river cruises were when AbD launched its partnership with AmaWaterways in 2016. Expedition Cruises aim to capture a different sort of travel demographic than people who might be interested in a Caribbean DCL cruise or a European river cruise.

If we had to venture a guess about what's next, we'd say that Disney will continue to mine *National Geographic*'s expertise for water-based adventure travel, as well as bring AbD river cruising to additional parts of the world, possibly as DCL nears completion of its large new ships. When we asked a Disney executive who happened to be on a Danube sailing with us about expanded river-cruise offerings, he simply smiled and said, "There are a lot of rivers out there."

We wouldn't be surprised, however, to see Disney eventually launch its own branded small-ship fleet after having tested the waters (literally) with a marketing partner. Keep your (Mickey) ears peeled.

DCL GLOSSARY

A CRUISE VACATION means you'll encounter a great deal of specialized lingo unique to the industry. That goes double for a Disney cruise, which has its own lexicon as well. Here are some general and Disney Cruise Line–specific terms that you may encounter both in your planning and on the ship.

ABD **Adventures by Disney,** the world-travel arm of Disney Destinations LLC. In addition to its adventure-focused vacations, AbD offers river and adventure cruises.

ADJACENT STATEROOMS Staterooms that are next to each other but aren't connected by an internal door. You must enter the hallway to travel between the rooms. (Also see **Connecting Staterooms.**)

ADULT DISTRICT The area on most DCL ships where the majority of the bars and lounges are located. The adult districts are typically restricted to guests ages 18 and up after 9 p.m.

ADULT DINING Describes the premium restaurants on the ship that require guests to be age 18 or older to attend and that carry an additional fee.

AFT The rear of the ship.

ALL ABOARD The time at which you're required to be back on board the ship following a day in port. If you're not back at the ship by all-aboard time, you'll be left behind.

ALL ASHORE The time at which guests may disembark the ship for a day in port.

ASSISTANT SERVER This is the person on your serving team who is primarily responsible for your beverage orders and for making sure your plates are cleared between courses.

BACK TO BACK Booking two consecutive cruises. This is most common on the *Disney Dream,* where guests with a fondness for Castaway Cay can book a three-day and four-day cruise one after the other. You can sometimes keep the same stateroom for back-to-back sailings.

BACKSTAGE Behind the scenes. Refers to any area of the ship that is not normally accessible to guests. (*Backstage* has the same meaning at the Disney parks.)

BLACKOUT DATES Specific sail dates for which onboard-booking (OBB) discounts (see page 104) are unavailable.

BOW The front of the ship.

BRIDGE The area at the front of the ship where the captain and his staff navigate the vessel.

CAPTAIN The leader of the entire vessel. Responsibilities include navigating, operating the ship's equipment, overseeing personnel, and tending to miscellaneous business. Many longer cruises include an opportunity to meet the captain.

CAST MEMBER Disney-speak for "employee." Everyone who works for The Walt Disney Company is a cast member.

CASTAWAY CAY Disney's private island in the Bahamas. (*Cay* is pronounced "key.")

CASTAWAY CLUB Disney Cruise Line's "frequent flyer" program. See page 85.

CLOSED-LOOP CRUISE A cruise that starts and ends at the same port. (Compare with **Repositioning Cruise.**)

CONNECTING STATEROOMS These are staterooms that are next to each other and also have an internal door connecting them. (Compare with **Adjacent Staterooms.**)

COSTUME Anything worn by a DCL cast member.

CREW MEMBER Generally, the employees of a ship. On DCL, cruise staff (see below) are distinct from crew members.

CRUISE DIRECTOR Holds responsibility for onboard hospitality, entertainment, and social events; serves as the public face of the cruise line on his or her ship. (A good reference for Gen Xers is Miss Julie McCoy on *The Love Boat*.) On the DCL ships, you'll hear the cruise director make most onboard loudspeaker announcements. He or she also will appear in the theater on most evenings, giving opening remarks.

CRUISE STAFF You'd think this would mean all of the crew who work on the ship. On DCL, however, *cruise staff* refers to the dozen or so attractive, personable, and hyperenergetic cast members who run the onboard family and adult entertainment activities: bingo, karaoke, dance parties, and so on.

DCL Disney Cruise Line. (*Duh!*)

DCL NAVIGATOR Mobile app for keeping up to date about daily activities on the ships; also gives you access to details about your DCL cruise.

DECK Nautical verbiage for "story," "floor," or "level." For example, your stateroom isn't on Floor 6 but Deck 6.

DOUBLE DIP Slang in the Disney-cruise community for an itinerary with two stops at Castaway Cay (see previous page). Each year there are just a handful of double-dip cruises, making them particularly coveted.

DVC **Disney Vacation Club,** Disney's time-share program.

EXCURSION Known in Disney lingo as a **port adventure,** this is any organized land-based activity in the ship's port of call.

FISH EXTENDER Next to each stateroom door on the *Magic, Wonder, Dream,* and *Fantasy* is a shelflike metal fish sculpture that functions like a mailbox. Some guests also hang fabric pockets from the sculpture, thus *extending the fish;* the pockets are used to accept gifts from a group of like-minded cruisers in a Secret Santa–like exchange. This is completely optional, and not recommended during your first sailing as it can be a considerable time commitment. (If you'd like to participate in an fish-extender exchange on a future sailing, search Facebook for a group specific to your cruise.)

FOLIO Your stateroom account.

FORWARD The front part of the ship.

GALLEY The ship's kitchen.

GANGWAY The ramp or staircase that guests use to embark and disembark the ship. Depending on the specifics of a particular port, the location of the gangway may vary.

GTY Abbreviation for **Guarantee.** Some guests book a stateroom without knowing the exact room number. Such bookings are known as guarantees because Disney guarantees that it will be in the category that the guest pays for or better. This is a nice way to book a room if you're not picky about its location.

HEAD SERVER The waiter in charge of the entire dining room in Disney's rotational restaurants. You may not see your head server much, but that's because he's extremely busy making sure the entire dining operation runs smoothly. If you're having any trouble with your primary serving team, speak with the head server.

IGT Abbreviation for **Inside Guarantee** (see **GTY**). This is a nonrefundable fare for an Inside Stateroom, typically booked at the last minute. You won't get to choose your exact stateroom, but you will get the category of room you want.

KEY TO THE WORLD (KTTW) CARD The card you receive upon check-in at the ship that functions as your room key, identification during onboard photo opportunities, and a charge card for merchandise and additional-cost food and beverage items on the ship. You will need your KTTW Card many times throughout your day on board, as well as to get on or off the ship. *Always* keep it with you during your cruise.

KNOT A unit of speed equal to 1 nautical mile (1.852 kilometers) per hour, or 1.151 miles per hour.

MDR Short for **main dining room** (aka **rotational dining room**). Each DCL ship has three MDRs.

MUSTER The required first-day safety drill.

NAUTICAL MILE See **Knot**.

OBB Abbreviation for **onboard booking,** or booking your next Disney cruise while you're on your current cruise. All DCL ships have a dedicated Onboard Booking desk. If you book your next cruise on board, you receive a discount on the OBB sailing (typically 10%).

OFFICER A member of the leadership team of the ship. On Disney Cruise Line, officers typically wear white uniforms.

OGT Abbreviation for **Oceanview Guarantee** (see **GTY**). This is a non-refundable fare for an Oceanview stateroom, typically booked at the last minute. You won't get to choose your exact stateroom, but you will get the category of room you want.

ONBOARD CREDIT "Gift" money that you can apply to your folio. Travel agents often give DCL onboard credit to clients who book cruises through them. You also can win onboard credit at bingo games on the ship and at promotional presentations for DVC, Senses Spa, and shopping. You can use onboard credit to pay for shore excursions, adult dining, shipboard merchandise purchases, and so on.

PFD Abbreviation for **personal flotation device,** or life vest.

PLACEHOLDER A deposit for a future sailing, at a nonspecified date, made while you are on a DCL ship. Placeholders get the benefits of booking a future cruise, such as a reduced deposit, etc., but can choose their sail date later.

PORT (ADJ.) The left side of the ship, as you face the front of it.

PORT (N.) A town or city with a harbor. The ships makes stops in ports.

PORT ADVENTURE See **Excursion**.

REPOSITIONING CRUISE Cruise in which the embarkation and debarkation ports are different (compare with **Closed-Loop Cruise**). Disney primarily uses this term to refer to its 10-plus-day Transatlantic and Panama Canal sailings.

ROTATIONAL DINING ROOM See **MDR**.

SERVER Your dining room waiter. Your server will guide you through the menu each night, take your order, and ensure that it's delivered to your table properly and promptly. If you have dietary issues or food idiosyncrasies, your server will be the one who makes sure that those needs are met.

SHIP A large oceangoing vessel—*don't call it a boat!* With a few exceptions, the general rule of thumb is that a ship can carry a boat but a boat can't carry a ship.

STARBOARD The right side of the ship, as you face the front of it.

STATEROOM Your room on the ship. Most other cruise lines call them cabins; DCL calls them staterooms regardless of the size or location of the room.

STATEROOM HOST The person who attends to your room. Your stateroom host will also turn down your bed at night, deliver messages, and generally assist with any aspect of your room's functionality. Don't forget to tip!

STERN The back of the ship.

TENDER A small boat that transfers guests from the cruise ship to land. Tenders are used when a port's waters are too shallow for a large ship to dock next to a pier.

TRANSFER The Disney-arranged method of getting you to the ship prior to sailing or to another form of transportation after sailing. For example, you can purchase transfers from a hotel at Walt Disney World to Port Canaveral or from Port Canaveral to Orlando International Airport. Transfers are available at all home ports.

VGT Abbreviation for **Verandah Guarantee** (see **GTY**). This is a non-refundable fare for a Verandah stateroom, typically booked at the last minute. You won't get to choose your exact stateroom, but you will get the type of room you want.

VPP Abbreviation for **Vacation Protection Plan,** DCL's trip insurance (see page 58).

INDEX

Page numbers in **boldface** indicate extended coverage of a particular topic. **DCL** refers to Disney Cruise Line, **RCI** refers to Royal Caribbean International, and **AbD** refers to Adventures by Disney.